SOUP STREET

A memoir by Food Not Bombs co-founder Keith McHenry

For information contact:
Keith McHenry
PO Box 422
Santa Cruz CA 95061 USA
keithmchenry.net

Soup Street / by Keith McHenry 2026.
332 p. : ill. ; 9 x 6
ISBN: 979-8-234-00487-1

Contents:
1. Anarchism. 2. United States -- Economic conditions -- 21st century. 4. Food -- Political aspects. 5. Food relief.

I. McHenry, Keith.

320.57

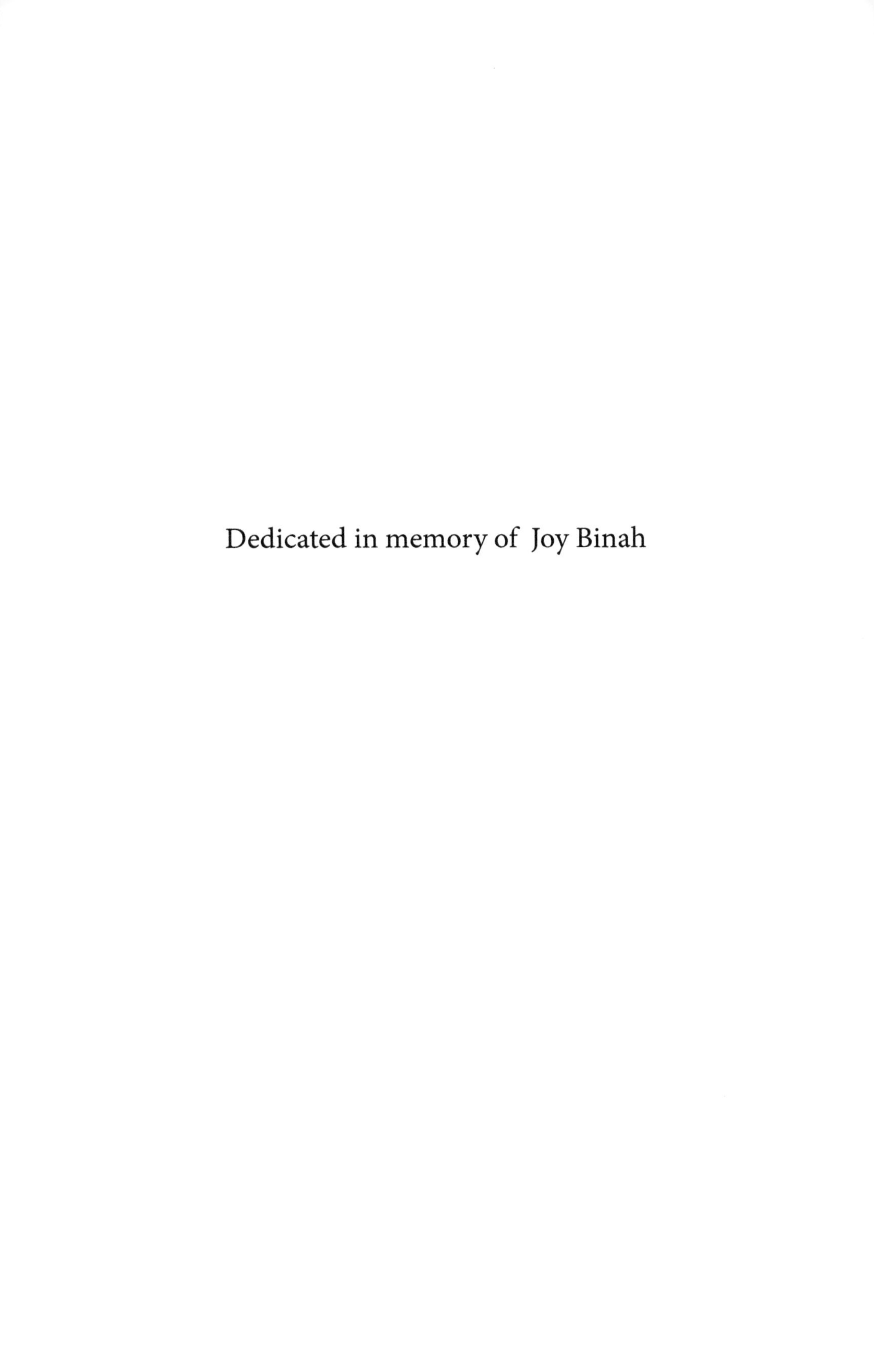

Dedicated in memory of Joy Binah

"A vivid, unflinching memoir, Soup Street traces Keith McHenry's journey from wild American landscapes to front-line activism and torture survival, revealing how a life of hardship, courage, and compassion gave birth to Food Not Bombs and a global struggle for justice, dignity, and hope."

—John Kiriakou, CIA Torture Whistleblower

Keith McHenry is the real deal, a warrior for peace. His book on feeding the hungry begins with outrage at the desecration of the pure air at Four Corners by the Peabody Coal generating plant, generating his youthful vow that, "Any political and economic system willing to desecrate the sacred lands of the southwest was a system I vowed to dedicate my life to ending."

I worked supporting Hopi friends and we closed that plant down, so without ever shaking hands, I can say I know who Keith McHenry is. The San Francisco Diggers (of which I was a founding member) fed a lot of people, but we can't touch what Keith, and his partner, my friend Diamond Dave, (who worked the Food Not Bombs tables in San Francisco) accomplished. This book is a slice of history you haven't read about or known if you haven't lived it. Learn the story of this remarkable man. Model his courage and dedication. Read this book and pick up the banner he never dropped.
— Peter Coyote, actor, author, Zen Buddhist teacher.

I've been a fan of Keith McHenry for decades, but I always had simmering questions: What sparked him to start Food Not Bombs? What sustains the strength it takes to endure police beatings, countless nights in jail, and a lifetime of struggle—all in service of feeding people? And how does he so deftly stir together the dirge of war with the scourge of hunger? I found the answers in his beautifully written Soup Street memoir—a nourishing blend of grit, grace, and radical compassion. This book is soul food for activists and a recipe for resistance. Bon appétit.

—Medea Benjamin, co-founder of CODEPINK

Keith McHenry shares how the background of his decent parents who were part of the "greatest generation" impressed upon him to share the good fortunes of living in this country and how it translated to him so as to dedicate his life to making things better for those feeling less fortunate. To improve upon the inequities of life here in our country by the simple act of sharing food. This would seem to be a beautiful thing except far too many of those in power saw hungry people congregating as a threat and as an eye sore. Keith celebrates his life by pointing out and protesting out this petty mean spirited view of feeding fellow human beings/countrymen in public as a negative worthy of arrest and harassment. It has been Keith's McHenry's mission in life to perform these good acts. He shares the adventures, the challenges and the arrests through his life. My punk band MDC made music for and supported "Food Not Bombs" through the decades and I am proud to know him and to have supported him. He has served millions of people with free vegan food. Bless him and pick up his read on the adventures of challenging mayors, the police and powers that be who would suppress the simple act feeding people in public with free food.

—Dave Dictor - MDC Hardcore Punk

FREE RADIO
HOMES NOT JAILS
HAVE FUN
FOOD NOT BOMBS
FOOD NOT BOMBS

CONTENTS

ENJOYING THE JOURNEY

My father loved his powder blue Corvair with the engine in the rear. A back end feature he proudly explained also propelled the Army tanks he flew above in his L-19 reconnaissance plane while stationed in West Germany.

My father accepted a transfer in 1963 from his position at the Rock Creek Nature Center in Washington DC to become a District Park Naturalist on the South Rim of the Grand Canyon. My mother, brother Bruce and I headed out with my father across the country at a time when the four lane Interstate Highway system had yet to scar America's landscape. I was liberated from those kindergarten Duck and Cover nuclear war drills at Bethesda Elementary excited to see what I thought would be Wile E. Coyote and The Road Runner zipping across the desert. I was of course only five and while I peered out hoping to see them I was not disappointed in the stunning beauty we would pass on our way to our new home.

I was small enough to lay under the bubble window behind the back seat. The perfect vantage point to see the evening stars, majestic towering clouds and vastness of the American countryside. Route 66 was a thin ribbon of asphalt with endless horizons free of fences and chain restaurants. A land absent of ugly corporate sterility with its psychic numbing and the desperation that would come.

My childhood of living free in America's wilderness was confronted nearly a decade later as a teen while standing on a Wasatch Mountain peak looking across once pure valleys of Utah now filled with the black smoke from the Four Corners coal generating stations. That Thanksgiving heading south on US 86 I caught my first sight of those monstrous high tension power towers that marched across the pristine beauty of Painted Desert. That was all it took. Any political and economic system willing to desecrate the sacred lands of the southwest was a system I vowed to dedicate my life to ending.

Something had always stirred in my soul propelling me to follow my heart. To disregard the safety of conformity. To adopt the unbound life as a Henry David Thoreau "government is best which governs least" inspired anarchist living by my principles no matter the dangers.

From my days experiencing the thumping leather boots of Hopi boys clutching rattle snakes between their teeth in the dusty plaza of Old Orabi to days of torture in a San Francisco Stress Position Cage, each detail between these pages is my authentic effort to share what led me to helping start Food Not Bombs. What was it that motivated me to spend my life spending hundreds of nights in jail for the crime of "making a political statement" armed only with a ladle and the pursuit of a just world at peace?

This book is an adventure that seeks to understand the influence of my family's participation in formation of the nation, the character molding tragedies I survived, my many days of homelessness and the joys that molded my path. The influence of a self confident mother who lived with dignity but died too young.

A life shaped by an intelligence officer grandfather who was proud that he directed the world's most deadly bombing campaign torching Tokyo whom I also witnessed arguing over the phone with his friends Secretary of Defense Robert McNamara and General Curtis LeMay on the logic of dropping a nuclear bomb on Hanoi. Another grandfather who spent his life as a National Park Ranger who held my hand as we waded through the tidal pools at Natural Bridges State Park in Santa Cruz or wandering through the vanilla scented Ponderosa Pines along the rim of the Grand Canyon, teaching me the latin names of the creatures that clung to the black rocks on the coast of the Pacific and the sage and Indian Paint Brush of the Coconino Plateau.

Travel with me across Northern Mexico in a 1979 blue school bus with a broken gas guage on tour with 17 members of two Mexican hardcore punk bands and our discovery of a of a peyote patch while waiting for the return of our band members with gas cans of fuel. Join me on two tours of Nigeria speaking on West Africa's largest radio station, buying a stolen van on the side of a rubble strewn road at the port of Lagos, escaping a kidnaping and speaking before the country's most powerful student organization. Cross eastern Europe on crowded Polish trains, taking an overnight train to visit the Food Not Bombs survivors of Wesley Clark's war on Belgrade and riding in freezing Serbian railcars stripped of hardwear joining a Sikh from Modesto California on holiday and two Bulgarian National Police transporting a Kurdish "terrorist" to the Turkish border.

My memoir is my honest search to reveal what motivated me to take this unusual journey and perhaps this book will inspire you to live more fully or reflect on the struggle and beauty of your own travels across time.

Enjoy the journey.

Keith McHenry
Co-Founder of Food Not Bombs

PART ONE: BORN WITH A PAST

My father and coworker floating down the Rio Grande with reporter Nancy Dickerson

Chapter 1

A RIO GRAND OF CHOLERA

The mystery of our destination excited me. All I really knew was that my little brother, Bruce, and I would soon be playing on the southern edge of our nation. Our baby sister, Dolly, must have cried for every inch of the 1,200 miles of pavement our family covered from the Grand Canyon to the heart of the West Texas wilderness.

The nearest grocery store was more than two hours away by car. I loved the feeling of living at the end of the world. No between-meal snacks or analog TV for us in the Big Bend National Park of 1963. Just the pure open skies and endless vistas punctuated by my father's tales of candelilla wax smugglers winding their burro trains through the washes under the cover of moonless nights. I have fond memories of the one-room schoolhouse where thirty of us would start each morning tooting on our plastic recorders. And I remember that hot day when President Johnson's wife Ladybird shook my brother's hand.

The biting scent of the greasy, bright-green creosote bushes cooking in the 100-degree heat hung over the alluvial fan that was our limitless playground. Bruce and I woke each day with the sun, shoved cheap, crumpled cowboy hats over our stubbly, blond crewcuts and dashed out into the 1,000-square-mile Chihuahuan Desert. We armed ourselves with a favorite stick or lariat and slapped our own thighs as if they were those of the horses we pretended to ride. We were free among the ocotillo, teddy-bear cholla and prickly pear pads laughing as we chased pods of prehistoric peccaries up and down the sandy washes. The only thing that called us home was our growling stomachs. Big Bend National Park was as God had left it, littered with the life and stones rejected on the seventh day. At least that was how it was explained to me.

My life free of boundaries, was bliss.

Our excursions to Boquillas to visit with the District Park Ranger Dick Strange and his family always promised to be interesting. The fun would include afternoons playing with the young rock sellers who spent their days on the banks of the swollen Rio Grande, crouching beneath the limbs of a droopy Salt Cedar. They were young boys about my age whose job was to wait for tourists to wander down to the river crossing to take their obligatory glance at Mexico.

My Mexican friends waded across the meandering green waters each day with their filthy rags of colorful stones to collect a few quarters. In their determination to survive, they tried to earn a quarter or two by selling a selection of transparent quartz crystals, sea blue and rose opals, labradorite, calcite, aragonite, and selenite of every hue scavenged from the mines deep in the Sierra del Carmen.

Sometimes my companions interrupted the quiet by launching a bottle rocket or two towards the southern bank. They let my best friend Nicky and I in on their secret: we could buy our own fireworks at the saloon in the tiny village of Boquillas, only a few hundred yards from the crossing.

The stone merchants laughed with us when an American lady shrieked at the sight of a Mojave Rattlesnake slithering into the willows. Nicky and I often crossed the greenish border waters to join our friends in an occasional game of basketball under a large cottonwood or to compete in the skipping of dull-colored river stones across the currents. We were a tough lot.

The smell of smoky willow fires and the murmuring of a burro, the angry crow of a rooster mixed with the soft clang of a lone cow's bell drifted north on the gentle breezes and pulled Nicky and me through the knee-deep waters to the mud buildings of Boquillas. On one blistering day when we tired of floating tree branches downstream into the shadows of Boquillas Canyon we decided to look for the fireworks saloon. How could two eight-year-olds resist such mystery?

The cool waters were refreshing, swirling above our spindly knees as we waded south towards the dusty village of Boquillas, on the northern edge of Chihuahua, with a population of less than a hundred people, a few tired old horses hobbled with rough rope, and that one old cow that hugged the shade under the waving thicket of giant reeds.

We followed the powder dirt trail that emerged from the wet sand into town and quickly stumbled upon the saloon, a windowless, old, one-room, adobe building. Nicky followed me past the filthy rug of a door into the mystery: a darkened cavern, lit only by the sunlight that leaked through the ragged threads of the doorway blanket and a flickering kerosine lamp at one end of the bar. Three or four old men in cowboy hats showing various degrees of damage sat quietly around a heavy, beat-up, wooden table. They were the toughest looking men I had ever seen. Nicky was just as impressed. I thrilled at the idea that they might have been outlaws, killers, or worse.

A rusty old metal Coca-Cola sign was the room's only decoration.

"Señor…fireworks? Fuegos artificiales?" I asked, remembering the rock boys' name for the coveted distraction. I held out a dollar bill that I had snuck from my mother's purse. A smile slowly emerged from the expressionless faces. One of the old men stood, slowly walked to the end of the counter, struggled to bend down and pulled out a dusty package of Black Cat Rockets from a crumpled box on the floor.

I looked up at the guy, handed him the dollar saying, "Gracias, señor," before turning to the others. "Buenos días," I said, and nodded to the saloon patrons as we walked confidently towards the door, flicked the dust-caked rug to one side and stepped through. As soon as we were outside, we sped to the river. We were really not as brave as we tried to appear.

Our rock-merchant playmates helped us launch our armaments, laughing as our rockets flew out over the Rio Grande. Once we exhausted the pyrotechnics our friends invited us to join them in another game of basketball. The court was a patch of dirt that I then knew was just north of the saloon. Our basket was a wooden beer crate nailed to the blotchy trunk of a village cottonwood. The basketball had long been deflated, so dribbling was out of the question. Instead, we held the limp ball while running in circles making quick passes to our bare-chested teammates. One team was shirtless, the other wore their shirts. We used a long stick—a pole that had its permanent place of honor leaning against the cottonwood—to poke the ball out of the basket and back into play. We all won because winning wasn't the point. Being boys and having fun was all we cared about.

I woke the next morning to a heavy sweat, stomach cramps, and explosive diarrhea that soaked my bed sheets. I heaved bloody vomit onto the floor. A yellowish swirl of delirium dominated my brain.

It was the fear in my father's face that frightened me. The terror in my mother's eyes made it worse. My father carried my feverish body to the family Rambler, placed me in the back and sped off at top speed north towards Alpine, Texas. My mother sat in the back dabbing my forehead with a cold, wet face cloth while struggling to make sure my black-speckled vomit didn't miss the sauce pan.

It took a little more than an hour to make the 120-mile trip. By that time, I was reduced to puking up a foul-smelling gas. My underwear was soaked in liquid diarrhea. My father scooped me up in his arms and rushed me through the swinging doors into the emergency room. Startled nurses pulled my father to the nearest gurney. Panicked hospital staff hustled to insert an IV into my thin arm.

An hour passed. The dry heaves stopped. The adults started to relax and I drifted off to sleep.

I woke, exhausted, in a room of white walls, white sheets, and white curtains. I overheard the doctor tell my parents that I would need to have two injections a day. A nurse that lived at the park would stop by our house to administer the shots.

We returned to our small cinderblock home in Panther Junction and, as promised, the park nurse came that evening. She had a kind smile as she held her fingers on my wrist to take my pulse and listen to my chest with her stethoscope. "Keith, I will be giving you a shot in the thigh so I will need to pull down your pajama bottoms. It will sting, but you are a big boy now."

She pulled a huge syringe from her black case, filled the reservoir with fluid and pushed a few drops out the end of a very long needle. Then she dabbed my thigh with a cotton ball wetted with alcohol and told me to take a deep breath. She quickly plunged the needle into my flesh, and it hurt. Really hurt.

"You did good. I'll be back in the morning," she explained while packing her medical case. And she did return, giving me the injection in the opposite thigh. That was when I overheard her talking with my parents about my illness.

"You are so lucky. I heard the others didn't make it," she said sadly. "I heard that of the twenty-eight people with cholera your son was the only one that survived." Such was the good fortune of living north of the boarder, having a family with a car and a hospital at journey's end.

A few months later our family returned to Boquillas to visit Nicky and his family. My friend was eager to tell me that several of our rock-selling playmates were among the dead.

"Yes, Keith, really dead, dead just like in the movies."

Keith while in the Cub Scouts in Luray Virginia

Chapter 2

RATS AND THE RED SOX

It was a steamy August afternoon in 1962. The Boston Red Sox had lost again. But that didn't matter to this five-year-old, blond, blue-eyed boy. I loved the excitement of the crowd, the salted peanuts, and the determination of the bat boys. I loved our annual summer visits to my grandparent's home in Massachusetts.

My mother's father had season ticket seats behind the Sox dugout. They were prime seats he first bought while studying law at Harvard. One of my grandfather's greatest joys in life was taking his family to see those arrogant Yankees play our beloved Sox. "Peanuts here, peanuts here, get your peanuts!" yelled a vender in a paper cap as he stretched to pass a cone of salty treats to a fan four seats from the aisle. My grandfather bounced my giggling little brother in the air to chants of, "Go Sox, go Sox"! My father reminded me to be ready to snag a foul with my new, leather baseball mitt. I was ready.

The chatter in the stands drained to a near silence and old men struggled to stand as they heard the music, "O say can you see, by the dawn's early light / What so proudly we hailed at the twilight's last gleaming." I stood proudly at attention, my hand over my heart, secretly knowing that it was our family's own song about a flag that was flying over the fort named after my father's great, great grandfather's great grandfather, Dr. James McHenry, signer of the U.S. Constitution and best friend of George Washington.

A fast ball cracked off Carl Yastrzemski's bat into left field. A roar swept the park. My mother faithfully filled in the box score. She didn't miss a play. I watched every move the bat boys made. I loved seeing them grab the bats that had been flung to the dirt at home plate. I joined the other fans in making the Fenway whoosh as the foul balls cascaded down the netting behind home plate and into the glove of a uniformed boy. One youngster was always stationed out in Fenway Park's left field under the Big Green Monster, hanging the metal runs under each inning on the scoreboard. I dreamed of having his job one day.

We streamed out of Fenway Park joining hundreds of other fans in the rush towards the parking lots and my grandfather's boat of a Buick. One of our many family traditions was the post-game trip downtown for ice-cream at Bailey's. East-bound Tremont Street was bumper to bumper. Carloads of Red Sox fans crawling through the forgotten South End.

My grandfather rested his left elbow on the open windowsill as we inched, block by block, towards fudge-dripping ice cream sundaes and banana splits. The adults were busy chattering about adult stuff, oblivious to the world beyond the interior of the cushy automobile.

My attention was riveted on the world of desperation outside our car. The once elegant brownstones along this part of Tremont were ragged and ignored. People sat on the steps in the shadows of the crumbling brick buildings seeking any hint of a cool breeze. Some sat together enjoying lively conversations. Others clutched the small paper sacks that, I would later learn, concealed bottles or cans of booze.

A man draped in filthy, stained rags of brown and gray lay motionless on the top stoop below a boarded-up door. He was missing a shoe. I stole a closer look. His pants were torn, exposing a blood-red chuck of muscle in his thigh. A large Norway rat was chewing on the man's flesh. The bright white of his leg bone glistened under the late summer sun. A second rat scurried across the man's bearded face. An empty bottle sat on the step below his dangling hand.

I couldn't take my eyes off the scene: a young boy's fascination with the unusual. We coasted on to the next block. No one was being eaten by rats on that block, but that wasn't so at the following light. Several giant rats with rough, wiry tails waving in the sun, crawled across the chest of another man cloaked in the blotchy, gray remains of his months-old clothing. Two rodents were gnawing on their self-embalmed human meal. They had already eaten several fingers and it looked like they were about to finish devouring his forearm.

The Buick pulled up to Bailey's and we stepped into the refreshing cool of the air-conditioned ice cream parlor. Loopy wire-framed chairs with acid-pink, vinyl seat cushions surrounded the round tile-topped tables. I stood wide-eyed, peering into the glass case at the colorful tubs of strawberry, pistachio, vanilla, and rich chocolate ice cream. A teenager smiled at me as he coiled hot fudge over my vanilla sundae. I devoured my delicious treat. On that sweltering day, my family was a winner even if our Red Sox weren't.

Maybe rat-eaten men were to be expected.

Keith playing with the Warnock kids at Shenandoah National Park headquarters

My Uncle Keith standing at the bank of the C & O Canal July 1942

Chapter 3

AM I KEITH, OR AM I KEITH?

I was born into someone else's past. I arrived replacing my grandmother's better son Keith, my perfect uncle, in 1957, a few months after his death from Lupus. I took my first breath on the banks of the Main in US Military Hospital 48 while my father was deployed with the 3rd Armored Division.

"He was the first male ever diagnosed with Lupus," my father often reminded me. Keith was perfect even in death.

That would be my first illusion and become my first question: am I Keith or am I Keith?

A brass plaque mounted on a lichen blotched granite stone at Pioneer Cemetery on the South Rim of the Grand Canyon includes the names of my father's mother, Bona Mae, and my grandfather, Donald Edward. But Keith's name is first. Raised letters read: DONALD KEITH McHENRY, 1936 – 1957, SON.

My grandparent's ashes were scattered around the lichen-covered stone. I know this because some of those ashes sifted through my tiny, child fingers into the Ponderosa pine needles surrounding our family's rock at the edge of the mighty canyon.

Keith's remains weren't scattered at this South Rim rock. He donated his corpse to science. A last selfless act in a life that made uncle Keith the flawless son. The perfect brother. The better of the two.

I can't remember when my father first told me Keith was the first male to be diagnosed with Lupus or that he was an Olympic skier, things he repeated like a mantra. My father may have told me all this even before I could speak. Like most people's memories of Keith, my father remembered his younger brother as bigger than life.

The family story claimed that his Lupus was triggered by an extreme case of sunburn acquired while skiing shirtless on the blinding, white spring slopes of Badger Pass, Yosemite when he was training for the Winter Olympics. The 1958 Wasatch Academy high school yearbook was dedicated to his memory and a brass plaque with his name adhered to the entrance of the Craighead Humanities Building.

Even though I never met him, I knew he was perfect: a handsome young man pure of heart, graced with compassion and humility, and extremely intelligent. I wasn't sure how I was going to live up to his dramatic death let alone his saintly life. But I knew that that was what was expected of me.

My little brother was named Bruce, after my father. He was born two years after me in Logan, Utah on a brisk April 19th. He could have been a musical shot heard around the world but he surrendered to his name.

My father made sure we all knew that he was never as perfect as his brother, our uncle, Keith. His mother was quick to remind the family of this essential fact. She would add my little brother to this pronouncement marking me as the better of the two.

Yet my brother was a talented musician, vocalist, composer, and lyricist who played the trumpet with perfect pitch. Women would run their fingers admiringly through the curly, blond locks that framed his always positive expressions.

I remember Bruce and I standing together on a snowy December morning at the Grand Canyon Clinic amazed at the sight of our tiny sister. We skirted above the canyon cliffs together following our father across the rockslides of Sinking Ship Butte.

A couple of years later Bruce and I tagged along, a mile or two behind the adults, on a three-day hike around the top of the Chisos Mountains in Big Bend, Texas. After we moved to Shenandoah, we would spend those three miserable, rainy days together on the Appalachian Trail. Bruce was the star catcher for Luray, Virginia's little league team, the Red Sox, while I spent the summers standing unnoticed in my bleach-white little league uniform in right field waiting for the fly ball that never came. For most of our childhood I was not only his friend but I was his guardian. While I couldn't relate to his flamboyance and relentless chatter, I appreciated his kindness and innocence.

He was full of hope the day I dropped him off at the Tanglewood Music Camp on that first summer after he graduated from high school. From the moment we headed west on Route 2, Bruce couldn't stop talking with exuberant optimism about the three months he would spend studying music with members of the Boston

Symphony. But the rejection of his summer romance with the cellist snuffed out that spark and reinforced his belief that he was the lesser son Bruce of the lesser father Bruce. In desperation, he started to drink. And he started to hate our father.

On reflection my brother knew his place in our family. He had a much better understanding of the dynamics than I did. But like me, he was also born into our particular past, absorbing the legacy of being named after my father, a man he saw as caught up in a desperate attempt to escape his own fear of being second best.

Our past included a great grandfather, Reverend H. Cresson McHenry of the Church of St. John the Evangelist, who was one of a long line of New World Protestants that led back to the twenty-year-old James McHenry who had stepped on to a Philadelphia wharf in 1773. Cresson McHenry's son, my grandfather, also tried his hand at being an Episcopal minister before he slid onto a coffin in a muddy Wyoming grave during his first funeral service. According to my grandfather, he quickly mailed a resignation letter to the bishop explaining his change of plans believing that his plunge into an open grave was a bad omen.

When it was my time to join the Episcopalian tradition, my father proudly drove our family through the oak and hickory forest, snaking up the narrow pavement to the old white church in Smoke Hollow, Virginia.

The service started with two hymns, a psalm and then the moment of confirmation arrived. The minister reminded us that we would take an oath to the only true faith. He recited a passage pledging allegiance to the Episcopal Church, to Jesus, the Trinity and all that it stands for "for the rest of our lives, Amen."

I couldn't repeat the words. A realization struck me like a bolt of lightning. I was too young to make a commitment for life. I was only twelve. What did I know about religion, God, and truth?

Even so I stepped up to the altar, knelt before the pastor, took the host, and sipped the sweet wine, but I felt uneasy. The body and blood of Christ didn't convince me that I was ready for a lifetime of believing.

Then the service that changed my life finally came to an end. The congregation flooded through the red doors and out into the sunlight. Thirty or forty people dressed in their Sunday best milled around on the street engaged in lively conversations. Children relieved to be freed from their pews ran around the chapel grounds laughing as they let off steam.

My father greeted me with a big smile and a bear hug asking me, "Keith, how does it feel to be an Episcopalian?"

I responded, "Dad, I just don't have enough information yet. The Episcopal Church might be the only true church but I am too young to make a lifetime commitment."

By that time in my life, I had witnessed the Hopi Snake Dances. They seemed pretty authentic to me. What about Buddhism or Hinduism? Those were religions I had heard of but knew little about.

I felt his heart break. His smile vanished into a tight-lipped frown. My father coldly announced, "Anyone living under my roof is going to be an Episcopalian," and released his hug. But then he added, "Keith, you are too honest, that's your problem."

My father might have been wounded by an honesty he had also known in his perfect brother, Keith. I never asked. It could have been just the pain of rejection of my needing to follow in his big footsteps. But it was a wound that shattered our bond as father and son. At least as far as he was concerned. But that moment was also a proclamation of my own truth and independence. I may have stepped through that red church door a child but when I emerged into the warm spring sun, I had become an adult. Just not the adult my father had intended I become.

That light feeling of having broken free from my father's control, however, I would learn to be an illusion. Yet there was a lesson in my father's response. A lesson I was about to take advantage of.

My life had been idyllic before we moved to Appalachia. It would be difficult to find a wilderness playground as free as Big Bend National Park or the South Rim of the Grand Canyon. My imagination knew no boundaries in the vast Chihuahuan desert bisected by the green Rio Grande or the limitless chasms of America's greatest canyon.

Park Service children didn't have many rules but the ones we did have were meant to keep us from an early grave. We were told that the rim of the Grand Canyon was off limits without an adult, but that never stopped us from venturing to the edge to witness the vast abyss cut by the Colorado. It might have been wise for this first and second grader to head home before sunset, but even that was not necessary in the wilderness of the early sixties.

But then it happened. Our family moved to Shenandoah National Park and I started the fourth grade. I had been the Keith that whistled a happy tune on my daily walk to school or trailed a quarter mile behind my father and his friend Napier as we strolled along the tow path of the Chesapeake and Ohio Canal towards Harpers Ferry. But that changed in Page County, Virginia where I climbed aboard a yellow school bus, taking my seat on the padded green benches with the other squirmy white kids.

Park Headquarters on Pumpkin Hill was the first stop on the route to school and the last stop each afternoon. The busload of increasingly noisy elementary students bounced past fields of yellowing corn stalks and slopes of green grass eaten close to the rocky ground by sheep. A couple of scrawny cows foraged for tall blades of grass missed by the furry flock.

After splashing through a tiny creek, the bus jerked to a stop below a weathered frame house with a rusty tin roof. The paint flaking building appeared to be sliding towards the road. Three toothless blond boys, with straw for socks and ropes for belts, pushed one another up the bus stairs. A little girl dressed in a red and white checkered dress climbed on board at the next bend and two boys with clean white shirts and black pants scampered to their seats at a second stream. Child after child joined us as we swayed back and forth along the dirt ruts towards an education.

Forty-five minutes later a huge two-story, yellow-brick schoolhouse loomed out of the Virginia soil like a prison. That first sight of the imposing yellow citadel made my heart sink. The immense brick facade rose from the barren dirt and weeds towards an early fall sky making even the tallest student seem insignificant. I was already doomed and I had only just arrived.

I climbed the cement steps behind the parade of arriving students entering the austere corridor of ocher tile. The musty smell of the hallways and the bitter ammonia of urine combined with the sinister echoing of screaming kids to signal the catastrophe I was about to endure. Students thundered up and down the concrete stairs towards their next class after the tinny school bell screeched the end of each period.

That sick feeling of dread would become familiar. The most popular kid at Springfield Elementary found a place behind me as we lined up to head back to class after my first recess. Of course, being the new kid in school he pushed me hard in the back. He laughed as he asked what planet I came from, made some nasty remarks about my strange accent and shoved me again. He got the attention of the other students which encouraged him to shove me with more vigor.

I asked him to stop but he kept teasing me. I had never been treated badly by a fellow classmate so this was a totally unique experience. At some point I turned around and punched Mr. Popular in the nose. The fight was on. He grabbed me and we fell to the ground and rolled through the schoolyard and across a wet ditch.

He started to cry when he realized he had a bloody nose. A teacher finally arrived to break up the fight. She took Mr. Popular to the first-floor toilets to wash his face. I returned to the line of students stunned and dusty.

I got the best of him that time, but later that week his friends cornered me in the second-floor bathroom. Springfield Elementary had no need for segregated toilets or water fountains. It was a whites-only institution.

Three friends of my bloodied classmate cornered me by the stalls. They glared at me with the evil grins of children anticipating the ecstasy of violence. The eerie glow of sunlight streamed through filthy windows. Two of the boys, both much bigger than me, grabbed my arms. A third boy clasped the back of my neck in his huge hand.

My screams echoed off the yellow tile walls but no one came. My head was plunged into a toilet of shit and piss. I struggled to break free but couldn't. A water-soaked log of crap smashed into my tightly closed lips. Another turd stuck in my left ear. Feces-stained toilet paper glued across my closed eyes.

They pulled me out for a second then smashed my head back into that fetid bowl. It was on the third plunge into the stench that one of the kids pushed the lever. A loud swishing sound sucked the air out of my ears as the tornado of shitty piss swirled around my head. My blond, crap-covered head sucked towards bottom of the bowl. Fortunately, my head was too large, otherwise I may have been pulled into the septic tank. I emerged, dripping with wet toilet paper and chunks of shit dangling from my eyelids and crewcut. The tough boy leader gave me a kick. "You better watch your backside hog jaws. This won't be the last time we will whop your ass," he growled, spitting in my face for good measure.

I wasn't eager to return to class but I was a fourth grader and had no other options. I extracted shreds of excrement-stained toilet paper and chunks of crap from my hair, ducking under the tap to rinse off what I could. I must have smelled awful. Being new to such violence and not knowing what else to do, I silently took my seat and continued with my education. I guess, looking back, that I must have thought this was normal since the teacher made no comment and I didn't mention it to my mother. She had no sense of smell and this may explain her lack of concern. My classmates of course laughed on learning of the second-floor swirly and hoped they would have another chance to gloat about my being treated to another plunge.

That was the beginning of four years of swirlies, bloody noses, punches to the side of my head or to the pit of my stomach, and daily threats that another beating would be waiting for me in the morning. Those rare days free of physical violence were a slog of taunts and insults and long, sleepless nights obsessing over my next promised pounding.

The violence at school was not limited to brutal beatings by classmates. Teachers got into the act. Miss a math problem, slide a hamburger bun back to its owner, or fail to wrestle the baseball bat from a fifth-grade bully named Tex and a teacher would get out their bread-board paddle drilled with strategic holes for optimum suffering.

Go to the front of the class. Bend over and grab the bottoms of your jeans and pull hard to experience maximum pain as ordered. Then there were the tears running down your face as your classmates smiled with pleasure.

The years of terror at school were bad enough but things at home also turned for the worse. There is only one time that I can recall my father's anger being directed at me during the years before our family moved to Shenandoah. Never once at the Grand Canyon or Big Bend or when we lived at Yosemite or Yorktown. That one outburst was when I flooded the dogwood trees he had carefully transplanted to the back yard of our home in Bethesda, Maryland when I was a kindergartener. Other than that one incident, I don't believe he ever raised his voice at me.

Thinking back, I remember him expressing frustration with his Shenandoah boss which may have contributed to his change in personality. One thing or another threw him into a blinding rage.

I left my bike in the driveway one afternoon and he had to move it before he could park. That was one insult too much. "Didn't I tell you not to leave your bike here," he screamed stomping into the house. I slipped from his wrath, dashed into the yard, and sprinted as fast as possible around and around our tiny mass-produced Mission 66 house, fleeing from my 200-pound father as he screamed at me to stop and take it like a man.

The entire neighborhood couldn't help but witness these dramas. Exhausted, I would rush through the back door, down the hall, and jump into my bed, feet raised to protect my little body from his belt or hairbrush. My poor mother would yell at him to stop but it was too late for reason. After my beating he would grab a chair and order me to sit facing the wall until he told me I could get up. For extra punishment he would place a clock in view and order me to stay until the big hand crossed the appropriate number.

The violence was interrupted with twice monthly camping trips. My father and fellow scout master Mr. Johnson led Boy Scout Troop 100 in to the mountains above town, out to Camp Lake Eden, where I was tapped out into the Order of the Arrow, and even took us on a week-long campout in Cinnamon Bay, Saint Johns, Virgin Island. Mr. J and my father would often entertain us around the campfire, with tales of the light aircraft wrecks they had survived while in the military. These vacations from violence with my scout friends may have saved my sanity.

I also escaped the terror by retreating to the forest behind my parent's home to paint pictures of laurel trees and rhododendrons with my tin of water colors. My mother also offered relief by letting my friend David and I steal time with my little sister's Easy Bake Oven to experiment with her cornbread recipes. She would also recruit me each spring as muscle for the task of double digging the dark Virginia soil of her vegetable garden. A clip of the shovel against a stubborn Sassafras root launched the fragrance of sweet root beer.

Even though I would never become the Christian my father wanted me to be, I participated in the pageantry of the church every Sunday. "I saw you trip on the unhemmed black robe this morning," he'd say, laughing at the site of me stumbling up the steps on the way to place the processional cross in its stand next to the alter. He would glory at the memory of my brother and I being, as he called us, Wise Guys in the Christmas play.

The violence was also psychological. My father sat with me on a stone wall outside his office at park headquarters one late summer afternoon. I was eight. "Keith, I am not ready yet to have children," he announced. "I am going to need your help." I recall being confused but ready to do my part. One thing was for sure, it did not instill confidence in him.

My mother and the other Park Headquarter parents decided the free bus ride to the poor education of Springfield Elementary in our school district wasn't worth the convenience and agreed to take turns driving us to Luray Elementary.

The beatings at Springfield Elementary followed me to fifth grade and the elementary school in town. I couldn't even escape the nickname, "Hog Jaws," given to me by my Springfield tormenters. I was placed in Special Education which mostly consisted of a classroom of white children with Down syndrome. I had dyslexia even though this was referred to by the school officials as retardation but probably more importantly I had the apparent illness of not having been born in Page County.

Our Special Education class had a boost in attendance when I entered the sixth grade. Racial desegregation in public education was finally forced on Luray. The white administrators and teachers tried to fight it by deeming the kids from the black side of the tracks to be retarded and thus making sure they didn't get too close to the children of our town's upstanding white Christians. This was in a town where you could buy mass-produced "Whites Only", "Colored Only" and "No Jews Allowed" signs at the Ben Franklin Five and Ten on Main Street.

The violence didn't stop when I advanced to high school which in Luray started in the eighth grade. There was no middle school in our rural community.

One day during the last months of my first year as a Luray High Bulldog, an incident finally made an impression on my parents and the school administration. It started in the dim fluorescent light of the locker room. Sweaty socks and the bitter smell of disinfectant smothered the cramped room. My classmates hurried to change into their gym clothes, jostling against one another and the Band-Aid-beige tin lockers. One of the bullies, a kid named Willy, squeezed past me muttering, "I am going to kill you Hog Jaws." When we crowded onto the basketball court, he made sure to dribble past me, taunting me and reminding me that he was going to beat me after gym. Then one student after another rushed past, mocking me with threats that Willy was really going to kick my ass this time. They claimed that I had insulted him. I was confused since I had never made any comment about Willy. I had the impression that they made that up just to see what Willy would do. It was hopeless and I became increasingly terrified by his escalating anger as he was egged on by the others.

I plotted my escape through the only exit from the locker room. I quickly dressed and headed for the door but Willy was waiting on the other side and slugged me on the side of my head. Then a fist to my belly, then another fist to my head, followed by more blows, one after another. Whoever told him a tale about me insulting him had caused Willy to become unhinged. I tried to block his swings with my arms; I tried to move around him to safety with no luck. He finally stopped beating on me when I fell to the ground. But then he finished me off with one hard kick to my head as I was crawling towards the principal's office. The next thing I remember is the principal's secretary bending over my bloodied frame sprawled out on the floor below the lobby counter.

"Keith, Keith, sit up," she repeated as she dabbed my face with a rough, wet paper towel. My blood ran across the linoleum tiles.

She called my mother. My parents arrived a few hours later. The principle announced Willy would be suspended for two weeks. Hardly a punishment for someone who hated school. But this was a turning point. My parents finally seemed to hear what I had been saying about the violence I had endured for four long years. At least that is how I remember it now.

After Willy's beating I had had enough of the terror and realized that to escape the violence of Page County, Virginia, I had to appeal to my father's desire that I follow in his footsteps and continue the family traditions. This is when I employed the lesson that I learned at the Confirmation Service at Smoke Hollow. While I couldn't fake my devotion to the church of my patriarchs it dawned on me that there were a number of other sacred traditions I could adopt. The one that would most meet my need to flee this hell was my father's alma mater, Wasatch Academy. So, I started to let my father know that I wanted to be just like him and attend the high school that he and his perfect brother Keith had attended. Mount Pleasant, Utah might be far enough to liberate me from my suffering.

My strategy worked and my parents flew to Salt Lake City with me in tow. We caught a Trailways bus at the downtown depot and took a long strange ride to the little village of Mt. Pleasant. Utah was a dry version of rural Virginia. The mountains much younger, with treeless peaks of granite. The houses of unpainted lumber and tin roofs were just as rundown as those of our Page County neighbors.

Although excited to be free from Virginia I was also anxious about the unknown. My emotional baggage was a lot heavier than the two cardboard suitcases of underwear, socks, dress pants, long sleeve shirts, and mandatory neck ties that I retrieved from the compartment under the bus. My father pointed out the landmarks as we walked through the downtown towards his high school alma mater. Yes, my baggage would prove to be very heavy. It didn't take long for me to learn I had huge shoes to fill. There he was again, uncle Keith, the better son.

"You look just like Keith. He was such a good student," Mrs. Ellsburg said, gazing towards the heavens as though she might see her perfect student up there, and then taking us to see the school bell dedicated to the virtues of Keith.

Headmaster Hansen was also eager to let me know about Keith. My uncle was the star of his jazz band. He was the captain of the football team and the school's best skier, dancing through the powder at Alta and Park City like no other Wasatch student in the school's now nearly hundred-year history. The uncle I never knew was also freshman, sophomore and junior class president and voted student body president his senior year.

On the other hand, my father had bemoaned that unlike his little brother he was tone deaf, never played an instrument, was just an average skier and never held any office at Wasatch. He attended the school in the shadow of his younger brother who was two grades behind him.

It was unanimous. Keith's English teacher, Mrs. Ellsburg, Headmaster Hansen, several cafeteria cooks and administrators all made sure I knew that I was expected to be as great as my perfect uncle. At least that was the message I believed they were expressing even if it was not their intention.

So, at age 14, the question again came into sharp focus: was I Keith or was I Keith?

When Uncle Keith's health started to fail my father was away in the military. He had signed up to fly L-19 surveillance planes with the Third Armored Division. As he tells it, he enlisted to avoid being drafted into a unit that could be stationed in the bitter cold mountains of Korea. A Korea that might include a real war and a lower rank of private. But Keith's suffering overshadowed my father's military service and his deployment to West Germany created a distance during his brother's illness that seemed to add to his guilt and reenforced a belief that Keith was the more perfect son and that he would never be enough.

I had replaced Keith one sunny day in May 1957 nine months after I was conceived on a canvas cot in a sweaty Army barracks in Bavaria. A detail my parents were not shy to share with me.

I don't think my mother's father would have let her marry a man who lacked an Ivy League pedigree if he had not been a Second Lieutenant and the descendant of a founding father. As it was, he did, and the young couple was soon off to Germany after a spectacular New England wedding.

The fact that I was born in West Germany was a source of pride for me. It made me feel special even though when I announced my place of birth on the first day of first grade my classmates responded by yelling out "Nazi, Nazi!" That didn't really bother me at all. They hadn't been born anyplace special. They were just standard Americans.

I remember a photo that placed me in that special place, Frankfurt. It was a square Kodachrome print I retrieved from the wicker basket of family pictures. It showed Uncle Keith's tiny replacement wrapped in a white blanket, lovingly held in his mother's arms.

I believe my father was the photographer. In the photo, my mother smiles as any mother holding her first born might. She is tiny in this color photo and I am, as one would expect, much smaller. So small, in fact, that my existence had to be pointed out to each person who saw my first baby picture.

Two huge Nazi swastikas take up the top right and left corners of the picture. Concrete swastikas on the frieze of a hospital built especially for Hitler's elite airmen of the Luftwaffe and transformed in defeat into the temporary home of the 97th General Hospital of the US Military. A field of blood-red tulips fills most of the bottom half of the Kodachrome.

This was my father's first photo of his first son. He was no amateur. His first photography teacher was Ansel Adams. His first camera, a single-lens reflex Exa, was a gift from that famous black-and-white nature photographer. That beginners Exakta 35 millimeter would be passed on to me to become my first camera years later.

Was the snapshot outside the hospital really the best photo my father could have taken of his first son? Was the first photo of the first son a message to me that it would be difficult for my father to welcome Keith's replacement? Was the picture a reflection of guilt that the better son died and he survived?

But my father, Douglas Bruce McHenry, was finally able to find his place. He would become a ranger in the National Park Service just as his father had been before him. He would begin by leading campfire programs and nature walks at Estes Park, Colorado, the very same National Park in the Rockies where he had met my mother a few summers before, during a geology camp.

My future mother drove west to Rocky Mountain National Park with her Wellesley College classmates. They did this more for the adventure than an education in rocks. My grandmother, Bona Mea Ford also met my grandfather at the same geology camp a quarter century before. My father completed the cycle by becoming a husband, a father, and a naturalist in the Park Service just like his father.

My little brother, Bruce, was born in Logan, Utah at a time when my father paid the bills by testing the impact of blast cones made to reflect conventional explosives towards the nuclear pay load of the first-generation Minuteman Missiles. When he wasn't helping with America's nuclear defense, he was working on his Master's Degree in Zoology and finally, after a year, he started to spend his summers leading tours in Rocky Mountain National Park.

My family began its three generations as national park service naturalists in 1932 when my grandfather, Junior Park Ranger Donald Edward McHenry, started some of the first National Park nature walks along the South Rim of the Grand Canyon. He helped design the Yavapai Geology Museum, and provided articles for the popular visitor's guide, Grand Canyon Nature Notes.

The Great Depression was still raging when my grandfather was transferred to National Capital Parks. He moved his family into the thick stone Lock House Seven below the Glenn Echo Amusement Park. Before long he had acquired a navy barge and modified it to look like the historic Chesapeake and Ohio canal boat, adding rows of theater seats. He obtained several mules and pressed them into service to tow the heavy barge-load of tourists past Great Falls as he stood on the bow telling his audience about the natural and human history of the Potomac and its canal.

My socialist grandmother cultivated vegetables on the hillside above the Lock House, raised goats, chickens, and rabbits and promoted the cause of the Victory Gardens. Uncle Keith and my father fished in the eddies of Great Falls, caught snakes, and bound along the tow path bare foot. Black-and-white photos of the pair could have illustrated Huckleberry Fin. This is where my father would learn the art of butchery, scrambling the brains of roosters and folding away the fur of fat rabbits.

The McHenry's moved again, returning to the American West, the iconic valley of the mighty Merced, and the granite towers of Half Dome and El Capitan. In the 1956 publication, Self-Guiding Auto Tour of Yosemite National Park, one may find the following entry: "According to Theodore Hazen, Donald McHenry presented the first campfire program east of the Mississippi River in Picnic Grove #1, across the road from Peirce Mill in 1937."

It goes on to discuss Donald McHenry's time before arriving at Yosemite saying that, "He presented a program in Georgetown which was attended by so many people, he had to climb a light pole to present his program. Ranger McHenry even tried guiding from above in a plane with a megaphone, but that was short-lived as the motor drowned out the talk."

My grandfather would retire to a home that clung to the mountain slopes above San Jose, California. He would die holding my father's hand in the glassed-in porch that overlooked the gigantic hanger at Moffett Field, the citrus and avocado groves that became Silicon Valley and out towards the San Francisco Bay, Alameda, Oakland, and the Bay Bridge. I would celebrate my first birthday in that glass room and hold my grandfather's hand as he guided visitors across the tidal pools at Natural Bridges State Park in Santa Cruz.

In his journey to follow in my grandfather's footsteps, my father took an assignment as a permanent ranger in law enforcement. Not exactly the position he wanted, but it was a good career move, he told his young family, that could lead to a full-time job as an Interpretive Park Ranger. I really didn't understand the significance of this, but his announcement seemed monumental to my preschool ears. Before he could start his full-time job, he was required to attend several months at Albright Training Center in Yosemite.

So, my father took his young family to Yosemite while he attended "Ranger School." My mother lovingly bathed my little brother and I in the sun-lit kitchen sink of a trailer on the banks of the rushing Merced River in El Portal. There were snake holes to probe with a stick and river rapids that could wash me to my death. I dared the subterranean critters to get me, poking a favorite stick in each hole. Not one snake or ground squirrel took the challenge.

We were forced to spend the winter in the valley when my father contracted appendicitis. "It was fascinating, I held a mirror in one hand so I could watch the surgery." My father laughed.

Black bear cubs in the snowy valley floor took to our galvanized tin trash-cans as though they were performing in a circus. My mother made sure we didn't miss the show. "They're on this side now," she said, excitedly ushering my brother and I from window to window in our tiny log cabin home.

Six months later we traveled east to Yorktown, Virginia and his law enforcement job patrolling the Colonial Parkway between Jamestown and Williamsburg.

The Navy personnel stationed in Norfolk found the parkway to be a perfect road for impressing their dates, speeding to Williamsburg and back. What fun that must have been until they crashed into a mammoth live oak or a stone wall.

My father was supposed to chase them down and issue speeding tickets. But, from what little I remember, he wasn't very interested in the high-speed chase aspect of the job. It seemed to me that he mostly took eight-by-ten glossy photos of cars hanging in the trees, pancaked into historic stone walls, or half submerged in the creeks.

By then I had already lived for all of my four years attending a nursery school in a historic church, carefully hiding my poops behind my mother's clawfoot bathtub. I was forced to pose outside our family's white picket fence next to my mother's father in my Easter best: matching green shorts and blazer.

I joined my father in the darkroom where I would sit under a red lightbulb and agitate floating sheets of photographic paper with a pair of metal tongs. The bitter, biting chemical odor of stop bath and developer suffocated his tiny office. I swished the paper in the chemical bath. The light grays darkened. What is this, I wondered with anticipation. The image darkened, grays turning to deep blacks. A decapitated head of what seemed to be a beautiful blond woman emerged from the grey lawn. She was staring up from the grassy edge of the parkway, her eyes wide open. Her screaming mouth frozen. Once dark enough, I slid the horrific image into the stop bath. My brother and I showered with my father in his outdoor bath when he returned from fighting house fires and we dangled fishing lines into the York River hoping for that big catch.

My father was finally able to really follow in his father's footsteps. He took the district naturalist position at Rock Creek Nature Center at National Capital Parks in the District of Columbia. My grandfather had also been a district naturalist in Washington during the last days of the Great Depression.

My father's planetarium show was innovative and a huge hit with the public. I felt special getting to sit on the carpeted floor scrunched against the pitch-black wall while the visitors found their theater-style seats in the round. The boom of a thunder bolt recording jolted the audience to attention. The audience let out a gasp as a violent thunderstorm moved west and the imaginary clouds parted to reveal the setting sun and a star-filled sky. Once the planetarium sky was dark my father asked the visitors to imagine they were Indians sitting around a campfire three thousand years ago. The elders would point to the constellations Orion or the Bear and Hunters teaching the young braves the life lessons in the heavens.

This was the time of the Cuban Missile Crisis and kindergarten at Bethesda Elementary. Classes were interrupted with Duck and Cover drills and visions of the Red Army marching in columns of fifty down Constitution Avenue towards our little red brick house on Bells Mills Road. John Glen orbited the Earth and my mother suffered through a perfect family Christmas sprawled out on the couch blistered with measles. She smiled through her illness to see my joy upon discovering a white Styrofoam astronaut's helmet emerge from the glossy Santa-decorated wrapping paper.

Fourteen months after moving to suburban Washington DC my father took his second National Park naturalist position on the South Rim of the Grand Canyon.

My family puttered along Route 66's thin ribbon of asphalt in our family's blue Corvair stopping at a Stuckey's or one of those family-owned fried chicken diners parceled along America's rural arteries. My brother fell ill in Shamrock, Texas. I remember being proud to hear my brother's name included in the list of the hospitalized that was broadcasted on the local radio station as we watched our clothes tumble in a clanky laundromat dryer. "Oh, we are so sorry to hear your son is ill," a bulky woman gently said to my mother. I guess the town was so small that she knew the others. What a sweet service to provide your community: with the list read on the radio, the infirmed and their families could receive cards, flowers, and meal deliveries from listeners. I would make my first snowman with my father in the yard of our motel. It was an adventure.

Texas flat became New Mexico mesas. I was glued to the landscape hoping to see Wile E. Coyote and the Road Runner. Then New Mexico became Arizona as we left the red-walled canyons of Gallup and Grants. The thin ribbon of pavement took our little Corvair through the pink pearly logs of the Petrified Forest, dusty Winslow, the Wigwam Motel, and into the muddy logging town of Flagstaff.

A twelve-point buck towered atop a snowbank greeted us, its head raised proudly above the entrance to the South Rim as we arrived. A Mayflower truck of household furniture met us at our cramped park housing. I joined the neighborhood gang, armed with a metal trashcan lid and a pointed three-foot wooden surveyor's stake. We dared one another to sneak up to the cliff's edge and we sunned naked on the sun-warmed boulders across the rim road from the visitor center. We were park service brats!

Then the president was killed in Dallas. A first-grade classmate demonstrated the assassination by hoping up and down, crowing like a rooster and laughing. She said that Kennedy had run around like a chicken with his head cut off. When I got home, I found my mother leaning in, sobbing, trying to make out the grainy-green images on the television. A few days later we joined America watching the horse drawn wagon slowly take the flag-draped casket to the Capitol Rotunda. I organized a funeral for a bird shot in the head with a BB by the mean backyard neighbor kid. I wrapped John F Kennedy Sparrow in my little American flag, placed him in my red wagon, and lead a memorial march of park service children around the neighborhood.

My mother's belly soon grew to the size of a basketball. She waddled behind my father as he led us over the sandstone paths of First and Second Mesa. She clutched the dashboard of the Corvair, moaning in distress as we bounced over washboard roads through canyons that would soon be flooded behind the Glenn Canyon Dam: a criminal act that would submerge hundreds of ancient Anasazi cliff dwellings and petroglyphs under the stagnant waters of Lake Powell.

My mother's discomfort ended in the screaming pain of labor on a cold December night at the clinic on the South Rim. It was a girl. My father, his parents, my brother, and I strolled through the fresh white powder to the small stone hospital. My new baby sister was wrapped in a white flannel cloth. Pink cheeks and squinty eyes peered out from under a pure white stocking cap. A tiny red arm wiggled free from a crease in the blanket.

"She is a dolly!," I blurted out in awe.

Yes, my sister Dolly had entered the world ready for cotton diapers, nights of crying, and a cheap Sears Bathinette. It wasn't long before I was struggling with her poopy bottom, safety pins, and the correct way to wrap a baby sister in clean diapers.

She also shared the matriarch's first two names, Martha Margaret, and those long blond locks that were never to be shorn. She was fortunate to attend a kindergarten class held by my grandmother just for her and the other Luray children her age. I don't recall any other details of her elementary school years. Dolly expressed disappointment in life at Barnstable High School when she retuned from an exchange trip to Indonesia. That special feeling of desperately poor people fawning over her pearly white complexion and wavy blond hair had come to an end. She was just another American student struggling with their homework. I got the idea that her impression of me as someone to fear came from hours upon hours of my fathers' hand wringing about my having gone bad while away at high school in Utah. We never became close. In her eyes I was the first-born Cain forever wandering in the land of Nod.

My little sister would follow my father into the National Park Service, cementing our families great honor as one of the few third generation rangers. She would meet her architect husband on the South Rim of her birthplace. They would have a son Matthew, whom they would made sure I'd never get to know.

My father was still busy making a difference in defense of mother Earth, fighting the occasional ponderosa forest fire, rescuing unfortunate visitors from a cliff ledge, leading nature hikes below the canyon's rim, and pioneering his extravagant new campfire programs that featured the use of a modern slide carousel projector with lap-dissolved color photos. As his father had before him, he started his program with a sing-along of "Home on the Range" and a round of "Row, Row, Row Your Boat." He gathered his rustic chorus around a roaring fire of pinion while waiting for the evening to grow dark enhancing the brilliance of his color slides.

But if my father's side of the family liked to play with fire, they had nothing on my mother's side of the family.

As far back as I can remember I was fascinated by the sixty-three framed, black-and-white, 8x10, glossy photos that captured the burning of Tokyo from 20 thousand feet and hung in neat rows on the walls of my grandfather's den in Needham, Massachusetts.

My mother's father, John Vanderpool Phelan, was a graduate of Phillips Exeter Academy, Dartmouth College, and Harvard Law School. He was a Harvard Crimson Football star and a loyal defender of capitalism. My grandfather was invited to join the elite Office of Strategic Services where he was assigned to the 468th Bombardment Squadron.

His squadron of B-29 Superfortress planes rained firebombs down on the civilians of Tokyo sixty-three times in Operation Meetinghouse. Death made abstract in his high-altitude glossies that failed to show the terror of the hundreds of thousands of Japanese men, women, and children that burned and suffocated to death on those nights of 1945. My grandfather boasted of his central role in this, a campaign that, according to Daniel Ellsberg's book, The Doomsday Machine: Confessions of a Nuclear War Planner, is still regarded by historians as "the single most destructive bombing raid in human history."

My grandfather organized at least two conventions of his 468th Bombardment Squadron during my childhood. One was held at a motel in Alpine, Texas. I was eight and I soaked up every war story. I also taught myself to swim after giving my plastic blow up life-ring to a little girl I wanted to impress while also feeling that it wasn't fair that I could paddle around while she had to cling to the pool side.

The jolly long-retired pilots talked of their fear that they would run out of fuel and be forced to abandon their planes over the swamps of China. There were tales of gunners who, fearing obliteration, opened blasts of their cannons on the swarms of Japanese Zeros. I sat mesmerized, listening to a grey-haired bombardier describe how, as bullets pierced the thin metal skin of their mighty high-flying Superfortress, he had crawled on his hands and knees across the bomb bay to fix a broken latch so he could release a load of incendiary bombs before the bomber had to rush back to the safety of Burma. The old men laughed about what would have happened if their bombers had run out of fuel as they lumbered high above the jagged ice of the Himalayas.

At first my feelings were confused. Any little boy would be awestruck by such exciting stories. I thought the B-29 was the coolest plane ever. Much better than those B-25s of the European theater I would say to myself with pride. Four remotely controlled turrets armed with two .50-caliber machine guns. I imagined how exhilarating it would be to sit in a Plexiglass bubble hanging below the fuselage and fire away at on-coming Japanese Hayate Ki-84's or to sit in the nose cone downing swarms of attacking fighter planes.

But at the same time, the thought of thousands of people burning alive didn't seem right. In my vivid childhood imagination, I visualized Japanese children like myself clad in light pajamas, living in bamboo-framed houses with paper walls that burst into flames as they slept.

I could imagine my own fiery death during a "duck and cover" nuclear conflict with the Soviets. Would we burn to death like those Japanese kids? My little classmate smiled at me from under her desk. "Do the adults really believe we will survive under our cheap little yellow laminated desks?"

If preparing for a nuclear war by ducking under a desk wasn't odd enough, there was a war I occasionally got a glimpse of on TV. Soldiers firing machine guns, waves of helicopters brushing the tops of palm trees, and death scores at the top of the news: five Americans killed, two thousand communists dead. We must have been winning the war in this place the adults called Vietnam.

My grandfather paced around his den of framed firebombing photos screaming at his former colleagues, General Curtis LeMay and Robert McNamara, as his family sat in the next room celebrating the birth of the Prince of Peace beneath an always-perfect blue spruce. Heavy lead tinsel and dozens of delicate glass ornaments from West Germany decorated the boughs. Packages wrapped with bows were piled high. It was the season that, even then, seemed to be more a celebration of capitalism than the birth of Jesus of Nazareth.

I could hear my grandfather yelling, "You have to drop a hydrogen bomb on Hanoi or the Communists won't take us seriously! They'll think we wouldn't dare do another Nagasaki."

Though he was my mother's father who graduated from prestigious Ivy League schools and spent World War II as an intelligence officer, his pleas to drop another atomic bomb didn't seem very smart. I might have been a child, but that sounded horrific, a plan not connected to any reality I could understand.

Reality may not have been all that important to my mother's parents. My first name, Jonathan, was also not based in a physical reality. I was named after my mother's imaginary playmate, an invisible boy that came to dinner every night and sat before his very real place setting. Jonathan was an illusion that would become me.

Another namesake, however, was quite real. The Vanderpool of John Vanderpool Phelan was the Vanderpool of Karl Vanderpool, the inventor of the electric trolly. Karl Vanderpool designed one of the first electric dynamos and was the man who introduced outdoor lighting at the World's Columbian Exposition in Chicago in 1893.

Family lore has it that he knew Tesla and that they shared innovations with one another. Thomas Edison and Vanderpool, on the other hand, were rivals. As the story goes, my great, great grandfather Karl was trying to perfect color photography when he died at the age of forty-nine. It was then that two men from Edison's company showed up at his widow's door in Revere, Massachusetts. They offered her one million dollars if she signed over the house and everything in it including his designs and inventions.

I may have first heard this impressive family history from my mother's grandmother, Adeline, while sitting at her bedside in her tiny second-floor room in our family's big house on Cape Cod. Adeline would share stories of her amazing life until she became exhausted and dozed off. My mother said she was diagnosed with "Delusions of Grandeur" but we all knew that she was grand and it was no delusion. According to Adeline, her mother and three daughters took the money from Edison and sailed to Belgium, Karl's birthplace. She recounted how her mother bought what she called "a castle" and threw elaborate parties that were attended by young, unmarried European royalty. She had set herself the goal of marrying her beautiful daughters into the comfortable world of Continental aristocracy. Adeline told of studying painting at the Royal Academy of Fine Arts in Antwerp. That part of the story sure was believable: her painting and original needle point were beautiful.

My West German birth certificate shows that I was named Jonathan Keith McHenry. I was named after my mother's imaginary playmate and my father's perfect brother. I bore a historic last name, one that said that I was born with a heavy past. Born into privilege.

I probably made my first pilgrimage to Fort McHenry at age four. Photos show my brother and me sitting on a cannon aimed towards Baltimore's Inner Harbor. That was the year that I first saw Fort McHenry's "Star Spangled Banner" hanging in the lobby of the Smithsonian Museum of History and Technology. We were the family with a National Anthem.

The McHenry of the fort was Doctor James McHenry, who sailed into the port of Philadelphia in 1773 when he was eighteen years old. His parents and brother followed, sailing out of Belfast a couple of years later. Together they established a shipping business on the wharfs of the colonial port of Baltimore.

Official U.S. Military accounts say James was introduced to Doctor Benjamin Rush and the Sons of Liberty soon after landing in the New World. Young McHenry was recruited by the rebels and asked to travel up to Cambridge Port, Massachusetts to organize a field hospital in anticipation of potential casualties during what would later become known as the Battle of Bunker Hill. McHenry met George Washington after the battle and, according to both family lore and his letters published in the 1907 book The Life and Correspondence of James McHenry, they hit it off. McHenry was invited to join Washington's staff, crossed the Delaware in the Christmas surprise attack on the King's Army and spent that cold, desperate winter of desertions at Valley Forge with Washington and his staff.

Remembering that harsh winter, a colorful National Park Service sign at Valley Forge says that Washington wrote, "McHenry's easy and cheerful temper was able to bear the strain which we suppose must sometimes occur between two persons thrown so closely and so constantly together in a position of social equality and military inequality."

McHenry was the chief surgeon of the 5th Pennsylvania Battalion. Young James was captured by the British at Fort Washington, New York in 1776 and held on one of King George's prison ships on the Hudson River until he was paroled in January 1777 and officially exchanged for British officers in March 1778. He wrote of caring for the ill prisoners and guards during the often-freezing days of his incarceration.

McHenry led an attempt to capture the traitor Benedict Arnold and was present at the surrender of General Cornwallis in Yorktown, Virginia that ended the American Revolution. He participated in the Continental Congress and his signature is on the United States Constitution. President George Washington tapped McHenry to be Secretary of War, a post he held into the administration of President Adams. At that time, he broke from Washington's belief that a professional military would prove dangerous to a democracy and lobbied Congress to fund a permeant standing army.

McHenry also obtained Congressional funding for the design and construction of a fort to defend the harbor of Baltimore. That fort was commissioned Fort McHenry, the fort whose flag was still standing in the "dawn's early light" of the "The Star-Spangled Banner." My father first taught me to lower and properly fold the red, white, and blue on the lawn outside visitor center in Yorktown reminding me to never let colors touch the ground. We made that final triangular fold that concealed the red under the star-studded blue and gave a snappy salute to punctuate a patriotic task well done. That was a lot of history for a young McHenry to bear, but I didn't know of anything else.

But there was even more American history in my blood. My father's mother was Bona Mea Ford. Those Fords with that dirty little secret. A secret kept from me for four decades, until my Kansas City girlfriend, Bonny, gave me a thin and unassuming book on Valentine's Day 1999. The book, Jesse James and the Civil War, was a quick read. It detailed the bank and train robberies of the James Gang and their participation on the edges of America's Civil War. I had bragged to Bonny that my grandmother had two uncles in the James Gang, though she didn't think much of her father's brothers. She referred to them as no-good Bob and Charlie. That's all that was ever said about my outlaw great uncles.

Then I sat on the porch of Bonny's Brookside home and read her present: the last pages of the book revealed our family's secret. Bob was the "Dirty Little Coward that Shot Mr. Howard" in the folk song every young American had learned in elementary school. Uncle Bob shot Jesse James in the back of the head while they were preparing one last robbery. Bob's murder of Jesse at his rental in a Saint Joseph neighborhood inspired a lifetime of hatred against my great uncle until he met his end at the barrel of a shotgun outside his own bar, The Ford Exchange, in Creed, Colorado. Uncle Charlie became a morphine addict and shot himself to death on May 6, 1884, seventy-three years to the day before my birth. Did I replace Charlie on May 6th instead of Keith? If I replaced any historic figure, I secretly hoped it was Henry David Thoreau, who also died on May 6th.

So yes, I was born into a past, a heavy past that shaped my future. In my case, it was a past that told me, my perfect uncle Keith's replacement, descendant of a founding father, an inventor, a murderer, and a mass murderer, that I too might be able to shape history.

US troops in the Germantown neighborhood of Philadelphia

Chapter 4

THE FLAMES OF MARTIN LUTHER KING JR

What a beautiful April morning. The nuthatches flitted in the hardwoods behind our house. Dogwoods were pregnant with new buds. I was an excited eleven-year-old eager to embark on another of my family's journeys to Cape Cod. Among other things, those trips gave me a break from the horrors of the Page County public school system. My mother said we would visit my father's Aunt Ethel in Philadelphia on the way north.

The whole family was busy hauling suitcases and paper bags of vacation items out to our old Rambler. My parents had turned on our staticky TV while we packed.

"American Civil Rights leader Martin Luther King Jr. was fatally shot today at the Lorraine Motel in Memphis, Tennessee," we heard in a crackled voice from our old, almost pictureless black-and-white TV.

I already knew something about what the adults called civil rights. I had even heard of Martin Luther King Jr. and his protests. Luray Elementary had done something for civil rights that most people in town hated and that was called desegregation. There was also a speech at the Lincoln Memorial that had something to do with Martin Luther King Jr. and his civil rights movement.

Black children started crossing the railroad tracks from the westside to attend our school when I was nine. Desegregation had finally arrived to rural Virginia. They joined me and the white classmates, many with down syndrome, in our special education class. I overheard white students say things about not touching the skin of Black kids, about making sure you don't get too close to "them" because they smelled bad, and about never swimming in the same water that "they" swam in.

Our mandatory, fourth-grade Virginia history textbook glorified the war to defend slavery. We started every school day singing Dixie before we said our pledge of allegiance to the flag and the Lord's Prayer. Racism in that community was unvarnished.

Such hate wasn't limited to Black people. My parents spoke out at a PTA meeting against mandatory bible classes defending the children of our town's one Jewish family from being taunted by the Christian kids for having murdered Jesus. The other parents were so angry at my mother and father that they came to our house that evening armed with torches, rocks, and insults. We gathered around my parents' bed and prayed that the we would not be killed by the other Christians. From what I witnessed living in Page County, it wasn't surprising that someone would shoot a Black man like the Reverend Dr. King.

The news seemed to have little impact on my parents and our family started out on another vacation. My father backed the Rambler out of the driveway, lumbered through our neighborhood, climbed Virginia Highway 211 past Mary's Rock, the Blue Ridge Parkway and then went north towards the Nation's Capital.

Two hours later we were leaving the rolling horse pastures of northern Virginia and turning onto the new high-speed highway that went west around Washington, D.C.

Instead of the normal commuter traffic that I had witnessed on past trips around the capital the two outer lanes where filled bumper-to-bumper with green camouflage army trucks. Eight or ten soldiers sat along two benches under the canvas tarps. I could see the fear in their eyes as they watched the highway disappear behind them. We passed hundreds of such eyes, all with that same haunted look.

Then we saw tanks on flatbed trucks and dozens, or perhaps hundreds, of jeeps loaded with combat-ready troops driving south. Two rows of double-bladed helicopters streamed overhead like two parallel lines of giant caterpillars. The lines spanned horizon to horizon, the helicopters all racing towards the clouds of black smoke rising from the east. I wondered if the capital was burning.

Our family sat in unusual silence as we motored around Washington, D.C. on the Beltway, surrounded by the military. My parents didn't say a word but it was clear that they were concerned. Their silence said it all.

But I couldn't take the silence. I was becoming worried that something bad was about to unfold.

"Dad, why are there so many soldiers driving around?"

"Well, Keith I don't really know. Maybe it's something to do with the death of the civil rights man, King," he said in a manner of expression that showed my father had little interest in the political events of the time.

My mother unconvincingly added, "It isn't anything. We'll be fine," trying to shield us from the terror she might have been experiencing. She probably had little information about the crisis even though she was interested in current events. All my parents knew was that Martin Luther King Jr. had been killed. I suspect they had little knowledge of King's campaign for civil rights outside of the occasional derogatory news report they might have caught from time to time on TV or in the press.

It wasn't long before we arrived outside Baltimore. I could see huge clouds of smoke billowing from building-size flames. The traffic came to a stop at the toll-booth for the Fort McHenry Tunnel. This gave me time to glance at a burning Baltimore on the other side of the harbor. As we reemerged from the tunnel, I saw that much of the city was in flames.

Interstate 95 took us quickly away from those fires and back to the rolling hills of corn and red barns of Maryland before arriving at the Philadelphia exit. My father steered the station wagon off the highway toward downtown and Independence Hall crossing the Schuylkill River through the eerily empty streets.

My parents commented that they were surprised to find parking on the street across from Independence Hall. My father put a coin in the meter and led us across the road to see where the Declaration of Independence was signed.

A ranger stood at the door in a grey shirt, green pants and the iconic Smoky the Bear Stetson. The National Park Service "family" was small in 1968 and we naturally felt like every National Park was our own. My father shook the ranger's hand and started to open the door when he was stopped.

"Sorry sir, but we're closed."

My father was surprised and asked, "But why? It's only 3:00."

"We had to close early today."

My father turned to the four of us with a puzzled expression. "Well, let's walk around the area and take a look. Aunt Ethel isn't expecting us until later tonight."

He took us down to the Automat, a cafeteria where you could buy sandwiches, plates of steamed vegetables, fried fish and chicken, and their famous pies from a wall of glass boxes. But it too was closed. We walked to another historic site also to find it closed. There wasn't a store or museum open in all of downtown Philadelphia.

"I guess we should go visit Aunt Ethel now since everything is closed down here," my father suggested still unaware of the cause for this mystery.

We returned to the station wagon and drove over to Germantown Boulevard. Aunt Ethel lived at the west end of the boulevard and had reserved a room for us at the old wooden hotel next to her apartment.

My father said that Aunt Ethel had lost her sight since the neighborhood had been a "better off," white part of town. He said that the area had been changing while she was going blind. This seemed to imply, I thought, that she didn't know she lived in an all-Black neighborhood. I am not sure my father's story really had any basis in reality but he would repeat it several times that evening.

As soon as the station wagon turned onto Germantown Boulevard, we came to a blinking stoplight. Each corner of the intersection was lined with four-foot-high walls of sandbags. Two helmeted solders aimed a huge machine gun towards the center of the intersection from the top of the fortifications. My father waited until a young officer clad in combat gear waved us on.

Nervous Black men rushed across the street in front of us, slipping down the side streets. Several young men were so keen to not attract attention that they seemed to glide on air past the heavily armed troops, moving like ghosts.

About twenty soldiers in heavy flak jackets stood holding their M-16's at the ready at each intersection. Belts of giant bullets were coiled through the gatling guns, each of which was operated by two helmeted soldiers peering nervously from their perch above the wall of sandbags. German shepherds strained at the ends of their leashes as the soldiers tried to control them. They growled angrily at the Black pedestrians, who tried to stay clear of the snarling teeth. Each army man had grenades or bands of bullets hanging off his uniform. The only people standing still were the soldiers. Everyone else was determined to clear the area darting corner to corner, eyes always looking down at the pavement as though it wasn't safe to glance at the military personnel that were occupying their community.

To me it seemed that everyone was frightened. The residents were terrified. The soldiers, too, seemed scared. They were mostly young white men who, if they had ever been in combat at all, it would have been in Vietnam. And of course, the residents of Germantown were even more visibly frightened. Many of them may have also seen combat in Vietnam.

A soldier waved us through that intersection as three other soldiers strained to hold back their dogs which seemed to smell the fear of everyone dashing past them.

My father drove slowly to the next crossroad where we encountered another fortified corner, this time controlled by a tank, several more machine-gun nests, and more dogs. A dozen nervous Black civilians darted through the intersection, some clutching shopping bags under their arms or against their chests like footballs.

We came to one tense intersection after another. Every corner fortified with sandbags, heavily armed troops, German shepherds, machine guns, and tension, lots of tension.

I remember staring out the car windows in amazement. I was passing through a real urban battlefield. Something I had only seen on our fuzzy black-and-white TV set. This was the kind of drama complete with heavy weapons and tense combatants that any eleven-year-old, white, middle-class boy would feel lucky to experience.

We arrived at the hotel next to Aunt Ethel's apartment building.

Our entire family followed my father to the lobby where he asked about our room. There was no way he would have left his family in the car after driving through that war zone.

The hotel manager was an older African American gentleman. He placed a form on the counter for my father to sign and then directed us to the stairs. We followed him hauling our suitcases up to the second floor. The musty smell of dried wallpaper made the hotel feel as old and flammable as it really was.

The hotel man unlocked our room. He switched on the TV explaining that one dial controlled the volume and the other changed the channels. He switched the television off then guided my father and mother to the bathroom and the clean white towels. My father gave him a dollar; he nodded in appreciation and walked back down the tiny hallway to the stairs.

Mom pushed the door closed and quickly turned the locks with a sigh of relief. She set out some clothes and disappeared into the bathroom for ten minutes as my father used the hotel phone to call Aunt Ethel. She wanted us to come over right away, dinner was ready and she was excited to see the children.

We scurried next door and climbed up to her apartment on the third floor. The smell of boiled cabbage greeted us even before Aunt Ethel opened her door: a tiny lady happily calling to us as we entered. "Welcome, welcome, please come in and make yourselves comfortable."

We sat around her little wooden table as she set platters with sliced ham, boiled peas, steamed cabbage and small caramelized pearl onions.

I could hear the TV in the corner. "Martin Luther King Jr. was shot today in Memphis, Tennessee. He had planned to speak to striking garbage workers when a gunman shot him outside the Loraine Hotel. A state of emergency has been called here in Philadelphia."

Aunt Ethel turned the TV off, "Oh, we don't need to ruin our dinner listening to the news," and led us in grace.

Dinner was over fast enough. My father told Aunt Ethel that we would see her in the morning and we hustled down the stairs and out into the dark. Our eyes stung from tear gas and wood smoke as we dashed around the corner to the hotel. The manager greeted us with a look of concern which I remember was not comforting.

Mom rushed us upstairs and quickly shut and locked the door to our room. My father turned on the TV to see what all the fuss was about. It seemed to me he still didn't understand the magnitude of the events.

The TV flickered images of people burning cars and houses going up in flames. A young Black man ran out of a store with a TV and then police rushed in and clubbed him to the ground. Then the TV showed thousands of people walking slowly towards Independence Hall. Community leaders were shown speaking to the crowd and then the program turned to an advertisement about enjoying life with Coke. Smoke crept into our room giving the images on TV a bit more reality.

After the ads, the news returned to explain there was a curfew across Philadelphia. It showed some more rioting with the text "Germantown Rioters" in white below a burning building that looked similar to our hotel. Just then a deafening screech interrupted the program. I went to see what the noise was. It was a streetcar pulling into the maintenance yard behind our hotel.

My mother yelled at me, "Keith, get away from the window! Get over here!"

Mom got down on her knees facing one of the tall double beds that crowded the room. Wood smoke drifted under the window frames. White whiffs of hazy smoke clung to the ceiling.

"Come on everyone. Let us pray."

My father kneeled next to my mother. They closed their eyes and put the palms of their hands together. I motioned to my brother and sister to join them and my father started to pray out loud.

"Oh, dear God, please protect my family. Please Lord, spare our building from fire and protect my wife and children. Dear Jesus, we pray that you protect my family from harm. Forgive us for our sins and save us from evil. In the name of Jesus, Amen." He finally seemed to realize that we were in danger.

Mom also said a prayer as we continued to kneel around the bed, palms pressed tight against the fear.

"Ok kids, it's time for bed." Mom guided us into the bathroom and handed us our toothbrushes and the toothpaste. "Hurry now, we have a big day tomorrow."

I am sure my parents didn't sleep at all. I barely slept. It was finally sinking in. The building was likely to burn and we would burn with it.

But we didn't die. As soon as the sun came up my mother got us out of bed. We dressed quickly. It was clear from my mother's frantic movements that we needed to act fast.

We followed my father down the stairs and out into the sun, to the diner across the street. I paused to read one of the white sheets of paper stapled to each tree.

In big black letters, the flyers said: "Curfew - Anyone outside after dark will be shot."

My white family crossed Germantown Boulevard to the front door of the diner. My father pulled opened the shiny, steel door to a surprised gathering of regulars.

"Please, sit right here," a silver-haired Black man said as he stood from his chair. The entire restaurant joined him in standing and those nearest the door pulled out their seats and motioned us to sit down.

"Coffee?" called out a heavy-set African American woman with a welcoming smile as she walked swiftly towards our table with a pot of black coffee and a fist full of thick, white coffee mugs.

"You have to try the cinnamon rolls. There the best in all Philly," called out a young, well-dressed woman from the far end of the diner.

It seemed to me that everyone in the diner was surprised to see a white family join them for breakfast after a night of neighborhood rioting.

A diner of twenty or so African Americans made this frightened white family of five feel welcomed.

My mother's father John Phelan and I on Easter Sunday in Yorktown, Virginia

Chapter 5

A WHITE MAN'S BURDEN

It was the summer of my fifth year and I was sitting attentively on the front bench of my family's blue dingy, floating on the placid fresh waters of Cape Cod's Middle Lake. The oak oars fanned towards the shores, clanking softly in the galvanized ore locks. My mother's father scooted to the stern. He took a black freshwater mussel from the damp hull, cracked it open on the bench and showed me how to pull out the slimy grey guts and then slide the goo onto my barbed hook. He flipped his sinker and hooked bait out into the glassy pond to show me how it was done. I followed his example.

My grandfather always spoke to me as though I were an adult. He never let me win at cards or checkers. His grandson needed learn to face the hard facts of winners and losers. I was not to be coddled: a philosophy he shared with his son-in-law, my father.

Our nylon lines disappeared into the dark waters as my grandfather described his time in the Pacific War. While drifting on the calm waters in front of his ten-acre property he shared a bit of his history. He described sitting on a plush, red-and-gold cushion and smoking fragrant black opium tar while meeting with Aung San, the leader of Burma. Dozens of the king's servants flitted around their deliberations. My grandfather told Aung San that he would need a hardened runway for his squadron of heavy, bomb-laden B-29's. He continued telling me about his making a promise to protect the leader from the Japanese Emperor. From his description, I imagined that the thick, humid air was cloudy with a sweet-smelling blue haze mixed with the enticing aromas of brazen pork and onion-grilled sea bass served on gold-plated platters and followed by trays of exotic deserts. He smiled while recounting the silk-draped women of magnificent beauty that drifted through the room. Old, white-bearded shamans sat in the corner gently holding long clay pipes while young boys rang bells. His account was so vivid I could see every exquisite detail. Recalling the black-and-white photo of thousands of people balancing reed baskets of hammer-crushed stones among nearly naked men pounding the rocks into pavement that sits on a ledge in his Needham, Massachusetts home, added to the power of his tale.

This dreamy story was interrupted when my rod dipped suddenly toward the water. Something took the bait. My grandfather told me to snap the pole, and I did.

"Reel it in," he said, pointing to the crank on his own rod.

The line was heavy, bending my pole in an arc to the pond water. A little perch wiggled in desperation as he approached the surface. I swung the rod over the center of the row boat. The fish flopped off the center bench onto the deck and then back to the bench.

My grandfather calmly told me to grab the struggling yellow fish. I did. "Hold tight. He is big enough to eat," my grandfather said with a hint of pride. "Now smack his head against the gunwale. Smash it really hard or he will suffer." I looked at the perch's big eyes looking up at me. I whacked its head against the boat killing the innocent little guy.

Back on shore we walked to my grandmother's kitchen. My grandfather showed me how to slit open the fish's stomach, scrape out the guts from the cavity and sever its head. The big eyes continued to stare up at me from the bucket of organs. Those sad, haunting eyes refused to look away.

My grandfather continued with his story of Burma, calmly explaining that I was born into a special family. I would grow up having to decide who should live and who should die. I might even have to kill tens of thousands of people. He said this to his five-year-old grandson. I imagine he was speaking about people like those smudged out in the blackened images of the sixty-three framed aerial photos hanging in his den. Photos he took when directing the world's most deadly bombing campaign, the of the firebombing of Tokyo. He explained that those I might have to kill would never face such difficult decisions as the ones I would need to wrestle with. That was our burden, he announced with certainty. "The white man's burden."

My father's father Edward McHenry with members of the US Congress and their wives

Chapter 6

THE SACRED GIFT

My father's father gently grasped my tiny, child hand. A leather-faced old man walked bowlegged with my family along the four-thousand-year-old sandy ruts that his ancestors carved into the earth. We were heading towards an ancient two-story stone pueblo on the banks of the Oraibi Wash. Red-tailed hawks and falcons tied to the roof tops sneered down at us, straining from their leg leashes. A steady, hot wind swirled with the incense of burning pinion from the coals of the round adobe hornos. The comforting scent of Piki Bread and roasted corn spread through the flat-roofed village, mixing with the golden rays of a late afternoon sun. The prison of electricity and coal hadn't yet desecrated the sacred, high Arizona desert. Old Oraibi was as it had been for generations.

Years before, in 1932, my grandfather's journey to take up his position as a Junior Park Naturalist at the Grand Canyon was dramatically interrupted by a sandstone boulder a hundred miles east of his destination. Hopi farmers found him broken inside his mangled car. The vehicle was crushed against a bolder above their corn patch. He convalesced in the ancient rock homes of his hosts for nearly half of that year before continuing on his bumpy drive to the South Rim. They would become life-long friends. Our graying guide, his hair bound tight in a red headband, had been one of the young men who carried my father's father to the safety of their cliffside community. My grandfather cheerfully placed his now frail arm on his friend's shoulder in response to his jab about my grandfather's shiny bald skull. They both laughed with the familiarity of brothers.

My grandmother scurried up the leather-bound rungs of a long pine ladder ahead of my mother. She scooted comfortably onto the mudded rooftop. An older man gently pulled my mother onto the dusty platform. My father lifted my little brother Bruce up to my mother's arms and I scaled the rungs to the top and found a seat on the striped blanket, settling with my family and the elders into our spot on the sunbaked rooftop. Huddles of other families spread their woolen rugs into position high above the plaza making themselves at home above their homes.

I was just six years old the first time I visited this holy pueblo. Jumbles of plump grandmothers laughed and teased one another as they shifted and turned in search of a comfortable perch. Bony and dusty children clung to their mothers and men helped settle the late comers.

The stone walls that supported our families had witnessed over two thousand years of boys becoming men and women celebrating the harvest. A small group of tall men draped in glossy buckskins, their heads crowned with tan antelope heads with devilish antlers, stood at attention beating a giant hide drumhead at the far end of the sacred grounds. I trembled with each thud and became aware of a comforting knowledge that I would always feel at home no matter where I walked on our sacred Earth.

Two clowns darted from pueblo wall to pueblo wall, their heavy, rich red helmets of desert dirt comically swaying in their colossal galactic battle. Tricksters playing in our waking dreams. I was mesmerized.

It wasn't long before two columns of young boys marched into view at the far end of the dusty plaza having just surfaced after weeks in the underground darkness of the round kiva. My grandfather shared his understanding that in the sacred cosmology of the Hopi life emerged from the underworld sipapu in the center of the kiva. Another cycle of the tilting Earth and another generation rises to the surface of the fourth world they called Tuwaqachi.

All rooftop conversations hushed. The tallest two boys at the lead were followed in size down to the shortest two, all of them stomping across the dance ground in a trance, retracing their path over and over again. Red fox pelts hung from the bright woven wool belts wrapped tightly around their waists. The white of their thick woven skirts made the red pelts even more vibrant. Juniper boughs bobbed around their necks, wrists, and ankles to the rhythm of the dance. The thunderous pounding of their high deerskin boots against the ground and the clapping of dried beans against tortoise-shell rattles cinched tight to their ankles reverberated to the even louder beat of the antelope clan's mammoth drum. Bits of fine adobe mortar sprinkled loose at the sound waves. A lonely raven gurgled and clicked as it floated above on a warm updraft.

One row of boys held deadly rattlesnakes and copperheads between their teeth. The serpents' tongues darted quickly between their sharp, poisonous fangs, as their heads bent towards the future men's jugular veins. A second boy mesmerized a desert viper with a bouquet of red-tailed hawk feathers collected from the leashed birds. Invisible ghost-spirits of all that danced below shimmered electric across my skin, sifting the sacred energy through my cells. A late afternoon golden glow of mystery blessed the atmosphere.

The boys becoming men startled me when they abruptly stopped and placed the serpents on the plaza dust. The rattlers slithered, flashing across the plaza, and disappeared into cloth sacks held open by the antelope clan. The undulating snake bags were secured with twine and whisked back to the desert while the drumming resumed. The initiated stomped to the rhythm of the antelope drummers, nodded in respect, and passed out of the plaza, disappearing into the depths of their mother kiva.

A silence of permanence weighed the Hopi families heavy to the pueblo roofs. The quiet of the gold setting sun held all in suspense.

A collective exhale from the rooftops announced the emergence of the graduates bearing woven reed baskets overflowing with yellow, red, and orange squashes, blue corn, and heavy loaves of richly browned bread. The sweet smell of pinion smoke and roasting corn and peppers fixed me to that place and time. The new men silently lifted their sacred offerings skyward to the holy families on the flat roofs of Old Oraibi.

I can never be a Hopi and yet still I basked in the glow of my transformation that knowledge that I will forever be tethered to the cosmos; a confidence that I will always be one with our universe, the warmth of that eternal wellbeing that embraces me to this day.

The Wasatch Academy Year Book photo class of 1974

Chapter 7

AN EDUCATION

This is how you mop a hallway: zigzag from wall to wall with a soapy cotton mop head tracing the infinity symbol foot by foot down the well-worn second-floor corridor of, for example, Darlington freshman dorm. The rickety, wood-framed dorm was condemned by the county when my father attended school there in the 1950s. Learning how to properly mop was the first, and possibly the most important, lesson I learned in high school.

Wasatch Academy, a ninety-five-year-old Presbyterian boarding school, was an island of diversity in a tiny, high-valley Mormon farming village stuck smack in the center of the Beehive State. Majestic cottonwoods quaked yellow along the town's irrigation ditches and golden aspens marched up the north-facing slopes of the Wasatch Range. Hay balers lumbered across the dry pastures gathering their harvest for the long winter. Shepherds followed cottony flocks of Rambouillet sheep to lower elevations and the inevitable, bloody sheering.

The Wasatch Academy student body was a collection of 150 teenage boys and girls. There were the kids who came from the National Parks, like me. There were the children of western state ranchers whose families lived too far from the nearest high school to make day attendance practical. And there were the wealthy "delinquents" spared a sentence in a California Juvenile Hall.

My academic performance at the start of my freshman year in 1970 was not as smooth as my mopping, but I was about to learn a second lesson, nearly as important as the first. I would learn to become disciplined and complete every homework assignment to the letter. Success in academics was just that simple. But before I learned that lesson, most of my classmates thought of me more as a comedian than a student.

Early on, one of my teachers took me aside and said, "You are going to flunk out if you don't take school seriously." With memories of Page County fresh in my mind, I decided to take it seriously.

At the beginning of my second semester of high school, Principal Larson came to greet the student body at the morning assembly. He spoke on the power of a good education as he probably had each semester since my father and uncle had attended assembly. The boys fiddled with their obligatory ties and the girls sat uncomfortably on the wooden seats in dresses that dropped below their knees. The morning sun, sifted by frosted window panes, bathed the chapel.

"I will read off the names of those students that received straight As this semester," he said, holding a sheet of notebook paper in one hand as he adjusted his reading glasses with the other.

"First on the list is John Elliot." The students clapped politely, not surprised at all that he had straight As. That was expected as he had a perfect score the year before. "Next is Debbie Grant," and more obligatory clapping. Debbie's classmates all knew she was smart. "Next on the list is David Miles," and more clapping but still no surprise even though it was his first semester. If anyone could be considered studious it was my roommate David. "And finally, the last student on the list to get straight As is Keith McHenry."

It was like a bolt of lightning shot up my back as the entire student body jumped to their feet screaming and clapping in surprise. I was the last person anyone, including myself, would have believed would have a perfect score.

My early scholastic success awakened in me a desire to make Wasatch a contemporary version of Henry David Thoreau's Concord. This would be the first time I would seek to construct a village of visionary artists, authors, poets, and intellectuals. Mount Pleasant's streets would be the paths of my modern-day community of Thoreaus, Emersons, Alcotts, and Hawthornes. Like the transcendentalists who walked the roads through the woods near Walden Pond, we would dedicate ourselves to the search for truth and beauty. This clarity of purpose engulfed my spirit.

Surely this was to be expected of a teenager whose first adult book was Walden. The war in Vietnam was my generation's war on Mexico and racism and segregation was akin to, and the legacy of, the slavery of Thoreau's civil disobedient night in jail. My mother's hardbound copies of Plato, Homer, Aristotle, and Latin grammar were my escape during the tortured years of elementary and middle school. Then The Beatles, Elton John, The Doors, Jimi Hendrix and Pink Floyd, combined with tabs of Orange Sunshine and Blue Windowpane, were the soundtrack of my liberation in rural Utah.

That first glorious school year came to an end and the promise of a magical summer stretched out before me. I rented a little glassed-in porch on the second floor of my roommate David's parent's house at First Avenue and T Street in Salt Lake City. I took a job as a janitor at University Books and Art Supplies, vacuuming past intriguing titles and delicious Windsor Newton pigments and sable brushes. When I wasn't polishing bookshelves or pushing a Hoover between canyons of books, I joined David's parents and their anarchist friends sailing on Echo Reservoir with a gallon of Boone's Farm, drunkenly discussing the finer points of Voltaire, Kafka, Coltrane, and Mozart. I spent dreamy afternoons in a friend's backyard art gallery feasting with friends while passing loose joints of skanky Mexican pot. It was a teenage version of Trout Fishing in America. David's father was "Jack Mormon" who was turned against church and state by the brutality of blood-soaked foxholes and storms of lead unleashed on the Pacific Islands during the Second World War.

I woke each morning to a symphony of chirps, peeps and the rustling of cottonwood leaves. On one day off without plans I rolled some Mexican pot, drifted down to Mrs. Miles' kitchen, cut a hunk of her limitless zucchini bread, quickly dusted up the crumbs and walked out to First Avenue. I had finished smoking my joint by the time my sneakers crossed S Street.

The morning sun warmed the high desert chill. Black-capped chickadee and dark-eyed juncos flitted about, darting between the branches and the lawns of the tree-lined neighborhood. The old stone and brick buildings along Temple Street kept getting larger and more beautiful as I meandered west towards the city center.

A particularly ornate mansion caught my eye. A stately gold-lettered sign on the grassy berm identified the beauty as, "The Utah Bicentennial Commission." The carved-oak front door was framed in an old Mormon style stained-glass and surrounded by a brick and sandstone edifice of unusual majesty. The glorious building pulled me up the walkway. I had to open that huge wooden door and peek inside. Apparently, that was some good pot.

I was startled by a smiling receptionist siting behind a polished cherry desk. "How can we help you?" she asked. I responded by saying that I found the building stunning and then blurted out, to my own surprise, that I had an idea for the Bicentennial Commission and would like to speak with the director. This request was inspired by the sign with "Director" painted in gold on the door behind her and my stoned desire to get a glimpse of what I thought would be another architectural wonder behind that door.

"Okay, may I tell the director who is here to see him," she asked, standing as though her blond bun was magnetically drawn to the ceiling above her.

"Keith McHenry," I responded.

"Great, please have a seat and I will tell him you're here."

I needed an idea fast if I was going to pull this off. I had just read one of the Foxfire books on the mountain life of the Great Smokies written by high school students. It dawned on me that the Utah Bicentennial Commission might be interested in a similar series about pioneer skills from the early days of the state. Sure, that seemed like a good idea to propose.

"Right this way Mr. McHenry," the receptionist said, directing me towards the office.

The director stood behind his beautiful antique desk before a picture window bordered with stained-glass, red roses.

"My name is David Swanson, what can we do for you?"

I thanked him for his time and explained that I was attending a high school in Mount Pleasant called Wasatch Academy and thought the students could produce a series of books about the skills of early Utah settlers. "Have you seen the Foxfire books?" I asked.

He had heard of the series and asked me to tell him more.

I excitedly explained that the students could interview farmers about irrigation or the raising of livestock. Maybe there could be chapter on the use of natural plants for medicine, soaps, or textile dyes. We could describe pioneer skills passed down from generation to generation.

"Well, Mr. McHenry, may I suggest that you write up your proposal and submit a request for funding from our Commission." He opened a drawer to his right and pulled out an application form. He must have noticed that I had been looking at the intricate molding in his office and offered to show me around the nineteenth-century mansion.

After the tour I thanked my guide and walked as fast as I could to a drugstore on Temple, bought a notebook and pen, sat against a shaded wall of the pharmacy and quickly jotted down the highlights of my plan.

The next morning, I returned to the bookstore and the honest work of vacuuming the graying carpet between the stacks. I spotted a book on how to write grants, slid the thick volume from the shelf and held it open to read with one hand as I shuffled the Hoover with the other.

I rushed home every evening to my treetop room excited to work on my proposal. The late evening thunderstorms and sheets of rain drowned out any distractions. After two weeks of late nights filling page after page in longhand my first draft was ready for the public typewriter at the main library. I carefully pecked out the proposal with a single finger.

I wrote that Wasatch Academy seniors could choose to work on the book in their final year. The project would not be available to the younger students. Participation would be the reward of three years of a standard high school education. Students could get math credits for their work on the budget for producing the book. Editing a classmate's interview or penning a chapter could be an English credit. A chapter on the use of native plants for healing remedies could qualify for a biology class. Like the Foxfire series, this annual paperback would be distributed to bookstores across the country. The promise of getting a high school diploma and your name on a popular book could attract new students solving Wasatch's crisis of a shrinking enrollment.

The click, click of the keys quickened as I banged out the last paragraph of the proposal. I stapled the pages together, slid them into the envelope I had bought for the occasion and rushed off to the Bicentennial offices to present my finished draft to Mr. Swanson.

The silence was abruptly pierced with, "You did a great job, Keith." Mr. Swanson explained that the next step I needed to take was to present the proposal to the Sanpete County Commissioners. If they approved it, they would send it to the state commission and by the beginning of the semester I could start work on the first edition. "I think the commissioners will be excited to see what you have here."

I was relieved. Mr. Swanson suggested I take a copy to the commission chairman before it would be formally introduced. "Let's call Mr. Olsen now and set up a meeting. He lives in Fairview. Can you go down to see him this week?"

I called my older, driving-aged schoolmate, Karen, and asked her if she could give me a ride. She agreed to be my chauffeur.

We found Mr. Olsen's brick house. He was standing in his well-groomed patch of front lawn dressed in baggy coveralls and directing a green garden hose towards a row of healthy rose bushes lining a classic Utah wire fence.

"Hello sir. Are you Mr. Olsen?" I asked.

"Yes, I am. You must be Mr. McHenry?" he responded with a welcoming smile.

"Yes, and this is my friend Karen." He shook our hands and turned off the tap to his hose.

"So, Keith, I hear you have been to Boston. Did you visit Paul Revere's house and Old North Church?" he asked with a glint in his eyes that said he had seen at least seven decades of central Utah but only dreamed of the world beyond.

Mr. Olsen shuffled up his steps, reached out and pulled open his rickety screen door. "Come in. Please, have a seat and tell me everything you know about colonial Boston."

I told Mr. Olsen all about Boston. I described how wide the Charles River was when the Revere of Longfellow's poem had rowed across it that dark April evening. I described the height of Old North Church's white spire and the walled pews that protected the congregation from the cold New England winters.

My weathered, old host radiated a child-like pleasure listening to the tales of someone who had actually seen the historic sites that were the birthplace of our country. "So, you want to put together a book about the pioneer life in Sanpete County?" he said getting down to business.

"Yes sir. I read a book about Appalachian Mountain life and thought we should have one for pioneer life here in Utah."

Mr. Olsen walked around his tiny living room crossing from his stuffed chair to his front door and back. "Keith, it is so important to have young people like yourself interested in our history. I fully support your project."

I shared a bit more about the vision I had for the book and handed him a copy of the proposal. He rose from his favorite seat once again in a motion that emphasized his delight. "Thanks so much for coming by and we will see both of you tomorrow at the county commission."

Karen and I found a pleasant piece of ground to roll out our sleeping bags at the mouth of the canyon above town and spent the day hanging out on the lush green lawns on the grounds of the Manti Temple. The long shadows of the sandstone spires meant it was time to get ready. I retrieved my thrift store slacks, white button-down shirt, and almost stain-free red tie from the back seat of Karen's VW and crossed the deserted lawn to a secluded corner behind the Temple.

The Sanpete County Commissioners met at six. I felt I needed to arrive early to indicate my sense of responsibility. As we pulled into the parking lot, we could see several elderly men dressed in sagging old sports coats and blue coveralls slowly hobbling towards the entrance.

We followed them through the lobby into a majestic auditorium of blond paneling, high ceiling, lacquered handrails, and podium. A hundred theater seats faced the arching half wall that separated the public from the officials who sat at the helm of the community.

Several of what would be a total of fifteen commissioners stood near their high-backed seats discussing the urgent news of rural Utah life. Mr. Olsen ambled into the hall from a side door, glass of water in one hand and a manila envelope in the other. While he was talking to another commissioner, he noticed me sitting in the front row and motioned for me to approach.

"Keith, this is Commissioner Parker." Mr. Parker reached across the rail and gave me a hardy handshake.

The blue-haired clerk knocked on her microphone before saying, "It's six o'clock, Commissioners. I will ask everyone to take their seats."

She turned to the crowd of about sixty people, most of whom were standing in the aisle and busy in conversation. "Attention, attention. Please take your seats," she announced with the authority of her decades.

The chatter subsided. Folding chairs squeaked open and the audience settled down. Mr. Parker stood over his microphone, tapped it twice and addressed the room. "Welcome everyone. Please stand to say the Lord's Prayer."

Everyone stood, their seats squeaking back into place. The assembled bowed their heads and Commissioner Parker's deep voice slowly lead the room in prayer. Even though I normally would shun such a ritual, I joined in out of respect for their sincerity.

Then the commissioners lifted their heads in unison with the audience and turned towards the American flag placing their hands over their hearts and joined Mr. Parker in the Pledge of Allegiance.

Mr. Parker banged his gavel with a thud.

Everyone sat, chairs squeaking again. First there was old business, a report on the county emergency radio system. A second-grade girl from the local elementary school received a gift certificate for a quart of ice cream from Dairy Queen for her public service organizing a trash pick-up around the campus during summer vacation.

Then there were some questions about the repair of the fence at the back of the cemetery. "Bob Johnson said he would provide $100 towards fixing the broken section. He feels real bad about his cattle grazing at the west end of the cemetery and he promises to make sure they don't leave his pasture again."

The Commissioners agreed to provide whatever additional finances were needed not to exceed $500 with the project set to be completed by the first of October. "Everyone in favor say aye. Everyone opposed say no. The ayes have it. The fence will be repaired."

Mr. Olsen looked over at me and the clerk announced the business of a request for a $9,000 grant by the Utah Bicentennial Commission.

Mr. Olsen slowly lifted himself out of his seat. "Dear fellow commissioners of the great County of Sanpete, I am honored to introduce you to a fine young man from over in Mount Pleasant, Mr. Keith McHenry. I think you will be very interested to hear his proposal. He came by my house yesterday and I was interested to learn that this young man has visited Paul Revere's House and has seen the Old North Church in Boston, Massachusetts with his own eyes. Please give Mr. McHenry your full attention."

I approached the microphone at the front of the auditorium. "Thank you so much, Mr. Olsen, Commissioner Parker and all of you here tonight. I have provided you all with a copy of my proposal for a book on the knowledge and skills used by the first pioneers to Sanpete County." I described the main points of the proposal and then said, "High school seniors will have the option of getting credit for their participation, such as interviewing the older residents of Sanpete and their descendants about the knowledge and skills unique to pioneer life in Central Utah that have been handed down from generation to generation." I added that the book would be sold in bookstores all over the west and attract interest in our community.

Mr. Olsen stood again and said, "I encourage every commissioner to vote in favor of this proposal. The money will come from the Utah State Bicentennial Commission so it will not cost the county a cent. And you all know we aren't getting any younger and if we don't tell our stories now, they may go with us to our graves."

The commissioner took a sip of water and continued, "I am just so happy that this young man has gone to all this trouble to help record our history and I believe we all should vote to adopt this proposal. Anyone second the proposal?"

Mr. Thompson responded, "I second it." Commissioner Parker asked, "All in favor?" Everyone replied aye. "All opposed?" Silence. "Then hearing no objections, the motion is adopted."

Mr. Olsen reached over the counter and shook my hand saying, "Job well done."

A couple of weeks later I got a package from the Utah Bicentennial Commission. "Dear Mr. McHenry, The Utah Bicentennial Commission is honored to announce that we are accepting your grant request of $9,000. Please fill out the enclosed form, have your principal sign and date the authorization and return it to our office."

Karen and I headed back down to Mount Pleasant and Headmaster Hansen's house. I skipped exuberantly up to the front door. He answered, beaming his familiar welcoming smile and invited us in.

I excitedly told Mr. Hansen that the Utah Bicentennial Commission had awarded Wasatch $9,000 for the book proposal I had told him of earlier that summer.

"That is fantastic news, Keith. Following in your uncle's footsteps I see," he said before reminding me again that my uncle was a great trumpet player, student body president, and had been accepted to the US Olympic Ski Team.

I let Mr. Hansen know that the reason we came to see him was to get his signature on the contract so we could start work on the book as soon as classes started.

"Well, Keith, since we last spoke, I decided to retire. We have a new headmaster coming in a few weeks. I am sure he would be happy to sign the contact."

Soon yellow aspen advanced towards the valley marking the end of summer and a return to school. My dorm mate, David, and I relaxed in the back of his father's 56 Chevy pickup as it passed the decaying steel mills on the shores of Lake Provo, the cliffs of Mount Timpanogos, and then winded into the sage and alfalfa pastures of Sanpete Valley. It wasn't long before we were slowing by the drive-in theater and the Dairy Queen and lurching to a stop outside the boy's dorms at Wasatch.

Early the next morning, our dorm parent, Mr. Gardner, stopped by our room to give us our institutional assignments. "You get clinkers again, Keith. I know that's your favorite job." I had graduated from mopping hall floors to the prestigious task of shoveling out the flaming molten clinkers and fly ash from the roaring coal furnaces. My warm classmates appreciated this, giving us shovelers celebrity status.

But what I was most eager to do that morning was to visit the new headmaster and get the contract signed. I raced over to the administration building. Secretary Murphy thought he might be at the Hansen's old place.

A tall, bald man peeked through the screen door and said, "Yes, may I help you?"

"Hello, I am a student at Wasatch and I gave Mr. Hansen a contract from the Utah Bicentennial Commission for you to sign so the senior class can get credit producing our book on pioneer life," I confidently reported.

"Oh yes, he did give me that contract. Well, I am worried that the State of Utah won't accredit the project and being new here I don't want to rock the boat by introducing such an unusual item to the curriculum," he replied.

"So, Wasatch isn't going to accept the funding and we aren't going to produce the book?" I asked, not able to conceal my disappointment.

"Yes, that's right. We aren't going to accept the funding. It's too risky, just too risky to do during my first year," he bluntly explained.

I was speechless. I silently turned away and walked back to campus.

Our first assembly would provide a glimpse of what would be in store for us that year. The electricity and excitement of my classmates reverberated throughout the chapel as we took our seats and greeted the friends that we hadn't seen all summer.

"Attention! Attention please! We are about to start. Please sit down." The dean of students, Mr. Chin, struggled to bring the opening assembly to a start. The wooden seats squeaked open and everyone eventually directed their attention towards the Dean.

"Welcome back everyone. I hope you had a great summer. We have some exciting changes this year. First, I want to introduce you to our new headmaster, Mr. O'Leary. Mr. Hansen retired this summer and moved to Cedar City. I am sure he will be up to see us again this year."

The Dean continued, "Mr. O'Leary comes to us from Claremont High School in California. Please give Headmaster O'Leary a warm welcome."

Mr. O'Leary rose from his front row seat. He was a towering middle-aged man with a shiny, bald head. A tepid clapping greeted his introduction.

"Thank you, students. I'm proud to be your new headmaster. We will finish class registration after assembly. First, I will announce a few new rules." He detailed his policy requiring students to request a pass to leave campus even if they only planned to go downtown. He said we had to return no later than the time requested on our pass and never later than evening study hall at 7:00.

"Is that clear?" Headmaster O'Leary asked not really interested in an answer as he crossed slowly across the front of the chapel, eyes fixed on the floor. "As Dean Chin explained, I was principal of Claremont High School, one of the top private schools in California. I was hired by Wasatch because of all the discipline problems here last year. I expect everyone to cooperate and help me make this a productive year." The drugs, sex and theft of the student bank were among the problems he was sent to resolve. Several more changes were described and our new Spanish teacher was introduced before Dean Chin announced the end of the assembly.

My daily routine began with the heroic early morning institutional chore of shoveling clinkers, a valiant attempt to shower off the accumulated black soot, and a hot breakfast. I would then head off to chapel where Headmaster O'Leary would introduce his daily list of new rules and punishments: detention if tardy to your institutional job; ten hours digging in the "sewers," a leech field of muddy ditches west of campus, if you are late to detention; and more detentions and additional hours in the sewers for leaving campus without a pass and on and on.

A few weeks into the school year and we were finally going to have our first guest speaker at assembly, a photographer from Salt Lake City who planned to show us slides of his recent trip to Asia.

Headmaster O'Leary opened the assembly with some more rules. "Students are still failing to go to detention on time and some of you have failed to show up to dig in the sewer so I am announcing an additional penalty of five more hours at the sewers for every day of detention you miss. And by the way, I don't like looking out and seeing the bottoms of your soda cans, so from now there will be no more drinking sodas during assembly."

That was enough of the new rules. I stood up to leave, requiring the row of classmates to rise to their feet to let me pass. "Come on, this is too much. New rules every morning and penalties on top of penalties. I'm leaving," I said loud enough for most the chapel to hear.

David stood to let me by. The rest of the students in my row also stood. "Come on let's go," I suggested as I passed each student. My row followed. As I stepped into the center aisle students throughout the assembly were rising from their seats. I reached the back door as Dean Chin called out that the assembly was adjourning for the day.

The students followed me out into the football field chanting, "Strike! Strike!"

As my friends and I were sitting at the end of the football field ranting about O'Leary, several other students retrieved a sound system from their dorm room. It wasn't long before Alice Copper's anthem "Schools Out for Ever" was blaring across the campus.

Two classmates asked me to sign their handwritten petition that started, "We will not return to school until these demands are met." The demands began: "We don't have to attend class," and continued with, "No restrictions on smoking. All students can smoke pot. All students can take acid, mushrooms, peyote and any other drug whenever they wish. All students can drink alcohol on campus. All students can be in any dorm at any time. Morning assembly is optional. No one has to do homework. All students can go to the tracks or into town any time they want. All students can have sex with their lovers when they wish. Anyone can dress however they want. There will be no restrictions on dorm hours."

The list was two pages long. Twenty or thirty students had already signed the back page in support.

"I don't think the school administration has the authority to legalize drugs and teenage drinking," I suggested. "We might want to have demands that the school can actually meet."

They argued their case a little more saying we should have all these rights and more but soon they both agreed it was probably just wishful thinking.

"Why don't we demand that all rules made since the beginning of the school year be revoked or something like that? Maybe demand that any new rules must be agreed to by someone in the student government, a faculty member and someone from the administration," I suggested, adding, "We can announce that we won't return to class until the administration agrees to meet with us and suspend all of this year's new rules."

They thought that sounded good. I wrote up the text for the proposal on a sheet of blue-lined, notebook paper.

I spoke with the student in charge of the sound system which was now blasting Steely Dan across campus. "Do you have a mic we could plug into the sound system?"

He did and by the end of the song I was standing on the top step to the back entrance of the main building addressing my classmates, several of whom were passing around a joint.

"Tom, Brian, and I have a proposal. Please listen up," I announced and then read the statement.

"All those in favor of staying out on strike until these demands are met raise your hands," I said.

Every hand went up.

I continued: "Ok, who should we choose to represent the students in negotiations?"

Tom yelled out, "Keith, you should be our negotiator."

A vote was taken and I was chosen unanimously by the crowd. "Take our demands to O'Leary," yelled out a student from the center of the field.

I found Mr. Chin. He suggested I speak with the teachers and ask them to send two instructors to the negotiations. I returned to the top of the stairway to the main building and interrupted the music again. "Mr. Chin suggested Student Body President Jim Noble be included in the representation of the students and suggested that we ask two teachers to participate."

I realized I needed to take another vote if I wanted continue to have the support of my classmates. I have no idea where I obtained that political wisdom. "All in favor of including two teachers and Jim to the negotiations raise your hands." Every hand went up again. Some of the now very stoned classmates shouted yes to the proposal.

The meeting started in a second-floor classroom soon after the vote. "Go Ask Alice" by Jefferson Airplane serenaded the deliberations from the yard below.

It was clear that Mr. Chin was concerned despite his attempt to maintain a poker face. O'Leary didn't bother to hide his angry expression. His sneering lips and beads of perspiration telegraphed his dismay at our challenge to his authority. Mr. Gardner smiled nervously and Mrs. Olmsted had a serious air. Jim was his relaxed self and I was all business with a laser focus towards ending O'Leary's tyranny. Dean Chin made an offer. We debated it for nearly an hour. I got some concessions. Mr. Chin made some good points. O'Leary made some promises.

"I need to take your offer to the students. Let's take a short break," I suggested.

On the way down the stairs Jim whispered that he wasn't sure O'Leary could be trusted. I agreed.

I went back to the top-stair perch above the football field. Our sound man turned off the music and handed me the mic.

"Attention, please. Attention," I called out over the sound system.

The strike-turned-party that had sprawled across the sports field quieted down.

I started: "O'Leary said all new rules will stay but that from this time on he would make the new rules in consultation with the faculty. I don't think we should agree to this. What do you think? All in favor of Mr. O'Leary's offer raise your hand."

Not one hand went up.

"All opposed?"

Everyone thrusted a hand towards the sky punctuated with a loud roar of "No!"

I returned to the second-floor meeting with news that the offer had been rejected.

O'Leary paced the room insisting his rules stand. Mr. Gardner tried to calm him down pleading with him to take the position of the students seriously. Jim reminded O'Leary that we had solid support of the students who were quite pleased to stay on strike and enjoy their new-found freedom. I pointed out that Jim and I were the reasonable members of the student body and told them that the first petition included demands that we be free to do whatever we wanted regardless of the wishes of the school. Everyone but the headmaster had a history at Wasatch Academy and this trust in one another gave Jim and I an advantage; that and our popularity with our classmates. We agreed to return to negotiations in the morning.

Music blasted across campus late into the night. A dance party broke out on a nearby tennis court. A small circle of students continued to pass around joints below the loudspeakers. A couple made out, just short of intercourse, near the goalposts.

There was no assembly the next morning. I joined my crew before sunrise removing clinkers from the furnaces. The chilly nights of the high desert fall didn't join our walkout.

Negotiations resumed. By noon our proposal had been accepted by O'Leary. It turned out that Mr. Chin had been supportive all along as were the two teachers.

I brought the agreement to the students. "All the rules made this year are to be revoked," I announced. A thunderous roar of "Yes!" rose up from the students.

"All new rules will be made by a committee of two students, two teachers and two members of the administration. All in favor raise your hand!"

My classmates screamed yes as they raised their hands.

"It's unanimous. I will report back to the negotiating team," I exclaimed over the loudspeaker adding, "It looks like classes will resume tomorrow."

I went back to the second floor to share news of the student's support. The music was turned up full volume. After I told the negotiating team about the vote everyone stood and shook hands. We picked up our notes and Mr. Chin snapped off the lights as we left.

A week later I was visiting with several friends at a student hangout we had assembled using sticks of cottonwood for walls and furnished with rough plank benches. We were skipping the Sunday service which had not been a punishable offense for over a year now. The Presbyterian Church had founded and provided the school's funding, making it affordable to families like mine. But the Presbyterians were divesting from the school and thus relaxing their rules on attending religious services.

"I dare you to streak the Mormon Church," joked my friend Tom.

Twenty or more students had run naked across campus a month before. Afterwards an even larger number of classmates streaked naked through downtown Mt. Pleasant late one night. Few locals witnessed the historic evening prank. Streaking was the latest harmless fad made nationally famous by sports fans racing naked across stadium fields during televised football games.

"I'll do it if both of you join me," I said to my two female friends, Peggy and Jane, who were laughing at the dare. To my surprise they agreed.

We walked up to the Ward on South State Street. I suggested we take off our clothes and hang them on the fence behind the north side of the church, walk out to the front lawn and sit naked on the grass. My two accomplices agreed to the plan.

We draped our jeans, shirts, and underwear on the top strand of barbed wire, scurried out to the front of the church and sat in a circle on the soft green lawn. The timing couldn't have been more perfect. It was a brisk late fall morning so we were pleased when the two huge, red doors opened a few minutes after we had taken our naked positions.

The two young men who had just swung open the doors had to take a second look. Were there really three naked people sitting outside the church? I could see that they were not sure of what they were seeing. Five elderly church ladies led the congregation out into the bright Sunday sun. Their eyes were struggling to understand what they were witnessing. The two doormen finally regained their senses and started to run towards us, but they were too late. We had already jumped to our feet and were racing behind the building towards our clothing. I helped my two classmates over the fence before climbing over the strands of barbed wire. We ran through the backyard of the house north of the church, holding our clothes in our arms. A couple eating breakfast jumped to their feet, alarmed, as they saw three naked teenagers run past their kitchen window.

We stopped in the next yard and quickly pulled on our clothing and walked swiftly towards campus exhilarated from the close call.

Our classmates were in suspense. Two other female classmates and their male friend were accused of the crime. An embarrassment to the school who had always struggled with community relations. But finally, the administration dropped the charges on the falsely accused and figured out who the real streakers were.

We went before the discipline committee that had been reestablished after the strike. The sentence came down. Guilty as charged. Twenty hours cleaning out the sewers. The harshest penalty one could get and still remain enrolled.

At the same time my new relationship with a mysterious blond sophomore from Texas named Cullen was heating up. We agreed to consummate our relationship the evening of the hearing.

Our art teacher, Mrs. Olmsted, stopped me as I was leaving that day's last class. "Keith, I want you to meet Mr. Thomas from Commercial Press. He came down from Provo to speak with you. Can you join us at the cafeteria tonight?"

Of course, I could. Mrs. Olmsted was more a friend than a teacher. Dinner with her was an honor.

Mr. Thomas liked my designs for the yearbooks he had printed at Commercial Press. He was proud to feature our National Scholastic Press Association award-winning publication to high schools and colleges around the state.

We collected our meal and found a seat on the edge of the cafeteria. "Keith, I want to offer you a job. After graduation we would love it if you spent the summer working in our design department."

Mrs. Olmsted said that it would be a great opportunity. She would talk with my parents and help me find an apartment in Provo.

I hadn't seen that coming. I told Mr. Thomas I would be honored.

That evening I scaled the icy fire escape to the top floor of the Fink Dorm and knocked on the glass pane with my knuckle. There was no answer. I was shaking with cold. I knocked again. I couldn't be too loud or I would attract attention from a night watchman or a classmate not tipped off to the plan. I knocked again. A dark figure moved behind the frost-covered window. The window slowly slid up. I belly-crawled in, crossed the sophomore's bed and shivered down the hall to Cullen's room.

She pulled aside a corner of her quilt and I squirmed under, shaking with cold. My hands were chilled and she recoiled when I first touched her warm body. The room had a cold blue glow from the street light. Cullen's roommate rolled over to face the wall. The Fink Dorm girls had a protocol they learned from the older women at Alice Hall. All hush hush, as a boy visitor was a punishable offense.

I was still pretty cold but Cullen wasn't patient. The fear of discovery and excitement of our first rendezvous accelerated events. She pulled me on top of her warmth. Her soft hands pressed against my back. Her fingers glided along my ribs. When the bed springs squeaked, we slowed ourselves. Our lips pressed together to absorb the sound of heaving breathing.

My extremities hadn't yet thawed when it was time to sneak back down the icy fire escape and scoot over to my bed at Sage. It must have been about 4:00 in the morning when I heard a knock on my dorm-room door. It was Mr. Olmsted.

"Come with me Keith. Get all your things. We are heading to the airport." I had no idea what was happening.

Mr. Olmsted led me out to his truck, taking my suitcase. "Keith, Mr. O'Leary spoke with your father yesterday. They agreed you needed to leave. You are flying to Boston to live with your parents."

Keith's father and the Boy Scouts at the Virgin Island

Chapter 8

THE BLAZING GUNS OF HOMESTEAD FLORIDA

Two years before the strike, I had drifted away from my sophomore year at Wasatch Academy inspired by the text of Hemingway's last book, Islands in the Stream and hitchhiked into the mysteries of the American Southwest. An adventure that ultimately landed me at my parent's home in South Florida and a semester at Dade County Colonial Christian School, a Klu Klux Klan dominated educational institution where I took geometry and English.

One Sunday I went to the school to retrieve my geometry text and got a much different lesson while passing through the dining room. "Where in the Bible does it say Jesus had long hair?" and the more disturbing Sunday School psalm of "Where in the Bible does it say we have to love Negros" (though not in such polite terms) always followed by the tossing of candy into the auditorium of screaming white kids. The principal of that Christian school was kind enough when I refused to order a white hooded uniform and join them at the mall raising funds for God Bless America Day and turned down an offer to be their "star quarterback" in a varsity team that as of that year had yet to materialize.

South Miami Dade High might just be the school for me after that: a public school with several thousand Black students mostly of Caribbean decent and not a single identifiable young Klansman to be found. To accommodate the huge number of students half of us attended in the morning and a second half in the afternoon. But I soon discovered that pubic school would not be the solution to that other more openly racist institution.

I joined a dozen or so students in Room 124 at 8:00 am. The teacher sat in the front corner opposite the door reading a magazine while trying not to make eye contact with the students. Several girls in the front of the room danced the Bump to "Give Up the Funk" and "Lady Bump" blasting through the tinny speakers on their boombox. A lusty couple was deep kissing in the back row. Several others would be arguing over a drug deal. When the bell rang it was off to another unidentified class featuring the Bump and a frightened white teacher who thought it better not to interact with the students.

The men's room outside the principal's office served more as a weapons bazaar than a place to relieve oneself. Young men placed black or purple clothes between the sinks, stalls and urinals to display their shiny, silver-barreled pistols. An occasional rifle or two would be leaning against the tile wall. There weren't many automatic weapons, but an occasional assault rifle would show up. The merchants tried to get your attention while you were busy doing your business, claiming their prices were reasonable and their merchandise of particularly good quality.

There was one class where the teacher would not be intimidated, even though his room was next to a corridor guarded by armed students who demanded a tariff of $5 to pass. I imagined that that hallway led to the section of South Miami Dade High where the better drugs, guns, and hookers were available. Mr. Johnson was a giant Black man with a shiny, bald head. I knew this class was American history because the teacher had two grubby history textbooks on his desk. He opened his copy to chapter one and asked a tough guy in the front row to read the first line of the one copy of the book he had to share with the students. The student muttered, perplexed, struggling to imagine what the text might be saying. "In" the teacher said and the student repeated "In," but was not able to read the second word, which wasn't a word. "Fourteen ninety-two," the teacher patiently mouthed followed by the student saying, "1492." They continued word by word like this until the entire sentence had been read out loud to the room of twenty. The classmate sighed in relief and passed the book to the person to his left who continued the struggle to read the second sentence. When the book came to my hands, I sat silently for a contemplating the pros and cons of a public display of literacy, but I couldn't help myself and recited the next sentence without any assistance. I looked up at the teacher to see if I should read the next sentence. A subtle nod of his head and a look towards the classmate next in line made it clear I was to hand the text over to my neighbor.

Those of us not occupied with the business of crime ate lunch in little clumps of students sitting on the sticky Bermuda grass, self-selected by race. I sat with the white kids who were mostly the children of military personnel from Homestead Air Base. Other than our race and a shared dislike of the brutal heat we had nothing in common and sat quietly trying to ignore the humidity and the equally oppressive school atmosphere.

The occasional gunshot or two were to be expected. One lunch period was interrupted by a white student in a car racing through the parking lot firing a pistol at another white student fleeing on foot. The incident was so trivial none of us bothered to flatten to the stubbled lawn. No one was hurt. A few weeks later the roles were reversed. A white student ran through the parking lot, firing at another student careening about in a Ford pickup.

A month or two after those shootings, there was a rumor that a girl was stabbed in the forehead by her classmate. Someone then fired off a few rounds in the direction of the supposed slasher. Another student responded by shooting back and before long dozens of students were darting around campus popping off rounds at one another.

I had just stepped onto the school bus for my ride home when I heard the first gunshots. I saw two students running behind a concrete school wall, firing off several bullets as they dashed from one hiding place to another. Three more students stepped out from behind a parked car and blasted off a few dozen shots at the other two kids. A serenade of pops and bangs emanated from areas out of view. A cloud of cinderblock dust bellowed into the air, indicating a failed effort at hitting a fellow student. A ping pierced the bus just missing my crouched neighbor. A few more bullets tore through the metal fuselage spraying slivers of steel and yellow paint across the seats. The still, sweltering air was the least of our problems then.

Most of the students who were not invested in the shootout had run to the far side of the school. Eight or nine members of the Dade County Sheriff Department's Swat Team stood just off campus, outfitted in helmets and flak jackets and armed with M-16s. They didn't advance on the school until the gunfire went silent.

No one spoke of any casualties. The hour-long battle wasn't important enough to make the news. But it was important enough for me to know I wasn't interested in surviving another firefight.

PART TWO: FOOD NOT BOMBS

Keith and his brother Bruce in the alcove of the family's home on Cape Cod

Chapter 9

TRUE BROTHERS

Once again, the regulars lined up along the North Street sidewalk that led to the bleak, brick warehouse of the Hyannis Salvation Army Soup Kitchen. Long pine shadows stretched across the street and made the fall chill that much colder. People pulled their jackets tight against them as they talked of the latest Boston Celtics game, housing searches, and the problems they have already had with the new guard as they waited for entry to that night's meal of canned green beans and cheap Stop and Shop hotdogs. My younger brother, Bruce, and his wife, Ruth, were among the hundred or more people who had gathered for dinner on that brisk early evening of October 14, 1998.

Bruce passed out slamming hard to the pavement. An ambulance arrived and rushed him to Hyannis General. Ruth must have been distracted by her own thoughts or a desire for dinner since she didn't join Bruce in the emergency vehicle. If you knew Ruth it would not be hard to believe she was too absorbed in her own illusions.

The emergency room doctors said they believe he blacked out from undiagnosed diabetes, and that he had been further weakened by more than twenty-five years of weather, soup lines, and alcohol.

Ruth found shelter that evening in a collapsing wooden shack by the railroad tracks, joining two men she had just met at Cape Cod's finest soup kitchen. Ruth was passionate about the Word of the Jehovah's Witness. My sister-in-law could recite chapter and verse of the true bible and it would not come as a surprise if an argument about religion were to erupt in conversation with her. Something definitely erupted that night.

Court documents would later state that one of Ruth's shack mates, Jon Little, may have stabbed the other man, Paul Peterson, to death. The prosecutor would say that Ruth may have also participated. Perhaps Paul was a sinner. We will never really know for sure.

Regardless, it seems that Ruth was quick with a plan: take the sinner's wallet and buy a gallon of diesel, pour it over the body, light Paul's bloodied corpse on fire, rent a hotel room, and blow the rest of the dead guy's money on vodka and mixers at the local package store, as liquor stores are still known in Massachusetts. Dead Paul didn't need the cash anymore.

His smoldering body, however, got the attention of the Barnstable Police. The stench of charred flesh was unmistakable. They sent Paul to the coroner. They asked around. A number of soup kitchen regulars told the police that my brother's wife had left the meal with the now deceased. In fact, they told the police, Ruth was throwing a party at Hyannis's cheapest motel. The police arrived uninvited and cuffed Ruth, her sidekick Jon Little, and another friend, Elliot Long, who may or may not have participated in the diesel purchase and the subsequent torching of Paul Peterson.

Ruth had safely hidden the murder weapon in her purse. The police found the still bloody knife amongst the chaos of her bag and she was incarcerated at the historic Barnstable County Jail.

Bruce woke up to a warm hospital bed with a view of the harbor and the news of his wife's predicament plastered across the front page of The Cape Cod Times.

Court records would later say that, "The defendant and McHenry were taken to the Barnstable police station for questioning immediately after the fire and discovery of Peterson's body. For a time, the defendant obfuscated and tried to shift the blame for the killing to McHenry and Elliot Long, another vagrant who at the defendant's behest had purchased a can of diesel fuel and torched the shed. As a quarrel between the two men erupted, she turned toward them and saw Peterson swing at the defendant with a knife, which nicked his nose. To assist the defendant, she grabbed Peterson's hand and pried the knife out of his grasp. She threw it over her shoulder."

In a later appeal, court records say that Ruth first testified to the following: "Thus disarmed, Peterson stood face-to-face with the defendant, who also held a knife with blood stains on the blade. Then the defendant, according to McHenry, grabbed Peterson's right arm under the elbow and stabbed him twice in the chest. Moments later, he stabbed Peterson twice more in the chest."

Ruth McHenry described Peterson lying wounded on the floor and crying out, "You've killed me, let me die in peace."

Upon repeating what may have been Peterson's last words, nearly fifteen months after the murder, Ruth told the court that Little repeatedly jumped on the man's chest and said, "die, die, die, die."

Bruce, taking this all in from a hospital bed, got some more news from the medical staff at Hyannis General. They told him that he was definitely diabetic and that he might also be bipolar. They suggested that they could give him medication to help quiet his mind.

I didn't know about any of this until I got a call from my brother. I was scrunched under a blanket in my freezing second-floor bedroom at the Leonard Peltier Defense Committee house in Lawrence, Kansas typing on my Performa when the phone rang. I think this is might have been the first time Bruce had ever called me. He was frantic and told me what he could about the crisis. "I need to raise money for Ruth's bail. Can you help me?" he pleaded with the dignity he was known for.

He shared what he knew of Ruth's arrest. He described the events as they had been told to him over the phone by his incarcerated wife. He was told she had been arrested and charged with accessory to murder. The details weren't clear, he said, but of course Ruth was innocent. He did not tell the story of a killer but that of the woman he loved, then an inmate who helped other prisoners and was respected by the guards. A woman who was kind and would never intentionally hurt anyone and who always wanted the best for everyone. That had also been my experience of Ruth, if tempered by her zeal for vodka and the true Word.

Twelve years before this tragedy I had given my brother a ride to Western Massachusetts, dropping him off at the prestigious Tanglewood Music Center in the Berkshires. There he'd spend the summer of 1976 studying music with members of the Boston Symphony. His beautiful signing voice had been praised by his high school choir director, Mr. Nelson. He was a natural on the trumpet, a choice of instrument that I believe was influenced by my father's small record collection featuring the Herb Alpert and Tijuana Brass green-covered album Whipped Cream & Other Delights. Bruce was a talented musician. It was no wonder why his teachers suggested he attend Tanglewood.

And it was there that Bruce fell madly in love with the Boston Pop's cellist. It must have been glorious from what he would later tell me, suggesting that she was his first lover, but was too much of a gentleman to say so directly. At the end of the summer, he wistfully told me how beautiful she was and about their shared passion for the magic of music. One chilly late-summer night, however, she let him know that their romance was over, that it had just been a summer fling. It was over, she said, before adding that he would soon be off to study music at Boston University and she would return to the Boston symphony stage. His romantic soul was crushed.

He didn't stay in school long. After a couple of semesters, he returned to our family's place on Cape Cod. The woman he started dating then, Carol, was smart and clearly cared for him. They shared a similar fashion sense, influenced more by Liberace than Sid Vicious. Carol was attractive under her thick makeup and lavish wardrobe. She had a good job as a cashier at the Osterville A&P Grocery and had her own apartment in Centerville. But Bruce began to drink. He struggled with an itch born from the thwarted dream of a future with the Tanglewood cellist.

Alcohol, pot, and chain smoking started to rough up his singing voice. The booze and the permanent party at my family's cottage on Middle Lake inspired a war between Bruce and my father. After six months of party-related damage to our family's "Little House," my father sent him packing.

He started driving a cab. Ruth was a regular fare. Medical issues, I believe. She was an enthusiastically devoted Jehovah's Witness and before long Bruce broke up with Carol and went to live with Ruth in a tent in the forest behind the Hyannis Police Station.

Bruce got fired from that taxi company. A customer had complained that they didn't feel safe riding with a drunk behind the wheel. Bruce went to work for another taxi company. Another customer found his enthusiasm for "the one true religion" a bit too much and complained to the dispatcher. And so, he also lost that job.

He took a job at Cape Cod Potato Chips. He had trouble operating the machines when sloshed and it wasn't long before he was fired. He took another taxi job, and got fired again. He started playing the piano for alcohol at a Chinese Restaurant until he wasn't even worth the free drinks.

My brother and I always had very different temperaments. I was quiet and serious and he had always been flashy and talkative. But since I was the first born, he looked up to me. I encouraged him to join a band in Boston. I had some musical connections. Ric Ocasek had performed at a couple of New Year's Eve parties at the collective house I shared with eleven other artists in Allston. I had also booked punk shows at the Rathskeller in Kenmore Square and helped out with an illegal squatted club on the top floor of a derelict office building on Boylston Street. My brother's musical talent would have an audience.

But he just couldn't live in a city. He told me of spending a miserable month in London, England at what was supposed to be his first record deal but he had been too terrified of the urban environment to leave the hotel and lost the gig.

And so it was that he, his new wife Ruth, and her daughter Jennifer all retreated to the back roads of Cape Cod in a damaged yellow Duster with a shattered windshield. Ruth's daughter Jennifer curled up next to Bruce and her mother in the back of their dilapidated car. But even though she could have had a roof over her head with her father the household drama there was worse than the roofless tranquility of my brother and her mother.

They secured a room in a cheap hotel when the Plymouth bit the dust. When they couldn't make those payments, they made other arrangements in the woods of Hyannis. And from time to time, they would scrape up a tarp or a tent only to lose it during the next crisis or police eviction.

One cold day during, his first year of homelessness I was able locate Bruce at a rundown weekly hotel room by the Hyannis Airport and took a seat at a tiny table in his room. Ruth and Jennifer sat on the bed. Bruce removed the butt-filled ashtray knowing the smell bothered me, and then bent over and slid his electric piano out from under the bed. "I have a new song to play for you," he said, "True Brothers." Then he sang:

Are you like me that you can see the way things are eroding?
And can you sense that something big is coming?
Heed the warning! Hope is there if you know where to look.
The light is shining. Stand outside the world and see alternatives arising!

There are gifts in men who show us when the danger will be mounting.
They are guiding lights for all to see the truth
that we are counting on to know just how
to go the distance we are running.
These, the men the teacher sends, unselfish to the end.

Humble men, who take the lead in caring for the people,
lending a hand to reach every man, woman, and child living in every land.
We can call them OUR TRUE BROTHERS!

They plant the seed and cultivate to see which of us grows.
They feed us truth with integrity. But only heaven knows
if we will listen to them long enough to make it to the end,
these the men the Leader sends undaunted for the friends.

I want to be able to carry my load;
able to rock and able to roll with the times.
I want to be able to stay on the course
and follow examples of men from the source of life

Ruth mostly talked with me about the truth that could be found between the pages of her bible. She also lamented her failure to save JFK's life and her fight with P.T. Barnum over his treatment of the big cats. Ruth was about five-years-old when Kennedy was killed yet she anguished over her failure to take the bullet. If only she had jumped more quickly and taken that bullet. Ruth also let me know that she had been in charge of the tigers and the lions at the circus and had refused to mistreat them, telling P.T. Barnum that she just couldn't hurt them anymore. But P.T. insisted on this inhumane treatment and so she quit. Ruth had principles, her delusions, her faith, her family, and her daughter Jennifer from a first marriage. And she also had Bruce.

Bruce had even less to say outside of theology. He rarely talked about music, recalled our times as children playing in the wilderness of the National Parks, or even much about what had been his obsession: his hatred of our father. An hour of bible stories and my mind would shut off. I felt I was losing my brother to the Jehovah's Witness, a cult that I believed preyed on those like my brother who struggled with difficulties. Bruce would also lament that his devotion to alcohol had excluded him from membership in his local congregation. My brother's mind had been both soaked and kidnapped.

But then Ruth was in jail, and then indicted for murder on December 1, 1998. Bruce started to call me almost every day. His conversations were mostly about Ruth and thankfully strayed away from his usual, long theological ramblings. It seemed as if the new crisis in his life and the medication against his bipolar condition had freed his mind from two decades of drunken religious fog. He excitedly told me that everyone in the Barnstable Jail thought the world of Ruth, even the guards. He described how she helped the medical staff and took care to make sure that everyone her life touched was happy. He also reported that she was well respected for her knowledge of the bible. Bruce was proud of his inmate wife, but was desperate to win her release. Unfortunately, I couldn't raise the bail. The best I could do was add to her commissary.

Bruce stopped drinking. The fight in his mind quieted as a result of the medicine prescribed at the hospital. He proudly announced that now that he was sober, he could attend services with the congregation. Social workers helped him get on the Section Eight Housing list. My brother called with news that he was moving to an apartment in East Dennis. He told me that he was confident his wife would join him soon. The district attorney would see that she was innocent. "She will be coming home soon, Keith," he said, ecstatic that he would be able to welcome her into their first stable housing in a quarter century.

Between the vodka, the fire, Ruth's creative grasp of reality, and Little's desire to pin the murder entirely on my sister-in-law, the details are cloudy. All we really know is that Paul Peterson was stabbed to death and then set on fire. And that the bloody knife that killed him was found in Ruth's bag. It was a dramatic scene fitting for the Ruth McHenry I knew.

The Appeals Court summarized the case in a May 2002 decision this way: "On October 14, 1998, the defendant, a thirty-six-year-old homeless man, had an altercation with the victim, Paul Peterson, over an abandoned railroad shed in Hyannis. Their argument, warmed by vodka, burst into violence. While the defendant's female companion, Ruth McHenry, looked on, the two combatants, armed with knives, fought one another. The defendant, with assistance from McHenry, prevailed, and Peterson died almost immediately from multiple stab wounds."

Since Ruth's testimony changed so often the district attorney told the court in frustration that he wanted to settle the case and agreed to a plea: credit for time served, regular visits to a psychiatrist and a lifetime on probation.

My brother called again. Ruth was free.

Bruce took her to the apartment where she made herself at home in a thrift-store easy chair, a throne for my brother's wife. Finally, they didn't need to fear that they would have to pawn the electric piano for a few nights in a cheap room. No one would force them to move along. Bruce was at peace and celebrated Ruth's return by composing a tribute to his companion, "My Love for You" and a second song, "Princess." The lyrics of his love for his partner gushed from his cigarette-damaged voice.

I visited my brother and his wife while traveling across the country with the Australian filmmaker Liz Tadic in the fall of 2003. Liz and I sat squished together on a cheap puffy couch in their spotless, well-cared-for basement apartment. Ruth sat on a kitchen chair crammed next to their two-burner stove and full-size refrigerator excitedly telling us about the bible, the circus, and her position in the Secret Service.

A few years later my brother's true love finally succumbed to her decades on the street. Thankfully, she died under her own roof, joining the other deceased Witnesses in the paradise she had spent a lifetime describing in exquisite detail.

My brother continued her work, making sure no one was denied entry into heaven. But one day he failed to attend a bible class. He missed an afternoon of knocking on doors. He didn't attend that week's service. His stepdaughter, Jennifer went to check on him. She could see his body on the floor through the window and dialed 911. The paramedics arrived. Our cousin Chris was the first person through the door. Bruce was unresponsive. He died, indoors, two weeks before his 56th birthday. Bruce was reunited with Ruth in their paradise.

Jennifer called to give me the grim news. There hadn't been a day since he came into the world when I didn't have a younger brother, even if it was a Jehovah's Witness-obsessed little brother. That was a shock and a reality I had never considered.

Jennifer is the sanity in the family. She raises three energetic children and runs a landscaping business with her Cuban-American husband out of a small rented duplex. My brother's only asset was a used Toyota Odyssey. We needed $3,000 to cremate Bruce's body. She tried to stall the mortuary.

I called our sister Dolly in Bellingham. Bruce is dead, I told her. While to Dolly the brother she had known as a child had died long ago in her mind, she was also in shock.

Jennifer shared my number with Bruce's friends in the congregation. They asked me if I wanted to attend a memorial and I accepted the invitation. Dolly agreed to join me on Cape Cod and attend the service even though, like me, she felt the Jehovah's Witnesses had robbed our brother's mind. She was still an Episcopalian and from what I gathered she believed he had become nothing more than a lost, homeless, alcoholic heretic that had abandoned our father's faith.

Soon I was talking with Bruce's friends nearly every day, making plans for the memorial. We settled on a date. I designed and printed a program to share with the congregation.

The mortuary finally agreed to reduce the price of cremation. His three-hundred-pound corpse had worn out its welcome.

I met my sister at her motel. We ate at one of those stuffy Cape Cod restaurants on Route 28 before heading off to the Kingdom Hall in Dennis. Dolly said polite words to me about her big brother, mentioned his struggle with our father in her often guarded, uncomfortable way of expressing our family's turmoil.

Dolly and I were welcomed by the congregation as family. The service was honest and down to Earth. They loved my brother, whom they also knew as their own brother. My conversations with members of his congregation were nothing like those I had had with Bruce. There was not a word about a true bible.

We spent the afternoon at a church member's house, in a huge room full of Witnesses of every age. The woman of the house pointed out all the vegan dishes they had made especially for me. They shared stories about Bruce singing for his friends and the time that he had come to someone's aid to help them change a flat tire during a snow storm. Someone recalled the time Bruce brought a cake he had baked to a church potluck where he learned he had used salt instead of sugar. Laughter filled the living room and there was no mention of god's kingdom other than a couple of good-natured jokes about the peculiarities of being a Witness.

"There wasn't a mean bone in his body. Bruce was always kind. We will miss him," someone said and we all agreed.

The Jehovah's Witnesses hadn't taken Bruce's mind. They had been the family he didn't find in the family of his birth. A family that celebrated their true brother, Bruce, a man who lived without possessions but had something much more valuable.

Keith and Liz Hurwitz in the kitchen at 41 Gardner Street in Allston, Massachusetts

Chapter 10

NEW BALANCE

It was 1977 and I was out of work again. Dented pots and frying pans hung above the sink in our drafty, decaying kitchen at 41 Gardner Street in Allston. I sat at the kitchen table scouring the Help Wanted ads of the previous day's Boston Globe. I circled one possibility and then tore out the page: "Thompson Tool & Die Inc needs a manager. Good pay. Apply in person at 135 Lincoln Street any time from 8:00 a.m. to 4:00 p.m. Ask for Ted."

I washed my coffee mug and headed off to the thrift store on Harvard Avenue to look for something that a future manager might wear to a job interview. Among the twenty plaid shirts on the men's rack, I found five white dress shirts. I tried on a large and it fit. I found a pair of black slacks at the back of the store and an almost stain-free, red "power tie" on the next row.

A very old, withered-looking woman stood behind the counter tagging incoming books. After a few minutes she realized that I was ready to check out.

"Can I help you, sir?"

One of the books in her pile caught my eye, 1984, so I grabbed it and put it with my four items.

"Five dollars, please," she said.

I placed my five crumpled one-dollar bills on the cloudy glass counter as she slowly folded my clothes and put them into a reused brown grocery bag. I grabbed the used, paperback copy of Orwell's novel, added it to the sack and wandered home.

I found the 135 Lincoln Street building early the next morning. It was a depressing four-story brick monument to industry rising into the foggy drizzle from a parking lot of mud. A metal sign with, "Thompson Tool and Die," painted in black Helvetica was screwed high on a windowless wall. A second sign above a person-sized door announced: "Office." I snaked across the highest dry parts of the parking lot, pulled open the heavy door below the sign and found myself standing before a large metal desk covered in papers. A frail-looking lady absorbed in her search through a precarious mound of forms failed to notice my arrival.

"Hello Ma'am, I am here to apply for the management position," I announced, attempting to get her attention. She slowly turned toward me, showing an almost toothless smile, and said, "Oh yes, honey, just a second."

She opened a valley through the formations of papers, located an application, and handed it to me. "Fill this out and Ted will see you."

The application form consisted of slots for one's name, address, phone, a few lines of job history, three references, and a signature attesting to the truthfulness of one's answers. I got her attention again and she took my application and disappeared into a cave-looking passageway beyond the clutter.

"Come on in, I'm Ted," a man said while pushing his office door shut. "We need a manager here. Someone that can work with these Puerto Rican speaking people. Can you speak Puerto Rican? I see you lived in California."

"I know a little Spanish," I replied with the required confidence. "I'm sure I would be a good supervisor and I wouldn't have any problem with the language."

"Great then, we will see you here in the morning. We start at eight," he said.

That was fast.

The next morning, I finished my daily oatmeal and rushed out into the light drizzle and over the turnpike to the factory where I found Ted submerged in what appeared to be all manner of invoices and memos.

"Hi, oh, what's your name again?" he asked.

"Keith, sir."

"Oh yes, that's right, Keith. I'll take you upstairs." Ted set down his papers and led me up two flights of concrete stairs, down a long hall, and through a door of heavy plastic strips.

Ted explained, "We play a special type of music that helps keep everyone motivated. The guy we get the music from was in the CIA. Mind control type stuff you know," he said with a smile and then went on: "We have to cut it off during the breaks. State law you know. We have one fifteen-minute break in the morning and one in the afternoon and a thirty-minute lunch break in between. When the music starts everyone must be at their stations working. You understand?"

Ted showed me where I would be working and told me my staff would show me the steps to producing the order of nearly five million pairs of vinyl New Balance Ns required by early that spring. You know the shoe, the one with the letter N glued or stitched on the side.

Ted led me to a second room. "This is Jose," he said, nodding towards a slight man in his mid-thirties who smiled as he shook my hand. "He leads the silk-screen crew."

Walking back to the first room, Ted continued: "Once the vinyl blanks are silk screened you bring them over here. The holes are punched so you can slide them on these pins on the bed of the Electro Thermotron." He then pushed a sheet of Ns onto the metal plate on the prehistoric-looking machine. He showed me how to step down on the peddle and told me that when the top plate is down the operator needs to push the red buttons on each side.

"Be careful. You could get zapped," he said, glancing over at me with a demonic grin, and then stepped around to the rolling laundry bin full of bagged Ns.

"The most important part of your job is to make sure you have the Ns for the left side of the left shoe in one bag, and that the right-side Ns for the left shoe are in another bag, left side Ns for the right shoe in yet another bag and the right-side Ns for the right shoe are in still another. If you don't do this correctly the next step in the process will be a mess and I will hear about it. The production line stitching them to the shoes will come to a crashing halt when they discover they have the wrong Ns. Do you understand?"

I nodded yes.

A cold glow from the twelve-foot-high windows illuminated the factory floor. Jose helped me set up my station pointing to the piles of blank pre-punched sheets of vinyl and I joined the line with Jose, Hector, and Juan pulling our squeegees across our screens, inking out one set of Ns after another to the rhythm of the repetitive, quick-paced, CIA-informed elevator music. With a single swipe, I pressed a coat of ink through the screen with the corner edge of my almost two-foot-wide squeegee, lifted the screen frame, grabbed the vinyl sheet of ten blue Ns, and placed it on the metal drying rack to my right. I then placed another hole-punched sheet of vinyl in position, lowered the screen, added another dollop of ink, and pulled the hard rubber blade across the silk mesh, squeezing out another ten letter Ns. Sheet by sheet, over and over again, as fast as was reasonable.

Every fifteen minutes or so a large woman named Maria stepped into our room to collect our sheets and distribute them among the women operating the

Electro Thermatron. They slid the still tacky wet Ns onto the pins, depressed the peddle, pushed the two buttons and, Ca-boom! the ink was cooked dry and the ten Ns bubbled up to that familiar pillowy, athletic-shoe look as they were cut free from the pinned sheets.

The loud electric bell clanged and the obnoxious music went silent. My co-workers left their posts and hurried out of the work area and down the stairs to a coffee truck parked outside in the puddles. They quickly filled their paper cups with coffee, grabbed a muffin, and rushed back upstairs to enjoy their break, chatting in Spanish.

Unfazed by my first day on the letter N line, I woke up ready for day two. I pulled on my manager's pants and white shirt and after three attempts secured my tie and grabbed my copy of Orwell's 1984.

At the factory, the cold brick rooms were silent. Then the bell rang and the music started. The silkscreen men squeezed Ns onto our vinyl sheets while the women banged out Ns on the die-cutting machines.

The bell rang for our first fifteen-minute break. I perched on a high metal stool near the light of a dirty window and opened my yellowing paperback to chapter one. "It was a bright cold day in April, and the clocks were striking thirteen. Winston Smith, his chin nuzzled into his breast in an effort to escape the vile wind, slipped quickly through the glass doors of Victory Mansions, though not quickly enough to prevent a swirl of gritty dust from entering along with him."

I was ten pages in when the bell rang. The music started and I joined my co-workers printing that week's order of dark blue Ns until the bell screeched again and the Electro Thermotrons went silent and I returned to the pages of 1984. Orwell's Winston was waking from his own personal prison: "Weeks or months must have passed. It would have been possible now to keep count of the passage of time if he had felt any interest in doing so, since he was being fed at what appeared to be regular intervals. He was getting, he judged, three meals in the twenty-four hours; sometimes he wondered dimly whether he was getting them by night or by day."

My damp overcast days merged with Winston's desperate search for reality. How has Maria lasted two decades at the Electro Thermotron? Would I be squeezing out my twenty-millionth N by the real year 1984? I had only worked there a week and it impressed me that this would be a dreary way to spends one's adult life.

Thirty minutes after lunch one day, Jose and I were cleaning up the blue so we could start printing the red. I stepped into the Electro Thermatron room with the last armload of blues. Maria depressed the buttons on her machine. Sparks crackled from her fingers as she flew off her stool into the gritty brick wall and crumpled with a loud thud to the cold concrete. Her stool toppled over and clanged against the foot of her neighbor's machine.

“Patricia! Patricia! See if she is breathing. I’ll block the door,” I yelled. Jose dropped his oily rags and rushed over to Maria’s side. Patricia pulled off her sweater and placed it under Maria’s head. I tossed my blue sheets on top of the bagged Ns and wheeled the canvas cart to the door to block access from any rare appearance of my boss Ted. I didn’t want her employment to be threatened by her absence from her station.

Patricia raced from the second-floor toilet with a Dixie cup of tap water and splashed half over Maria’s bluish lips. Maria lay flat across the filthy cement floor, blood returning to her limbs. Then her torso heaved and she groaned back to life. Jose pulled on Maria’s left shoulder as she tried to push herself to her feet. I guided her slowly to her stool and mimed “rest your head” with my temple tipped towards my two praying hands. She laughed as she struggled to climb back on her high stool. There was little chance that Ted would fire her now that she was at her station.

We all returned to our stations relieved that Maria had survived.

The alarm interrupted the monotony, the hellish music stopped and the world of Orwell took me away from the factory floor. “War is Peace.” Endless war and big brother were always watching. My fifteen minutes of 1984 with the “Outer Party” and their “Two Minutes Hate” against the enemy Emmanuel Goldstein came to an end with the buzzer, the motivational music, and hours of more Ns. The final bell rang and my crew wished one another buenas noches.

I fled home along the chain-link fences above the Turnpike to Lincoln Street and my room at 41 Gardner for dinner and bed. Only 4.5 million more Ns to go. I would finish Orwell’s 1984 long before that.

Sharon and Keith at 41 Gardner Street in Allston, Massachusetts

Chapter 11

ROBBING McDONALDS

Five decades of rancid olive oil and pasta sauce had left their mark on the Italian diner's red vinyl seats. Strands of spaghetti flowed from oval porcelain platters onto the stained, red-checkered table cloth. It would prove an adequate, if possibly not the most sanitary, of feasts.

The laughter from the next room almost drowned out our tired conversation. A 350-pound patriarch rocked back in his chrome chair, roaring with hilarity as his family and friends tossed back chalices of vino and gobbled twists of spaghetti soaked in marinara sauce. From the hilarity and boisterous conversation several comments about "doing twenty upstate" gave me the impression this might have been the Godfather's welcome home, or his last meal before doing time.

For our road-weary group, it would be our last meal together. We had spent over a week on Lester Rall's outlaw transcontinental "hippy" bus line, the Grey Rabbit.

The journey began at the fog-and-rain-shrouded entrance to Golden Gate Park, at the blunt end of Haight Street where I had joined thirty or so others, all similarly clad in blue jeans, tie-dyed shirts, ankle-length skirts, and pony tails: all of us flower children, a few lugging guitars, refusing to wilt in the long days of the late 1970s.

The tribe scrambled onto the gutted and refurbished Greyhound. I found my place in a sea of blanket-covered mattresses and opened my copy of Ferlinghetti's, On Leaving San Francisco. Soon we were chugging up the west end of the Bay Bridge and on our way to the east end of America. It was a kind of post-industrial magic carpet ride equipped with granola and cheap Mexican weed punctuated only by the occasional stop to use a funky gas-station restroom. The spell would remain unbroken until coming to a stop in a Boston Combat Zone alley behind the Naked I.

I had traveled east with no real plan, just the hope that I could move back into some crevice at the Gardner Street house I had helped mold into an artistic left-leaning community of Boston University students in the mid-1970s. I entered through the never-locked back door and found my former girlfriend, Freddi, drifting through the kitchen. I asked her if any of the Victorian's eleven rooms happened to be available.

"I believe there's a free mattress in the band practice room in the basement," she said, adding that I would need to ask the other occupant if he would mind having a roommate.

The practice room was still mostly as I remembered it: stained, whitish carpets nailed to the walls and one slit of a window that opened to what passed as a side yard of ailanthus trees. The drum set had been replaced by two single mattresses. A man about my age woke from his bundle of blankets with a groan. "Hey, do you mind if I share this room with you?" I asked. "No problem, man, help yourself." I placed my backpack at the end of the mattress and headed out to find employment.

It wasn't the first of my Allston job searches, but it would turn out to be both the fastest and the one that led to the outcome closest to home. I landed a job that first day at the Budget car rental place that shared our parking lot. This job was closer by a block than my previous stint at Riley's Roast Beef, known for hockey team violence and the weekly shattering of the floor to ceiling windows. It was also closer than my short-lived employment at the Allston Twin Theaters which ended a week after I started when patrons injured themselves tossing sodas and shoving one another during a New Year's Eve showing of Animal House. And closer as well than my four-month position at Sharp Electronics repairing adding machines. I didn't do any repairing, but instead collected the broken machines from banks and corporate offices around eastern Massachusetts that my boss was supposed to repair leaving temporary lenders in their place. I came to work one morning to find heaps of adding machines strewn across the shelves and floor. Black motor oil dripped from the ceiling panels. My boss quit in anger at the institutional chaos of a corporate policy that discouraged the employment of Black men. A policy I would learn was based on a belief that banks and other clients would assume that any Black man with an adding machine was a thief. Since the only people the temp agency sent over for the position were Black and thus only worked one day before being let go it meant that my boss had to retrieve many of the computers himself and had no time to repair those we were bringing in. I overheard him shouting at his supervisor demanding that he be allowed to hire the Black man that had started that day but he was told it was against company policy.

My boss's boss greeted me at the door to the repair shop. "You are going to have to pay for every outstanding product not retrieved," he told me as we both inspected the destruction in a state of shock. By my quick calculations the roughly one hundred adding machines I had scattered around town at a price of $150 just wasn't worth the risk so I quit. A week later I learned that my replacement, Happy, had traded a car load of machines and the company car for a few hours with a hooker in Quincy and that his body was discovered crushed on the tracks near Coolidge Corner after staggering into a Green Line Trolly on the Cleveland Circle Line.

My new position, basically next door, started during the interview: I was handed a terry cloth and told to dry off a just-washed Budget Rental Car return. The owner, Mr. White, ended the interview mid-sentence distracted by his own concerns leaving the rest of the training to a burly tough armed with a green garden hose and a rag.

The old three-story brown Victorian Mansion that I had been calling home on and off for several years was surrounded on two sides by the Budget Rental parking lot. The police could be found nearly every night parked under a street light next to our building counting the sports betting take from the Linden's Superette across the street.

My coworker insisted to me: "We need to keep the cars in perfect condition," and bragged about the ease with which he turned back the odometers on the rental vehicles to the required new car milage. By the end of my second day and twentieth vacuumed-and-ready-for-sale Lincoln, I was promoted to the Sunday opening manager. Mr. White explained that if the bell above the counter rang, I had to lock up the rental office and run the two blocks east down Brighton Avenue to the Clark and White Lincoln Mercury dealership because that would mean there was a break-in or a fire. I was to give him a call once I secured the property.

I opened the rental car office on my first Sunday, swept away that morning's light snowfall from the entrance and then the bell started blaring. I raced down Brighton Avenue. Flames were bursting from the dealership's second-floor windows over-looking Gardner Street. Plastic-smelling black smoke bellowed out of the building blowing over the neighborhood. A bright red hook-and-ladder fire truck pulled up and cranked its ladder to the roof. Firemen uncoiled hoses and two men cranked open the brass fitting to a fire hydrant across the street.

Mr. White was already on the scene when I arrived, so I walked towards him but he waved me away, saying in a low voice, "You talk with the fire marshal but don't tell him I am here," before slowly drifting out of sight. The fire chief rushed over to me. "Were you here when it started?"

"No," I said adding that I had heard the alarm when I was opening the Budget Car Rental office at Linden Street and ran down to see what was happening.

Another fire engine arrived as the first squad of fire fighters scrambled up their ladders with heavy hoses over their backs. By now all four floors were burning. Fire fighters crashed their axes into the heavy metal garage doors as others frantically uncoiled hoses and screwed them to hydrants. Mr. White reappeared and walked slowly past me whispering, "You'd better get back to Budget," before disappearing once again down a back alley. Clark and White Lincoln Mercury would reopen in the suburban community of Newton, the apparent beneficiary of fire insurance. The Brighton Avenue location would be redeveloped as a luxury condominium project.

My twelve-hour Sunday of fire and car returns finally came to an end. I had to get to a meeting with a relative. I picked up my brother Bruce near Boston University in a dilapidated orange Volkswagen Beetle with a rusted-out passenger seat floor and sun-stiff wipers I had borrowed from a housemate. My father's cousin, Machin, had pressured my brother and I to attend "a secret meeting of great importance," he said, and asked that we meet him at his place in Sudbury. Machin, always a bit disorganized, greeted us and then rushed out to a store to get alcohol to lubricate the conversation. He came back with a bottle of sake.

Machin was the same age as my father. He had been a logger in the Pacific Northwest. He had several children from a first marriage, was raising a couple of his second wife's children from her first marriage and was struggling to raise two children that they had had together. His step children had difficulty moving beyond the criminal lifestyle of their father who was still incarcerated at the Concord Correctional Institute. Machin was a kind man who found it difficult to find a path in life that suited him.

Not long after Machin returned with the apparently necessary social lubricant his friend joined us. Machin started the meeting by introducing us to this friend. "He is with the Minutemen," he explained as he poured sake into our porcelain, Chinese restaurant tea cups. The four of us were huddled around a cheap card table in the garage. "Machin tells me you are against president Carter and might want to help our cause," he said, adding that the president is a Communist with something he called the Trilateral Commission and planned to hand the country over to the Chinese. "That's why we have such bad inflation and the energy crisis. He's even planning to give away our Panama Canal, can you imagine?" Machin poured Bruce and I another cup of sake and coaxed his friend to get to the point. "We need your help boys. We want you to become members of our group, the Minutemen, and help us take back our country. We know you are against communism just like us," he said. "We want you to help us kill the president and we have a solid plan and you two are just the ones who can do it." I don't generally drink alcohol so I was getting pretty drunk but not too drunk to realize I wanted nothing to do with this. Machin misunderstood, my problem with Carter was that he was too conservative and militaristic. But since Machin was always the awkward older relative it wasn't surprising to learn he had been lured into a bazaar far-right fantasy.

My brother and I thanked them for the sake. I told them that we would think about it and get back to them as we staggered out into the snowy evening. I successfully started the VW and we crept back to Allston, Bruce's dorm, and my warm sleeping bag on the basement floor mattress.

"Keith, Keith, you look yellow," Freddi said as she shook me back to consciousness. In a jolt, I emerged from what I would learn was more than a week of semiconscious, fever-nightmares of swirling reds and yellows. I was both hot and cold. My sweat-soaked, down sleeping bag clung to me. My clammy, wet blue jeans and sweaty shirt stuck to my skin. Freddi lifted me to my feet, pulled my damp bag and perspiration-drenched clothes from my body and helped me get dressed for a bus ride to the emergency room at Saint Elizabeth's Hospital

The doctor said I had hepatitis and prescribed Compazine saying it would help me get my appetite back. He also told me that I had to let my housemates know they needed to get a gamma globulin injection or they might also contract hepatitis.

I stopped into the Budget office to let them know I wouldn't be in. "No worries, you were fired seven days ago," the clerk said. My housemates were not too happy about paying twenty-five dollars for a shot of the gamma globulin.

I went back to my sleeping bag and passed out. I faithfully took a dose of Compazine twice a day for about a week. Then, one morning a sensation that felt like the twisting of my jaw jolted me awake. I climbed out of bed and went to the basement toilet and checked out my face in the mirror. The twisting wasn't so obvious in the reflection. I stumbled upstairs to get a better look in the better lit first-floor bathroom mirror. I grasped the two sides of my face with my hands trying to keep my face from twisting. The torque of my neck was more visible now. I wondered if I might be tripping. I struggled to keep my face from spinning but it was of no use. I leaned over the kitchen sink splashing cold water on my face but the twisting only increased. My housemate Paul wandered into the kitchen. He said I looked frightened and wanted to know what was going on. My neck and jaw were screwed so tight I couldn't speak. Paul rushed me to the bus and back down to the emergency room.

A nurse helped me onto a gurney. The doctor on duty arrived. She looked distressed. She asked me a question. I grunted pointing to my mouth with a thrust to dramatize the twisting. Paul had little information to share with the doctors and nurses. He had found me this way. The doctor lifted a huge book from a shelf and started madly flipping through the pages of the pharmaceutical digest.

My neck and face were twisting with such power I corkscrewed off the gurney onto to the floor. Paul and a nurse pulled me back to the bed. The nurse exclaimed in a sweet Irish accent, "Oh shit, we can't wait for the doctor. I'm injecting you with a barbiturate."

She drained a small glass bottle and wham, plunged the needle in my arm and held me to the gurney. I relaxed and the doctor solved the mystery: a severe allergic reaction to Compazine. "Take two tablets of this barbiturate a day for thirty days," the doctor instructed.

My housemates still weren't too happy about the shots. To add insult to the discomfort of the injection, they had to fork over what then was a lot of money for the privilege. That included housemates and their lovers. My housemate Sue was dating a neighbor, John, who also happened to be a Christian Scientist. He refused the injection on religious grounds. While he didn't get the pleasure of a stick in the arm, he did get the opportunity to enjoy nearly two weeks of hepatitis delirium.

I was evicted. I rolled up my smelly sleeping bag, shoved my meager items into my pack and dragged myself out to the snowy streets of Boston. I found some warmth sitting at Riley's Roast Beef but it was back into the snow at the 3:00 a.m. closing.

My legs were cylinders of ice. My feet burned numb and the delirium of lingering hepatitis and the barbiturates to fight the Compazine had me staggering along the frozen streets. I was too weak to do more than stand in a doorway out of the direct wind. I needed money and a way to get to a warmer environment. I needed a bus ticket south.

The snow was a few miles per hour short of a full blizzard. I made my way east down Commonwealth Avenue and past a McDonald's crowded with dozens of warm Boston University students.

That gave me an idea: "I'll rob the McDonald's after the lunch crowd when the cash registers will be stuffed with money. It won't hurt McDonald's. What's a few hundred dollars to this global poison profiteer. It's probably my political duty anyway. A direct attack on a symbol of American greed."

I paced back and forth in a doorway across the street reviewing my possible moves. "I will walk up to the register with my hand in my coat pocket and announce that I have a gun and demand all the money," I thought. I repeated the plan over and over in my head. I walked back and forth in front of the McDonald's. I tried to strengthen my resolve, to build confidence with each slog past the storefront. I was freezing but the adrenaline of the mission distracted me from the pain.

"They won't miss the money," I said to myself. "And they're evil, anyway." I repeated and repeated to myself the line I would say at the counter: "I have a gun, give me all your money."

The hours slowly ticked by as I practiced: "I have a gun, give me all your money."

Lunch passed but I still didn't have the courage to go inside. There would be more money after dinner anyway, I told myself. So, I kept pacing and practicing: "I have a gun, give me all your money."

Shards of sleet bit at my checks. Another half inch of ice wrapped around my jeans. Dinner came and went and soon the restaurant was nearly empty. It would close and I would miss my opportunity.

I walked across Commonwealth with as much confidence as I could, opened the door, and walked swiftly towards the cash register on the far left. A teenage blond girl with a McDonald's cap and uniform stood at the ready to take another order. The only other person around was a frat boy drunkenly trying to read the menu. I would walk up to her and say, "I have a gun, give me all your money."

I took a step towards the cashier but the guy reading the menu moved to the counter first. "One double cheese burger, small fries, and a medium coke," he slurred.

The bubbly employee responded, "That will be $2.35." She rang up his order, took his money saying, "thanks," and then turned to fill a bag with the burger and fries and pass it to the frat boy.

The inebriated hamburger buyer stepped away. It was my turn. My hand was in my pocket pretending to be a gun. Now I had to say it, "I have a gun, give me all your money."

I stepped up to the counter. I looked at the school girl in her reddish brown and white McDonald's dress and little pointed hat.

"A small vanilla milkshake, please," I stammered.

"That will be seventy-six cents," she said.

"Oh, I don't have that much," I said and then turned around and walked back out into the frozen night.

A holiday photo of everyone at 41 Gardner Street in Allston, Massachusetts

Chapter 12

JUDY

A cooling mist shrouded the Shawmut Peninsula on a cold fall day in 1978. She disappeared into the damp fog of Back Bay Boston. Was that our Judy that we buried the year before walking beneath the brown arches of Boston's Trinity Church? That must have been Judy with her shiny, jet-black hair stepping elegantly along the tulip-lined walkway towards the graceful Swan Boats on a sunny May afternoon in 1979. Her long dark Members Only wool coat swishing as she drifted from view, heading down tony Newbury Street.

I thought I saw my deceased friend again six months later, her inky locks then a tangled mess. Was that her standing outside Riley's Roast Beef glancing suspiciously up and down Harvard Street and shuttering nervously with her arms folded across a food-stained white blouse? Her pale, thin legs jutted awkwardly from a threadbare brown skirt. I wanted to go to her but I couldn't abandon my struggle to cut free the rubbery veins from a twenty-five-pound side of beef I was preparing for that evening's torrent of roast beef sandwiches. I thought I could see the fear in her eyes before she scurried into the dark. Was that really my Judy?

Judy was my collage girlfriend Liz's older sister. She was more than a good a friend, Judy was family. Her deep coal eyes seemed to have seen more than her years spent as a UCLA art history student would suggest. They were dark pools of thought that I loved to dive into. I was honored that she let me.

Judy came to spend a few summer weeks with me in the Brookline, Massachusetts apartment that her sister Liz and I shared. The two sisters were coast switching: Liz went west to visit her parents in Studio City.

Judy had a passion for the Beatles, paisley shirts, pachouli oil, and really anything with a sixties, flower-child aesthetic. She had missed celebrating the hippy era, having been bound by the chains of her protective mother.

Judy soaked up my tales of psychedelic adventures and wanted to try LSD. She had the impression that I would know where to buy some D-lysergic acid, but that had been a long time ago in my still-short life. I had no connections then, but her enthusiasm could not be ignored so I set out to help.

First, I called some of my friends who were more likely to have a lead, but like me their LSD experiments were in the past. Judy's downturned lips wouldn't let me disappoint her so all I could think of was to drive down to the Greyhound Bus Station on the edge of Boston's Combat Zone. That was where one could always be sure to snag some trouble.

It didn't take long to find someone that knew where to score. A tall, well-dressed Black man was broadcasting his likely access to mind-expanding substances at the curb, strutting around and sporting a purple felt fedora and matching purple tie.

He was a proper gentleman, opening the door of my car for his girlfriend as he asked us our names. His name, in turned out, was also Keith. I wondered, however, if his name would have been whatever I had offered. He explained that we would need to drive out to a house in Roxbury. He would bring his girlfriend as "collateral."

"Ok, if you think that is necessary. The collateral bit. We would be happy if she joined us," I responded.

We drove about twenty minutes to a house bordered by empty lots of brick scraps, broken bottles, spindles of rebar, and other debris. A lonely yellowish triple decker with most of the window panes knocked out.

My new best friend Keith stepped out of my car explaining he would have to go it alone: the residents were nervous about visitors. "Surely you can understand," he said. He left his girlfriend with us as insurance against the theft of Judy's twenty-dollar bill.

He gracefully danced across the post-apocalyptic landscape towards the east side of the ruins and disappeared. It was a long, long wait. Keith's girlfriend tried to engage us in a lively conversation about a world that seemed to consist mostly of local criminal activities, and slang of which we were generally ignorant. When she saw we were getting worried about Keith's return she would sweetly assure us that he would be down shortly.

That turned out to be a long shortly, but he did eventually bounce out of a side door with a less than comforting grin.

"I've got some good news and I've got some bad news," Keith reported with the cool exaggeration of a tacky used car salesman.

"I couldn't get you any acid but I got you something even better, mescaline, pure mescaline from Mexico," he said as he handed me a wad of tinfoil folded into an inch square envelope.

I opened it. The mescaline looked more like dried snot than anything I knew of as mescaline. I didn't want it but of course Keith didn't want to insult the dealer so after some back and forth I realized we were in a very weak position to change events and this didn't seem like the safest street to experience a sunset. So, we agreed to take Keith and his girlfriend back to the Commons.

One of the friends I had called on my search for LSD was Judy's childhood friend, also named Judy. I called and invited her to come over to get a third opinion on our mescaline.

Judy's friend Judy arrived later that afternoon and while she was not impressed with the product, we agreed to divide the grey matter into thirds. Maybe it was mescaline or maybe it wasn't but we would never know unless we tried the crusty, vile-looking thing.

The three of us sprawled out on my queen-sized bed and waited to see what would happen. We spent our afternoon engrossed in an enlightening conversation about the influence of the sixties on society but by sundown our vocabulary had decreased significantly.

"Elbow, elbow, elbow," we yelled in unison pressing our right elbows together.

"Knee, knee, knee," we said, with our right knees touching in identification as we rolled across the bed with laughter.

"Head, head, head," and the tops of our heads touched and we burst into more laughter.

The sun rose and we were still touching and naming our anatomy. The sun set and we were still fully clothed and wiggling around on my bed laughing and touching each other all over. Sometime that night we fell asleep. It wasn't mescaline.

The summer ended and Liz and I moved out of that Brookline apartment and headed to Portland, Oregon with plans to stay with my Uncle Jack and Aunt Becky until we got settled.

Liz found work on the graveyard shift burning computer chips for Intel. I joined a crew painting a hangar for Intel's private jets but rain soon ended that job so I took work as a janitor at the Portland Art Museum. Liz and I also found a studio apartment with a Murphy Bed at the Belmont Arms at Belmont and South-East 14th.

A rainy Portland encouraged attendance at the local independent movie theater matinees. Liz and I saw Woody Allen's Annie Hall at the Avalon. A perfect film for a Jewish girlfriend and a young man raised in a Protestant family. Liz and I could see ourselves in the humor of that film.

One day after cleaning the museum's art school I went on my own to another movie at the Avalon also staring Diane Keaton. The rain was unrelenting, making for a miserable, depressing afternoon. Liz was away visiting her family in Southern California. I needed another dose of humor.

Looking for Mr. Goodbar was not, it turned out, a comedy. My mind could not quite adjust to that reality and I left the theater a little off balance.

I found a parking space right in front of my place at the Belmont Arms and started to back in, but two men on motorcycles, draped in heavy rubber rain gear pulled in behind me. I couldn't complete my parking and my first thought was that I must have lost something like my muffler and the two bikers had pulled in to help.

I turned off the engine, half parked, got out and walked towards the motorcyclists.

"What the fuck are you doing?" one of the bikers yelled as he lumbered towards me. He shoved me against the back of my Chevy truck. The other guy grabbed my right arm, twisting me sideways and pressing my flame-red, bearded face against the glass of my camper shell while screaming at me, mostly just vulgar names.

The man that had first shoved me pulled my wallet from my pants, found my Massachusetts license, clicked on the radio clipped to his shoulder and called in my name as he whipped out a ticket book from under his rubber poncho and started to mark it.

It was now clear that they were not the two helpful Hells Angels types I mistook them to be. They were, instead, two of Portland's finest. The officer who was now crushing my chest against my truck spun me around to face the ticket writer who shoved the soggy citation book at me demanding I sign at the X. I did. I can't recall what that ticket accused me of.

He dashed off another ticket. "Moving Hazard Violation," he said, ordering me to sign the second citation and, again, I did.

His partner had my back pressed up against my truck. The ticket writer tore one citation off his pad and handed it to me. I took it. He ripped the Moving Hazard Violation ticket from the book and thrusted it towards me. I tried to grasp the damp yellow ticket.

The boisterous barking of the police had attracted nearly a dozen of my neighbors. Several witnesses were screaming at the police to leave me alone.

An officer spun me around slamming me hard, yet again, against my camper shell. The glass door bent but didn't snap. The tickets slipped from my hand and dropped into the flooded curb.

The author of the tickets threatened, "I will show you who's 'Food for people, not for profit,'" quoting the bumper sticker on my camper shell. The guy who had been smashing me against my vehicle grabbed my neck and pushed my head down towards the floating citations.

"Pick up the fucking tickets, you asshole," he yelled, rubbing my face into the gutter, my long, blond hair swirling in the curbside stream.

More neighbors had by then joined the crowd and most of them were angry and loud. Some were pleading with the two men to stop. A woman reached out towards one of the officers as though she were planning to pull him away from me.

Somehow, I was able to retrieve the tickets from the stream of rainwater with my teeth. That's how I remember it now anyway.

One of the cops ordered me to get back into my truck, demanding that I finish parking.

I slid, soaking wet, behind the wheel and pulled forward next to the last car on the block planning to back into the space I was originally attempting park in. I put my Chevy into reverse and eased back, trying to fit in the space without tapping the two motorcycles that were next to one another occupying a third parking space. I didn't quite make it and I could see through the drops on my rearview mirror that I had knocked one of the Harleys to the pavement. I saw one of its operators jumping up and down punching the rain with his fist. I was not going to get out of my pickup, not now.

The idea of escaping across the Columbia River to the safety of another jurisdiction flashed through my mind. A quick dash to Washington State would give me time to think things over; give me time to call Liz in Studio City.

Anyway, I was not interested in finding myself at the wrong end of a billy club or steel-toed boot so I pulled forward a couple of feet, put my truck into reverse again and backed over both motorcycles crushing them into two balls of metal. "They won't be able to pursue me now," I thought.

The two patrolmen were jumping up and down as I took a last glance in my side mirror. Mr. Ticket was zigzagging to and from one of the twisted bikes, grabbing a radio mic as he frantically waved his other arm in some vain attempt to get me to return. His partner was trying to lift what was left of his Harley. Several of my neighbors were clapping and three of them were now out in the street surrounding the two cops. The scene in my mirror vanished as I turned onto 15th.

My mind was racing. I didn't want to speed or run stop signs or red lights. "This will be a very law abiding get-a-way," I thought as I struggled to find the entrance to I-5 North. I saw a patrol car speeding along the west bank of the Willamette. I crossed onto the Morrison Bridge and realized that I had missed the onramp to the highway.

I was then driving head-on towards a speeding police car, blue lights flashing. Another patrol car was racing down Second Avenue from the north. I made a left, still obeying the speed limit. Red and blue flashes illuminated the cab of my beloved 65 Chevy. Lights that flashed to the rhythm of my panicked thoughts.

Several police cars were rushing towards me from the south and I could see two more cruisers darting behind the buildings on Madison. I turned on my blinker to indicate I would be turning left and bumped onto the steel grating of the Hawthorn Bridge.

A web of patrol cars and police vans had made a vehicular wall at the end of the metal trestle. As I drove closer, I saw policeman ducking behind their vehicles, aiming all sorts of pistols and rifles in my direction: maybe twenty or more officers, barricaded behind their vehicles, each with an eye closed, and the other squinting down the barrels of their guns. Guns aimed at me.

I stopped, shifted out of gear and removed the key from the ignition and put it into my pants pocket. I put both hands on the ceiling hoping not to be shot.

A loud crash rained glass across the cab. The army of officers jumped to their feet, with their guns drawn. The steal barrel of a service revolver hit the left side of my head. Another metal pistol smashed my skull from the right. The driver's door swung open. I was pulled from the truck and thrown to the metal teeth of the bridge. A boot stepped on my neck with a swift movement that followed my descent to the roadway.

"Resist and I'll blow your brains out and say you had a gun," the patrolman calmly announced as he put the barrel to the back of my head.

He was joined by others. I was handcuffed, lifted to my feet and placed in the back of a police vehicle. The rain amplified the flashes of red and blue lights. My pants were filled with window shards.

Time rushed. I ended up in an elevator. I was led past a wall of closed-circuit TV monitors. Black and white views of city parks and street corners that comprised a startling discovery in the innocent days of the late seventies.

I was placed in a cell with a young man who was yelling that she deserved it. The officer removing my handcuffs mentioned that my cell-mate had just stabled his mother to death. His long, black overcoat, black shoes, long, black hair, and jackal screams were a brutal introduction to life behind bars.

Was my life already getting snuffed out before I had a chance at adulthood? Would I never dip another wet brush into a tray of pigment? Would that still-life of light filling the void between my arrangement of red, white, and blue household products be my last painting? My future suddenly looked bleak.

I was finally removed from the cell with the mad mother-killer and ended up with twenty disgruntled men in a larger cell furnished with metal bunks for twelve. Police dragged a young woman in handcuffs past our lockup. Six or seven guys jumped to the bars, grabbing toward her as they begged for a blow job or a good fuck.

More women passed through the gauntlet. The men in the next cell would also call out similar threats, desires, and obscenities at these already disheartened ladies. One woman yelled back suggesting she had experienced this humiliation before. I couldn't imagine how disturbing that must have been for them.

The night was uncomfortable. No matter how vigorously I tried to shake the glass from my wet blue jeans and underwear there seemed to be even more. I sat on a lower bunk with three other guys. One old white man in a plaid wool pants was in despair, worried that his wife would be angry at his having been arrested with a sex worker. The neighbor on my other side insisted he was just walking to his car when he was arrested for hiring a prostitute. Their conversation turned to cunnilingus and before long our unit was alive in debate. I was taken back by the racial division. The Black men in my cage were to a man repulsed at the idea speaking vigorously against the practice while the white guys praised the act declaring that it was wonderful. Fishy tasting or the sweetness of a flower was the question. It was going to be a long night.

When the morning finally arrived, a prisoner pulled up to our cell pushing a cart with a coffee urn and cartons of milk. Coffee. I so wanted a cup of coffee, as did everyone else. The more experienced inmates elbowed their way to the bars prepared with their eight-ounce Styrofoam cup. Once I saw an opening, I asked the trustee if I could have a cup of coffee.

"Where's your cup?" he barked. "I don't have one," I replied. "Use an empty carton," was his callous retort.

I asked for a carton of milk. He reluctantly handed me one. I drank most of the milk casting aside my decision to stop consuming dairy and passed it through the bars.

"Coffee, please," I said with authority.

He gave me a confused look. I guessed "please" wasn't a common jailhouse word.

A tiny box of stale Cheerios and second small carton of milk arrived an hour later. "Breakfast," I was told.

A heavy wad of oversized keys clanged against the bars to get our attention. The jailer then boomed out the last names of the eight or nine cellmates. I understood from the conversations that they would be off to court and maybe their freedom. My name was not among them.

The next big event was called lunch. Each tray featured two pieces of white Wonder Bread with boloney sliced so thin I could see the dark lines of the bars through it, and two inch-and-a-half-long sticks of celery. I scored a coveted Styrofoam cup with the apple-juice.

Men arrived from court angry at the outcome. A dinner of thin lunch meat on that same spongy white bread and a grainy apple ended my first day of incarceration. I won a slab of mattress to myself that evening, hiding my treasured cup from the view of any possible thieves.

The pattern was repeated. Coffee, breakfast, call to court that didn't include my name, lunch, disappointed inmates returning from court, and then dinner. I wanted to call my uncle but didn't know his number and asked every jailer that went by to help me. They said they couldn't : "its policy."

On day six we were marched down the hall to take our mandatory weekly shower. A man was sitting at a desk at the first turn and there was a phone on that desk. I asked him if I could call my uncle in Hillsborough. "He's a lawyer," I added. He couldn't let me do that, he said, "its policy." But on my way back from the shower, he waved me over and asked me for my uncle's name. "John Phelan," I said. He dialed information and asked to be connected with John Phelan and a minute later he handed me the phone. I shared the basics with uncle Jack, telling him that I was in a jail on the top floor of the courthouse and that I would really like to get out. It hadn't yet dawned on me yet that I might be able win my freedom.

There was then another dinner of transparent boloney on gummy white bread and parallel celery sticks and another night spent guarding my Styrofoam cup. And once again I woke to another morning of coffee and cardboard-tasting Cheerios.

The keyring banged against the bars, last names were being called and then I heard, "McHenry." It finally happened, the toneless barking of my last name suggesting I still had a future.

It seemed like I would have to spend eternity crammed into a holding cell before I once again heard, "McHenry," and was then led out into a courtroom. My uncle nodded my way when he saw me. I stood where placed. My uncle told the judge that I had never been in trouble, that I was going to an Ivy League School in Boston and that he would make sure I returned for trial. The judge said that I had been charged with Hit and Run and Eluding a Police Officer. The District Attorney confirmed as much. The judge then released me into the custody of my uncle; I would be set free by dinnertime.

The born-again Christian night watchman at the Portland Art Museum who took my obligatory one free call the night I was arrested failed to share the information with anyone at my job. He had probably returned, unimpressed by my situation, to the bible lessons aired over his favorite radio station. Thankfully no one missed me, so I returned to my position managing the janitorial staff as though nothing had happened.

A week later a docent told me that the fountain between the museum and the art school was malfunctioning so I climbed around the pump room to see if I could find a solution, coating myself in black grease in the process. I couldn't find the problem so I called the fountain repair company, cleaned up a bit, and walked over to Safeway to buy breakfast. Safeway was introducing a new feature, offering both plain and maple granolas in wooden barrels, mimicking the popularity of bulk bins, like those at the Boston Coop where I had been a member for the past three years.

I tasted a pinch of maple and then sampled a pinch of plain. I didn't think the maple was worth the extra cost so I scooped a breakfast amount of plain granola into the bag they provided. I wrote the bin number on a sticker and stuck it to the bag, and then picked up a can of V-8 juice on the way to the check-out line.

I heard, "come with us," and turned to look for the person whom that voice was addressing. Two stock-boys grabbed my arms. I protested demanding to know what was going on. They told me that I was under arrest. "This can't be possible," I thought. "I haven't done anything wrong and there's no way am I going back to that frightening hell of a jail. Seven days was enough."

I shoved one of the clerks into a wall of canned goods, sending tinned vegetables and soups rolling across the linoleum. The shelving cascaded into the bread and pasta aisle. Jars of tomato sauce shattered. I tried to free myself but they were able to haul me into a backroom cage that held cardboard waiting to be recycled. The police came, handcuffed me, and marched me out to their car.

That's when a switch turned on in my mind. From that moment on I couldn't help but imagine that my eyes were firing bullets at every police officer I saw, an uncontrollable impulse that finally vanished sometime during the food arrests of San Francisco a decade later.

Fortunately, Liz was at home when I called. The bail was small, so I was released that afternoon. I was starting to dislike the rainy Rose City.

My uncle suggested I get witnesses to the Hit and Run and Eluding a Police Officer case. I went to the house across the street. The woman there said her son watched the whole thing but that he was so frightened that he left town. The cheery couple at the end of the block invited me in for tea. They were eager to support my defense, saying that what the police did to me was horrible. Their young daughter pranced around the living room apparently happy to have a guest.

I took a sip of warm Earl Grey and asked about the aerial photos of an industrial facility that decorated their walls. "Those are pictures of the Trojan Nuclear Power Station where my husband works as an engineer," the woman of the house said with pride. I didn't let them know I volunteered with the Trojan Decommission Alliance seeking to end her husband's radioactive occupation. I was relieved to get their cooperation. I don't recall speaking with any of the other witnesses about the incident but I may have.

The court appointed a defense attorney to represent me and I made the trip to the northwest side of town and visited his office. His framed diplomas on the wall behind his desk indicated that he had graduated from Reed College and received his law degree from Lewis and Clark.

I sat before his impressive oak desk and watched him thumb through the police report. He offered his counsel as follows: "Hit and Run and Eluding a Police Officer, I see. You will get seven years in Multnomah County Jail if we go to trial. I can assure you of that. You are only eighteen. You will spend the best years of your life locked up. I suggest you leave the state. You had Massachusetts license plates and long hair. The powers around here just don't want people like you in Oregon. My advice is leave and don't come back."

Like a good country song, Liz broke the news to me a week later as we sat before our truck's disassembled carburetor that was spread out, as was customary, over sheets of old newspaper. She explained that she had been seeing our former housemate, Sharon, for over a year. She had taken the graveyard shift at Intel to avoid the temptation to cheat on her with me. We hadn't been lovers in months. She just hadn't had the heart to tell me.

So, I took my lawyer's council and disappeared into the underground abandoning my social security number and all other connections to formal society. Even in this young computer age I knew that the SS number could lead to trouble and possibly my capture. I had already been leery of the digits since I was repeatedly warned by my mother that one should never share them with anyone other than one's bank and the Social Security Administration. I believe she was also the one that first told me that a similar system designed by IBM had been used by the Nazis during the Holocaust to catalog the victims and that here the government had limited its use to alleviate the public's concern that America could be heading down a similar path. After reading Henry David Thoreau's "Civil Disobedience" as a fifth-grader I was already primed to be a War Tax Resister. I also had come to the conclusion that the Social Security system was unlikely to exist by the time I was 65. It was time to melt into a world free of the Empire's chains.

Somehow Liz and I bounced back emotionally. Our lives were so intertwined that our romantic rupture failed to crush our friendship. For many, a break-up would have meant an immediate separation but we remained close. We were family.

Liz and I headed south together in my pickup and moved into a garage on Deakin Street in Berkeley with one of our past Boston housemates, Helen. The cement floor was layered in rugs against the cold. We nailed electric space heaters to the wooden wall to ward off the damp Bay Area chill and slept in a bundle with Helen's furry, blue-eyed, white husky.

Liz joined Helen working at the Marrakech Falafel Restaurant on Euclid. The owner plied me with his latest Falafel mix dreaming of making it big with a prepackaged instant falafel. "Was that as good as the last batch?" he enthusiastically asked. I looked for work, filled my sketchbook and spent an afternoon with Wavy Gravy as he relaxed with one elbow on a Telegraph Avenue curb and his feet stretched across an empty parking space.

"Oh hell, the Bay Area is getting crazy. I'm not sure I want to live here anymore," the African-American man at the next booth told me as news of the assassination of San Francisco Mayor George Moscone and Supervisor Harvey Milk aired over the radio at the crusty, old University Avenue diner. Less than ten days before that, that same cafe radio announced the news that over 900 members of Reverend Jim Jones' People's Temple had committed suicide in Guyana. Maybe that guy in the diner was right, it was time to leave the crazy Bay Area.

But in the end, it was the bitter cold of our garage and the lack of money that forced Liz and I to head to her parent's home in Southern California. Liz found a job with another computer company and I signed up with a temp agency.

This was when Liz's sister Judy and I started to really cement our friendship. She still lived with her parents, worked at a bookstore and was enrolled at UCLA.

I drove Judy to her job at Brentano's Bookstore at the Beverly Wilshire Hotel and I had some idea that I might be able to find an art patron by painting landscapes of Rodeo Drive. I set up my easel outside a shop that I recalled featured $200 shoelaces. Not one person ever walked on that sterile street and the atmosphere didn't inspire much in the way of art.

When not selling books or attending class, Judy eagerly tried to prove to me, and the entire art world really, that Los Angeles did have an architectural history. She refuted the conventional thought of the art historians she had been studying with. This premise was the subject of her thesis at UCLA.

She gave me the full story on the origins of food-mimicking restaurant design as we stood outside the Tail o' the Pup in West Hollywood. We scooted over to the Fine Arts Museum. "Yes, you can find masterpieces in the walls of the museum behind us but to understand the cultural pride connected to the Tar Sands is to understand the City of Angels," she said.

Next it was off to the Mayan Theater with its glamorous history. We parked on the nearly vacant, trash-strewn street outside the beautiful old theater plastered with huge full-color photos of nearly naked women promising raw sex.

Judy was determined to show me the interior details, so I convinced the sour-looking box office attendant that we had no intention of watching his films and he let us in for free. Judy pointed out the electric reproductions of flaming pots of oil illuminating the plaster faux stone passages, a creative attempt to mimic the imaginary caverns of a Mayan pyramid. "Follow me," she whispered enthusiastically, clutching my hand as she led me through the darkened maze to the auditorium. "You must see the majesty of the crown jewel of early Tinsel Town." We popped into the mammoth theater where we were met with the image of a five-story-tall throbbing erect penis spewing oceans of thick white semen across the screen. "Look at the beautiful details in the ceiling," Judy encouraged me softly, pointing to the exaggerated gold Mayan medallions and feathered godlike figures. "You see what I mean?"

While we drove around investigating all that Judy knew to be of cultural significance, we made the decision to share an apartment together some place in

Santa Monica. We both liked the area. It was still affordable. A paradise for two friends embracing the beauty and magic of their times. This would be another chance to mold my own visionary renaissance, a Concord of the Pacific.

I had been in Studio City for about a month when my mother and her brother, Jack, started to call. "You have to return to Portland to stand trial. Your uncle won't pass the bar if you don't," my mother pleaded. Jack was even less kind, "You're the one that ran from the police. You can wreck your life but you won't wreck mine."

On call after call, they made their impassioned pleas, insisting that my failure to return would jeopardize my uncle Jack's ability to work as a lawyer. "You must make it to your arraignment. You must or your uncle's life will be ruined," my mom pled. The stress of their calls finally got the best of me. My mother and uncle had the impression that I was still scheduled to appear in court on the date announced at my bail hearing. That gave me two more weeks to make it north to Portland. Judy said she would continue the search for an apartment while I was away. I was sure she would find the perfect bohemian place.

I grabbed my red backpack and headed out to the freeways. To avoid as much of Oregon as possible I put out my thumb and headed towards Las Vegas. I planned to take Interstate 15 towards Salt Lake City travel through Idaho and along the Washington State side of the Columbia Gorge. It seemed that the less I came in contact with the Oregon authorities the better. I learned that one should never try to hitch out of Vegas: no one will pick up a what they would assume was broke, losing gambler. I was lucky, however, and got a ride through the City of Lost Wages all the way to my high school roommate and friend David Miles' home in Salt Lake.

David wasn't sure of my future as a defendant and neither was I, but my mother had David's home number and continued to beg me to continue my trip towards justice. I headed north crossing the Cascades and bounced along the narrow roads north of the mighty Columbia to Vancouver, Washington.

I caught a last ride with a plaid-shirted lumberjack crossing the Columbia River arriving in time to make my court appearance. I hid my pack in a hedge behind the county court house. A bailiff directed me to a wall of name-filled pages where I was to locate my court room. "Jonathan McHenry - Department 7."

I slipped into the designated courtroom and asked a uniformed officer to point out the prosecutor. She stood at the front, talking with some other legal professionals. I stepped up and interrupted her conversation asking, "Is Jonathan McHenry's case on the docket today?"

"No, there is a warrant out for his arrest," she said and returned to her conversation".

Ok, I will let him know, thanks," I responded and swiftly left the court room.

I had saved $27 for just such an emergency. You don't forget details like that. I walked over to the Trailways Station. My $27 could get me to Ashland, Oregon. It would cost $12 more to reach the freedom of California. I bought a ticket for the first bus south. I would figure things out there.

The bus arrived in Ashland late that night. A teenage girl was sitting on a step in the rain. As it turned out that step also doubled as the Ashland bus stop. I asked her if there was a park with a picnic table where I could sleep protected from the downpour. She suggested I stay at her apartment. It was half a mile away. She wouldn't be back until the next day. The sliding door was unlocked she said, giving me her address. "You can crash in my bed. Make yourself at home."

It was a long half mile repeating her address on Siskiyou Boulevard as I dragged along the cold, wet street. I found her place, which I had imagined was her parents' home, since she seemed too young to have her own place. I slid open the glass door calling out to the parents but no one was there. A few hours later a woman about my age with long black hair hovered above me in the dark. "The bus to Eugene never arrived," she said as she snuggled next to me wrapping her arm across my chest.

When we woke up, I discovered that she was a beautiful woman in her thirties. We hit it off. She told me she had intended to go to Eugene to finalize her divorce with photorealist painter Richard Estes, pointing to photos of her and Estes. I had admired his work as an art student. I took her at her word. Anything seemed possible since I had stepped into a world where police could pull up out of nowhere, slam you into the gutter and charge you with crimes. I looked for work in Ashland and spent the evening with the teenager who was actually intriguing older woman. After a couple of days, however, I got nervous about my legal situation and wished her well, hoping to see her again.

I stuck out my thumb and minutes later an ebullient blond stopped her yellow VW bug next to me and called out to see if I needed a ride. She told me that she was an art teacher at Medford High School. I, of course, didn't let on that I was a fugitive. We clicked and by the time she pulled next to the I-5 onramp to drop me off, I was magnetized by her joyful spirit. I stood on the southbound lane, worried the Oregon State Police might pay me a visit. But I could tell something was missing. I had left my bag of art supplies and my sacred sketch book in her car.

There was nothing to do but cross the freeway and hitch north deeper into the Oregon that I was fleeing.

The school district office wasn't difficult to find since it was the first building off the Medford exit. I stepped into the lobby and was greeted with enthusiasm: "You must be the boy Alice spoke of, she found your bag in the back seat and called the State Police to find you."

So, now there were two reasons for the Oregon State Police to look for me. The receptionist directed me to the high school where I would have a second meeting with the beautiful art teacher, Alice, and recover my art supplies. Then I returned to the southbound lane of I-5.

God works in mysterious ways, they say, and sure enough a Christian Rock Band picked me up in their funky old school bus and delivered me straight to the Tenderloin in San Francisco, and freedom from the Oregon authorities.

It was a long walk through the cold mist to a couch at my friend's place in the Richmond District. I woke early the next day and left before anyone else got up. I didn't have a penny to my name. I sung to myself, the lyrics of "Me and Bobby McGee" repeating, "Freedom's just another word for nothin' left to lose." The words lifted my stroll west to Ocean Beach.

The thought of that first day meandering south on Highway One still thrills me. I can't help but relive that sense of freedom every time I motor past the now empty hillside where an ostrich kept me company from its perch north of Half Moon Bay. A pumpkin farmer let me off at the Pescadero turn off. Another ride took me along Mission Street and dropped me off at River Street in Santa Cruz. I crashed with a household of lesbian friends over by Emeline. They donated a place on their couch, adding in a jar of liquid acid from their refrigerator. They told me they didn't need it anymore.

I strolled over to the Ocean Street entrance to the coastal highway. I hadn't eaten much over the past few days, having finished the last of my granola before passing Chico with the Christians.

I stuck out my thumb, but then I saw a faded sheet of Martin Luther King Jr. postage stamps in the sand. That was money. I walked across the street to Denny's with my treasure. A young surfer-type girl about my age in a white, perfect-fitting Denny's uniform greeted me. I could see that she was responsible for waiting on the counter customers. I nestled onto a stool and showed her the stamps. I turned on the charm and suggested that she could buy them from me and then I could buy breakfast from her. She didn't want to. The sand-stubbled, sun-bleached sheet of twenty 15-cent images of Doctor King Jr. were valuable, I persisted, explaining that all she needed to do was squirt a dab of glue on the back and they were as good as money. She finally gave in, with a sympathetic smile, and brought me a plate of crispy hash browns, oatmeal and a coffee. I gave her all but one stamp. I told her I needed it for a memory on a page of my sketch book. That yellow and brown stamp is still pasted snuggly to the page between the hard covers resting in the Food Not Bombs archives at the University of Victoria.

I pass this intersection often these days and I intend to share this happy memory with the young woman who sits in the sand where I found those stamps holding her "Hungry" sign the next time she graces our meal at Food Not Bombs.

I returned to the road. It was two rides to Moss Landing and then a third driver was going all the way to San Simeon. I took it but the sun was setting when we approached the naval station at Point Sur so asked him to let me out by the river.

"But this is in the middle of nowhere, are you sure you want to get out here?" he asked, puzzled.

I explained that I couldn't drive through Big Sur in the dark and miss the spectacular views so he pulled over and let me out. I found a comfortable place to sleep in the dunes by the banks of the Little Sur River.

The first rays of sun poked over the mountains and woke me the following morning. The air was warm and still. It was Easter Sunday, so I took a sizable sip of my donated liquid LSD and scrambled over the sand dunes to the road. It was pure bliss. Wild roses kissed by bees and butterflies swayed gently along the roadside, high above the glistening waves of a limitless Pacific. The early morning sun warmed my back. I stood motionless next to my pack, gazing at the long grassy pastures, sweeping and dotted with brilliant orange poppies that stretched out towards the naval outpost. Untethered cottony clouds drifted freely above the high slopes of chaparral to my east.

The acid was starting to grip my synapses. The already vibrant Easter Sunday sparkled with increased intensity. I contemplated my relationship with my father. It must have been that it was Easter or maybe it was the bees darting from rose to rose that brought him to mind. Psychedelic thoughts about his influence on me that he would never recognize and my forgiveness of his cruelty bathed me in a bliss of empathy for all I had put him through. The pain he must have felt when I disappeared from Wasatch my sophomore year or the Christmas when he feared that I had died after I passed out from alcohol and my mother's valium. A sea of love washed over me like the waves lapping against the resurrection of craggy stone shores below.

I meandered around a sharp bend in Highway One where I came upon a group of four women. Their long straight hair gently blew as if in unison in the light Pacific breeze. My sudden appearance was a surprise. They laughed and greeted me. One girl asked where I had come from. I pointed to the dunes below. They smiled at the news and encouraged me to hop into their van and join them on their adventure.

I accepted the ride from my new companions. We swerved around the curves and I was tossed against the two women I had joined in the seatless cavern of their cargo van. They told me that they were secretaries from Sacramento. One girl screamed with laughter as she slid across the metal van floor. I flew into her friend who caught me in her arms. The tin box of the van started to swerve in an uncomfortable way. That much I remember, that and their matching long hair and matching bodies which made them indistinguishable from one another. My cargo comrades seemed to have a puzzled expression at my laughing response at flying across the metal deck. We all struggled to gain control of the seating as the vehicle navigated the curves of Highway One. The woman sitting closest to me asked me where I was going.

"South," I replied, "I'm just heading south." A prophetic feeling of bliss washed over me at the simplicity of the idea that I was "just going south" to no place in particular.

The van pulled up to a gift shop tucked in a grove of redwoods. The back van passengers tumbled out to the warm asphalt. They invited me to join them for breakfast but I declined. The four women looked perplexed but didn't insist. I flung my backpack over my shoulder and disappeared south. The two-lane road clung high above a gently dancing forest of giant kelp. I was the lone occupant on the ribbon of America's western-most road soaking in the colorful world of gliding sea gulls and squadrons of whitecap nipping pelicans. The lonely moaning of seals called from waters lapping at the edge of the continent several hundred feet below. My path along the Coastal Highway hugged the cliff, coiling ahead and disappearing into a distant canyon only to reappear still clinging to the mountainside. The peace was never interrupted that afternoon by even a single vehicle.

I spotted the dark outline of a man walking north. He grew larger as we moved towards one another. We met on the cliff side. He reported on the great dumpsters he had found in Moro Bay and San Luis Obispo. The Safeway in San Luis Obispo was the best, he said. He was a coastal dumpster diving expert and let me know that they would get better the farther south I went. He handed me an apple as he bit into the other red delicious he had recovered the Safeway garbage near Cal Poly. I took a bite. We shook hands and I continued south as he plodded towards the trash bins of Carmel.

I accepted a ride once the best of Big Sur was behind me. My driver was quick to ask if I was gay. He asked if I wanted to stay at his place. I told him I was straight and was trying to get to Los Angeles by nightfall. He was a perfect gentleman all the way to San Luis Obispo.

I stood at the flower-lined entrance to the 101 still glowing from the psychedelics. A pickup with a camper shell pulled up and the young Latino driver asked if I wanted a ride to LA. "You can rest on the mattress in the back," he said. I did so, and soon drifted off to sleep bathed in the sweet fragrance of lemon and orange blossoms. The scent of citrus flowers always takes me back to that lazy afternoon.

The truck pulled to a stop outside one of those classic Southern California diners. This one had a view of the San Fernando Valley. The driver and his friend invited me for dinner. "It's on us," they said. I agreed to join them, and also asked to borrow a dime so I could make a call to my ex in Studio City. Liz said she would be out to pick me up in about an hour. Perfect, I thought, I can finish supper before she arrived.

We were no longer lovers, but we were both happy to see each other after several months of my having been on the road. I enjoyed telling her of my adventures during a pleasant drive to her family's home on Milbank Street. She told me about her job at a computer company. We both agreed that nothing much would ever come of the computer chip industry. It didn't seem very likely at the time that computers would have much of a future. Who would ever need one? Perhaps it was a big waste of time, but it paid well, she said.

I followed Liz through the front door of her parent's home. The phone was ringing. Liz's mother lifted the receiver from the kitchen wall telephone and answered. She jumped up and down, shrieking. "No, no, no," she screamed pleadingly to the phone. It was like her face had vanished and life drained from her, her essence dissipating in a flash. I had never witnessed such defeat. Mrs. Hurwitz's normally enthusiastic self was instantly extinguished, switched off like a light.

She thrust the receiver at Liz, who then held the phone to her ear. Then she too joined the madness, lost grip of the phone, and started kind of hopping up and down screeching her own painful "no, no, no," as tears streamed down her face.

Liz's father was on the phone. He had found Judy. A tear-soaked suicide note hung from the lifeless fingers of her week-old corpse. She took her last breath on the carpet of the Santa Monica apartment we had planned to share.

It was only the tone of Mr. Hurwitz's voice that made the news sound plausible. That and the reaction of Liz and her mother. Mrs. Hurwitz paced around the kitchen in quick circles, eyes staring towards an undefined emptiness with her trembling knuckles crammed into her quivering lips.

I was alone in the ability to function. My plans, as ephemeral and optimistic as they were, had vanished. The Hurwitz family needed support. The tragedy immobilized the three of them.

The family started to sit shiva. Liz's mother stood by the dining room window staring at a world that was no longer there. Mr. Hurwitz slumped in his favorite easy chair and stared at the floor.

Judy's corpse lay on a refrigerated tray at the Los Angeles County Coroner's office and we would have to wait for the autopsy. It had been a busy month for murders and other unnatural deaths. Liz wandered from room to room as though Judy would be waiting around the next corner. Her parents sat silently hour upon dismal hour.

The doorbell rang with the first delivery of kugel, a potato and egg pudding, and my introduction to sitting shiva. One loving neighbor after another arrived with food. At seven o'clock, Nelly and Tom arrived with bagels, lox, and smears. At seven-twenty, Maggie and Mores appeared with bagels, orange juice, and fresh coffee. At seven-forty, that morning's kugel swung onto the dining room table. Each delivery was accompanied by a warm hug, tears, and expressions of shock: no one knew that Judy had been in such pain. Flowers, kugel, lunch meat, thinly sliced cheeses, breads, fish, bagels, more kugel, and all manner of casseroles continued to arrive with words of sympathy.

At seven the next morning, the parade of Brooklyn-style Jewish deli food and homemade dishes started again beginning with the mandatory bagels and smoked lox. Judy's mother continued to stare out at an emptiness from her post at the dining room window. Mr. Hurwitz was burning a hole in the living room carpet with his vacant stare.

I answered the door, directed the platters of food to the kitchen, and brought the well-wishers to greet the silent Mr. Hurwitz, sitting in his lounge chair and always balancing a half-eaten bagel with cream cheese in one hand. With each visitor he would slowly set the sandwich on a plate at the end table and slowly stand to hug his guest. The scents of smoked fish and onion bagels were not powerful enough to smudge out the smell of death that seemed to cling to his clothing.

Liz escaped the house each morning in her ocean of grief, dragging herself past the first wave of breakfast deliveries on her way to the distractions of work. The sympathy of an ex-boyfriend could never be enough to console such loss. How could it?

By the third day, every surface of the kitchen and dining room was overflowing with food. I couldn't pack another tub of cream cheese into the fridge. Judy's father made his first call to the coroner's office to see if the autopsy was finished so Judy could be laid to rest. I continued to greet the well-wishers, call family and friends and struggle to find room to receive the increasing waves of food.

Day twenty and the food was still coming. Another call to the coroner at nine o'clock and still no autopsy. Judy's mother had taken to sitting by the kitchen window staring blankly into her torment. I organized a major food rotation program. So, this was a sitting of shiva.

The Los Angeles County Coroner's Office finally got around to Judy. "Yes, Mr. Hurwitz, your daughter died of an overdose of a combination of tranquilizers and other medications. We are sorry it took so long; it's been a bad month for murders."

A family friend scheduled a funeral at Forest Lawn and secured a burial plot. A list of those to call was made. I dialed Judy's best friend Judy. She would fly to LAX in the morning. I made more calls and the parade of food and friends continued.

The doorbell rang and rang and rang. And then it rang and it was Judy. We hugged at the threshold. My dear art historian friend's death finally hit me. We soaked one another's shoulders in tears.

Judy was my first death of a friend. It was the first lifting of a casket, the first dead weight that cannot be forgotten. The casket was lowered. Judy, Liz, and I threw handfuls of red clay into her grave. We sat in the dirt and threw clods into the six-foot hole and we remembered.

Mr. Hurwitz began to disappear into his work as a carpet broker. I took Liz's mother grocery shopping. She timidly fingered the shopping cart as she shuffled vacantly down the aisles. I kept the house organized and moderately clean. I tried to lift her spirits with conversation but it was no use. When I was not striving to keep Mrs. Hurwitz going from task to task, I was working a nine-to-five shift at the Mode-O-Day clothing warehouse in Burbank ticking black marks on the tags of incoming bras and house dresses.

The warehouse closed because of the gas crisis. The gas lines began. Even though tankers heavy with fuel were anchored off the port of Los Angeles, gas stations found it difficult to fill their reservoirs. Frustration at the long waits and the odd/even license plate rules sparked more than a few gas-line fights. I saw an opportunity and agreed to gas up the neighborhood cars for $5 an hour. I got a lot of reading done. This was my first legal, though off the books, business venture.

There was a little more life in the Hurwitz family and someone suggested that we go out to eat to break the spell of sorrow. It had been nearly a year since Judy's death. So, Liz, her parents, and I went for Chinese. I'd announced my intention to return to Boston. Mrs. Hurwitz had begun to venture out for food and supplies on her own. Liz and her father had settled in to a routine. I wasn't needed any more in Studio City.

The pot stickers and greasy chow mein arrived. Liz's father claimed I would always be what he called a dead beat and would never amount to much.

"Who would trust a vegetarian?" he asked rhetorically. I didn't respond. I talked about the environmental damage caused by urban growth. He argued that Los Angeles would never run out of water. "We could pave the Mojave Desert," he said. I was mortified at the thought. I let him know that I found his suggestion to pave the desert to catch rainwater disturbing. He bet me a hundred dollars that I would be broke and homeless in twelve months. I set out to prove him wrong.

Liz took me to the Grey Rabbit, the outlaw bus line. Soon the old reconditioned Trailways rumbled through the streets of Los Angeles towards Boston. I was ready to make something of myself.

That's when I first thought that I saw Judy walking through Copley Square before the arches of Trinity Episcopal, where I later thought that I glimpsed her standing suspiciously outside Riley's Roast Beef as I struggled to slice the thick grey veins from the side of a cow. That's when I started to go about defying Mr. Hurwitz's prediction.

An early literature table at Brattle Square, Cambridge, Massachusetts

Chapter 13

THE BIRTH OF A MOVEMENT

I had attended a year's worth of meetings in the stuffy second floor hall at the Clamshell Alliance Office in Central Square Cambridge in preparation for the October 6, 1979, occupation attempt of the Seabrook Nuclear Power Station construction site. This was my introduction to the decision-making process called consensus and the affinity group organizing structure. The effort to reach a consensus on each proposal drew our meetings out into the wee hours of the night. While often tedious, it also inspired creativity, depth, and greater commitment to the decisions we would agree to.

An affinity group, as the name suggests, is a small team of people who share affinity with an idea, location in the community, friendship, occupation, or artistic interest. My affinity group formed mostly around our shared neighborhood and participation in the work of the Mobilization for Survival, a group that organized against the nuclear arms race. Our group was named Silver Seed from the Neil Young lyrics, "Flyin' mother nature's silver seed" in the tune, "After the Gold Rush."

Our affinity group planned for success. We started getting fit for the action by jogging around the Allston and Brighten districts every weekday morning for at least an hour. We prepared the necessary equipment like gas-masks and camping gear. Our affinity group participated in the Boston cluster meetings at the Clamshell office as well as the New England-wide planning meetings. This was how the process worked and I found it very promising as a method of organizing for social change even beyond the immediate task of stopping the construction of the nuclear station on our northern coast. Our near daily interaction was designed to build trust and it did just that.

The Boston cluster met several times along a fenced industrial area near the Massachusetts Turnpike in Brighton. We practiced pulling down chain-linked fences and filmed our sessions with super-eight movie cameras. We reviewed the footage at our cluster meetings, like high school football teams reviewing their past game films, and critiqued our strengths and weaknesses. In the days just before heading north Silver Seed distributed gas masks to the cluster and packed our gear. Our excitement was mixed with the anxiety of facing off with a police force dedicated to defending the investment in nuclear power.

Soon it was time to join the others in the wooded lot on the edge of the construction site, private land offered as a staging area by a man named Toney.

The night of October 5 was difficult. The ground under our pup-tents was cold and hard. The sour odor of fermenting fall leaves scented the drama. A bulldozer dragged its noisy blade across the graveled construction site under the glare of high intensity flood lights making it impossible to get a restful sleep.

The designated wakers walked quietly from tent to tent to let us know it was time to mobilize. The Silver Seed affinity group joined the long line of activists silently winding through the hardwood forest in the inky dark. The survival gear of our imagined future on the construction site was strapped to our backs in used backpacks. We emerged outside the chain-link parameter just as the sun was peeking above the Atlantic. State police and national guard troops with water cannons and clubs stood caged behind the wire fencing. I could see several protesters at the fence armed with bolt cutters struggling to snip a hole in the wire links. Several others yanked on the surrounding tatters of chain link trying to pull open a path into the site. Teargas dropped from military helicopters. A fog of acid gas swirled around us biting at our eyes. Snot and tears drained from my gasmask-covered face. I gasped for air and fell to my hands and knees coughing.

The masks didn't work. One by one we tore them off to avoid suffocation as we careened into one another, blinded by the bitter white smoke. Someone fell into me, unable to navigate the chaos. I tried to help them to their feet but torrents of road salt and pepper spray blasted from a water cannon positioned behind the fence and forced us back to the ground. I tumbled back into the brittle weeds. A frontline activist clinging to one of the gaff hook ropes smashed over me propelled by the water pressure of toxic soup.

There was a short break from the teargas and water cannons, so we regained our composure and tried again. I pushed up to the group ahead of me. Several of us pulled the opening in the fence wider. That unleashed the baton armed troops as dozens of national guardsmen rushed through the hole swinging four-foot-long clubs. A swift smack to the head dropped a woman near me. I tried to reach her but more teargas cascaded down from the helicopters blinding me. She disappeared into the fog of confusion.

I will never forget the cruel smell of CS gas. I doubt anyone who has filled their lungs with the stuff can forget it. Even though I was filled with a sense of determination I also had a first twinge of concern that our effort to breach the site might be doomed. Then I put that thought of failure out of my mind.

Clouds of biting gas suffocated our patch of marsh. Two state police officers continued to blast pepper spray and road salt into the torrent of the water cannon smashing our front line to the ground. My eyes burned as I fell coughing to all fours on the wet stubble. It was too much. Several people had already retreated to a grove of oaks just out of reach of the authorities. I joined them.

Nearly thirty protesters were captured during the first two days. These political prisoners were held without bail in the Rockingham County Jail.

On the morning of October 8 several hundred of us drove to the small white New England court house where our friends were scheduled to appear before a judge. We planned to free our comrades, fully rejecting the legitimacy of the government to hold them. We linked arms in two circles surrounding the court house. Someone started to sing "We will not be moved." The singing caught on.

Before long, our voices were drowning out the hearing. Some of our prisoners opened the windows and joined in the chorus. The proceedings were impossible. I remember one police officer with tears in his eyes as he hung onto to a fire escape above the blockade. I felt he was honestly moved by the passion of our convictions.

The police tried to remove the prisoners, attempting to push through the lines of singing activists. Many of us sat in their path our arms still linked. One officer scraped me across the pavement by my red wool Mexican poncho tearing the neck hole with the weight of my frame. A cold rain started.

I could see that some of the officers were struggling with the decision to beat back the chorus with clubs. Police gripped the arms of our prisoners and forced them into patrol cars. The officers started their engines preparing to back into the blockade. The patrol cars found it difficult to move. C.T. Butler and several others had let the air out of the tires.

The drivers were surrounded. They panicked and lurched through the singing protesters on the rims and screeched out onto the main street. Some of us were knocked to the soaking pavement. The rain was miserable but we pressed on, first drying out in a laundromat then it was off to the doors of the jail or back to the woods outside the power station.

The snow started to fall on our conversations. The week-long siege cemented friendships. I was one of those idealistic young people who came to New Hampshire to interfere with a failing political system. This confirmed it. I would never belong to the state of the United States of America again. Never participate in the government's wars, its greasing of the corporate wheels of extraction and exploitation, its demands to comply. I was free!

The October 6th Occupation Attempt of the Seabrook Nuclear Site was life changing for me and my friends, the group of friends that would become Food Not Bombs.

Once back in Boston we settled in for another round of marathon meetings. The Coalition for Direct Action announced plans for a May 24th Occupation Attempt of the Seabrook Nuclear site. The friends I made during the first snows of 1979 planned to return. We would continue the struggle against nuclear power.

Scads of protesters once again wagged mock battles against highway fencing in Brighton, wheat-pasted the tough-looking posters produced by Hard Rain Press, and organized local events to build interest. Danny Schechter, "your news dissector" ran short announcements on a local rock station WBCN about the action to the song "Volunteers of America." Other activists scrawled "May 24th Occupy Seabrook" in spray paint on cement walls across New England. We were going to put an end to this nuclear threat.

On May 23, 1980, I hitched a ride from Boston to Seabrook to join my affinity group. They had already pitched tents and had started a cooking fire when I found them.

I woke to a brisk spring dawn. The sounds of birds chirping and flittering around in the thin oaks of the New Hampshire coast greeted me as I emerged from my cozy pup tent. I stepped out to the first morning light excited about another attempt to stop the dangers of nuclear power.

Breakfast was an apple or a few handfuls of granola. We had no time to cook. Several thousand people had gathered in the marshes and hardwood forests surrounding the Seabrook Nuclear Power Station construction site prepared to make the promised May 24th occupation of the nuke a reality. The brilliant blue sky and comfortable temperature were encouraging.

One of my friends, the Boston University law student Brian Feigenbaum, had volunteered to be the media voice of our protest. He faced the cameras speaking about our nonviolent intentions and the urgency of blocking the reactor before it was contaminated with nuclear material. I remember hearing that Brian's real name was in graphics on a number of TV reports covering the day's events. While most of those participating in the direct action felt no need to share their identity, Brian was the one person the police could positively identify. This would prove to be a mistake.

Brian was wiry. He had a dancer's frame and a thin, scraggly beard and mustache that partially hid his mouth. He was articulate but not in a lawyerly sort of way. In his interviews he must have come across as an earnest young man enthusiastic to protect New England from a catastrophic nuclear accident that could release deadly radioactive material across the community causing birth defects and cancers. I didn't see the reports on TV, but I can imagine his thin arms moving through the air to emphasize the message that we intended to breach the fence around the site and camp among the heavy equipment and concrete walls until the

Public Service Company of New Hampshire agreed to stop the project. Maybe we'd even plant vegetables and an apple tree or two if we succeeded in securing the thirty-four-acre construction site.

A few hundred battle-ready protesters gathered at the main entrance protecting themselves with an assortment of bicycle and motorcycle helmets. Many of us also sought safety from police clubs and rubber bullets by duct-taping foam and cardboard sheets to our torsos and limbs. If the October 6, 1979, occupation attempt taught us anything it was that we could expect serious violence from the state police and the national guard.

Our cluster of a few hundred protesters advanced on the front gate in a wave. Hundreds of others swarmed the chain-link fencing surrounding the site from the marshes, forests, and tidal streams. Hundreds of police in riot gear stood nervously beyond the fence poised to repel our advance. Several young men in the lead tossed metal gaff hooks over the top of the wired links. Once the cord was pulled tight, lines of protesters grabbed a section and pulled. The fencing bent towards the demonstrators tearing a swath from its mooring and slicing a gap for the police to rush through.

Swatting a bee hive would have been just as wise. Riot police and national guard troops swarmed onto the street. I was smothered in teargas and was soon coughing and blinded. I stepped out of the way of the advancing clubs and pepper spray until I regained my breath. Thankfully the protective gear did ease the pain of the clubbing and our bandanas and goggles helped protect some of us from the biting sting of mace and the teargas dumped liberally from a low-flying helicopter.

We stood our ground and the officers that breached the fence returned to their position inside the construction site. It was a standoff for the moment.

There were a few more attempts to pull down the fence and enter the site but it was clear we didn't have enough people to force the police to completely retreat. People started to sit on the asphalt entrance and before long the protest had become an unplanned sit-in. Some of us laid on the black pavement soaking up the warm May sun. Others became absorbed in animated conversations with members of their affinity groups, the tight-knit groups of friends who had spent the past year together preparing for this day of nonviolent direct action.

News that one gaff hook had snapped off the line and flew towards the police apparently striking an officer on the head circulated through the conversations.

Three or four hours passed and many of the activists had drifted off to get food or use the toilet. The crowd had thinned. I sat with my friends near the main gate discussing our next move. Should we call for everyone to meet or just do our own action? Maybe we should walk back to our van and smoke a few bowls of pot and think things over. Then suddenly without warning five or six police in riot gear, their plastic visors down, marched up to us and yanked Brian out of our deliberations.

Brian's arrest was a shock. A spontaneous chant rose from the crowd, "Let him go! Let him go!" One of our friends, Jo, jumped to her feet and followed Brian to the gate but he soon disappeared into the sea of helmeted police and national guard troops.

"Let's go!" I yelled to my friends. C.T., Sue, Mira, Jo, and I raced towards our van. We climbed into the old green Dodge and sped off to the Rockingham County Jail where the police had taken prisoners during the October occupation attempt.

Once we arrived at the jail, Jo ran across the street to a laundromat payphone and franticly dialed the numbers on our small list of activist lawyers. Sue, Mira, and C.T. kept the desk sergeant busy with questions about Brian's charges. I ran between Jo and the jail, passing messages.

At one point I returned to the jail lobby with news from Jo, "We have a lawyer and the bail is $20,000." A few more calls and Jo found a supporter willing to post the bond. We would not be intimidated by the state. I don't recall any of us having any doubt we would raise the bail or fail to otherwise win his release.

Five hours of sitting in the Lysol-reeking lobby was a bonding experience. Brian finally emerged from the inner recesses of the Rockingham County facility to smiles and hugs.

Brian needed a shower and good meal and couldn't risk a second arrest so we gathered up our equipment from the woods and headed south on Route One.

Ideas flew around the van as we headed home towards Boston. "We need to start a defense fund and pay back the bail." "Let's organize a caravan to the arraignment." "Let's use the trial to generate more opposition to nuclear power." "It was a false arrest and shows how dishonest the authorities are," and so on until we finally arrived at Sue and C.T.'s flat in Inman Square, Cambridge.

We started to organize a defense committee over dinner.

"We can hold bake sales outside the BU Law School. Maybe even in Harvard Square and outside Park Station," suggested an enthusiastic C.T as Brian sauntered down the hallway a bit wet and wrapped in a towel.

I was excited by the vision and added, "That's a great idea, and we can talk with people about why we are organizing to stop the Seabrook. We could bring leaflets about the dangers of nuclear power." The brainstorming of those days was exhilarating. Thankfully this excitement at forming ideas and then bringing them into reality has never left me.

C.T. and Brian planned the first bake sale. Brownies, cupcakes, and two apple pies to be sold on the plaza at the entrance to the law school. After buying the wholewheat flour, sugar, and other ingredients they returned to Sue and C.T.s Tremont Street flat to bake not only the desserts but their minds in a haze of high-test Maine barn pot.

Before long the sweet smell of burning sinsemilla was overtaken by the warm chocolate aroma of brownies. Even with the drug-induced distractions the bake goods came out of the oven in great shape. Nothing was burned and they were tasty looking, if not so uniform or symmetrical in shape. No mind-altering ingredients were added.

Brian and C.T. were off to Boston University with their first batch of baked goods and the attempt to raise a defense fund. Brian's classmates rushed by the card table of pastries mostly ignoring the unusual display. Every so often a student would ask about the purpose of the bake sale seemingly unable to grasp the message, "Support Brian Feigenbaum's Defense," that was scrawled out in black marker on the side of a well-worn banana box.

After several hours and five dollars in donations it was time to pack up.

Brian tried to make the best of it, "Looks like we may be eating dessert for dinner tonight."

It was around this time that our crew had started a little moving company, Smooth Move, hauling people's furniture and household belongings. Like my later design business, this was a strictly off-the-books operation. Our largest job was moving the contents of the New England Free Press to their new location. We were happy to take their overprinted booklets and pamphlets off their hands.

Among our household clients was a local activist family who needed to move from an apartment in Cambridge to a house in Somerville. I saw a poster mounted on cardboard leaning against their "to discard" pile.

"Are you really throwing this poster out?" I asked.

"Yes, you can have it," they responded.

The large poster showed children in a playground printed in dark green ink on yellow textured paper with the text, "It will be a great day when our schools get all the money they need and the Air Force has to hold a bake sale to buy a bomber."

The perfect addition to our bake sales.

"Let's each buy a used military uniform at the Central Square Army Navy Surplus, make some colorful cardboard general's ribbons, take the poster and invite the people who walk by to help us buy a bomber," I suggested. So, we baked a batch of cookies and it was off to Harvard Square to set up our bake sale to "buy a bomber."

The sight of three scruffy-looking, young, pretend-Air Force generals did attract attention. In addition to the poster, we placed a ¾-inch brass nut showing we were making progress on the purchase of our first bomber. News of the US military spending $1,200 for that same five-cent hardware nut was making headlines.

"What is this?" was a question we heard more than once that afternoon from puzzled pedestrians glancing at the poster and plates of cookies and brownies.

"We are raising money for a bomber," we responded. "See, we have already made enough to buy this nut. Get a cookie and help us buy our second $1,200 nut," we went on, while pointing at our hardware.

"No really, you don't look like you're in the military," they would insist often with a knowing smile.

We would quickly add that Brian had been falsely arrested during a protest against a Nuclear Power Station being built in a marsh forty miles north of Boston and that we were raising money for his legal defense.

This was enough of a hook to get people talking but it really wasn't enough to increase the sale of our baked goods. It was, however, a valuable lesson in political organizing. A lesson we would return to.

The cover of the Boston Collegiate Coupon Book designed by Keith McHenry

Chapter 14

TRASH

I forged the course of my journey in the trash bins of my life.

One cold fall night in 1980, there it was resting in a galvanized garbage can that stood silently in the evening mist of Harvard Square, in Cambridge. Bright white sheets of paper pierced the fog and snagged the eyes of my housemate and political coconspirator C.T. Butler as he strolled home. He was exhausted after a sweaty night working in a steamy kitchen, but still he rushed back to our place on Harvard Street excited to share the news of his discovery: free drawing paper. There was a curbside bin of treasures waiting for us in the Square, he announced as he slogged into our living room. Then it was a race against the drizzle. We wasted no time in returning to the promised mother lode. We found the metal barrel still protecting its precious office debris. But it wasn't just drawing paper that we found there. It was the remains of a graphic designer's layouts of that year's IBM annual report. For C.T. the contents said art supplies. I saw something else.

I yanked the hard-surfaced sheets from the can. C.T. and I reverently stacked the bounty in heaps on the floor of our Dodge. I left the miscellaneous scraps for the early morning collection.

This garbage-can discovery was all I needed to transform my life. A simple piece of tracing paper covered each sheet. There was evidence of an X-Acto knife incision neatly slicing the thick strip of white tape that still half-adhered to the smooth board, the lower half stuck neatly across the top of the tissue. I surmised that the translucent parchment must have been applied to protect the type, ruby red film, and inked rules of the boards from the dust.

But the layer below the tissue provided the real key. A light blue pencil outlined a rectangle that looked to be seventeen inches by eleven inches in size. I knew enough about offset printing to understand that the black-inked dashes outside the blue-lined box were the cutlines, just like those the printer at Red Sun Press asked me to draw when I delivered my first offset printing job to the activist press in Jamaica Plains area of Boston.

A blue line marked the annual report's center. Columns of shiny photographic paper carried the text. I pulled a second board from the pile. I could see that the blade had knifed the four edges of a red film also bound by faint blue rules. "I think they call this a window," I said to C.T. "It leaves a clear box on the film for a photo."

While the type and lines populated the sleek sides of the sheets, the back side of each piece provided a clue to the material. The name "Letramax 2000" was streaked diagonally in rows, deep grey type across a field of lighter grey. There was a lesson in these thirty or so boards.

The next morning, I was sitting on a city bus bouncing down Mount Auburn Street on my way back home. The late fall sun cast a dappled golden tone through the oaks, black walnuts, and elms. Yellow and red leaves rested against the stone cemetery wall. The sweet vinegar smell of decay drifted past the rattling window frames.

The name came to me like one more flash of those tree-strained sun beams: Brushfire Graphics. The secret to be a professional graphic designer was revealed to me in that stuffed can of trash. I started my company that evening inking the flaming paint-brush bristles of my logo on one of those discarded IBM annual report mechanicals.

The Food Not Bombs logo

Chapter 15

THE PURPLE FIST

The TV on the first floor of the Somerville, Massachusetts rental droned on with election results. My housemates and their friends hung on every return: New York goes to Carter; North Carolina goes to Reagan; California is too early to call. The occasional groan of despair signaled that President Carter wasn't doing so well in his reelection bid.

My friends Sue, C.T., Mira, and Brian were sprawled across my queen-size mattress in my second-floor room passing around a joint. Screams of terror from the first floor increasingly interrupted our conversation about the virtues of anarchism relative to the electoral theater playing out that night on America's TV screens. It seemed to me there was little hope for change in elections controlled by corporate interests. Both political parties supported war even if Carter's wars were covert like the genocide of East Timor. We agreed that it's the system that needs to change, not political parties or candidates. Even so Reagan provided a particularly apocalyptic energy.

The loud shrieks of anguish drowned out the TV indicating Ronald Reagan would be America's next President and as if to mark the occasion our shared dog, Yoda, started chewing the back cover of Volume One of Emma Goldman's autobiography, Living My Life. In our pleasant state of intoxication, we knew that Yoda was sending us a message.

"Let's trip until the end of the world," I announced on the eating of Emma Goldman's words. So that's what we set out to do. Sue slid out a sheet of Mickey Fantasia blotter from her purple bag of tricks. One hit for each of us with more left in reserve if necessary.

Once properly dosed we floated downstairs past a living room of people drinking away their distress. One older woman was on her hands and knees pounding the floor in front of the TV as Reagan was giving his acceptance speech. My housemate, Frank, spun behind her, drunkenly sloshing whiskey onto our hardwood floor. Another woman curled up on our couch, protecting her head with her hands.

The six of us anarchists scampered out to our van, which we had pre-stocked with cans of spray paint in anticipation of the no-matter-who-wins electoral disaster. We were prepared to graffiti the city until the first nuclear strike took us out. Reagan was our real-life Dr. Strangelove, even more terrifying than the Peter Sellers of Stanley Kubrick's movie. We stopped two blocks from my house. I vigorously shook my can of red, elated by that beautiful sound: the sensual click, click, click of a full can. I sprayed "General Strike Not Nuclear Strike" on Congressman Tip O'Neill's long wooden fence. He must have been tired of sending someone out to wash off my painted communications to the Speaker of the House.

We all had our favorite walls. Brian wrote out, "If voting worked it would be illegal," on a white expanse of the Shawmut Bank on Massachusetts Avenue. "Duck and Cover," looked nice on the Firestone Dealership and, "Vote to die," equally fine in purple on the back of the Harvard Coop Bookstore. White was nice on the red brick walls of Harvard. Maybe the acid made us invisible but we never noticed a single cop all night. By the early dawn glow, the best our tripping selves could do was smear images of flowers and clouds on the blank canvas of Kendall Square and the Salt and Pepper Shaker Bridge.

It was dawning on us that we would not be able to trip until the end of the world so we found an early morning diner and started to rethink our plans.

We drifted into a red vinyl booth. The wiry C.T. suggested that our collective rent a house. Sue seconded that, describing her dream of a workspace full of puppets and other make-believe things. She threw her arms around C.T.'s neck to emphasize her agreement. Brian's vision included a huge kitchen and large meeting room. Mira thought a basement darkroom for developing photos and a silkscreen studio would be helpful.

I sat at the sticky plastic tabletop sipping my third cup of industrial Folgers soaking in the enthusiasm. Living together sure would make our galaxy of projects much more focused. We would face fewer logistical issues with our food distribution and street theater. I suggested we shouldn't invite anyone to live with us that didn't share our passions. With that I was all in. This was another chance to create and participate in a new version of my Thoreau's Concord of visionaries.

We found the perfect place. Joan Blout's newly renovated rental at 195 Harvard Street in the Jamaican neighborhood of Cambridge. A two-story, single-family home freshly painted in grey and white. The long slender leaves of a thriving ailanthus tree sifted the midday sun across the facade. Mira and I were sitting on the front stairs when Joan arrived to show us her property. We were dressed in our thrift store best trying to imply we were a couple with means.

Mrs. Blout agreed to rent her two-story house to us signing a $600-a-month lease on a countertop in the kitchen. I handed her $1,200 in cash, money secured in a series of pot and acid deals and from our low-wage jobs.

We were the first to soil the new wall-to-wall carpet and to burn splashes of dinner onto the shiny surface of the new gas stove. The first to replace the stench of new carpet and fresh paint with the smell of coriander and sweet sinsemilla.

The first floor was one open space with a south-facing bay window that overlooked the street. A rough brick chimney defined the border between the kitchen and the living room.

Joan Blout not only renovated and rented houses in Cambridge, she was also an important member of the art community. I had the impression that she was a person of high-society but I didn't know the details at the time. Her connections with Cambridge Community Center, The Cambridge Art Association, and other local institutions would prove to have a huge impact on the future of Food Not Bombs.

Then it happened. Mrs. Blout called our house six months after we signed the lease inviting us to join her for lunch. We agreed of course but we also assumed this would be our eviction lunch. A last supper of sorts for our young experiment.

Joan seemed nervous when she invited us to sit at her table. A bad sign.

She started the conversation. "I can't attend any function without hearing about you guys."

Not a good omen, I thought.

"Your impact on Cambridge is impressive. My friends are so taken with your work, your creativity and enthusiasm," she paused, her expression becoming serious. "But I don't need to remind you that you have never paid rent."

Oh no, here it comes.

"It's clear that $600 a month is too much for you to pay so I will lower the rent to $400 but you have to start paying at the first of next month," she told us.

We wasted no time looking for part time employment to supplement our income from moving jobs and drug sales.

Joan's request for rent turned out to be a blessing for me. I found work at the Passim basement coffeehouse in Harvard Square preparing sandwiches and soup during the shows. Bob and Ray Anne owned the historic folk venue. Bob took the door and introduced the performers, Ray Anne made the coffee drinks, I made the dinners, and Nancy was the waitress.

A delivery of pea soup and a turkey and Swiss on a baguette to poet Allen Ginsberg could inspire a pinch of my butt and a suggestive comment in a playful attempt to get a reaction from his boyfriend. I didn't mind since it also provided me with the opportunity to soak in snippets of his "be here now" philosophy and radical left politics. He treated me as an equal even though he was a giant in American culture. He occasionally asked me for my opinion on a line or stanza of that evening's poetry and told stories to his dressing room audience about the San Francisco Police in North Beach.

That was also a time when I was blessed to escort the graceful Odetta through Harvard Square cradling her arm in mine as we floated along on a warm summer's breeze. Bob would introduce her as the "Queen of Folk" or "The Voice of the Civil Rights Movement," two titles she deserved. Odetta moved along the dreary Cambridge streets with strength and dignity, her wide smile and sweet voice warming the late fall cold. I remember thinking that she looked taller than me even though we were around the same height. She made our conversations one of friends always ending with a warm hug and kiss on the cheek at the steps to her hotel. This was my introduction to a humble kind of fame.

It wasn't long before our house became popular with anyone we happened to meet during our travels. A second-floor room of wall-to-wall mattresses was designated "the bedroom" and every square inch was occupied by midnight. My girlfriend, Jane, and I tried to make the little backroom our own but it too was often stuffed with friends. Our resident guru, Asis, packed the basement with his harem. Amy might be wrapped around that month's guitarist or sprawled out across the yellow laboratory counter turned dining room table. At one point, Jane and I gave up searching for floor space and started to sleep under the stars along the Charles River in the hedges of MIT. And then, as winter set in, we found sanctuary in the women's lounge in Building 77 on Massachusetts Avenue.

Besides being a home to parties and crowds of people in need of a place to sleep, 195 Harvard Street became the center where our friends came to make their preparations for their demonstrations. One such protest was against an October 30th speech by Vice President George H. Bush on the effect of what he called "the Soviet disinformation apparatus" of European antinuclear protesters. This imagined Russian disinformation threat sure had legs. Those antinuclear protesters in this case were huge sectors of the German population who did not feel safe having US Pershing II nuclear missiles roaming around the country on the backs of trucks.

My friend Carl brought two dozen sturdy locust poles, a roll of burlap, kerosene, wax, and twine to make torches: Halloween being the one holiday where pyrotechnics might escape police interference.

Brian, Mira, Amy, C.T., and several other friends frantically chopped vegetables to add to a cauldron of potatoes and butternut squash. Mira and Amy activated our overused blender creaming tofu for what would become our famous tofu pumpkin pies.

. Sue and I were upstairs making the first Food Not Bombs banner. We rolled out a five-foot bolt of black cloth speckled with slivers of silver threads retrieved from her steamer chest of fabric across the floor. She found a sheet of fire-engine red and a strip of orange cloth that would be just right for the carrot and leaf green for the carrot stock. The perfect colors for our carrot and fist logo.

"What color should we use for the fist?" I asked remarking that white, brown, black, red, or yellow would be inappropriate since people will think we support one race over another.

"How about purple?" Sue bubbled as she slid a strip of purple fabric from her wooden chest laughing as she called out: "Purple people eaters! Purple people eaters! Purple is the color of all races."

Sue and I stitched the last leaf of green to black cloth. The stew was ready and Brian slid the pies out of the oven. Dinner was piled into our Dodge van among a tangle of makeshift tables, paper products, torches, and literature. C.T. and I drove the stuffed vehicle over to the plaza outside the MIT Student Union where we quickly unpacked below a stand of yellowing poplars.

The only one of our collective members missing from this mad party was Jo. She was in hiding. Her boyfriend had borrowed her car to wheat paste posters announcing the October 30th protest. He impulsively spray-painted "Shoot Bush First" on the wall of the Student Union and the car was traced back to Jo and her home at 41 Gardener Street in Allston. The Secret Service arrived too late to arrest her. She had already disappeared.

A damp stagnant air choked the Halloween night in mist. I strung our new banner between two small trees. C.T. and I set the two plywood tables below the banner placing bowls and spoons with the stew and pies. A second table displayed our literature, mostly the overprints from the New England Free Press we had scored when moving their Inman Square office.

The plaza pavement shimmered with a late October drizzle under the street lamps. Orange, crimson, and yellow leaves stuck to the cement around our feet. That familiar vinegar scent of fall drifted with the fog. The organizers tested their rented sound system. Activists dressed as ghosts, witches and goblins arrived with banners and signs reading slogans like "Burn Bush Burn" and "Health Care Not Warfare."

The heat radiating from our huge cauldron of stew became a magnet drawing a crowd of curious protesters. "What do you have here?"

"Squash vegetable stew and tofu pumpkin pie. Have a bowl, it's free!" Our guests expressed shock on learning the food cost nothing.

The costumed mob swirling around the plaza was so loud it was almost impossible to hear the speakers denounce Bush and the policies of President Reagan over the boos and cheers. A bottle rocket flamed through the trees. The damp night sparked with the electricity of resistance.

Speakers were still yelling from the stage when the rally stormed out to the far lane of Massachusetts Avenue. Worried we would be left behind to deal with the police we quickly gathered our belongings pushing through the knots of protesters towards our van. We tossed the as of yet unlit torches on top of our other equipment. I maneuvered the Dodge gently out into the middle of the crowded street.

Brian walked ahead asking people to move aside until I was surrounded by throngs of chanting demonstrators. The first order of business was to unload the torches. I grabbed an arm load and handed the pile to a passing friend.

"Here take these down to the drummers," gesturing towards a circle of doumbek-banging friends sitting in the middle of Mass Ave.

A stranger with long blond hair dressed in country club casual appeared at the door of the van eager to help. He had the air of a law enforcement agent trying a bit too hard to look like he was "down" with the protest.

I grabbed six or seven of the heavy wooden torches and thrust them into his arms yelling, "Who put these here?" in the hopes that he wouldn't accuse me of involvement in some pyrotechnic crime. He stepped back unsteady from the weight not only of the bundle but from the momentum of my delivery. His confusion gave me a window to complete my mission.

I grabbed the rest of the rag topped poles and hid them behind a hedge and jumped back in the van and drove out into the empty oncoming lane. C.T. saw the chief of police walking urgently in my direction and rushed towards him, "accidentally" blocking his path before he could stop me.

"Sorry chief, I didn't see you," C.T. said good naturally.

As I was driving away, I yelled out to C.T., "I tossed the torches into the hedge over there," pointing to the bushes that ran along the stone wall of MIT's main building.

As I steered out of the Halloween chaos, C.T. recruited five or six people to help him collect the stashed torches. They succeeded in firing them up. A pile of blue wooden Cambridge Police barricades was stacked in the middle of the street and set on fire. C.T. and Sue passed out psilocybin mushrooms from our impressive stash. A golden light flickered from the smoky flames seemingly in rhythm with the drums as a few hundred other protesters danced in the glow of a bonfire of burning barricades. Cries of "Burn Bush Burn!" rose with the flames.

I recognized one of the goblins dancing around the Halloween fire by her gestures. The Secret Service never found Jo and Bush was not shot first.

People lining up to eat with Food Not Bombs in Washington DC in 2018

Chapter 16

SOUP LINE TO THE FUTURE

"God bless you. God bless you," he said, smiling.

I carefully poured a full ladle of vegetable soup into a hot paper cup. A carrot slice floated to the surface: a pleasant dash of orange to the otherwise thick green stew. I passed the cup of warmth to the bright-eyed man with a scraggly grey beard. The remains of a plaid shirt hung in tatters from his arms. Two soiled hands reached out from the rags to take the cup, his blue eyes sparkling like light house beacons from his smudged face. We smiled at one another. The soup warmed the late March chill from his fingers.

"God bless you," he said again, gracefully bowing his head before stepping aside to let the man behind him receive the Sacrament.

One man after another stepped up to our near-scalding, thirty-six-quart pot. The long winter shadows of our soup-line stretched across the sidewalk. We were joined by a stooped-over woman, her arms and neck wrapped in a rainbow of ribbons and her grey head protected by a knit cap of bright blue, pink, and green with streaks of sparkly silver. She closed her eyes as she nodded reverently to her cup of thick stew.

Most of those first thirty or so people of the streets smiled silently, looking me in the eyes as I carefully passed them a hot cup of soup from behind our make-shift lunch counter. But then there were those who softly said, "God bless you" as they grasped their eight ounces of sustenance.

We wanted to bring the memory of the Great Depression to life on the sidewalk in the shadow of the cold steel Federal Reserve Bank. Maybe shock the public out of complacency and awaken the desire to resist the financial theft promised by America's new president and allies.

C.T. and I were among the handful of anti-nuclear activists who decided to bring the struggle to stop the Seabrook Nuclear Station home to Boston by forming "The First National Bank Project." The First National Bank of Boston and its board members ruled the nuclear energy and weapons industry in New England. They financed the Public Service Company of New Hampshire and the construction of the nuclear power station being built in the marshes of Seabrook. The chairman of the bank was Richard Hill who, I learned while writing this book, had attended Phillips Exeter Academy and Dartmouth College at the same time as my mother's father. I have no idea if they knew one another. After directing the Bank of Boston, he sat on the boards of military contractors Polaroid and Raytheon.

Six or seven of us met at a dingy Central Square coffeeshop to critique our first action and discuss our group's future. We decided to organize a second action outside the bank's March 26, 1981, stockholders' meeting at the Federal Reserve Bank at South Station. We also agreed to try another street theater performance.

"How about dressing as hobos and setting up a Depression era soup line during lunch?" I suggested. "After all, their policies and those of the Reagan administration could lead to a future where people really will need to eat at a soup kitchen."

I added that we could make soup from the produce I was recovering and another activist suggested we dress in our most raggedy clothes, get a few sticks and tie bandanas at the end like the bindles hobos carried in the old black-and-white movies.

Two weeks later it was time to make this protest a reality. I made my food delivery to the projects and returned home to carry several cases of organic produce into our kitchen. Peter Gabriel's "Biko Biko," the revolutionary song about the young South African anti-apartheid activist Biko who was killed by the police was blasting from our stereo.

September '77
Port Elizabeth weather fine
It was business as usual
In police room 619
Oh Biko, Biko, because Biko
Yihla Moja, Yihla Moja
The man is dead

C.T. adjusted the heat on the stove while swishing a giant spoon through the pot full of vegetable soup. Brian, Jessie, and a friend named Karl scrubbed the mud off our collection of carrots and potatoes. The pleasant fragrance of onions and garlic sizzling in olive oil wafted through our home. Amy kept the glass pipe stuffed with pot and Sue, Mira, and I assembled our hobo attire.

It was nearing midnight when we realized we had a lot more soup than would be necessary to feed the small handful of friends likely to join the protest. And, moreover, with such small numbers we wouldn't have much of a Depression-era soup line.

"Maybe we should go to the Pine Street Inn and let the shelter know we will be sharing food at South Station," I suggested. The Pine Street Inn was a small homeless shelter founded during the Great Depression that provided a warm place out of the winter cold for thirty or forty men who otherwise lived outside. It is possible a woman or two may have also found sanctuary on those hard slabs but I never witnessed such in those days.

C.T. and I climbed into the old Dodge van and hustled over to the South End, parking under a street lamp on the narrow street outside the shelter. I rang the Inn's night buzzer and a staff person named Mark arrived cracking the front door open to see what we wanted.

"Hi, we are with the group Food Not Bombs and we want to invite your guests to join us for lunch and a protest at South Station." I am sure Mark had no idea who Food Not Bombs was yet, but he would.

"Come on in. Why don't you tell everyone yourself?" he offered.

Mark led us to a large yellow-tiled room that smelled of damp socks and urine. A street light streaming through the filthy windows provided just enough illumination to see that there were a couple of dozen men sitting along the walls. Others laid on the floor using knapsacks or garbage bags filled with personal items as pillows.

Mark flicked on a dim light. People sat up or otherwise adjusted their positions. "Ok men, we have an announcement. This young man, what's your name again?"

"Keith," I said.

"Yes, Keith. Well, he wants to talk with you."

"Thanks Mark," I said. "My friends and I have organized a protest against the Bank of Boston outside their stock holders meeting. We are trying to stop the Seabrook Nuclear Station. The Bank is funding the construction and supporting investment policies that hurt our community. We just finished making a huge pot of soup and we will bring it to South Station at around eleven o'clock tomorrow. Along with protesting their investment in the nuclear industry we want to impress on the bank's stockholders that their policies could lead to a financial crisis like the one that caused the Great Depression. Americans might find themselves eating at soup kitchens again if we don't stop them."

Several old guys groaned. A couple clapped. "This is great. A protest like we did in the 60's." Another stood to shake my hand, "I'll be there."

"Ok, we will see you at eleven in the morning," I said ending the announcement. As we left, I thanked Mark for giving us the time to speak to everyone.

The next morning, we walked our dogs around Fresh Pond, rushed off to collect the day-old muffins at Warburton's in Harvard Square and returned home to pick up the reheated soup, our hobo props, homemade table, and serving supplies. Sue blew up six or seven brightly colored balloons and off we went to South Station dressed in our best tattered hobo clothing.

I pulled the van up to the curb on Atlantic Avenue. A small group of the disheveled men we had spoken with at the Pine Street Inn were already waiting.

Our little band of "hobos" rushed into action setting up our saw horse and plywood table. Then our huge pot of vegetable soup was placed next to a stack of our brochures that described the bank's board of directors and their threat to our security. Sue tied the balloons to the van's mirror. As we had expected our protest failed to attract any of our activist friends.

"Welcome everyone! Please line up here," I yelled pointing to the Atlantic Avenue sidewalk at the South end of our rickety tables.

"Ok, ok," grumbled an old guy in a food-stained shirt.

More men from Pine Street shuffled into the line. The first guest stepped up to the pot when he saw we were ready.

Then there was that first "God bless you" that I would come to hear so often over the coming four decades. "God bless you."

A man of thirty or so dressed in a smart grey business suit sheepishly approached me. "What are you doing here? I haven't seen a soup line except in photos and movies about the Great Depression. Reagan's economic policies aren't already having such an impact, are they?"

I gave him our brochure and said: "You may be seeing more of this if we don't start organizing against Reagan and his banker friends."

A proper Bostonian lady, white hair and pearls, rushed past us vigorously, giving us the middle finger. Another older woman walked swiftly past, also decorated in pearls but she called out to let us know she was a stockholder and had come to vote against a bank policy she didn't agree with.

"That Richard Hill is a terrible director," she said, and then added, "Thanks for coming out."

"You should do this every day," suggested an older stubbly-faced gentleman that we had first met at the Inn.

"There isn't a free meal in this town," said another man in blueish mechanics coveralls. "We get our coffee and donuts in the morning before we leave and more donuts at night but that's about it."

Back home, the eight of us were electric with enthusiasm as we cleaned up our disaster of a kitchen. We talked over one another excitedly as we recounted the experiences of the day. "I never expected people to be so grateful for a simple bowl of vegetable soup," Mira said. "That sure was inspiring," Brian noted turning to Jo to say, "that was just what Julian had been telling us about how to create a living theater," referring to Julian Beck co-founder of the Living Theater. Brian, Mira, Sue, and C.T. had been invited by Jo to prepare meals for their theater workshops in New Hampshire.

"The most powerful thing about today for me was meeting the guys who otherwise hide in the shadows. Such beautiful people…proud with a kind of honesty that was self-evident even in the brief time we spent together," I said with the passion of someone whose life had just been transformed because that was in fact what was happening.

"We have to do this every day!" I suggested, "We should quit our jobs and do this full time."

So that's what we did. I gave my boss at Bread and Circus two weeks' notice and asked if I could continue to collect the store's discarded produce explaining that I wanted to keep handing out the food at the projects. He agreed, saying he thought that was a good idea.

I met the tofu delivery driver on the loading dock and asked him to see if his boss would let him drop off their scraps next to the discarded produce. A day later he let me know I would find two buckets on the platform that Friday.

For the moment, our meals were more theater than survival. Reagan and his administration's policies had only just begun. All that would change.

August 6, 1980 March to Draper Nuclear Lab in Cambridge, Massachusetts

Chapter 17

HIROSHIMA DAY

August 6th is one of those dates that is branded into the flesh of my soul.

And thus, with appropriate drama I lifted a gasoline-drenched copy of the white pages out of a bucket and held it up in the air, letting the gas drip all over the neglected patch of gravel. About fifty people stood in the noon sun outside the new glass and concrete Draper Laboratory on that blistering Cambridge day in 1981. Inside, all manner of engineers were busy designing the latest in nuclear weapons technology.

"Just imagine if a one megaton nuclear bomb were to be launched at Boston? Everyone listed in this phone book would be killed just like this," I said as I flicked a lighter and held it to a corner of the phonebook. In a flash the pages and the thousands of names listed on them all burst into flames.

The possibility was real.

I had read John Hersey's Hiroshima before I entered high school but that isn't what branded the searing pain of August 6 into my heart.

It was another idyllic New England Christmas at my mother's parents' house in Needham, Massachusetts. The Vietnam War was raging and I was an elementary school student. A blue spruce towered above a mountain of shiny wrapped presents. Real lead tinsel and delicate glass ointments from Germany glistened from the stately needle boughs in the corner of the living room. Snow drifts swirled against the white clapboards of my grandparents' suburban Boston home and dusted the red-bowed wreath that welcomed the holiday guests at the front door.

Christmas carols on the old Grundig Radio couldn't mask the loud conversation in the den. My grandfather spun around his office with the phone pressed to his ear. He paced beneath the sixty-three framed aerial photos of Tokyo burning. They were photographs that he had taken from the nose of a B-29 during his Operation Meetinghouse. My grandfather was engaged in a heated telephone battle with his friends General Curtis LeMay and Secretary of Defense Robert McNamara.

He bragged to me, his young grandson, that he had provided LeMay with a flight plan outlining the virtues of using one of his squads of B-29s to transport an atomic bomb over the Himalayas to drop on the city of Hiroshima during the days he was directing the fire bombing raids over Tokyo from bases in Burma. Hymns to the Prince of Peace struggled against my grandfather's argument for a nuclear detonation over Hanoi. "Send a message to those communists in China and the Soviet Union," he demanded.

A decade after my grandfather's holiday arguments with America's military establishment I was a busy 22-year-old organizing a march against the nuclear arms race co-sponsored by Food Not Bombs and the Cambridge City Council. Cotton puffs of clouds drifted across the perfect mid-July sky. I climbed the impressive Cambridge City Hall steps to the Council Chambers with laser focus, carrying my just-off-the-press posters printed in rich brown ink on a heavy goldenrod colored paper. "Please give copies to the mayor and all the council members," I said with a smile as I counted out the appropriate number of posters. I remember being so proud of my design and the quality of the printing.

The receptionist happily assured me she would. She then casually added that a man who had introduced himself as from the CIA had stopped in to inquire about the march.

"The CIA? Really?" I asked. And she assured me, "Yes, he said the CIA."

Though a bit flustered by this information, I was on a mission to place my newly minted poster in as many locations as I could and rushed out to the streets of Central Square without inquiring further. But the receptionist's comment kept gnawing at me. Why would the Central Intelligence Agency take notice of our little demonstration? The only thing I knew about the CIA was its history of coups, covert wars, and the stuff my grandfather did with the Office of Strategic Services before that branch of the military became the CIA. I thought the CIA only worked outside the country. This was unsettling news to be sure. Just how much danger had I gotten myself into, I laughed to myself.

But after posting at a couple of locations it occurred to me that I had better find out what was going on with the CIA thing. Let them know I was not intimidated and by doing so head off any threat to my safety. I slipped into the grungy Plough and Stars swiftly darting to the payphone by the toilets. That familiar bar urine stench bit my nostrils as I franticly flipped through the brittle, stained leaves of the white pages that dangled at the end of a wire. I thumbed through the Cs, no CIA or Central Intelligence Agency.

I did find a number for the Draper Laboratory so I popped a dime in the slot and dialed.

"Good afternoon. You have reached Draper Laboratories. How may I direct your call?"

Thinking on my feet, I responded, "Please put me through to the president of the Laboratory." I had no idea who that was, but thought that maybe introducing myself to him could reduce any threat by the CIA.

"Just one moment please," the operator said.

I heard a few clicks and then a voice said: "Hello, office of the president. This is Mrs. Sullivan speaking. How may I direct your call?"

"Please put me through to the president," I said with as much authority as I could muster.

"President Duffy is busy right now. Would you like to leave a message?"

"Yes, thank you. Would you please tell him that Keith McHenry called and would like to schedule a meeting?"

"Ok, let me see, the next available appointment won't be until August 21st."

"Oh, that is too late. I need to meet with him before our August 6th protest."

"Just a second please, your name is Keith McHenry, is that right?"

"Yes, please tell him I'm calling. My schedule is very busy but I would be free to meet with him on Friday at 4:00 p.m. if he is available."

" Please hold."

After a moment of silence, Mrs. Sullivan came back on the line and said: "Mr. McHenry, General Duffy is able to meet with you on Friday at 4:00 p.m. Please come to the main entrance and ask for President Duffy."

"Thanks so much. I will see you on Friday."

Friday came and I went to meet the general. I arrived at the front desk and asked for President Duffy.

"Are you Keith McHenry?" The receptionist asked.

"Yes, I am here for our four o'clock appointment."

An older roundish man stepped slowly forward from behind a pillar near the elevators.

"Welcome Mr. McHenry. I am General Duffy. Please feel free to call me Bob."

General Duffy gave me a hardy handshake and I followed him to a room off the lobby.

We shared some polite small talk, I explained that we planned to hold a nonviolent protest outside his building. The grandfatherly general told me a little about his time in the military when he was stationed in Panama Canal Zone and Algeria and then he got to his main point suggesting we were on the same side, both working for peace.

"I help develop the technology for the Peace Keeper Missile and you are marching for peace. We may have different ways of working, but our goals are the same. The only thing I ask is that you not damage our building during the protest," he requested in a serious tone.

I assured him we had no wish to harm his building or his employees and I invited him to join us.

Saturday, August 6th arrived. Small groups of people mingled outside City Hall. I passed out white poster boards with my stenciled design of a nuclear mushroom cloud and the question "Today?"

After about twenty minutes of speeches the group of fifty or so protesters stepped off the sidewalk onto Massachusetts Avenue and marched south towards Draper Laboratory.

C.T. and I drove to the final destination with food and a copy of the residential phone book that had been soaking in a bucket of gasoline.

The march arrived and people gathered on a triangular traffic island across from the lab.

I yelled out a few welcoming words getting the attention of our hot, bedraggled protesters: "The Soviet Union and the United States have thousands of nuclear warheads pointed at one another. Our nations are spending billions of dollars preparing for nuclear war when our taxes could be better spent on education, social services, and other domestic needs."

I held up the white pages dripping with gas, struck a match stick on the side of the box of Diamond Wooden matches and whoosh, tens of thousands of Boston area names burst into flames.

General Duffy watched from across the street. A year later he would ask to say a few words to our protesters.

Keith's photo of his mother milking her favorite goat Strawberry on her last Christmas

Chapter 18

MOTHER

I settled into my designated middle seat on a Delta flight from Boston's Logan airport to Houston. I had stopped in Boston to visit my father. This was sometime in the first few years after the turn of the millennium. I had probably dropped in to see him when I was returning from Europe or Africa. I introduced myself to the woman in the window seat. She offered her hand and told me that her name was Debra Lovell. We tried one of those cramped-airplane, elbow-into-your-side handshakes.

"Lovell as in Lovell's Lane in Marstons Mills?" I asked. Yes, she is one of those Lovells, she said. She tells me that she is a journalist with the Houston Chronicle. I told her my name and she remembered my mother. She mentioned that her mother had died of lung cancer in 1985. I said that my mother had also died of lung cancer that same year.

"There were at least sixty people in our village that had lung cancer back then," she said, adding, "I believe they traced the cancer to a chemical in the antifreeze used in the F-16 jet fuel of the military jets that landed at Otis Air Field." An invisible vapor that rained death across the idyllic ponds and thick woods of the inner Cape.

If I could call any one place home it would be the tiny village of Marstons Mills, Massachusetts on Cape Cod. What was an old cow pasture with a lone cedar in 1914 had become ten acres of hardwood forest by the time my skinny little frame first stepped foot on the sandy shores of Middle Pond. Our family's two-rut dirt road meandered more than a mile through a corner of the Hamblin Pond duck farm. Oak and maple leaves brushed the car windows as our family glided towards the paradise we simply called "The Cape."

My great-grandfather was the Lynn Shoe Factory magnate, Joseph Charles Phelan. He and his wife Adeline bought the barren hill and built a two-story lodge that became the centerpiece of my childhood. This, like all other monumental tales of family lore, was rooted in my core. Every time we passed under that old rusted railroad bridge in Lynn my mother would remind the family that her grandfather was the inventor of the shoe size and that striking factory workers had torched one of his twenty-seven buildings. She would always add the cautionary detail, "He didn't believe in buying insurance and the arson forced him to close down his operation." Those massive brick temples to the industry of capitalism had been empty since the fire in the late 1800s. Even so, like the red brick walls of Fort McHenry, I was taught from an early age that my family was part of the mortar that bound America.

My great-grandmother, Adeline, was the daughter of Charles Vander Poele, the inventor of the dynamo, the electric trolley, and a co-founder of General Electric. It was on a cold New Orleans day when I first caught a glimpse of his name painted in gold over the green of the Saint Charles Line. And it was as I waited on the street, one freezing night in Brno, Czech Republic in 2006, when I saw a trolly screech to a stop and was stunned to read the words Charles Vander Poele painted on each of the cars. That was our Charles Vander Poele.

Throughout my childhood, my mother and I would spend hours in the Big House kitchen, drifting around the island, locked in conversation. I may have been only ten or twelve but there were few subjects too complex to discuss.

Mother was self-confident. She had an interest in current events, loved filing in the box scores at Fenway and kept track of the stock margins on the ticker tape printed in the Globe. During a lesson on stock investments, she interrupted herself to slide open a drawer on our old rollup desk and lift her stash of elaborately engraved first edition General Electric Stock Certificates, pulling them from the safety of their huge onion skin envelope. I was made to understand that this was our General Electric.

As was often the case on those summer afternoons, a cooling breeze would drift off the crystal waters of Middle Lake and into my great grandmother Adeline's tiny second floor dormer. Adeline was the oldest person I had ever met, and she was wise and visionary all the way to the grave. It was no wonder my mother was so confident. Adeline's bony, blotched palms would grasp my tiny hands as she spent her days lounging in her custom-made bed that was built out of the giant cypress that paneled the rest of the interior of the house. She shared enchanting tales of her formal art training in Belgium. She gave detailed accounts of exotic toga parties and illustrated her tales with entire photo albums of black and white pictures that filled a basket in the alcove under the stairs that lead to her room.

Her Big House was modeled on an Italian hunting lodge designed by a relative. She said that the giant old-growth cypress trees were logged in the dark swamps of Florida and cut to the specifications required for the paneling in the two-story high living room: those timbers traveled by rail to frame our massive stone fireplace and held four generations of Christmas Stockings. Our electricity was generated in a noisy engine house at the entrance to the property and a red hand pump at the head of a graceful soapstone sink provided fresh water filtered by the sands beneath the cement basement. The musty scent of Cape Cod would be a life-long tether to my place on the land.

One of Adeline's Pre-Raphaelite paintings hung in a simple heavy dark frame above the fireplace. I spent many evenings considering the meaning of the dark four-foot-high goddess Circe turning Odysseus' men into swine. That little pig at sea would be a mystery to me until I first heard the siren's call in the pages of my mother's library. Two massive black iron chandeliers hovered above a lion's pelt spread over the hardwood floor. A baby grand piano rested silently in one corner of the grand hall, it's keys only brought to life at the whim of my mother's touch. The glass eyes of various trophy heads stared vacantly from the walls.

Two flights of stairs met at a balcony that led to four tiny rooms with custom-made bunk beds. A fine powder of sand permanently coated the hardwood floors, evidence of our days at the lake swimming, fishing, and sailing. I spent hours behind a lawnmower engaged in a brutal battle to clip back the advancing columns of green briar. An alcove beneath the stairs would be my cocoon of safety and comfort, its gravity pulling me and anchoring me there.

When I was seven, I declared war on a briar patch in the center of our turnaround. Upon victory, I dug up a spindly, three-foot oak sapling from the edge of the woods and buried its fragile roots there. The oak grew to monumental proportions, becoming more than capable of sustaining the rope swing of my childhood desires.

Sometime in 1972 or 1973, my lawyer uncle, Jack, put the family's heritage up for sale. He and his wife Becky wanted to sever all ties with my father. A conflict had grown between them and my parents. My parents assumed that Jack and Becky's devotion to Ayn Rand was to blame. Three decades later Becky told me they feared my father would accidentally kill one or both of their two nephews and couldn't live with the thought. They saw that my brother and I were unsupervised and running wild. She blamed my father for my having contracted cholera saying that was the last straw. I don't agree with her assessment.

My mother mobilized to buy out her brother's half and invested her stocks in a shopping center development, following a tip from her father's former law partner. It took her three years of anxiety and stress to complete the financial puzzle and secure the ten acres. But then she had the bug for easy money and sought to repeat her success. She plunked down her remaining profits on another mall project, but that one turned out to be a bait and switch and she lost everything except our family's place on the Cape.

My parents bought a couple of Toggenburg milking goats from a herd in Harvard, Massachusetts when I was a senior in high school and corralled them behind their split-level home in Acton. I think my father was in search of a kind of sanity he couldn't find at work under the Reagan Administration or at home in the sterile suburbs. His solution was to start his own herd of Toggenburgs. He had fond memories of his mother grazing alpine goats on the weedy hillside above Lock House Seven, their hooves balancing on the slope in the shadow of the Glenn Echo Amusement Park in Southwest Washington DC. My mother was reluctant at first but it wasn't long before she came to love her smelly girls.

My father retired from the National Park Service during my second year at Boston University, angry at the forced morning prayer meetings. He sold the Acton house and moved with my mother, me, my siblings, and the goats to the Cape. My once-spindly oak wouldn't yet shade the solar hot water panels my father installed on the roof. The hand pump had been retired to the basement with the soapstone sink. Electricity soon arrived from the power grid. My mother cheerfully took up work cleaning houses and selling milk, homemade feta, and eggs from a card table on Route 139.

When the family made our move to the Cape my father started Team Interpretation, a national park consulting business that took him to the Bodhi Tree National Historic site where he designed the self-guided tour and matching signs. That job led to another assignment a year later with the Indian National Park Service designing tours and museum exhibits. My parents then headed off to Kanha National Park, home to a tiger sanctuary in India. A neighbor milked my mother's does, fed her goats and hens, and collected the eggs in exchange for taking over her business out on the street.

I was then immersed in a world of my own making. There was my orbit surrounding the tasks of Food Not Bombs. I also had a bill-paying constellation of side gigs that included the sale of commodities like weed, acid, magic mushrooms, and cocaine that helped finance my expanding graphic design and poster distribution businesses: Brushfire Graphics and Up Against the Wall. Then the idea came to me to start an evening class I called "The Graphic Design Workshop," promising my students for the low price of $195 that they would qualify to take a position as a professional designer after just eight nights at my drafting tables. One of those early students that walked the six floors to my studio at 636 Beacon Street was the statuesque beauty named Andrea Albert.

One night, after I returned from dinner eager to start the first night of that round of classes, I found an angry note to a "Mr. Cenery" scrawled across a yellow sheet hastily torn from its note book. "I thought the design class started at 6:30." This would be the first of many missed connections involving the woman with the long brunet hair whom I would marry. Andrea was the daughter of a crane operator at the Delco Battery Plant and a tough no nonsense housewife who lived in the suburbs of Rochester New York. Andrea too was tough, just like her mother.

She basked in the excitement of Boston's eccentric community of artists and free thinkers roaming the life drawing classes of what we liked to think of as the Athens of the New World. We could talk with ease about anything, but we mostly talked of the details needed to tame the madness of our design company, Brushfire Graphics, or the drama of her sisters. Andrea and I became quick friends and it wasn't long before I hired her away from her clerical job with the Yankee Group. I couldn't have chosen a more competent office manager. Andrea was the most loyal companion I could have every wished for.

The pace of design jobs moving through my half-floor of drafting tables staffed with paste-up artists was frenetic. My 636 Beacon Street office was abuzz pasting-up sports calendars, coupon books, and fashion ad designs, all of which flew out the door as soon as they were press ready. We rushed to make tight deadlines sending sleek John Dellaria Salon display ads to Vogue, Mademoiselle, and a host of other publications. It was a $10,000-a-day operation with by-the-hour deadlines that could have been a seven-day-a-week venture, but Andrea and I did find the time to take the occasional weekend off to visit the Cape. So, when my parents returned from India sometime in the fall of 1984, we headed down to welcome them home from their exotic big cat adventure. I had heard from my mother that dad was excited to show off his tiger pictures. When we got there and sat down with my parents and my sister at the dining-room table, my father would say, over and over: "We could hear the tiger's breath, it was so close."

Andrea and I returned a month later and parked beneath the boughs of the giant oak I had planted decades before. As I approached the house, I could see the stooped-over silhouette of my mother in the kitchen.

I usually found my mother weeding the garden, soaking up to her neck in the lake, or fiddling around in the barn, but this time my mother was hunched over the island in the kitchen. She winced in pain and took labored breaths with closed eyes as she gripped the counter in preparation for my hug.

"Thanks for coming down," she said quietly, straining to smile.

My mother started to complain about a throbbing pain in her left shoulder when they returned from India. She struggled to milk her three goats and care for her hens. She said she was in agony when she unfolded her card table or set out her glass bottles of milk on her stand on Route 149.

She was sure she had contracted an exotic disease while out of the country. Her doctor sent her to Mass General to meet a team of tropical disease specialists.

"They think it might be Visceral Leishmaniasis," she said hoping to have an answer to her mystery. "I will get the test results next week. I will be so relieved when we find out what is causing this," she continued, convinced that it was something she picked up overseas.

Each time Andrea and I came to visit she would report that the pain had grown worse. I could see that her usual high energy was draining out of her; she seemed a little more exhausted each time we visited. And she was growing desperate, forced to abandoned her roadside dairy business. She just wasn't up to it anymore.

She had often expressed surprise at the number of her customers who said that cow's milk made them ill. "Most of them seem to have lung cancer and they say the treatments make it uncomfortable when they try to digest cow's milk, but that they feel fine with the goat's milk," she said.

By then, Andrea and I left Boston every Friday evening and headed south to the Cape. We wanted to take some of the pressure of caring for mother off my father and sister. My father was a mess each time we arrived. The strain on his face was becoming permanent. He circled nervously around the kitchen in desperation.

"I don't know what to do. I just don't know," he'd say.

The doctors finally came to realize that my mother didn't have an exotic disease and her insistence that she had caught something in India had diverted their attention from the medically obvious. That increasingly sharp pain in her left shoulder was a classic symptom of lung cancer. The very cancer that tormented so many of her goatmilk-buying neighbors. It seemed like most of the housewives in Marstons Mills were struggling to survive the disease.

Mom grew weak. Papery black-and-blue skin hung off her forearms. Her legs were becoming black strips of leather. I suggested she consider following the cancer fighting diet of Ann Wigmore. Her living food diet of sprouts might turn things around. Dad was growing more frantic. He had pinned his hope on the new program of chemotherapy, but it wasn't slowing the cancer. Then, at my suggestion he wanted mom to check into Ann Wigmore's Hippocrates Institute.

But mom just smiled lovingly, the sparkle in her eyes defying the pain she was enduring. "I'm not going to eat sprouts. I would rather die eating chocolate then live eating those godawful things."

I picked up a couple of Hershey's bars at the Cash Market that afternoon.

Soon she wasn't getting out of bed even to use the toilet. On a late May morning in 1985, as I was gently wiping her arms and shoulders clean with a warm wet washcloth, I thought her breath was shallower than it had been. By ten that Saturday morning, mom was pleading with my father to call the pastor at St. Peter's.

In anticipation of his visit, I brushed the remaining wisps of her grey hair—no more the long, flowing blond curls that had always been a source of pride. I finished by touching up her lips with a light application of lipstick I found on her dresser.

"Oh, Keith, every inch of my body hurts. I don't think I can change out of my nightgown. I'll wear my bathrobe when he comes," she whispered.

Pastor Webster arrived at five that afternoon. My father and I lifted my mother slowly from the bed as though she were made of paper-thin glass. Dad steadied her as I slid her favorite blue socks over what was left of her leathery black feet.

We gently placed her in a chair in the living room. She held herself with dignity. Pastor Weber gently clasped her hands and said a prayer.

"Savior of the world, by your cross and precious blood you have redeemed us. Save us and help us, we humbly beseech you, O Lord."

The laying on of hands was followed by the Holy Communion.

"Gracious Father, we give you praise and thanks for this Holy Communion of the Body and Blood of your beloved Son Jesus Christ, the pledge of our redemption, and we pray that it may bring us forgiveness of our sins, strength in our weakness, and everlasting salvation through Jesus Christ our Lord. Amen."

My mother's eyes sparkled. The pastor lifted the wafer to her mouth. Mom tried to help him, lifting her frail fingers to her mouth. After she took the body of Christ, I passed the silver cup to the pastor. He lifted the chalice pouring a few drops of the wine, the Blood of Christ, into mom's dying lips.

Dad and I helped mom back into bed thanking the minister as he passed my mother's room on the way to the kitchen door.

Not long after we returned Mom to bed she whispered, "Bruce, Bruce." I knew that she was desperate to see my little brother.

"I'll get him mom, don't worry. I'll find him."

I drove to a Chinese Restaurant in Hyannis where I knew my brother had played piano for drinks. He wasn't there, and I learned, in fact, that he wasn't welcome there ever again. I stopped at the soup kitchen. Someone suggested I look in the woods outside the Hyannis police station and that's where I found Bruce and his wife Ruth.

"Mom is dying and she really wants to see you," I said, but he wouldn't have it.

"This is just a scam to get me into an intervention. I know dad. He won't stop at anything."

I assured him it was not dad's idea. "Mom asked for you," I said. "The pastor has already given her the last rites."

It took a while, but I finally convinced him. He indulged in one last swig of gin and followed me out of the woods to his dented and shattered yellow Duster. Ten minutes later we were both parking outside the Big House.

Bruce and I walked to mom's room. A warm breath of love from my mother pushed the stale air of death from the room. She reached her trembling hand out towards my little brother. He knelt beside her and took her delicate fingers in his palm. Bruce said with his never wavering honesty how much he loved her.

Her dry lips almost parted with a shinning, satisfied smile. Bruce put his head near my mom's relaxed chest. I could hear her softly say, "You are a good man, Bruce. I love you." Then she let her hand slide slowly out of his palm and onto the mattress.

Bruce stood and slowly left the room. I thanked him, gave him a hug, and said goodbye. He couldn't conceal his distress. He needed another drink.

I returned to my mother's side and took her hand. My little sister Dolly knelt on the floor to her left and softy grasped her other hand. Dad sat next to her on the bed placing his right hand on my mother's heart. Her breath became more and more labored, and then softened to a gentle rhythm with one soft breath, then another. She closed her eyes and lifted her chin ever so slightly. Her smile radiated with something like the bliss of a woman satisfied with her time on Earth.

"I love you," she whispered as she gave our hands a little squeeze. Then her life quietly drained away with her last breath.

The cover of the Boston Celtics Calendar designed by Keith McHenry

Chapter 19

THE CALENDAR OF TIME

Over ninety-thousand, freshly printed World Champion Boston Celtics 1985 Calendars hung on some ninety-thousand walls all throughout New England. And yet, the green borders of the World Champion Celtics had not yet been flipped over to reveal Larry Bird jumping towards the basket illustrating February 1985.

"I designed this," I could say, knowing this was close to admitting that I had been touched by the gods of Boston's basketball dynasty. A quick look at the back cover proved I had made it into the realm of Boston's graphic design royalty. I would no longer need to rely on showing a portfolio for work. I had made it. And I owed the magic of my success to the sports photographer Steve Cadron.

The twelve months of the Celtics led to a winter of New England Patriots Yearbooks and then team posters and full color photos of cross checks and slap shots of Bobby Orr's Bruins. My off-the-books business appealed to my sports broker, who was eager to let me in on the point spread or a future World Series victory predicted during the midsummer heat. There was the intrigue of drizzly, late-night payments delivered via a black leather-gloved hand sliding from an electrically lowered BMW window. Pasting in the holiday of "Keith McHenry" on May 6 in the same Helvetica type as Valentine's Day, President's Day, Independence Day, Thanksgiving, and Christmas slowed the process down by at least a day. Once discovered it would need to be stripped black from the film and thus give me time to make sure the check cleared before the printing began. This was an extra security measure in the extra-legal world in which I was immersed.

You could call it, "Anarchist meets Mafia." I didn't have any hard evidence that Steve had ties to organized crime. It was rumored that his girlfriend, Lynne was the daughter of Joseph Covello of the Gambino crime family. Steve often provided accurate predictions of point spreads and up-coming victories to give me an edge in sports betting while suggesting that he should get a discount on his jobs. There were also the requests to have a truck load of University Coupon Books delivered to a rest stop on I 95 just south of the Massachusetts state line to avoid a hefty sales tax bill. All and all he seemed more like a proponent of disorganized crime, if anything.

One day Steve, my stealth connection to Boston sports greatness, glided over to one of my oak drafting tables. He wore a top-of-the-line custom-tailored Italian suit. I was reviewing a project with one of my paste-up artists. I could almost feel Steve's arrival before he darkened the door of Brushfire Graphics. It made me think of the feeling a diver must get before seeing a lingering shark in a coral reef.

"Keith, I need two sizes of display ads for the Boston Herald by the end of the week. A quarter page and a half page but I don't need a full-page ad," he said.

He set a scrap of notebook paper down on the corner of the drafting table. I could just make out the hand-written text and rough layout notes scribbled there in blue ink.

"Red Sox Calendar Day is in a week and a half, so these ads have to be to the Herald by Friday," he mumbled, almost as an afterthought.

"So, you want the usual quarter page and half page ads. No full page this time?" I confirmed.

"Yes, that's right," he said and started to leave.

"Great and who's designing the calendar?" I asked, puzzled.

"Didn't I get that to you?" he asked with an uncustomary look of shock mixed with his more customary effort to hide his chaos.

"I will be right back!" he blurted, before abruptly turning and dashing out of my office.

Three hours later he returned with a shoebox of 35-millimeter slides: Kodachrome photographs of Red Sox players in action mounted between two, two-inch by two-inch cardboard frames.

"Put this photo on the cover and say something like Celebrating the '75th Anniversary of Fenway Park,'" he said, picking out a slide that featured an aerial photo of a night game taken from the Goodyear Blimp.

The shoebox also included action photos of some of the greats: Jim Rice, Roger Clemens, Bill Buckner, and Dwight Evans.

"I don't care which photo you use for each month, because the calendar celebrates Fenway Park. But we need the seating plan on the back inside cover."

"Can you get me the artwork?" I asked. "If I am going to turn this around by Friday it would sure save time if I didn't have to reproduce it."

Steve returned the next morning to report that management was not able to find any multicolored seating diagrams. They didn't remember where they had sent them. I would take an old copy off another publication, double its size on my stat camera, separate out each section, clean up the edges with a pen and reduce the dozen or more layers to its final size.

My eight employees slid their parallel rulers about methodically, sticking each line of waxed type and logos to their mechanical boards.

"We have to have everything ready in two hours. Hang in there," I announced, trying to hide my sense of panic.

"I can't find Christmas... I can't find Christmas," yelled Barbara the woman pasting up December.

The tiny photographic slip of Helvetica was gone and there was no time to send the request to the typesetter to get us another copy.

"Everyone, lift up your right foot and see if it's stuck to your shoe! Now lift your left foot!" I shouted, trying not to sound too panicked.

"Here it is, here it is!" As I expected, Christmas had been waxed to her heel.

My wife and office manager, Andrea, reviewed each page, checking off the details. Her attention to detail was a blessing.

Andrea methodically read off each piece of type, image, and printer direction to me page by page as I confirmed her information. "Front cover has Fenway Park logo, Red Sox logo, Bud Lite and Budweiser logos, window for photo one. Slide marked this side up with front cover indicated."

We reviewed each month, one by one, taped the final sheets of tracing paper to the panels and tucked them safely into a large manila envelope. Andrea and I rushed to the FedEx office at Logan Airport hoping to catch the flight to Memphis before it took off.

The air crew was unscrewing the hose from the tanker of jet fuel. The conveyor belt had already been wheeled away from the bay. The plane was ready for its flight to the Memphis hub.

We ran up to the FedEx counter, gasping for breath. "We need to get this to Saint Louis first thing in the morning," we said, telling the clerk that it was the artwork for that year's Red Sox calendar. She relaxed a bit, picked up a phone and told someone to contact the cockpit. "Tell the pilot to wait," she said, "we have one more package."

Andrea and I got special treatment at FedEx. That same clerk had her own tiny brush with sports glory six months before when she penned the bill of lading for the pasteups of the Celtics calendar and helped us bundle off the New England Patriots year book a few months before that. The package zipped out to the plane and we were off to another deadline.

I had forgotten calendar day in all the excitement of landing another huge full-color project: two thirty-six-page glossy travel brochures for a selection of all-expenses-paid excursions to Italy.

Andrea had all fifty-three thousand calendars shipped via FedEx overnight directly to the gates of Fenway Park. I remember that FedEx bill. It was more than nine thousand dollars.

Pallets of glossy full-color calendars celebrating the seventy-fifth anniversary of the stadium stood in four-foot-tall stacks at each entrance. "Get your free calendar here, get your free calendar here," yelled the concessioners, each with a Jimmy Fund button dangling from their red and white uniforms, as they gave each fan a copy of the free Fenway Park Calendar Day calendar.

I could tell when the game was over. The Red Sox faithful were flooding the streets below the open bay windows of my second floor Beacon Street office. It wasn't long before Steve flew into my office and slapped a calendar on the edge of the nearest drafting table.

"What's this? The Red Sox management is furious!" he said, drumming his index finger into the calendar's cover photo.

"What did you do? Look at this cover! Why is the Green Monster in right field?" I looked at the cover photo. Fenway's iconic left field wall was pictured there in right field. "They almost had to call the game in the fifth inning. Fans were tearing off the covers and throwing them into the field," adding, "you have to make this right."

"Get me the artwork and the slides. This is what happens when you don't allow enough time to proof your work," I calmly suggested.

Steve rushed out of the room without a word and an hour later returned with the FedEx package of mechanicals and slides.

"Look Steve," I explained pointing to the slide, "I wrote the directions clearly on the slide. The printers at Budweiser in Saint Louis were in a hurry and flipped the film. I guess they didn't realize that Fenway Park was not symmetrical like Busch Stadium. I'm sorry Steve, but that is the cost of being disorganized."

Mr Butch (Harold Madison Jr) in Kenmore Square

Chapter 20

WELCOME TO KENMORE SQUARE

I was standing in the chaos of my office, my attention temporarily focused on the graceful flotilla of white sail boats swaying with the breeze out on the Charles River. The phone rang, calling my attention back to the drafting tables and my staff of pasteup artists. I picked up the receiver.

"My name is Donna Franca," a woman's voice announced with a flourish. "I've heard such good things about you. I have a magnificent assignment for you," she said in a more sensuous than business-like Italian accent. "I need you to design two fantastic, beautiful, thirty-six-page, full-color travel brochures. We will print three hundred thousand copies of each. The press has been reserved for the end of the month. You can do this for me, yes?"

I said yes.

"Come by my place, General Travel on Commonwealth," she said and hung up.

I skipped out of my office, excited to get started on what seemed like a dream job. I'm ashamed to admit this but for some reason I silently repeated to myself some version of, "Not all Italian-Americans are in the Mafia," as I crossed Beacon Street.

I pulled open the heavy glass door and entered a long dark room with ten or more sleek glass desks all clean of papers. Only one lonely phone sat on each desk facing an empty black office chair. The low ceiling pressed a noticeable gloom across the cavernous and sterile-looking office. A smartly dressed college-aged woman stood shuffling through some papers on a table in the back. She approached, extended her delicate hand to greet me, and introduced herself as Veronica.

"Yes, I am here for my noon meeting with Donna Franca," I said.

An elegantly dressed woman in her sixties sat behind a huge glass desk. I thought laughingly to myself that the empty desks I had passed could have been the larger desk's offspring. The sweet rose-petal scent of an expensive Italian perfume suggested I was entering the domain of someone important.

This queen of Italian travel was impatiently yelling at someone on the phone. Her hand sharply struck the air near the outer waves of her ballooning perfectly coiffed hairdo adding unrestrained enthusiasm to her argument. Justified anger, I was sure. "I will not refund one single penny. I promised you Italy and I delivered you Italy," she exclaimed before dropping the receiver to the cradle.

"So, you are the Mr. McHenry I have been hearing so much about," she said, and smiled with a seductive nod.

"I am Donna Franca, the owner of the grandest agency featuring tours to my beloved homeland, Italy." She dramatically explained that her competition was trying to take her place. "But, we won't let him, will we?" she added with a twinkle, already suggesting that I was on her team in the race to remain number one in the all-important Italian tour industry.

"Every Travel Agency in the Midwest must hold your beautiful brochure in their hand by Labor Day. That's when the children start searching for travel packages to buy as Christmas gifts for their retired parents. You understand? If your beautiful brochures aren't in the agents' hands first, they will suggest these families buy our competitor's tours and those are not nearly as wonderful as my complete vacation packages."

She explained all this in colorful detail, expounding on the virtues of her magnificent product. It all sounded even more exciting in her flamboyant accent. She described wonderful tours that take lucky travelers to either Zürich or Rome and then to Palermo for a week.

"They will enjoy wonderful cuisine and beauty beyond their wildest dreams," she said, and then added, "let's write that down."

She asked Veronica to get her checkbook from the stylish cabinet behind her desk, filled out a check and handed me the deposit for the job, a ten-thousand-dollar check, and a fist full of text and photos for the brochures.

Her phone rang again and an excited conversation ensued as she waved to me like I was about to depart on one of her wonderful trips.

Many of my clients, including Donna Franca and the Red Sox, were members of a local business promotion organization called the Kenmore Association. I was a dues-paying member myself and volunteered to design many of the group's publications. So, when they called one day to ask for help, I didn't hesitate to swing by their office.

Kenmore Square was the intersection of academia, baseball, and the punk bohemia of the eighties. Hundreds of Red Sox fans burped in waves from the bowels of the subterranean Green Line flooding the gum-stained sidewalks of Kenmore Square on their sacred march to Fenway Park. Some of my tonier clients owned shops like Giacomo's Salon and Rondi's Clothing. Most Kenmore Association members operated hardscrabble establishments selling things like greasy pizza slices to the tides of Boston University and Mass College of Art students. Baseball memorabilia shop clerks, artsy punk rockers, and Shawmut Bank tellers surged along the wide sidewalks in a rush to snag a lunch of Gyros, burgers, or some sugary treat from Dunkin Donuts. Beefy cops weighed in at Charly's dingy twenty-four-hour diner. Frat boys armed with fake IDs prowled for coeds outside the Miles Standish Hall after draining their cans of Pabst Blue Ribbon purchased from the Golden Goose. My neighborhood was that classic Boston tough I loved.

The association's vice president and local realtor, Paul Valihura, welcomed me to his tiny, bleak office situated on the second floor above Kenmore Liquors.

"Thanks for coming in," he said, shut the office door, and directed me to a wooden chair in front of his paper-strewn desk. The dry dusty smell of a room whose windows had never been opened foretold the nature of subsequent events.

"Keith, the Association wants you to take a photo of that Black guy that stands outside Captain Nemo's Pizza and design a poster with a red circle and a line slashing over his picture like a no parking sign. The poster should say, 'Wanted out of Kenmore Square,' in big bold text."

"Well, Paul, I don't think that is a very good idea," I said. "People love Mr. Butch. He is called the Mayor of Kenmore Square, you know?" His expression made it clear he didn't know this essential piece of information.

"If you're trying to stop people from panhandling before the Red Sox games, I would be happy to provide free meals to everyone," I said, suggesting we could use one of the empty warehouses behind the outfield wall on Landsdowne Street and provide a free meal before every game. "Even so, I doubt it would really reduce the number of people asking for money in the square."

I could divert enough of the food I was recovering on my weekly Food Not Bombs schedule to make this happen. It wouldn't affect our Harvard Square or Park Street Station meals.

Paul thought that was a bad idea, "I don't think the Association would support you providing a free meal to these bums."

"Paul, there is no way to remove the homeless from Kenmore Square," I said. "It's the perfect environment for those without housing. The reeds and bushes along the Fenway provide a safe place for people to sleep and the Red Sox fans and college students are generous and happy to give people a quarter or two."

"Kenmore Square will never be a fancy upscale district like Newbury Street," I told him. "We should go with our unique strengths, promote our lively nightlife and artistic culture, and cater to baseball fans and college students. Visitors to our neighborhood will never have the money or desire to buy two-hundred-dollar shoes and fifty-dollar dinners. Our members would do much better financially if we promoted the special qualities of Kenmore Square."

"So, I guess you won't be making our poster."

"No, I couldn't do that but thanks for having me over. I will see you at the general meeting."

Years later I kind of wished that I, or someone else, had designed the poster. Not because I wanted to drive my friends like Mr. Butch out of the square but to prove to Paul that his proposal would have likely backfired and any shop that displayed such an attack against the popular King of Kenmore would have been sure to have lost business and may have even had to endure some verbal recriminations from former customers. Just imagine people's reaction upon seeing such an insult to the Mayor of Kenmore Square, a Hendrix-inspired beacon radiating love as he cradled his broken electric guitar. He was the one constant of Kenmore who would reliably kiss your newborn on the way to a Yankee's game, help you push your car out of a snowdrift, and greet you with one of his riddles.

A week later I attended the monthly Kenmore Association meeting. Sergeant James MacDonald spoke to the members.

"Good morning, I am Sergeant MacDonald of the Boston Police Department. I am here to tell you that the presence of vagrants and tramps in Kenmore Square is hurting your business."

He suggested that our members lock their dumpsters, ask customers to discard their returnable cans and bottles in bins located inside the stores to discourage those "dirty tramps" from redeeming them. Most importantly, he encouraged our members to photograph the vagrants, note the time and date that the photo was taken, and duly provide those photos and details to the police.

Paul closed the meeting by telling the members of the Association that, "the number one priority is getting rid of this eyesore we have here, which is the street people."

A few days later Andrea called me to her desk.

"Keith look at this," she said, pointing to the second page of the October 1986 issue of the Kenmore News. The typewritten newsletter of the Association mostly consisted of news from the Security and Maintenance Committee. I had attempted to participate in the committee's breakfast meeting but was turned away at the door because Kenmore's only upscale restaurant had a dress code and blue jeans and a t-shirt didn't meet the requirements. I followed Andrea's fingertip and started reading:

"The Security and Maintenance Committee encourages all KA Members to assume an active role in cleaning up Kenmore Square. In order to prevent the attraction of street people (especially the "rough element", new to Kenmore Square), the following guidelines were suggested at the breakfast meeting:

"Please don't give free food to these street people.

"Please lock all dumpsters. Unlocked dumpsters will be cited by the city inspectors and all infractions will be subject to fines. Open dumpsters attract street people looking for collectibles and food.

"Please refrain from throwing returnable cans and bottles in public trash receptacles. The street people find Kenmore Square a profitable location for collecting on these cans and bottles.

"Start calling the police if certain annoyances persist and keep a record of your calls (i.e., the date, time of day and response time)."

Andrea was outraged. They were writing about our friends, our family. Harold Madison Jr., better known as Mr. Butch, often joined Andrea and me for dinner on Fridays at our Kenmore apartment above Rondi's Clothing Boutique. I remember the night he sat before our little TV enjoying a chunk of potato casserole as he cheered on Reagan's bombing of Libya. Andrea would insist he soak his tired feet in our bathtub and after some ritual complaining he would roll up his jeans, sit on the side of the tub and sigh with pleasure at the warm water. He tried to ignore her advice about his fickle girlfriend and he was quick to share his latest tune. Our lives were entwined.

Andrea and I took a break from the urgent design projects dominating our day and sat down to write a response to the association.

"As members of the Kenmore Association we object to the dehumanizing statements against those living on our streets made by the Security & Maintenance Committee in the October newsletter. These people are our neighbors, friends, and family and they deserve our compassion and support.

"Dehumanizing people in this manor smacks of Hitler's Germany. The Kenmore Association is showing a total disregard for people being people. We urge the Association to support efforts to help our neighbors instead of adopting policing to drive them out of the community.

"There is no evidence that their presence is having any negative impact on business. We should celebrate the unique qualities of Kenmore Square that make it attractive instead of seeking to transform it into a second Newbury Street."

"Sincerely, Andrea and Keith McHenry - 24-hour residents of Kenmore Square"

I shared the letter with several friends asking for their opinion. A copy sitting on a friend's table caught the eye of the editor of The Brookline TAB, a local weekly paper. "Would you mind if I wrote about this controversy?" she asked.

A front-page story in the TAB started to give the issue life. We sent the final draft of the letter to the Association but it was the public debate set off by the article that had the real impact and ignited a struggle in the neighborhood.

Andrea and I wrote a petition to Boston Mayor Raymond Flynn calling for "better relations with the police, residents, and visitors of Kenmore Square and to develop community unity as a way to reduce violent crime."

I hustled through the square gathering signatures, climbing stairs, and riding elevators to seek support from local business people. The employees at Platform Studio and the doctor's office on the sixth floor of the building that housed my office were happy to sign. I popped into the Boston Language Institute and convinced my client, David Arinsberg, to sign.

I had an even greater response at the other buildings. I ventured into another Beacon Street building. The fourth-floor elevator opened to the acrid smell of embalming fluid. A young man whisked past in a bleached white lab coat. A chrome sign said I had arrived at the New England Institute of Anatomy, Sanitary Science, and Embalming. I had no idea such a school shared my Kenmore Square neighborhood. I caught the attention of a woman strolling past the elevator distracted by the pages of a thick lab manual. "Would you sign our petition?" I asked. The first man returned and joined us in conversation. They were interested in speaking with their classmates about the issue. "I love Rocker Ronny, Sassy Tammy, and Mr. Butch," the male student said, suggesting we hold a meeting in their fourth-floor break room.

A day later we were huddled around their white Formica table in the school lounge. Eight or nine students of mortician sciences, James Ryan, master chef of the popular Hoodoo Barbecue, a spattering of Boston University students and a few other locals all joined together to map out a campaign strategy. We knew one thing for sure, we wouldn't let the Association drive our friends from our vibrant community without a fight. We formed a group called, "The 24-hour residents of Kenmore Square," and launched a, "Welcome to Kenmore Square," campaign. By mid-October we had secured more than four hundred signatures on our petition and planned our first event.

The crisp October 14th evening was electric as swarms of fans flooded through Kenmore Square on their way to game six of the American League playoffs between the California Angels and the Red Sox. Our welcoming party commandeered the grassy strip between the east and west lanes of Commonwealth Avenue. A small grove of red leaf maples lined the border of our open-air venue. Mr. Butch helped me string a Food Not Bombs banner between two tree trunks. Andrea set out the twenty-four-quart pot of potato and lentil soup and disposable plates and paper hot-cups on our wobbly plywood table. James Ryan delivered barbecue. Sam, one of the mortician students, and Rocker Ronny unfurled our, "Welcome to Kenmore Square," canvas banner. One half of this four-foot sign included my drawing of the pigeons flapping in the Kenmore air before the iconic neon CITGO sign. Motorists honked in support as they crawled down Commonwealth past our contingent of well-wishers. Mr. Butch waved to his fans.

The Kenmore Association President and local funeral home owner, Bert Scott, stomped past us, angry about our interference with their grand effort to "clean up" what he called Boston's black eye of tramps, vagrants, and punks. After a few nasty words he scurried across the street and disappeared into Waterman's Funeral Home. It had become a pitched battle between embalming professionals.

Boston University journalism student, Zia Siddiqi, scribbled my perspective on the matter in his notebook:

"Kenmore Square is an exciting place," I said. "There is a vast diversity of people that come here and these people (street people) love the culture. They like talking to the Red Sox fans. They enjoy hanging out with the BU students. They like watching the Neon lights and cars of the people come here. This is where the culture comes from. These people contribute to our culture and traditions."

"All these people make up the Kenmore Square along with the businessmen and they are a part of us," I said, adding that Harvard Square and Copley Place were "Yuppified." I told Zia that I did not agree with the associations contention that the homeless people might be involved in the recent stickups. "We know the three guys who did all the armed robberies in the Kenmore. We can point them out but no one listens to us." He asked why we were ignored. "Because the issue is not to curb the violence of those people but to Yuppify the Kenmore Square."

I continued, "It is easier to sweep out the street people or the punk rockers, but it is much harder to deal with the people with guns."

Zia Siddiqi asked Mr. Butch what part of the day he spends at Kenmore.

"Six, seven, eight or nine...Kenmore Square rain or shine," he responded. "Reason that I come down here: lots of girls and I can drink beer."

Just as Steve Cadron had told me in July when he ordered designs celebrating the Red Sox American League victory and the World Series, the Mets would beat the Red Sox in the seventh game on October 27, 1986.

While we were organizing in opposition to the Kenmore Association's campaign against our friends, I was also immersed in the nuances of the two Italy travel brochures and making almost daily trips to General Travel.

"Come on back! Let's see what masterpiece you have brought me," Donna Franca called out one day from the back of her office.

I slid my "masterpieces" out of their envelopes and proudly placed them side by side. She read through each page.

“Wonderful, but I think we need to spice up the text a bit. Here for example, we can make our five dinners in Palermo come to life. How about ‘You will experience the traditional gastronomic explosion of Sicily’s world-renowned chefs. Magnificent! Never to be forgotten and offered by no other tours.’”

I reminded her that re-typesetting the copy would add to her costs. “No problem, Keith,” she said, “every word must be exquisite!”

Just then the silhouette of a short businessman darkened the agency door.

“Michael my dear, come join us,” she called out to what must have been a recognizable shape against the light.

As Donna Franca stood, she cocked her head towards me and softly whispered that our guest was the governor of Massachusetts, Michael Dukakis. “He’s a close friend of mine,” she added as he made his way past the empty glass desks.

“Michael, this is my new graphic designer, Keith McHenry. He is making me two beautiful brochures, really beautiful.” Describing me as her new graphic designer suggested that she wasn’t working with her past vendors but I didn’t pick up on that and ignored the red flag. I was so excited about the opportunity to produce such an impressive project; it was my biggest job yet.

Dukakis stepped over and reached out his hand, saying, “Great to meet you.” We shook hands. “Good to meet you too,” I replied.

Dukakis and Donna Franca talked about how wonderful the Boston Symphony season was and lamented the less than colorful fall foliage. The Governor would nod my way in that politician-wishing-to-give-you-the-impression-that-he’s-including-you kind of way.

After about thirty minutes of small talk Dukakis wished Donna Franca and myself a good day. Our conversation about the brochures had also concluded and I followed Mr. Dukakis out into the sunlight. His small frame climbed into the back of a shiny, double-parked black limousine with the Massachusetts license-plate: One. Yes, it really was the governor and Democratic Party presidential candidate.

They must have been good friends because Dukakis stopped in again two weeks later. At least such friendliness was my naive impression at the time.

I agreed with Donna Franca that these publications were masterpieces. It was very difficult in those days to curve type around a photo, in this case a lifted picture of Michelangelo’s marble David. And even though I knew none of her tours stopped in Florence the image was great and I didn’t think her prospective customers would fixate on such a detail.

Then the big day came when I would present Donna Franca with the two completed brochures. The thirty-day design sprint was about to cross the finish line.

The manicured tip of her index finger traced each line of text. A "very good" and "fantastic" punctuated her pleasure of her own writing. I glowed inside even as I worried that she would send me back to the drafting table.

"Keith, this is very good. Perfect," she said with a huge smile and familiar wave of her arm.

I presented her with the final bill.

"As I told you the bill is much higher than the original estimate," I said, "because you asked to re-typeset so much of the text. I am happy to let you pay the extra cost in installments if you need to."

"Let's talk about this after the printer takes a look at your work. Send it to him first thing in the morning and then we will talk," she replied.

The next morning, Andrea placed the oversized manila envelope of artwork promising those wonderful Italian tours in the cab driver's hand. I took off to General Travel, swung open the ceiling tall front door, and skipped past the still unstaffed desks.

She seemed happy to see me, waving her arms about as she called out in her exuberant Italian accent, "Keith, my dear, the printer says the job is perfect, just perfect. Thank you so much!"

"I am so pleased. It's been wonderful working on it with you," I said, and meant it.

We chatted a little more and then I asked for the check.

"Oh no, Keith, I will not pay you more. The price is just too high."

"But Donna Franca, you knew the contract said you were paying half up front and the second half would be due when the job was finished."

That happy endearing expression I had come to expect changed. She glared with a special cruelty that she must have been accustomed to. "Keith, Keith, I am sorry but I won't pay you another cent for the brochures. How about designing me a poster? Maybe you will do better with a poster."

Those words "maybe I will do better with a poster" mixed with the nausea of doom would be scorched into my memory for life.

"Please, Donna Franca, I am too small a business to eat so much money. I have employees and subcontractors to take care of. You must pay me today."

"Too bad Keith, I won't pay you another cent."

I stood up slowly, in disbelief, my mind racing, consumed in dizzying terror. My legs hung rubbery, disembodied from my stunned body. I had never lost that much money on one job.

I called my lawyer first thing the next morning but he couldn't see me for another day. A laser focus that I am now familiar with propelled me into action.

The first thing I thought of was that I needed to have some leverage over Donna Franca. A way to bargain with her.

I called the printer at 8:00 the next morning.

"Oh, as you probably can expect from Donna Franca, she has some more changes. Please send the mechanicals over to my office on Beacon Street and I will have them back this afternoon." At least I hoped this would be the case.

A cabbie soon arrived with the originals. Andrea and I hid half of the boards above the ceiling panels in our office, slid several under the photostat camera and took the others to our apartment.

A furious Donna Franca called me around two o'clock that afternoon. The printer told her that I had retrieved the artwork. His four-color press sat idle. Pallets of glossy paper filled his shop waiting to pass the inked rollers.

"You must return the art to the printer immediately. You don't know who you are messing with young man!" she yelled at me in the way I had witnessed with her screaming into the phone at unsatisfied tourists.

I replied that I would be happy to return them as soon as her second ten-thousand-dollar check cleared. I told her I would trust she would come through with the additional fees soon after the printing was completed to her satisfaction.

That evening Andrea and I crossed Kenmore to our apartment. The sheriff had taped a summons to appear in superior court the next morning on our apartment door. This must have happened soon after Donna Franca's angry phone call.

This is how I remember my visit to my attorney.

"We can work this out I know," he assured me as he dialed Donna Franca's lawyer. My attorney let her lawyer know that he was putting us on speaker phone.

"So, you are saying you represent Mr. McHenry, do you?"

My lawyer responded in the affirmative.

Donna Franca's attorney said, "Well sir, if I were you, I wouldn't represent him. Not if you value your life," adding a few more details to make sure his message was clear before Donna Franca's council ended the conversation banging down his receiver with a loud crash. My attorney got the message.

"Sorry Keith, I can't represent you. I am so sorry," he said, looking shyly at his desk in an effort to avoid eye contact with me. And that was that.

That evening Donna Franca's, "Terry the Nun," as the slight frail woman had been referred when she drifted pass our meetings at General Travel, shuffled into my studio around seven.

"We are praying for you Mr. McHenry," she said in a sorrowful Italian accent. "You need to return Donna Franca's artwork. If you do not give it to me right now two men will be coming over here to kill you. Please sir, give it to me and spare your life," she pleaded with an exaggerated air of compassion.

I asked her to pass on a message to Donna Franca, "I will be happy to give her the artwork as soon as I get paid."

I rushed up to the sixth floor, darting into the offices of my friends at Platform Studio and breathlessly explaining my dilemma. Two guys were coming to kill me and I needed their help.

Jeff said he knew of a nearby construction site with stacks of rebar and volunteered to get five or six bars. My typesetter friend Bruce stepped into a closet behind his Edit-writer 550 to retrieve his signed Red Sox baseball bat.

My office had a long hallway down the center with three rooms on each side. I sublet one of the window-side offices to a small company struggling to develop what we now know as Artificial Intelligence. The frantic commotion in the rest of the elegant wood-paneled office didn't seem to interfere with their work repeating "Hello" for hours. My allies stationed themselves in each doorway ready to bash the gunmen into a crumpled mess.

I darkened most of the lights and I sat as bait at the back of my office, a large wood-paneled room of oak drafting tables strategically positioned between me and my murderers. For a brief moment I worried that my self-confidence may have been misplaced. But this was not the time to exchange it for self-doubt.

I rolled my chair away from the bay windows so they wouldn't be able to shoot me from Raleigh Street, positioning myself in a location where the killers would have to pass my army of friends. A sweaty smell of fear clung to the stale office air.

Time seemed to move brutally slow, minutes folding into more tense minutes. I assumed each thud of a footstep or creaking of a door was announcing the arrival of my two murderers.

I nervously imagined that moment when the two men I had never seen would swagger towards me with their pistols drawn. For some unrealistically hopeful reason I kept ending my movie with the thought that they might give me one last chance before pulling the trigger. But really how realistic was that scenario? I also imagined my friends being brave enough to smash these guys over the head before they could unload on me. What I didn't consider was what would happen next once the killers were downed?

It seemed like we had been coiled and prepared for our brutality for at least two hours but my assassins failed to arrive. I thanked everyone and joked that the Mafia was too chicken to face the likes of us.

Having survived the threat of death I now had to face the legal system. The subpoena Andrea found stuck to our apartment door ordering me to appear in court at 9:00 am the next morning.

The bailiff called out, "All rise!"

The judge swooshed in to the Superior Court with his black robe flapping behind him. He seemed unsurprised by his friend's appearance. "Donna Franca! What a wonderful party you had last night," he called out. "The food was fantastic, just magnificent."

He pranced over to his Donna Franca, gave her an enthusiastic hug, wrapping her in his back drapery, and followed up with the kiss, kiss, kiss to one another's checks before gliding back to his throne.

He flipped through a few papers. "I see here that you took Donna Franca's artwork. I am ordering you to return it by noon today. We will discuss the rest of the issue in two weeks. So ruled," he bellowed as he slammed his gavel hard to the desk, stood up and disappeared to his chambers.

A fair hearing seemed out of reach with this court. I went to a payphone outside the courtroom, dialed my office and directed Andrea to retrieve all the mechanicals, slice them up with X-Acto knives, stuff the mess into a garbage bag and make sure the mutilated artwork was cabbed to the printer by noon.

Andrea and I returned to our office the next day. The door was jimmied open. Someone had broken in and walked off with many of our files. But that wasn't the worst problem.

Danna Franca's assistant Veronica stopped in to Brushfire Graphic on the afternoon of the court hearing.

"Keith, I am going to leave Donna Franca tonight but I must tell you some things," she said. "First, I will never see you again and I am sorry for that. I really like you and your wife. Donna Franca wiretaps the phones of those she does business with and one of my jobs was to transcribe some of the tapes. She is recording your phone conversations."

She went on to explain that General Travel isn't what we may have thought. "You heard her arguing with clients on the phone. That is because they are angry that they couldn't leave their hotel rooms in Palermo. You may have also read news of the mafia trials in Italy? There is a war going on in Palermo: bombings, gun battles, and murders. It's no place to enjoy a vacation."

"Let me tell you what she is doing," she went on to explain Donna Franca's business plan. She chartered jets and filled the seats with elderly midwestern passengers. She loaded the luggage compartment with drugs, guns, and money followed by the tourist luggage. The same was true on the return flight.

"Donna Franca can't even go to Italy herself, because she is wanted by the mafia courts." Veronica also had shared that my prosecuting attorney was also Donna Franca's lover. "You see, this is serious. You must be very careful. This is why I will disappear tonight. I know too much," she said, ending her startling news by giving Andrea and I a big hug as tears welled up in her eyes. Her news added fuel to our adrenaline-driven days.

I netted a criminal case for destroying the boards and I was forced to appear in a bleak windowless Boston Municipal courtroom a couple of mornings after Veronica's visit. The prosecuting attorney stood next to me as we waited for the judge. A dying florescent light flickered ominously above.

The assistant district attorney leaned towards me to share a little secret. "Well, Keith," he said, "I want to remind you that there is no death penalty in Massachusetts so if you are convicted, I can have you taken care of in exchange for some favors in the joint. They have nothing to lose. If you don't go to prison, I know people that really don't want to do time and if I help them out, they will help me out so either way you're finished."

His comments sounded comical, like he was a bad actor in a low-budget gangster movie. I don't remember what the judge said or if he set an arraignment or what. I do remember telling the assistant district attorney that he couldn't intimidate me and that he should tell Donna Franca to pay her bills.

When I returned to my office, I got a call from Lynne Covello the advertising director for hairstylist John Dellaria's salon empire. She had inspired me to do some of my most creative designs. Together we worked on display ads for the top fashion magazines of the time, Vogue, Elle, and Mademoiselle often featuring unique design techniques I invented for each assignment. Soon competitors would lift those techniques and we would see them in other advertisements in the following issues. Lynne inspired me to keep one step ahead of them all. We were a great team.

"I am ending our professional relationship, Keith," she said. "Please come over with the photos I gave you."

I found the photos, black-and-white glossies that burglars had failed to snag, and went to her office. I stood at her desk and she started to scold me in code that only she and I understood, her connection to Donna Franca. I knew she shared a luxury apartment with my sports client Steve Cadron, but it wasn't until I was being fired that I realized that Donna Franca was also a member of her circle. Her boss John Dellaria heard her tirade and stepped into her office.

"What are you doing Lynne? You can't fire Keith," he said. "He's won us several Clio Awards. You should keep your personal business out of this. You are not going to fire Keith and that's an order." I was stunned by John's admission. I guess clients generally don't want their designers to know about winning the prestigious award for fear of an increase in fees. The Clio is awarded to the advertiser and not the company who produces the advertisements. Anyway, I had no idea that the display ads I had designed for Lynne had won advertising's top award.

I remember spending most of Thanksgiving weekend alone in my studio pasting up display ads for Filene's Basement Christmas sales before popping into my sister-in-law's apartment in Brookline for a brief moment during their holiday dinner. Why was I trading time with my family and friends in exchange for meeting yet another deadline?

It was early December, the season of compassion. Time for those Red Salvation Army buckets to dangle from their iron tripods next to bell-ringing part-timers. Holiday tunes drifted across the icy sidewalks from shops eager to sell you that perfect gift. The struggle between the Kenmore Association and the people of the streets and their defenders made for interesting Christmas season copy.

The Boston Phoenix weekly entertainment paper and WGBH radio wanted the story about the angst in Kenmore and arranged an interview with me.

The Phoenix reporter called me one chilly December morning.

"Are we still on for the interview?" he asked.

"Yes, please come to my apartment at ten," I said and repeated my address.

Then he added, "I had a message on my answering machine this morning from someone claiming they were going to kill you. Do you know what that is about?"

I told him it was nothing and not to worry about it. Then I got a second call from the reporter at WGBH.

"Are we on for our noon interview?"

I assured her that we were still on. Then she asked: "I had a strange message on my answering machine this morning. The caller claimed that you were going to be killed. What's that about?"

Again, I assured the reporter that it was nothing.

As I was hanging up the phone, I could see ten or more Boston Police officers rushing up the stairs of our office building. More patrol cars were screeching to a halt in from of 636 Beacon Street, their armed occupants leaping towards the entrance. Our going away office party the night before must have gotten out of control after we left.

"Andrea, it's time to go. Those cops will be over here soon enough."

Our new Nissan pickup-truck was parked behind our apartment. We had packed it with another load of drafting tables and other items we planned to move to Andrea's sister's but there was no time for that now.

Andrea grabbed our cat and I took two suitcases of clothing and somehow in the panic was able to hook a leash into the collar of our Afghan hound, Bear. We scrambled down the back stairs shoved the last of or things into the pickup and left.

Andrea and I agreed to take the back roads south and concluded we shouldn't call or write anyone we knew, not even anyone in our family, not anyone. With a little over twelve thousand dollars in cash that we had slowly been withdrawing from our account so as to not cause any suspicion, a cat, a dog, two oak drafting tables we had intended to store and some clothing we disappeared into the streets of America on that blistery December 16, 1986.

PART THREE: LUNCH CRIMES

Andrea and her friend Linda over looking the bay in San Francisco, California

Chapter 21

THE SAN FRANCISCO TREAT

Andrea and I spent months snaking across the United States. We spent a few days seeking warmth in an elegant, heated, well-lit restroom in Kincaid Lake State Park in Kentucky, and then headed south to Corpus Christ and skirted the border until we arrived in California in late March 1987. As we were scooting north past Palo Alto along Interstate 280, I suggested we settle in San Francisco before we depleted what was left of our cash.

With luck, we found an old friend of Andrea's who hooked us up with a one-bedroom in the Richmond district and our new life began. I found the most common name in the white pages phone book, Dick Lee, and used it to hook up our phone and utilities. I took a job at Bob's Typing and Thumbtack Bugle and Andrea scored employment as a secretary.

My boss Bob was busy smoking pot and telling me about how I was going to make him so much money that he would finally be able to buy his dream Jaguar sports car. This distracted him from asking about such details as my long abandoned social security number or proof of my identity. To him I was just Keith McHenry, a graphic designer from back east who knew how to use the newly emerging personal computer. He had two such word processors and set me up at the one closest to the tiny office door.

My dreary days consisted of typing resumes for people seeking uninspiring jobs of toil. The cold fog floated outside the chilly Geary Boulevard office when a professionally attired woman in a grey, tailored suit who looked to be in her thirties stepped into our chilly second floor room. "I need my resume updated and a cover letter to go with it. Is this something you can do for me?" she asked with a warm smile. "Of course, that is what we do here at Bob's Typing."

She asked to have her Peace Corp entry removed from her CV and handed me a hand written letter to type addressed to the director of KCBS radio.

I still remember the address on her resume and correspondence, 333 Parker Street, San Francisco.

Her current job was Director of Military Intelligence for the Pacific Rim. Her education included a graduate degree in "information extraction" from Fort Ord and an undergraduate degree in "information extraction" from Fort Huachuca. Her letter requested a position as a field reporter at KCBS. It wouldn't dawn on me until decades later that she must have had her own computer and an assistant who could have met her requirements. Not surprisingly she landed the position. She would be interviewing me a year later at the entrance to Golden Gate Park and I would be addressing her KCBS microphone outside City Hall minutes before I would be arrested in a Santa Claus suit.

Andrea and I sat down for dinner on September 2, 1987, and flipped on the TV news. A munitions train had struck Vietnam veteran Brian Wilson the day before as he and several other protestors were sitting on the tracks outside the Concord Naval Weapons Station in northern Contra Costa County. The train severed both of his legs beneath the knee and severely fractured his skull. He and a small group of activists had spent the summer at the tracks in a campaign they called the Nuremberg Action in protest against weapons shipments to Central America.

I had met Brian and his fellow Veterans for Peace activist and track sitter, Duncan Murphy at the Fast for Peace action at the Boston Commons in the early days of Food Not Bombs.

Two days later Andrea and I joined a protest of nearly ten thousand people at the site. As the demonstration was ending people started to tear up the rails.

Later that day we tuned into the evening news to see how the media covered the rally. Andrea and I were in the foreground of the segment showing the people in bandanas prying up the tracks. It almost looked as though we were supervising the direct action.

"Well, I guess we aren't so underground anymore," I quipped to Andrea as we stood in our tiny living room on 4th Avenue. Andrea suggested that since our cover was blown, I might be happier if I started doing Food Not Bombs again.

I took Andrea's advice, quit my job with Bob's Typing and took an early morning job trimming produce at Inner Sunset Community Food Store and Other Avenues Grocery out by Ocean Beach so I would have time to organize a local Food

Not Bombs group. I started to recover day-old bagels from Sid's House of Bagels and produce from Thom's Natural Groceries on Geary. I began delivering my daily load to Saint Anthony's Soup Kitchen and Glide Memorial Church in the Tenderloin.

Once I had started to build a food collection schedule it was time to experiment with serving locations choosing to start with United Nations Plaza one windy lunch. I brought a Colman Stove given to me by Andrea's father so I could keep my stew warm. It was missing a knob and required a pair of pliers to operate. The pliers were stolen by the fifth cup of vegetable and rice goulash. An amped-up guy without a shirt who identified himself as Jesus Christ Satan hopped around me describing his dream of installing Oriental rugs and grills all around the plaza to add some culture to the City by the Bay. Two young guys new to the city stopped to talk with me. John and Darrick had just arrived from the east coast wishing to taste the hippy energy that they had studied about at the University of Maryland. I convinced them to help me start the new chapter of Food Not Bombs and we agreed to hold a planning meeting at a Chinese restaurant on Haight Street. By the end of that first meeting we had decided to start sharing meals at the entrance to Golden Gate Park at Haight and Stanyan every Monday at noon. A free meal was provided to those in the area every day, but the foot traffic that would pass by our information on our literature table on Mondays would allow us to reach tourists and locals alike, much like we had been doing in Harvard Square.

Then one misty morning as I was struggling to set out bunches of Russian Kale at Other Avenues my side started to ache. I told my co-worker that I needed to a take break and I curled up on the carpet in a back room. I never returned to the produce coolers that morning and had to force myself to drive home. That next morning Andrea handed me the phone saying it was my doctor. She had called him worried. "I will meet you at the emergency room in ten minutes. You could die," Doctor Shuller bluntly announced and hung up.

When I arrived at the hospital, a group of striking nurses was still walking slowly in line past the entrance to Saint Mary's. I had been delivering bagels and fruit to the union strike for two weeks and had become friends with the nurses on the picket line. As I staggered, blind with pain, towards the door, I yelled over to the three striking women I had delivered breakfast to the day before. "I'm sorry Janice I wouldn't normally cross a picket line but I am very ill."

Janice called back: "That's ok Keith, we understand." Another nurse added: "We hope you will be alright!" I heard their kind words and staggered through the wide sliding doors. Doctor Shuller met me at the massive stainless-steel door to the emergency room and guided me on to the gurney he had positioned at the entrance. He then wheeled me through the empty corridor to the operating room.

The operating theater had a hollow sound to it since Doctor Shuller and the anesthesiologist were the only people in attendance. A beep-beep-beep sound and the "five, four, three, two..." of the anesthesiologist echoed steely under the flood lights.

I survived the surgery and started my hectic recovery in a hospital bed overlooking Golden Gate Park. The frantic flood of calls started while my head was still pounding from the dissipating anesthesia. A bread pickup in the Sunset District resulted in the arrest of our driver John and a long night in jail: police charged him with driving a truck registered in California with a Maryland driver's license. His friend Derrick walked from the Taraval Street Police Station to Police Headquarters in South of Market seeking to win his release.

My first post-op meal finally arrived: a cube of fluorescent green Jell-O vibrating in the center of a plastic saucer. This offering was set on a placemat printed with an image of Christ on the cross. The lance thrust into his rib cage and crimson blood dripping from the wound presented a dramatic contrast to the hyper-green Jell-O.

Haight Ashbury activists Jim Rhoads and Calvin Welch warned that John's arrest was a sign of things to come. Jim and Calvin had invited me to provide lunch with a small group of rainbow-attired Dead Heads and bus dwellers at an emergency rally on the steps of City Hall. Country Joe McDonald sang to the gathering. A police campaign of ticketing, towing, and arresting people who lived in their buses along Lincoln, Folsom, and the panhandle was heating up. The local media stoked anger at the new mayor, Art Agnos, and the transients with an account of a man urinating on a tree near his bus. Something had to be done.

This conflict was shaping up to be a David versus Goliath battle between the local real-estate companies and property owners on one side and the Vehicular Residence Association, The Haight Ashbury Neighborhood Association (or HANC), and its members on the other. I had no idea of the political minefield before us. After all, we thought that San Francisco was America's most liberal city.

A month before my appendix ruptured my little crew made our weekly trip to Haight and Stanyan to share our feast. Birds flittered about in the scraggly pine and poplar branches surrounding Alvard Lake. A content circle of colorfully dressed pipe-passing Jerry's kids lounged on the warm grass. The morning's last fog evaporated over a grove of wind-swept cypress. Derrick scooted a sixty-quart pot of rice and beans into position. Jefferson Airplane softly played on a clunky boombox at the end of the food table. All was at peace.

An older hippy type, typical of those who wandered the Haight in those days, approached me as I placed the final stack of flyers on our literature table. "Did you know you can get a permit to feed the homeless? Just send a letter to Peter Ashe at the Parks and Recreation Office," the stranger said with confidence.

The suggestion seemed innocent enough. I mailed a letter requesting a street performer's permit for our weekly meal dated July, 11, 1988. I suggested that the city would be pleased to have us sharing food and ideas every week at the entrance to Golden Gate Park. I wrote that we had obtained such a permit in Cambridge, Massachusetts.

A week passed. The Grateful Dead would perform at the Oakland Colosseum again that evening. "Did you get your permit yet?" asked one of the two police officers that happened to stroll past the table once the line had thinned.

"We sent in our request. We should have it soon," I replied confidently.

Each week an officer would casually ask about our permit which I started to find curious but not of much importance. So, after one of the Monday meals, I walked over to the Parks and Recreation office to ask about the permit. The secretary didn't know anything. A commissioner who happened to walk through the lobby also had no information. I could leave a message for Mary Burns, they said. Then my appendix ruptured.

I emerged from Saint Mary's Hospital at 11:30 Monday morning, August 15, 1988, after a week spent recovering on the fifth-floor ward. Andrea brought my camera just in case there was something to photograph. Keeping my hands occupied was her way of making sure I wouldn't get in trouble. We drifted the two blocks shrouded in an August mist not sure of what to expect. The fog, a week on opioids and a nervous uncertainty of what I would encounter at the meal was surreal.

Andrea and I joined Jim, Calvin, and the Height Street attorney Sarge Holtzman at the entrance to Golden Gate Park. John and Derek pulled up in my truck. A group of Haight Ashbury residents helped unload the tables, signs and food. I snapped a photo or two. A line of guests formed parallel to Stanyan Street as had been the case every week since we had started in early April. A few people joined John and Derek behind the table with serving spoons and ladles at the ready.

Police captain Richard Holder strutted up next to our literature table. He announced over a bull horn that we were breaking the law and subject to arrest. A line of riot police marched up a path from the south, each tightly gripping a hard black billy club in their thick leather gloves. Another line of officers marched in from behind us. A patrol car and police van crept slowly up the asphalt path emerging from the Lincoln Street underpass. I snapped another picture and passed my camera to Andrea.

A few sharp jabs of the club pushed the waiting line of diners away from the meal we had brought them. The military-style operation separated the food from the families, Dead Heads, and travelers.

A motorcycle cop grabbed my left arm. "You are under arrest," he said in a hushed voice. I don't remember being shocked, but I may have been.

Andrea ran next to us demanding he be careful as all three of us arrived at the door of a police van. She yelled, "He just got out of the hospital!"

The officer lifted up my shirt. "Oh shit," he blurted, seeing I had a thick layer of slightly blood-stained gauze wrapped around my belly. Perhaps I wouldn't be getting that planned beating after all.

It wasn't long before four more volunteers were cuffed and pushed into the police wagon. Two women were stuffed into the front compartment. John and Derek joined us, metal handcuffs also tightened to their thin wrists.

We could hear people outside yelling, "Shame! Shame!" and, "Fuck you, Nazis!" in tones of profound anger. I believed this could have been the first time anyone had been arrested for sharing meals with the hungry. I knew it was a first for everyone gathered at Haight and Stanyan on that cloudy day. I couldn't have imagined such a thing was possible.

The police crammed nine of us into the van and as soon as the police shut the door we started chanting, "Food Not Bombs, Food Not Bombs," as we moved back and forth in unison shaking the vehicle for all outside to see. It wasn't long before many of the people at the scene joined us in the chant. After about fifteen minutes of chanting, we started singing, "We shall overcome." The people who had come to eat or to show support had been driven out to Stanyan Street or down towards Alvard Lake by club-jabbing riot police.

A local activist and photographer, Greg Gaar, was busy taking photos. He had spent his entire life in the Haight and knew there could be an opportunity to capture another snippet of history.

Deetje Boler was taping the event on a cassette recorder. I would hear the audio later that week. "Let's go across the street and loot Cal Foods. We will show those bastards," shouted an angry diner. But they didn't.

I was too excited to be tired. That noon foggy apprehension I had felt vanished in the euphoria. The other eight also showed no signs of being dismayed by our fourteen-hour visit to booking. An older man, John, his greying stringy head of hair coiling from beneath a knit rainbow-colored cap animatedly suggested we had made history, "This is the modern-day Salt March of Gandhi's campaign." Yes, there was something that felt important about our incarceration. We weren't sure what that was. It was just a feeling and when we were finally freed into the chilly night it was hugs all around and a commitment to return to the scene of the "crime" again on Monday.

Jim called me Tuesday morning. "I hope it's not too early. Did you see today's Chronicle?"

I hadn't so I walked down to Green Apple Books to get a copy.

A black-and-white photo was spread across all five columns of page three of the San Francisco Chronicle above the headline: "Volunteers Arrested at S.F. Food Giveaway."

Three San Francisco riot police with their plastic visors up stood guard in front of the tables of food and literature. A sign, with the text, "Food Not Bombs," and the carrot and fist logo, was visible between the legs of two officers. Commander Richard Holder stood to the side with a bull horn. The food was surrounded by other police officers. It looked bad. In fact, it looked really bad for the police and even worse for the city's new liberal mayor, Art Agnos.

News of the arrests shocked people. Phone calls poured in with offers to help. "Hello, Jim gave me your number. My wife and I are so angry about this. Are you making any plans to respond?"

Witnesses to the arrests mobilized. A meeting was organized. We agreed to assemble at Haight and Central before noon the following Monday. We would have a short rally and then march to Stanyan. David Solnit volunteered to make a flyer using the photo from the Chronicle. Other supporters volunteered to staple copies to wooden electricity poles, tape copies to store windows and hand them out to anyone who seemed likely to participate.

Monday arrived. HANC members sat on the grass on the Haight side of Buena Vista Park. Boxes of bread, bagels, and produce were lined up along the sidewalk. There were cases of melons stacked three boxes high, all recovered that morning from Veritable Vegetables. Five-gallon buckets of rice, beans, vegetable stew, and salad were stationed nearby. A crowd swirled at the corner. Some held signs. Others had arrived with pots and spoons to bang on while we made our way to Golden Gate Park. We brought together about one hundred people in all.

Jim Rhodes gave a speech on behalf of HANC. I spoke about the growing numbers of people made homeless by eight years of the Reagan administration. Max Ventura ended the short rally with what would become the Food Not Bombs theme song:

In sixteen forty-nine to Saint George's Hill
A ragged band they called the Diggers came to show the people's will
They defied the landlords, they defied the law
They were the dispossessed, reclaiming what was theirs

"We come in peace," they said, "to dig and sow
We come to work the land in common and to make the waste ground grow
This earth divided we will make whole
So it can be a common treasury for all

The sin of property we do disdain
No man has any right to buy and sell the earth for private gain
By theft and murder they steal the land
Now everywhere the walls rise up at their command

They make the laws to chain us well
The clergy dazzle us with heaven or they damn us into hell
We will not worship the god they serve
Their god of greed who feeds the rich while poor folk starve

We work, we eat together, we need no swords

We will not bow to the masters or pay rent to the lords
Still, we are free men though we are poor
You Diggers all, stand up for glory, stand up now

From the men of property, the order came
They sent the hired men and troopers to wipe out the Diggers' claim
Tear down their cottages, destroy their corn
They were dispersed, but still the vision carries on

You poor, take courage, you rich, take care
This earth was made a common treasury for everyone to share
All things in common, all people one
We come in peace. The order came to cut them down.

Supporters yelped their approval. It was our philosophy set to music. A Food Not Bombs sign led the crowd out into Haight Street. A protester rested a painting of Star Trek's Doctor Spock on a box of melons and stepped onto the street to lead the parade.

The tin banging of serving spoons against metal pots marked the pace. Some balanced cardboard boxes of produce on their heads. Two tables, both heavy six-foot-long fiberboard creations, joined the procession. Two people shared the task of transporting each bucket of food. All were chanting, "Food Not Bombs! Food Not Bombs!" Some spectators cheered us on, others were mystified by the procession, others waved from second-story windows.

Several of San Francisco's finest maneuvered their motorcycles behind the march. One officer repeatedly ordered everyone to get out of the street, threatening to make arrests. We ignored him.

The parade crossed Stanyan Street. We set up the tables and got ready to serve lunch, setting out paper plates and plastic ware. Those waiting to eat lined up. Three columns of riot police marched towards the food, their thick black-gloved hands tightly gripping their clubs. A squad of motorcycle patrolman dismounted.

The police surrounded the food servers and swept our literature from a table. One by one, they arrested the volunteers. Officers pushed plates of beans and rice out of the hands of the hungry. Our chant of, "Food Not Bombs," morphed into, "Food Not Cops!" Soon it changed again: "Arrest hunger not free food!"

Before long everyone started singing: "We are Food Not Bombs. We are going to change this world." When the police action started Andrea and I escaped down Waller Street. We crossed Cole. A motorcycle cop skidded up to a guy on Haight Street dismounted and bashed the young man to the sidewalk and kicked him in the ribs. Andrea and I rushed down Waller and disappeared into Buena Vista Park.

The next morning, I woke to a now familiar flood of phone calls. Most were calling to find out if Andrea and I were safe, but also to comment on the coverage in the Examiner and the Chronicle.

The arrests it turned out made world news. The New York Times August 30, 1988 story, "29 Trying to Feed Homeless Are Arrested in San Francisco," ended with the sentence: "Those arrested went peacefully." The story was also reported in The Times in London and The Times of India and aired on the then new TV network, CNN.

Andrea and I had rented a mailbox and answering service at Mail Boxes Etc. on Polk Street for ten dollars a month when we first moved to San Francisco and were living in the back our truck. I stopped in after the Monday arrests. The owner was stressed. "Mr. McHenry, you are getting too many calls," he said. "I don't know what you are doing but I had to hire two more employees to answer your line. I know the contract says unlimited calls but I am losing so much money just responding to your line. It would be kind of you to find some other way. Maybe one of those new answering machines?"

I agreed to pay him more and find another solution if he kept me on for another month or two. He was thankful.

The calls and letters were responding to news of the crackdown. People wanted to start their own Food Not Bombs groups in defiance.

Thankfully, I had been taking notes on the steps we were taking to start the San Francisco chapter and turned them into a flyer, "Seven Steps to Starting a Local Food Not Bombs Group," to mail in response.

Activists from all across the Bay Area were becoming even more angry at the City's assault on our act of compassion and met again to plan another march down Haight Street on the following Monday.

People gathered at Central Street. There were more speeches. Max sang the Diggers Song again. People hoisted crates of corn, melons, and peppers to their chests or balanced them on their heads and stepped out on to the street. Assorted, colorful, hand-drawn signs denouncing the arrests or celebrating the spirit of resistance sprinkled among the flotilla of lunch-transporting defiers. A case of apples also joined the procession along with boxes of bagels and buckets of soup and rice and beans.

The marching band of pots and spoons swept us towards the park. The chants of, "Food Not Bombs, Food Not Bombs," echoed off the Victorians of the Haight. Several people clutching carrots were among those who marched defiantly towards Stanyan Street.

People hurriedly spread out blue tarps on the Golden Gate Park lawn. The police stood in rows with their visors up and clubs at the ready. Reporters from local television stations maneuvered into position with their cameras and microphone-wielding anchors. The San Francisco Independent, the Chronicle, and the

Examiner all sent their seasoned journalists. Riot police yanked volunteers from the tarps as they attempted to share plates of rice and beans. One activist tried to pass out melons only to have their wrists cuffed with a hard plastic tie. The hungry darted to servers to grasp a plate of lunch or grab a bagel.

This was news.

But now the media was also getting fed the message from City Hall and business leaders. The more established reporters gathered around the police spokesperson, holding out their microphones for the official word. Our side of the story would begin fading from the local news.

"There has to be some kind of police action. At this point it seems to be a political statement on their part, not a food give-away issue," explained San Francisco Police Public Relations Officer Jerry Senkir.

Officer Senkir added that the city would provide buses to take the hungry out to the armory at the beach while also implying that there is a universal understanding that sharing food in a public location was wrong. He concluded that Food Not Bombs was "making a political statement and that wasn't allowed."

The following Monday was Labor Day. Hundreds of people gathered at Central and Haight Streets. The holiday parade was much larger than the past Mondays and the spoons and pots rang out even louder than before. A sea of signs and banners, cases of fruit and vegetables, bags of bagels and bread, and five-gallon buckets of rice and beans surged onto Haight Street to the chant of, "Food Not Bombs! Food Not Bombs!"

The police were helpless to stop the larger procession. They abandoned their meek attempt at Ashbury Street and it wasn't long before the first of marchers crossed through the grassy entrance to Golden Gate Park.

Blue tarps were quickly spread out across the lawn. Melons, many sliced for easy enjoyment, carrots, and bagels lined the edge. Young people, most in their twenties, nestled buckets of rice and beans and salad on the tarp before them. Others positioned themselves with paper plates of fruit or slices of bread.

"Melon anyone?" called out one of the kneeling women risking arrest.

It was a joyous feeding frenzy.

Rainbow-clad travelers and aging flower children rushed to secure their lunch. A smiling mother and her giggly daughters scurried to the tarp just in time to get plates of rice and beans and a fist-full of onion bagels.

Then it happened. The riot police, armed with their ubiquitous clubs, advanced on the servers and pulled them from the tarps. They twisted the arms offering melons and bagels behind their backs, pulling thick plastic cuff ties tight around each wrist. Not everyone walked to the waiting police vans. The police dragged those who refused to cooperate with the brutal arm of the law across the grass and gravel towards the line of paddy wagons parked along Waller.

Two, and sometimes three, police officers propped each criminal food distributor into position. An official police photographer snapped a polaroid mugshot. Then each detainee was whisked away to a black-and-white wagon. One by one, the food servers were cuffed, photographed, and stuffed into vans. Fifty-three times. Van after van lurched out of the park towards police headquarters.

KPIX-TV camera person, Hank Schoepp, captured the mass arrest. Young idealists offering food to their community as bulky members of the tactical squad plucked the meal-sharing "criminals" from the feast. This was apparently a problem of optics so the officer in charge, Commander Richard Holder, calmly stepped up behind Mr. Schoepp and with the force of both hands shoved the cameraman to the dirt. The original version of Steve Talbot's documentary, "The Art of Being Mayor," showed stunning video of Holder walking up behind the cameraman and giving him an energetic shove to the sod. I spoke with Hank Schoepp several years later. Commander Holder's assault injured his back, which would require surgery, and changed the course of his life. He lamented that his grumpy disposition from the chronic pain and financial difficulties of his medical challenges added to the stress in his marriage. "I survived several wars and riots and now after Holder pushed me to the ground, I'm only able to film clips for the weather segment," he told me.

And once again the media crowded around the police spokesperson Senkir.

"It's illegal to give away food in the park to more than twenty-five people without a permit," the Sargent claimed. "This outfit has never applied for a permit," wrote Chris Chrystal quoting Senkir in his September 5, 1988, report for United Press International.

But there was that letter to the San Francisco Parks official Peter Ashe dated July 11, 1988, that said: "We would be interested in a permit to provide free meals and information at the corner of Haight and Stanyan Streets in the park."

God, Jim and Keith drape banner from the mayor's balcony 1989

The San Francisco Police arrest 24 volunteers on August 22, 1988

Chapter 22

DON'T GET TOO COMFORTABLE IN THAT CHAIR

Police spokesperson Sargent Jerry Senkir was standing at the entrance to Golden Gate Park, trying to justify the 1988 Labor Day arrests of Food Not Bombs volunteers to the media. Riot police were dragging melon-sharing youth through the grass and gravel in the background as he explained: "It's illegal to give away food in the park to more than twenty-five people without a permit. This outfit has never applied for a permit."

The police made fifty-four more arrests of people sharing food with the hungry. Would we be able to sustain those numbers week in and week out? None of us were sure.

I was a bit naive at the time, but I thought that if we could talk directly with Mayor Agnos, he would agree to end the arrests to avoid any further embarrassments to the city. A short conversation was all we required of the former social worker. The mayor was also franticly seeking a meeting with someone in the community he could trust. He hoped to encourage us to move our meals out of sight. Jim Rhodes at the Haight Ashbury Neighborhood Council called me to say Agnos wanted me to come to his office on Wednesday at one o'clock.

I arrived at City Hall with a park resident, Nate, who frequented our meals. Nate called the stand of raggedy eucalyptus trees near Hippy Hill his home. His father had also lived on the streets of California and I thought he would be able to represent those who ate with us.

I stepped into Room 200 and walked up to the receptionist. She sat holding the phone to her ear with one hand while writing a message with the other. Two men in dark blue suits stood silently at the balcony window. I would learn that they were police officers assigned to the mayor. Haight activists Calvin and Jim were already standing in the lobby speaking with John Crews of the ACLU.

One of the mayor's aids ushered us past a copy machine tucked into an open closet into a large conference room. Mayor Agnos stood up. He was taller than he appeared in the media.

He proceeded to introduce the assembled city officials, gesturing towards Police Chief Frank Jordon standing to his side by the door to the mayor's public office. He motioned his hand towards his chief of staff, Hadley Roff, who was leaning dangerously far back in an office chair. "You all know my chief of staff Hadley Roff," he said. Being new to San Francisco politics, I didn't know who Hadley was in the power structure of the city. The mayor then directed our attention to Mary Burns of the Parks and Recreation Department, and finally nodded towards two lawyers and introduced them as Randy Riddle and Thomas J. Owen from the City Attorney's office. The ACLU attorney John Crew introduced himself and Jim and Calvin reminded the group of their role as neighborhood representatives.

The mayor tucked in his clean white shirt as he sat back down. He wanted to solve our issue that very afternoon. After all, he was the mayor of one of America's greatest cities. He was leading a government with a three-billion-dollar-a-year budget, a city that was—and is—a global tourist destination. And there he found himself forced to negotiate with a homeless-looking homeless advocate and his homeless friend: a humiliating and unwelcome interruption of more important matters.

Agnos suggested we set up outside the Haight Ashbury Soup Kitchen. That wouldn't be as visible as the location at the entrance to the park, but the idea was shot down quickly.

"The neighbors are already trying to shut the soup kitchen down because they are providing meals four days a week. Adding another day would only add to the pressure to close it," said Jim, who sat on the board of the soup kitchen.

One of the city officials agreed with Jim's perspective. Jim and Calvin made a solid defense of the weekly meal's location at the entrance to the park, speaking of the need to continue the public expression of our message: "Food Not Bombs is trying to speak to the public about diverting federal taxes from the military to domestic spending. You can't be opposed to that can you?"

Agnos grunted, seeming to recognize that he should be in support of our goals but that things were not that simple. He had to answer to money.

Police Chief Jordon claimed all Food Not Bombs had to do was apply for a permit. The ACLU's John Crew spoke up: "Food Not Bombs officially requested a permit on July 11th but the city responded with riot police instead."

“Is that right Mary?” the mayor asked, turning to the park’s director.

Mary Burns made an unusual facial expression that could have meant she was aware of the letter and our attempts to meet with her or it might have meant she didn’t have any knowledge of the request. As I would come to learn, Burns was quite adept at subterfuge. Agnos was visibly angry with her, but he had not yet realized that he didn’t have any power over her and her friends at the parks department.

I said very little until near the end of the meeting.

“I propose that there be no more arrests during our negotiations. That would be a good way to build trust,” I said.

Agnos seemed surprised at the proposal. What arrests? We weren't expected to share our next meal until Monday.

I continued: “The arrests have not been limited to the times when we share food. A volunteer spent a night in jail at the Taraval Station a week before the first food arrests.”

That observation didn’t please Chief Jordan who glanced at the mayor as if to say that I was insignificant and my comments not worthy of response. Once again Jim and Calvin backed me up. John Crew also came to my defense and soon the mayor agreed: No more arrests during negotiations.

Jordan sheepishly responded, “Ok, no more arrests during negotiations,” with the tone of a boy fearful of being caught with his hand in the cookie jar.

I also suggested that no one speak with the media until we had come to a settlement. We agreed on that as well.

A second meeting was scheduled for one o’clock the following day.

Before heading to the second meeting, I passed by the entrance to Golden Gate Park and stopped to hand out flyers reassuring people that we would return again on Monday. The authorities had not succeeded in stopping us. I taped a few of the announcements on the metal poles along Stanyan Street. As I was posting the last flyer one of our regulars, Glen, staggered up to me. He was a veteran dedicated to drowning the anguish of the war.

“Keith, I can’t take it anymore. I’m going to the bridge. If I had a gun, I would shoot myself in the head right here,” he moaned jabbing his index finger into his temple. He started to cry.

I offered to buy him a bottle, but that only caused him to blubber more. “I’ve got to kill myself today. I can’t take other night in this fucking park. You know me Keith, I’m a good man. I fought for America, Keith. I fought in Vietnam. This is too much.”

He pulled me into his large pudgy torso draping his balloon arms around me. I leaned into the weight of his desperation. We held each other tight. He shuddered in my embrace soaking my right shoulder with his tears.

"Mr. McHenry, Mr. McHenry, you are under arrest," said the voice of someone tapping me on my left shoulder.

The officer pulled my hand behind me and in an unusually gentle fashion slid his metal handcuffs over my wrists.

A patrol car had quietly pulled up behind me while I was consoling Glen. The officer opened the rear door, held my head and directed me into the back seat.

Glen started to plea with the officers. "Keith is a nice man, he feeds us. Don't arrest him. He didn't do anything. He was helping me."

Glen came to my window, "Keith, Keith why are you in there? Why, why?" he cried clutching is head in dismay.

I let the officer know that I had a one o'clock meeting with the mayor. There was some long conversation over the police radio as I sat handcuffed in the back of the patrol car. The noise of the still-running engine muffled the radio conversation.

Twenty or thirty minutes passed before the officer opened my door. "Ok Keith, we are going to release you into Glen's custody. Step out of the car," the policeman directed. He unlocked the cuffs and turned to Glen: "He's all yours now, Glen."

I eased Glen across the street to Cal-Foods, handed him a five, and suggested he buy a pint instead of heading for the bridge. "Sleep on it, Glen. You are a good man. It's not time to die."

I jumped into my pickup and rushed down to City Hall.

The receptionist took me to the conference room. The mayor jumped to his feet and angrily demanded to know why I was late. "You have kept us waiting for nearly an hour," he blurted, eyes blazing, standing straight as a board with both of his hands pressed hard against the boardroom table.

"I thought we had an agreement that there wouldn't be any more arrests. I was arrested on the way here. I also thought there would be no talking to the media, but Chief Jordan is quoted in this morning's paper saying that I wasn't someone to be negotiating with. That I couldn't be trusted. So, I'll just leave now and we can let the arrests continue," I announced and started to walk towards the door.

"No, no, wait Keith, wait. Is this true? Keith was arrested?" blasted the mayor as he turned towards Chief Jordan.

It looked like the meeting was heading towards chaos. Jim and Calvin started to stand. The two city attorneys had a look of panic. Jordan appeared to be searching for words.

“Please sit, Keith, please,” the mayor begged, trying to stifle his inclination to pat a sit-down motion with his hand. My allies started to defend me and called out the mayor for not being able to control his police department.

I turned back towards the mayor and stepped up to the back of one of the chairs. The mayor started to look relieved. The threat of more arrests was a gamble. The numbers of those risking arrest could drop and the opposition could feel things were starting to go their way. But on the other hand, even a few more arrests could be a problem for a mayor with otherwise great progressive credentials. But I kept those concerns to myself.

People started to return to their seats. Calvin gave a very stirring speech about the breach of trust and asked the mayor and the chief if they really thought a resolution would be possible seeing that they couldn’t keep their word for even one day.

We went back and forth. There was another attempt at moving the meal to a less visible location, I argued that the message of Food Not Bombs deserved the public’s attention. Mayor Agnos proposed a temporary permit at least until there could be a public hearing hosted by the Parks and Recreation Department. Mary Burns agreed to ask the commission to set a date.

We waited ten minutes while a staff person typed up a temporary permit. Copies were passed around the room. A few changes were made and an aid returned with a new draft for six weeks of Monday meals. A second, third, fourth, and fifth six-week permit were also prepared with the corresponding dates and times.

Mary Burns objected to the tables remaining at the entrance. I argued that our purpose was not only to share vegetarian meals but to inspire dialogue.

“We are not going to end hunger if we don’t change American politics and encourage a discussion about the urgency of diverting military spending towards the needs of the community.”

We battled on about the location until we finally agreed that we would set back from Stanyan Street but still be visible to those walking into the park. We sketched out a map showing the huge oak tree and our two tables in front of it.

As the meeting came to an end, the mayor whispered a comment to his deputy. It was apparently time for a public statement. Agnos’s staff rushed into action and we followed the mayor into his office. Reporters who clearly knew the drill were fanning their microphones out on the mayor’s impressive desk in a semicircle aimed towards his luxurious chair. Camera people adjusted their tripods and twisted their lenses into focus. Reporters flipped their notebooks to a blank sheet.

Agnos tucked in his pressed white shirt. Pulled up his pants and tugged on his red tie. Habits that seemed more about helping him prepare his mind than his appearance.

Silence took over the room. Agnos sat behind his desk and began to read his statement, typed copies of which had already been handed out to the reporters.

"When enforcing the law, we don't want to create a remedy that's worse than the problem," Agnos announced. "I'm worried about the violence that could occur. We will look for a permanent solution. We must develop a policy for this kind of program where people can be fed with dignity and in privacy."

Agnos described the next steps and the scheduling of a Parks and Recreation hearing to get the public's input on a permit process. He took a few questions but was interrupted by the Chronicle reporter who turned to ask me for my opinion. I started to respond but was interrupted.

"Wait, wait," called out several of his colleagues. "Let Mr. McHenry sit in front of the mics before he answers."

I headed towards the other side of the desk. A surprised Agnos stood to give me his seat. I began my response.

"We're extremely excited that we'll be able to share food and information with the community without having to fear arrest. It's encouraging to us that we're on a path to successful resolution to provide basic needs for the homeless."

The reporters yelled out their questions interrupting one another. "Do you feel this is a victory?" "How do you feel about the negotiations?" "Mr. McHenry Do you plan to serve again this Monday?"

I couldn't hear them amongst the confusion and pointed to one of the journalists, saying, "Could you repeat that?"

I then said, "I am pleased that we can continue sharing meals and information without interference," and invited another question by acknowledging another reporter. "Yes, we will be sharing meals this Monday," and then gestured to a third journalist, responded, and took another question.

Mayor Agnos stepped up behind me gently placing his hand on my shoulder as he said, "Don't get too comfortable in that chair, Keith."

Everyone in the room burst out in laughter.

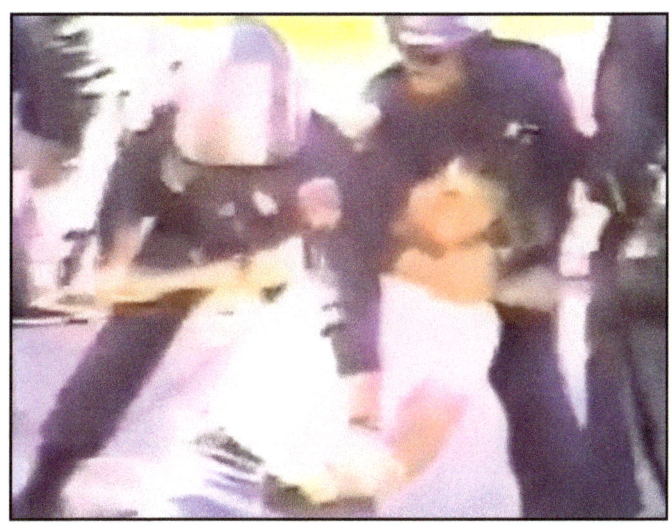

Keith arrested during Fleet Week protests at the Presidio on October 15, 1988

Chapter 22

THE ILLUSIONS

I stuffed my keys and change back into my pocket after stepping through the metal detector into the Hall of Justice's high-ceilinged, marble lobby. The particular smell of stress and aftershave was still unfamiliar to me on that warm October morning in 1988.

A tall, well-dressed businessman at the back of the line for the coffee kiosk recognized me: "Hey Keith, do you have any plans for the weekend?"

That seemed like an odd question from someone I had never met. As for my plans, I assumed he meant plans like going camping or to a concert. So, I responded, "No, nothing special," and continued on to the elevators and my quest for a signature on a Police Intelligence Department release form required to retrieve my confiscated property.

The Blue Angel F/A-18 Hornets had been rumbling through their terrifying ballet in the skies above San Francisco all week. A flotilla of battleships lumbered under the Golden Gate Bridge. The October spectacle of Fleet Week promised to draw thousands. Local activists asked Food Not Bombs to provide lunch at their protest against the US war in El Salvador. They planned to rally at the Richardson Gate to the Presidio Military Base. Other than the time and location, I knew little more in the way of details.

I did know that Eric Weinberger would be organizing a meal for the protest against the US war in El Salvador on the Boston Commons and that C.T. would be coordinating a meal for activists protesting the war outside the capital in Washington, D.C. I had spoken to C.T. by phone a little over two weeks earlier. We grew excited when we realized that this would be the first time Food Not Bombs would be providing meals at protests in three cities on the same day.

I pulled up outside our Mission District kitchen with a truckload of Sid's day-old bagels and donated produce from Thom's Natural Foods that would have been garbage if I had not recovered them on my morning route. The small two-story house on Albion was easy to make out in the row of identical rundown rentals. A stick-thin woman made the warehouse doorway across the alley her home. She didn't own a thing. Not a comb to tease her matted dreads, not her own crack pipe nor any of the progression of babies that seemed to double her bodyweight every nine months.

Our silent doorway neighbor wasn't the only landmark. An assortment of stuffed toys and broken sound systems decorated the front door gate. The previous night's party was morphing into preparation for that day's lunch. A passed-out stranger lay in a pile of clothing. Danny O'Connell, who was fond of introducing himself as "The Ten-Thousand-Year-Old Buddha," had left the comfort of his hammock in Golden Gate Park to help us prepare lunch. Danny was a Marine, a veteran of the Secret War in Laos. He reminisced with a Cheshire Cat grin about calling in airstrikes on US military positions. His unit volunteered to stay in Laos an extra tour so they could complete the job of defeating America's war machine in the land Danny loved. He was fluent in Laotian, Vietnamese, and Mandarin. He was no stranger to the tricks of spy craft and provided valuable tips on the science of disruption. Like many other veterans on San Francisco's streets, he had fond memories of a night or two with Grace Slick. It was no surprise that he was listening to Jefferson Airplane as he sat on a milk crate cutting up apples and pears: "When the men on the chessboard get up and tell you where to go… And you've just had some kind of mushroom, and your mind is moving slow… Go ask Alice, I think she'll know," mouthed my Buddha friend, accompanying our tinny-sounding boom box.

Even though the men on the chessboard of US foreign policy told Danny where to go and he did have some kind of mushroom before he deployed, his mind not only moved deliberately, it moved off the chessboard to places only Danny knew of, and things were not always as they seemed. He made that much clear.

When we pulled up to a traffic island at the entrance to the Presidio there were already about a hundred protesters milling around on the hot sidewalks. Filling my rearview mirror, I saw a line of soldiers in combat helmets and flak jackets armed with M-16s, ready to defend the military base.

The Blue Angels' roar shook the blistering pavement. The San Francisco Police Tactical Squad marched into formation behind a long line of metal police barricades. The trickle of protesters became a flood, many carrying banners or cardboard signs denouncing the massacres and mayhem of the Central American war. The sign wavers were soon joined by dozens of activists hauling two-by-fours and refrigerator-sized sheets of brightly colored cardboard. While the protest swirled around in the intersection, demonstrators hovered at our table snacking on cups of soup, bagels, navel oranges, and plates of stew.

A crowd rushed into Richardson Street blocking traffic to and from the Golden Gate Bridge. The activists assembled what they described for the media as a replica of a war-torn El Salvadorian village made of the wood and cardboard across the access to the bridge. People pulled colorful balls of yarn from shopping bags and wove themselves into a huge tangle. It wasn't long before fifty or more demonstrators were self-knitted into the village replica.

Police commander Richard Holder strutted up and down a line of riot police. He gracefully spun his hand in the air and out came the clubs and down went the plexiglass visors and off went the riot police, stomping into the knot of protesters and props. Officers pulled on the boards and yarn, dragging some of the woven ones across the asphalt. A battle ensued.

A chorus of, "No Justice, No Peace! No war with El Salvador!" could be heard over the roar of the jets, the blaring horns of frustrated motorists, and a police officer yelling, "This is an illegal assembly. If you don't leave now, you're subject to arrest," over a loudspeaker.

The traffic was snarled and backed up over the Golden Gate Bridge, past the Rainbow Tunnel, maybe even past the last exit to Sausalito. Traffic in the Marina was also at a standstill.

Ten or twelve riot police followed a bearded man dressed in a white t-shirt and jeans through the crowd of protesters pointing out the people identified as the leaders. Two helmeted policemen grabbed one of the women he marked and marched her off to a waiting police van. The man pointed to a second woman. She too was pulled from the demonstration, cuffed, and taken to the police vehicle.

My friends and I scurried to pack up the remaining food. We rushed our folding table and igloo jug of tea off to the back of my truck. It was time to escape.

I raced around collecting the last bits of litter, shoving the used cups, plates, and orange peels into a garbage bag. Then six burly members of the Tactical Squad surrounded me. One of them reached across my chest and neck from behind, choking me as he pulled me backwards off my feet. Another one pulled on one of my legs as another grabbed onto my pant cuffs. The officers twisted me over face down onto the concrete, sandpapering my left cheek into the traffic island. Metal cuffs snapped tightly around my wrists.

Events happened fast. Questions dashed through my mind like flashes of a mirror sending messages of sunlight in Morse code. One thought vanished into the next before I could make sense of the first. I wasn't sure why I was being arrested. Had I committed the crime of sharing free food? I didn't think so. I thought we had settled that legal dispute with the mayor a few weeks before.

I was stuffed into a black-and-white police van. Riot police kept the yelling for the crowd to back away from their vehicle, striking anyone who got close with a quick club jab.

The two women whom the bearded man had previously identified welcomed me to the cage. A helmeted patrolman appeared at the back door with a pad of yellow citations.

"Sign here," he said, pointing to the line marked by a bold X.

"Throwing barricades at the Tactical Unit," was the crime scrawled on the citation.

Did I really throw a barricade at the line of riot police? Was my memory so clouded by all the excitement that I didn't remember throwing something at the police? That didn't seem like something I would have done. I did remember standing next to the barricades to watch the blockade but I didn't think I throw anything. Maybe close proximity to the barricades was all that was required for such an infraction.

A couple of months later I got a call from a man introducing himself as Terry Messman. I didn't know him but he said he had been at the Fleet Week protest with his partner. "My wife Ellen has video footage you should see," he said.

Video footage? It was unusual for activists to have video of a demonstration in 1988. Terry and I arranged to meet during our Wednesday meal at UN Plaza. He walked up and handed me a plastic VHS cassette. I took the footage to my friend Sarge Holzman's Law Office at Opera Plaza as soon as the meal was finished and packed up.

Sarge put the tape into his VCR and pushed play.

The footage started with the protesters setting up their village and weaving themselves into it: a human-and-wood blockade of yarn-tangled demonstrators. Riot police tried to unwind the mess. They started to make arrests. They dragged the activists across the pavement while some were still tied to two-by-fours.

A bearded man in a white t-shirt and blue jeans unhooked a section of the metal police barricade and threw it towards a line of riot police. It bounced harmlessly to a stop ten feet from the nearest officer. The video then showed him turn and wade into the crowd. About ten or twelve riot police followed the guy. He pointed out a young woman. Police arrested her. He took a few more steps and pointed out a second woman. Several of the helmeted officers grabbed her and led her away.

The video showed the crowd yelling, "Shame! Shame!" at the bearded man. He backed against my pickup truck with his arms crossed as people stood around him yelling, "Nazi! Nazi!" and, "Fascist! Fascist!"

Then the camera spun around quickly and there I was. One officer in riot gear was pulling me to the ground from behind. His arm around my upper body and neck. Other officers started grabbing my legs. I struggled to get the keys to my truck out of my pocked and toss them underhanded towards a group of distressed protesters.

Someone yelled: “What are you doing? He was just handing out food!”

Others screamed at them to stop. A woman stepped towards the officer whose arm was around my neck as if she was going to pull him from me. But then she stopped, apparently having second thoughts. A woman in the foreground had her fingers in her trembling mouth. She looked horrified. Police were kneeling on my legs. Other officers were twisting my arms behind me. They cuffed one wrist to the other. The patrolmen then marched me towards the van like offensive line-backers in a football game, ready to block any opponent from tackling the quarter back.

Sarge asked me, “Well Keith did you notice something about the guy who threw the barricade?”

I didn’t know what he was suggesting.

“Look, he has a beard, is wearing a white t-shirt and blue jeans.” He rewinds the video a little. “Look, there you are. You have a beard and you are wearing a white t-shirt and blue jeans. Now what were you charged with? Remember the citation says you threw a barricade at the police,” he said.

He explained that someone in the police department had probably watched me leave my apartment and called in my wardrobe.

He continued, “They probably have a copy of your clothing in a locker at police headquarters or down at the academy.” This would happen again, he predicted.

Two months later Sarge and I were attending a heated police commission meeting. Why would the department send out half its force to violently attack a small peaceful Castro Street protest for AIDS funding? An angry crowd demanded answers.

“Look Keith,” said Sarge, pointing to a big guy with a beard.

I looked at myself and at the man in the corner: Black jeans, black t-shirt, and a scraggly beard.

“Your second shift double,” Sarge whispered.

Three years later I got news that the city had finally provided us with the documents we requested in discovery during one of our federal Civil Rights law-suits. District Judge Vaughn Walker would deny my complaint as being too long but he was great on our requests for discovery.

I went to review the files and found my attorney Randy Baker sitting on the floor of his Richmond District living room surrounded by boxes of memos, notes, and letters about Food Not Bombs. Seven boxes of police records were fanned out by the door to the kitchen. Two cases of Health Department documents blocked the view to his fireplace. Yellow ochre file folders dotted the hardwood floor like lily pads.

Randy was excited. "Keith, look what I found in the Health Department files," he said, handing me four pages with the familiar heading, "San Francisco Police Department Memorandum," across the top. This one was dated September 27, 1988, three weeks before my barricade arrest.

It was a short memo from Captain Richard Holder—the man giving orders that day at the Presidio—to Deputy Chief Frank Reed, who I then knew was the well-dressed man in line for coffee who asked me if I had any plans for the weekend. I was starting to get to know the players in the city's game to silence Food Not Bombs.

The memo started:

A. As per your request, I have conducted an investigation regarding the planned activity of the "Food Not Bombs" organizations October 15, 1988, at the Presidio. During my investigation, I was able to obtain the private phone number of "Food Not Bombs" organizer, Keith McHenry, who unknowingly was a great asset to this investigation.

I had to read that again. Holder "was able to obtain the private phone number of Food Not Bombs organizer, Keith McHenry, who unknowingly was a great asset to this investigation."

This memo was written in the time of telephone landlines and less scrutiny of the identity of utility customers. It was many years before mobile phones, digital communications, and Edward Snowden's revelations. This was still mostly the analog era. Yet even by post-Snowden standards this level of personal surveillance was special.

As I mentioned earlier, when I first arrived in San Francisco I opened the White Pages, the phone book that listed all the names and phone numbers of everyone in the city, and scanned through it to find the most common name: Dick Lee. I ordered my Pacific Bell phone service under that name. In Boston my phone was listed as Michael Sullivan. With twenty-six pages of Dick Lees and the police knowing me as Keith McHenry, you can see why obtaining my private phone number would be a bit trickier than simply looking me up in the phonebook. I believe that a police informant obtained my number by listening to me share it with Starhawk at a protest planning meeting in Berkeley.

I asked Randy if this memo suggested that they had tapped my phone.

"Yes, Keith it looks that way. You must have a secret supporter in the City Attorney's office because they moved this memo from the police files to the Health Department documents so the police wouldn't remove it during a final review."

Unlike today, most of us made very few calls in the late 80s, and long-distance calls were very expensive and thus even less common. This is Captain Holder's interpretation of my phone conversation with my friend and Food Not Bombs co-founder C.T. in Boston.

B. "Food Not Bombs" current and planned activity.

1. As part of a nationwide anti-war protest scheduled for October 15, 1988, "Food Not Bombs", plans to blockade all the entrances to the Presidio and support similar activity at the Pentagon and other military organizations. The goal is to shut down the Presidio all day by blocking and feeding demonstrators at the gates to the post. "Food Not Bombs" anticipates that this demonstration will draw more participants, 3000, than the last major demonstration at the Presidio on 03/24/88.

As I recall Food Not Bombs didn't anticipate anything other than offering a free meal. I was starting to understand that I wasn't the only one living my life.

Keith sitting outside a laundry on Clement Street in San Francisco

Chapter 23

PAY PHONE

A second round of couples counseling determined that Andrea and I were no longer wife and husband material so I moved out of our Clement Street flat and we agreed to get a divorce. I was recovering from a second sinus surgery in 1996 on the back porch of a friend's Section Eight apartment. A surprise visit from the Department of Human Services sent me onto the streets. But I was in luck. My friend Bobby Castillo needed a housemate. On my way to his place, I found a fairly new twin mattress leaning against an apartment wall at Geary and Beaumont. The sign said free, so I hauled it two blocks to my tiny new room on Spruce Street. My first order of business was to transfer my phone line of ten years. Pacific Bell told me it would be switched on later that week.

A few days later, I trundled home with two sacks of groceries. My housemate Bobby was getting some fresh air on our front stoop. He greeted me with a smile. "The phone company came today. They hooked a box on that pole over there," he said. He pointed out the box and added that it seemed strange that it had a small red flashing light on it.

Two months later I stumbled into our gloomy shared kitchen, poured my first cup of coffee, and squeezed into my mattress-filled room to start returning calls. I flipped open my notebook to the most recent messages. First on the list was a volunteer with a question about a protest where Food Not Bombs planned to offer a meal in Washington, D.C. I dialed their number on my yellow princess phone.

I heard that screechy beep, beep sound and then a recorded voice said, "To complete this call please deposit $1.35 for the first three minutes."

I hung up and dialed the number again, and again heard the beeps and, "To complete this call please deposit $1.35 for the first three minutes."

What is up with this, I thought. I retrieved the Pacific Bell white pages from the papers under my table, found the number for residential phone repair and dialed the listing. "To complete this call please deposit 35 cents."

Maybe I dialed the wrong number? I tried again, but again heard: "To complete this call please deposit 35 cents."

I returned to the white pages and found a second number for phone repair and dialed 611. "Hello, you have reached Pacific Bell's phone repair. Please stay on the line and the next available customer representative will be right with you," followed by that unpleasantly up-beat hold music.

"Hello this is Sally. How may I help you?"

"Oh yes, I dialed two different numbers from my home phone and I was told to deposit $1.35 the first time and 35 cents the second time."

"Ok, sir. Let's see what we can do. What number are you calling from?"

"415-330-5030," I responded.

"Thanks, I'll be right back." I was left with more of that annoying music.

"Ok sir, we checked the line and you are calling from a pay phone."

"How can that be possible? I am calling from my home phone. There isn't any place to deposit 35 cents."

"Sorry sir, but we show that you are calling from a pay phone."

Still stunned, I explained that I had been paying a monthly phone bill for this line since 1987.

"I am sitting in my bedroom," I protested, "and the phone is plugged into the wall. There is no place to deposit coins on my princess phone."

"Sorry sir, but the number you are calling from is a pay phone. We checked the line and it is definitely a pay phone."

It was clear that I would be getting nowhere with Sally, so I thanked her, hung up, and decided to get on with my morning. I grabbed my poster distribution lists, Scotch Tape and headed out to my pickup. I went to collect the day-olds at the House of Bagels, took an aqua aerobics class at the Presidio Y and then made a quick trip down Union Street and Chestnut Street taping ODC Dance Company and San Francisco Opera posters in each store window. Then I went over to Civic Center Plaza to drop off my bagels. At least a hundred regulars were already there waiting in line.

I taped more posters into store windows on Van Ness and Polk then returned to my Spruce Street room and my notebook of calls that I still needed to make. I picked up the receiver and redialed the D.C. number.

"To complete this call please deposit $1.35…" I had forgotten about my morning issue with the phone.

I woke up the next morning and stumbled into the dreary kitchen and made my first pot of Peet's dark roast and returned to my office bedroom to begin my day. Again, I dialed the D.C. number on my slim yellow princess phone.

"To complete this call please deposit $1.35 for the first three minutes."

I tried a Boston number only to hear: "To complete this call please deposit $1.60 for the first three minutes."

I called the 611 phone-repair number again and a woman introducing herself as Jane picked up and asked how she could help.

I explained the issue: "Every time I dial a number on my home phone, I get a recording instructing me to deposit money. I have a princess rotary phone that is plugged into the wall in my room. I get a bill from you every month and have been paying for this line since 1987. Can you fix this problem? I really need to make some calls today."

Jane asked me for the number I was calling from and I gave it to her: "415-330-5030."

"Thank you very much. I will check the line." She left me with more cheery music and then came back to say: "Sir, this is Jane again with Pacific Bell. I checked the line and 415-330-5030 is a pay phone. You need to deposit the required amount to make each call."

I repeated that I was sitting in my bedroom, that the phone had no place to deposit money and that I had been paying a phone bill for this line for the past ten years. "Please Jane, isn't there anything you can do so I can use my phone?"

She politely assured me that I am calling from a payphone. "You just need to deposit the correct amount if you want to make a call," she advised.

"May I speak to a manager?"

Jane transferred me to a manager. "Hello, this is Tom how can I help you?"

“Well, Tom, yesterday I started getting a recording telling me to deposit money each time I dialed a number,” I said and repeated that I get a monthly bill and that until yesterday I could make both local and long-distance calls.

He asked me for my name and number. “The phone is in the name Dick Lee and my number is 415-330-5030.”

“Thank you. I'll be right back,” he said and faded into more of that regrettable music.

Manager Tom returned. “Hello Mr. Lee, I did a number of tests and 415-330-5030 is definitely a pay phone. You will need to deposit the correct change if you wish to make a call.”

I protested, but he told me there was nothing he could do. I just needed to deposit the required change.

I borrowed Bobby's phone and called another phone repair number. They also told me I had been calling from a pay phone and suggested I deposit the correct amount if I wished to complete my calls.

After a week or more of this routine I considered another tactic.

One morning I asked Bobby if I could use his phone to make a quick call. I found the number for the San Francisco Chief of Police Fred Lau in my notebook.

I had a good relationship with the new chief. That connection started when Mayor Agnos was on his 1989 campaign of violence and misdemeanor incarcerations against us for the sharing our meals at City Hall.

At that time, we were still getting arrested nearly every day outside City Hall for felony conspiracy to share free food in violation of a court order. We had started our campaign, “Risk arrest One Day a Month with Food Not Bombs,” with the intention of outlasting Mayor Jordan's daily assaults and lockups. Local priests and nuns took up a day, handed out our decoy meals, were patted down, cuffed and carted off to the Northern Police Station. Community groups, student associations, political organizations and union members stepped up to take an arrest. The National Lawyers Guild unfurled their banner, grabbed serving spoons and dished out paper plates of rice and beans with those who thought they knew the game plan. This time, however, the police hesitated. Instead of clamping the cuffs on the attorneys the police brutalized the hungry who had come to eat.

One balmy evening in 1989 the police found us serving at a small sidewalk protest outside the Democratic Party headquarters on Van Ness near Market. The officers thought they were obligated to shut us down but as we were sharing food at a new location and time, they thought to call their superior Captain Fred Lau first. The captain arrived and asked if we intended to hurt anyone. Upon learning that we just planned to share food he told his officers to back off.

A year later Captain Lau's good friend and San Francisco's highest ranking Black officer, Commander Isiah Nelson, died when his motorcycle crashed into a concrete barrier on the abandoned portion of I-280 that had been damaged during the 1989 earthquake. Nelson was returning from a night of policing a Giants game at Candlestick Park. A year before his death Commander Nelson had won well-deserved praise from the people of San Francisco for safely and calmly evacuating sixty thousand fans from a lightless Candlestick Park when the Loma Prieta earthquake jolted Game Three of the World Series to an end.

Since I was immersed in a sea of lawyers, police officers, and police commission hearings I had come to understand that Isiah Nelson and Fred Lau were among those in the department trying to influence a new vision of a more progressive form of policing. A significant contrast to the institutional brutality of the department. They encouraged a shift away from enforcers working for the powerful to protectors of the community. Captain Lau's disinterest in making the mandatory food arrests was the first sign to me of his willingness to defy unreasonable policies. So, when we heard of Nelson's death my lawyer and friend Dennis Cunningham agreed that we could encourage this alternative direction in policing and become allies of this more just view by attending Nelson's funeral.

I dressed in my dark suit and red tie and drove over to St. Dominic's Catholic Church. Lines of police officers dressed in their finest stood at attention in ruler perfect rows. Every street around St. Dominic's was filled with rows and rows of police.

Dennis and I were among the few civilians amongst all the law enforcement uniforms. I was very conscious of the attention we were attracting as we stood in a clearing of asphalt outside the impressive facade.

Captain Lau stood alone outside the cathedral entrance greeting mourners. Dennis and I walked up to the captain and I reached out and shook his hand. He thanked me for coming. I could see his sincerity in his eyes. He led us into the nave filled with most of San Francisco's police force, and ushered us to an empty pew near the front. Heads turned, visibly surprised to see me.

Police Chief Richard Hongisto was finally fired after a protracted protest campaign against police violence, the Rodney King Uprising, and a week or so of martial law and a scandal connecting police Chief Hongisto to the confiscation of loads of the San Francisco Bay Times edition with the headline, "Dick's Cool New Tool: Martial Law." Mayor Frank Jordan picked Fred Lau to replace him. I stopped in at Lau's swearing in ceremony on the fifth floor of the Hall of Justice as I was on my way to get another release form signed at police intelligence. He made a point of coming over to shake my hand telling me to call him any time. I recalled thinking this might be his way of coopting the now well-established coalition seeking justice for the police murder of people like Aaron Williams and our movement to end the violent repression directed against protests. I knew I would need to be careful.

But now with this phone issue I felt it was time to take him up on his offer. I made the call from Bobby's phone. "Chief Lau's office. How can I direct your call?"

"Hello, this is Keith McHenry. May I speak with the chief?"

"Just a second," the receptionist said.

"Hi Keith, this is Chief Lau. How can I help you?"

I remember it as if this conversation had happened yesterday.

"Well, chief, I know you don't wiretap home phones, but I am having a problem," I said, making a show of shielding Chief Lau from any potential criminal liability. "My home phone has become a pay phone and I haven't been able to make any outgoing calls for the past week or so. The phone company hasn't been able to fix the problem so I was wondering if you could look into it for me."

He said he would be happy to investigate and asked me to give him another call if it remained a problem. "I will send someone over as soon as possible."

I thanked him. Bobby and I stepped outside to observe the results.

A half hour later an unmarked white utility van pulled up to the house. A man in a white shirt and blue jeans pulled an aluminum ladder off the roof rack and extended it up to the lines at the top of the wooden telephone pole nearest our apartment building. The pole with the box and the red blinking light. He strapped on a leather tool belt and scurried up the ladder.

A garage door at the home across Spruce Street slowly opened. Two middle-aged men dressed in neck ties and pressed white shirts with the sleeves rolled up above the elbow sat before laptops on a long, nearly bare folding table. Large padded black headphones rested on their heads and a thick coiled cord was plugged into their computers. One garage occupant lifted his hand to make a sign to the van driver who had climbed to the top of the ladder. The ladder man made some adjustments in that suspicious box. He looked over his shoulder and motioned back to the two men in the garage. He returned to the street, folded up his ladder and secured it to the roof of his van. One of the men in the garage stood, pushed a button and the garage door slowly closed leaving the two "businessmen" at their stations
.

The van drove away and I went to my room and dialed Chief Lau on my own landline to see if the problem had been fixed. Sure enough, I could call out again.

"Thanks so much, chief. Whatever you did, it worked."

That afternoon I walked over to get my mail at Mail Boxes Etc. On the way back I noticed a pay phone at the corner of Geary and Spruce. It finally clicked. The wires must have been crossed.

Keith interviewed before being arrested for sharing lunch outside City Hall

Chapter 24

LUNCH CRIMES

The police caught me again. They nabbed me down on the third level of the Civic Center Garage transporting a box of contraband bagels and a five-gallon bucket of illegal vegan soup. They knew it was destined for a crowd of diners waiting eagerly upstairs outside San Francisco City Hall on that sunny spring day in 1993.

The routine was all too familiar, the coarse light fluttering in the elevator, the buzzer and clinging open of that heavy, iron jail door, the screaming prisoner cuffed to the booking wall. The officer clicked me free from the cuffs. The contents of my pockets rattled onto the booking desk. It was another visit to the sixth floor of the Hall of Justice. Another trip to jail for Felony Conspiracy to Violate a Court Order against sharing food without a permit.

The double-thick steel door rumbled open. The transport officer directed me into the holding cell with a graceful sweep of his hand then slammed the door shut behind me. Another flake of grey marine paint fluttered to the filthy floor. A dark smudge of a prisoner groaned and rolled over on the thin ledge of concrete benches that lined the perimeter of the cell. Years of human residue were caked into the ocher walls and blood-stained floor. I found my place amongst the crud and made myself as comfortable as possible on the floor, far from the steel toilet. I had fourteen or more hours before I would be taking up my position at the ink pad.

The principal entertainment was joining the others in a fitful sleep on the cold cement and the periodic check of the two Filipino clerks rolling another inmate's ink-stained fingers over the boxes on the obligatory FBI forms. The drama of a latex-gloved expert twisting out six sets of perfect fingerprints was one of our only interruptions to the harsh monotony of the holding cell. The other distraction was conversation.

"That was crazy. I can't believe we got caught," laughed one of the two sharply dressed Black men in their mid-thirties as he smacked his thigh.

They said enough for me to glean that they had eaten a lunch of lamb chops and mashed potatoes at Charlie's Diner on Polk Street and tried to slip out on the check. Dine-and-dash, as we call it in the business.

On hearing their tale, an old grizzled white man wrapped in a wardrobe of accumulated rags announced that he was arrested for pocketing a deli sandwich at the Civic Center Seven Eleven on Market Street.

After a bit more conversation a young Latino man, his arms stuffed in his t-shirt against the cold, chimed in. He was arrested at the Safeway in the Castro trying to boost lunch meat and cheese.

"So why are you here?" asked one of the two Dine and Dashers, turning to me.

"I was caught sneaking into the Civic Center with bagels and stew for the Food Not Bombs lunch," I smiled.

"Lunch?" he exclaimed, realizing the irony. "We are all here for the crime of lunch."

"Lunch crimes! Lunch crimes!"

They were trying to get lunch and I was trying to give lunch, and now we were all in jail. We laughed at the absurdity of our culinary solidarity.

The first thing the police take from us is the Food Not Bombs banner

Chapter 25

A SIGNATURE

The police impounded my Nissan pickup again while I was attempting to deliver another covert meal in the fall of 1993. The clerk at Traffic and Parking explained that I needed another special release from the police and sent me to an office at the Hall of Justice.

I went into the Traffic Department at Police Headquarters. "No, not this office," the first-floor desk officer grunted. "See Police Intelligence on the fifth floor," he added as though giving such instruction were routine. I should have known, but still I had hoped that the process would be a bit more streamlined.

The elevator doors slid open to the fifth floor just as the doors of the department's auditorium flung open across the foyer. Dozens of men and women in their Sunday best flooded into the hallway.

"Hey Keith," called out someone from the crowd. A pudgy man in a grey sport coat and blue tie was waving at me. "I want to introduce you to my wife Helen and my daughter Mary. I've told them all about you and how I had to arrest you for feeding the homeless."

I shook Helen's hand and offered my hand to Mary, a cute little girl in a frilly white dress who was twisting about in embarrassment. She smiled shyly and pressed up against her mother. "It's ok Mary, you can shake his hand. Mr. McHenry is a really nice man," her father explained.

The patrolman handed me his copy of the program from the department's award ceremony that he and his family had just attended. "Can you sign this to Mary from Keith?" he asked removing a pen from his shirt pocket.

"Yes, I'd be honored," I replied.

Captain Richard Holder, a regular signer of intelligence memos strode pass us, glaring angrily at the friendly exchange. The family and I wished each another the best.

It was my time to get another one of Holder's signatures.

Keith charged with a Third Strike for possession of 24 "stolen" milk crates

Chapter 26

THREE STRIKES

Dawn struggled through the morning mist of San Francisco's Inner Richmond. That year's first warm cup of coffee steamed in the golden rays of that first sunrise of 1994. Dapples of yellow glistened across the shiny leaves of my ceiling, kissing the ficus canopy over my desk. I could hear the hard dry kibbles clinging against the tin bowls of our dogs Bear and Pluto as my wife Andrea poured their New Year's Day breakfast.

I clicked on my desktop Mac Performa. The internal fan whirred to life spitting out the pixels of electronic correspondence.

"Today We Say, 'Enough is Enough!'" I clicked on the email, "First Declaration from the Lacandon Jungle. A message to the people of Mexico," the Zapatista uprising against the Mexican Government and the North American Free Trade Agreement was proclaimed there in the glow of my computer screen. I tapped print and the rebellion of worlds clicked from the jaws of my Epson.

Andrea and I wrapped up breakfast and headed out for our first dog run of the year. We met Food Not Bombs co-founder Jo Swanson and her partner Richard Edmondson on the vast lawn of Sutro Heights high above the guano-stained Seal Rock. My good boy Pluto jetted after the ragged lime-green tennis ball I hurled across the close-cropped grass. Jo and Richard's blond Elsie flirted with our also blond Afghan Bear who was busy sniffing the ruins of long-deceased Mayor Sutro's garden wall. We casually discussed that evening's San Francisco Liberation Radio broadcast. Andrea would prepare the Hors d'oeuvres and bring the wine. I would bring the text of the Zapatista declaration. Jo and Richard would charge the car battery and select the music.

Richard's old Dolphin camper chugged through the Haight, climbed above the Castro to the summit of Twin Peaks and rumbled to a stop at a parking space below the triple-pronged Sutro Tower antenna. The sun disappeared into the foggy Pacific horizon behind us. A neckless of red break lights and silvery head lights crawled along the straight line of Market Street before disappearing at the Ferry Building and the Bay. The last reflections of the New Year's Day sun flickered dark and were replaced by the twinkling lights of Berkeley, Emeryville, and Oakland. Stephan Dunifer and his friends were busy at our sister station, Berkeley Free Radio, switching on its one-hundred-watt transmitter someplace above those distant lights.

I slid the microphone into the tabletop stand at the center of the camper table. Andrea opened our picnic basket, popped the cork of her favorite Sebastiani Sonoma red wine, filled the goblets, emptied a box of crackers into a bowl, and placed a white taper candle next to the mic. Richard adjusted our one-hundred-watt transmitter as Jo thread the cable through a side window securing the antenna end to the roof of the Toyota. Richard flipped on the power supply and the needle swung back and forth in the display of the twelve-channel mixer.

"You are tuned into San Francisco Liberation Radio serving the San Francisco Bay Area at 93.7 FM," I said, pulling the mic closer. "We will begin tonight's broadcast with an exclusive. We received an email from the mountains of Chiapas, Mexico this morning, with the First Declaration from the Lacandon Jungle."

"We are a product of five hundred years of struggle," the communique began. After reading the first paragraph I slid the mic over to Jo who read the next section of the declaration by candle light.

A police cruiser pulled up behind us. Andrea snuffed out the candle flame and Richard guided the antenna into the cabin. A flashlight beam flashed though the blinds. The four of us sat still and in utter silence. The beam darted in through another window. After about ten minutes we heard the officer rev up his engine and drive off. Richard threaded the coaxial back out the window. We were back on the air and the show went on.

Three days later I pulled up to the curb at my customary parking space on Polk Street across from City Hall. This coveted, unmarked parking spot did not have a meter and was the closest free parking to the location where we shared our twice daily meals. I climbed out of my truck and retrieved a huge cardboard sign proclaiming, "Viva Zapatista! No NAFTA" to accompany my bagel delivery. I positioned myself near the crosswalk to City Hall and waved my marked cardboard pronouncement. I was in a festive mood and arrived dressed in my white chef's hat and coat, both embroidered with Food Not Bombs logos. It was impossible not to notice our solidarity with the indigenous rebels of Chiapas and their resistance to the tragedy of the North American Free Trade Agreement.

An older couple walked up and thanked me for my protest. "Here's twenty to help you out. Thanks so much for all you are doing."

One of our dedicated volunteers, Tom Osher, dragged a damaged folding table into position at the face of the Civic Center reflecting pool. Several food bandits emerged from the underground garage with five-gallon buckets of rice and vegetable stew. The police must have still been on the holiday since they had failed to disrupt our meal the day before. But, since the raids were likely to continue, we maintained our security procedures. A line of regulars had already gathered in the chilly January breeze.

A wavy-haired man in white country-club shoes and a polo shirt darted back and forth near my vehicle. He held something to his ear franticly talking into it as though he were speaking on a phone. To my surprise it was a phone. One of the then-new mobile flip phones.

A yellow tow truck arrived and backed up to the front of my vehicle. The driver hooked his truck up to my bumper and drove off, bouncing my pickup out of sight.

I calmly leaned my sign against the lip of the fountain and walked over to City Hall's first-floor bank of phone booths. It was just another day at Food Not Bombs.

I found the phone number for Parking and Traffic in the white pages, dropped a quarter into the payphone and dialed.

"Hi, my truck was just towed from the Polk Street side of City Hall. What do I need to do to retrieve it?" I asked.

The woman on the phone started to explain the procedure when the frizzy-haired guy with the flip phone stomped up and shoved me repeatedly against the inside of the phone booth as he barked insults at me.

"I'm sorry, ma'am, someone is smashing me against the phone booth. Let me call you back from another phone."

I wiggled past the assailant laughing softly at the absurdity of events. He seemed more like some cartoon of an angry golf pro than someone with the intention of injuring me.

I climbed to the second-floor phones and continued my conversation with Parking and Traffic. The clerk provided me with the details and then I took that glorious descent down the gracefully cascading City Hall stairs to the first floor of the rotunda. You may have seen those stairs in movies such as Raiders of the Lost Ark.

I was about to pass two businessmen and a uniformed police officer who were busy in discussion when one of the businessmen called out, "Hey, Keith we want to talk with you."

"Yes, how can I help you?" I cheerfully responded and walked over to the gathering.

The man that had called my name tapped a little blue book against his palm, "Keith, you are under arrest under the new California Three Strikes Law."

I smiled thinking that it must be a joke. But he wasn't kidding.

The uniformed officer calmly asked me to put my hands behind my back. He then slipped his handcuffs over my wrists, snapped them tight, led me out to a waiting patrol car on Van Ness Street, and whisked me off to the familiar grey walls of Northern Station on Fillmore Street.

An officer fished my jean pockets clean of keys and coins. My chef's hat was then added to the paper bag of property. One of the suit-wearing officers took my driver's license and marked up a citation. Another removed the cuffs and then it was time to spread 'em—hands on the counter, legs wide—for the pat down. A cop flipped the ticket towards me. "Assault, Battery and Strong-Armed Robbery" were my charges. "Sign here," he said pointing to the line beside the bold X.

I found myself jammed into a filthy seventh-floor felony cell. Bail was set at $25,000. After a week on a smelly mattress cramped against a steel toilet a volunteer slapped the ten percent on his credit card and I returned to the streets.

My attorney, Dennis Cunningham, placed the police report on the desk of his Mission District office. The flip-phone man was Mayor Frank Jordan's Film Commissioner, Nick Roomel. The report claimed I assaulted Roomel and stole his beeper. The evidence that the beeper was a Three Strike Felony theft was an invoice claiming he replaced it for $99. There was no mention of a stolen beeper being recovered from anyplace in City Hall, my person, or my vehicle.

The parade of court appearances began. A small unit of officers in riot gear lined the wood-paneled courtroom walls. Two bailiffs staffed a metal detector in the hallway to make sure everyone entering Benson's court was weapon free. The hearing was quick. Assistant District Attorney James Chou landed my case. Judge Jerome Benson set bail at $45,000. Several friends call out shame, shame and I returned to a seventh-floor felony cell.

Apparently, Judge Benson wasn't eager to preside over this political hot potato. Judge Philip Moscone caught my case and again the courtroom was protected by a small squad of police in riot gear. Judge Moscone reduced the bail and my friends paid the ten percent. I was free again.

Coincidently or not, I had a status hearing, this time before Judge Dorothy von Berildingen. The felony food conspiracy trial of Food Not Bombs bagel server Robert Norse Kahn started that same morning before Judge Robert Barclay. Robert was one of the Santa Cruz activists that came up to the City in a show of solidarity. They had also been getting arrested for sharing soup without a permit in sleepy Santa Cruz.

Robert was hauled off by the police before our videographer, Hugh Mejia, had a chance to film the crime. This absence of evidence was just what District Attorney Arlo Smith needed to finally take a meal server to trial since no jury would convict them if they saw the "crime" on film. Since there was no video, I would be the key witness in Robert's case able to testify to the Kafkaesque twisting of hearings, permit deletions, and dinner disruptions.

While Robert's lawyers were sparring with the prosecutors on a fourth-floor courtroom at City Hall I was nervously waiting on a hard bench in Dorothy von Berildingen's court at the Hall of Justice. My accuser, Nick Roomel, sat near the front. I sat with my lawyers Mary Sterns and Dennis Cunningham a few benches away.

According to the district attorney a homeless survivor of Roomel's cramped house of recovery and forced labor, the court diversion program he ran called, "Freedom from Alcohol and Drugs," was waiting to appear before the judge in the same courtroom I was. When he saw his tormentor, he told him to "fuck off." The prosecuting attorney told the court that I had asked the guy to intimidate Roomel. Was this a chance opportunity or a preplanned setup? I may never know.

My bail was returned to $45,000. I was cuffed and whisked off to the Civil War era stone jail in San Bruno. Guards escorted me along a third-floor tier. Prisoners clustered along the railings some yelling at friends across the five-story atrium. A dirty glow from wired windows increased the gloom and grey of the blackened granite walls.

As I stepped into my cell, a tinny loudspeaker blasted out: "Lock Down." A hopeless expression rolled across the face of the prisoner whose cold stone cell I would be sharing. He mumbled that he'd had enough. Thankfully my bail would be reduced, but not in time to testify in Robert's case. He was convicted by Judge Barclay and sentenced to two months in jail for violating the court order against sharing food without a permit.

When Robert started his jail time, we made sure to do our best to undermine the power of the mayor and the court by sharing food every morning to San Francisco's community of the arrested, their council, family, and friends. We would ask everyone making their way towards the Court House metal detector, while offering them breakfast bagels, fruit, and oat meal, this question, "Did you know that there is a man named Robert Norse who is doing time in jail here for sharing food with the hungry?"

At some point I learned that my former teacher and author of A People's History of the United States, Professor Howard Zinn, would be visiting San Francisco. His visit may have been announced on a KPFA radio program. Our volunteers were still sneaking in two waves of decoy food plus the real meal every day at United Nations Plaza and it was common for several of us to get snagged and charged with felony conspiracy.

I reached Professor Zinn and he agreed to participate in a press conference to speak out against the travesty of arresting volunteers for sharing meals with the hungry. Authors Starhawk and Ron Kovic (the Born on the Fourth of July memoirist) also agreed to speak against the criminalization of the homeless and the disruption of our meals for survival at the media event.

We met at United Nations Plaza. I built a podium of four Berkeley Farms Dairy milk crates borrowed from the vegetarian restaurant Ananda Fuara. A small gathering of reporters formed a semi-circle before the four of us. One by one each speaker stepped up to the podium and denounced the campaign of arrests and violence against our servers. I don't remember there being any news stories but the one thing I do remember is that Howard Zinn made the suggestion that we organize a campaign requesting that President Bill Clinton's Justice Department start an investigation into the repression against our volunteers and the miscarriage of justice in my first strike assault case.

He reminded us that the Kennedy administration had sent members of the Justice Department south to protect Civil Rights activists from the violence of local law enforcement and the Klan, suggesting that it might be worth it to ask Clinton to intervene in San Francisco's repression.

We initiated a letter writing campaign asking our supporters to draft letters to the attorney general, Amnesty International, and the United Nations Human Rights Commission requesting that they initiate an investigation. We also created our own packet of information and submitted it with our request for support.

Our video coordinator Hugh Mejia produced a "Video Press Release" showing the beating and arrests of volunteers and other documentation of the city's brutality. We included the video and internal police memos showing my home phone had been wiretapped and that the police and mayor's office had conspired to silence our work using the courts and violence. Hugh also arranged to have this packet of information and video tapes delivered to the United Nations offices of Libya, Cuba, China, and other countries we believed might be interested in exploiting America's domestic human rights problems.

Our first response was a letter from Amnesty International announcing that they would investigate our claim. My friend Jessie Mejia, Hugh's father, and I walked through the second-floor of City Hall, delivering copies of the letter to the offices of each member of the Board of Supervisors an hour or so before their weekly meeting. The aids, even those who wanted our meals to stop were polite and accepted our correspondence. That was until we arrived at the offices of the well-known radio personality Supervisor Barbara Kaufman on the Southwest corner of City Hall.

Sunlight illuminated the hall through Kaufman's open office door. I knocked on the door frame announcing our arrival as we stepped through the open door. Her chief of staff, Nancy Kitts, was busy standing at her desk shuffling through a pile of papers. I stepped towards her, holding out a copy of the document. "Here is a letter from Amnesty International," I explained.

"Get out of here!" she yelled, thrusting her right hand against Jessie and pushing us towards the door. As we fled her fury, she angrily shoved the door closed, threatening to slam Jessie in the back. I instinctively raised my right hand to protect Jessie from the door assault. In doing so, I accidentally smashed my hand through the wafer-thin glass and sliced a gash my palm.

A bloody trail followed me to the second-floor men's room. I wrapped the throbbing red mess in paper towels and rushed downstairs, out to Van Ness and across to my truck at a meter outside Opera Plaza. I left Jessie standing at the shattered door in a state of shock and believed he went out to the meal to tell the other volunteers that I had cut my hand.

My stomach was churning. I needed more than paper towels to stem the flow. I happened to have parked outside the office of one of my lawyers, Sarge Holtzman, and rushed in to see if they had a bandage. They didn't, so I asked for something to help my stomach. They looked but couldn't find anything.

I returned to my truck intent on driving to the closest emergency room but before I could turn into traffic a half dozen members of the sheriff's department surrounded my vehicle with their guns drawn and ordered me to step out. I complied.

The city police arrived. They handcuffed me, put me in a patrol car, and whisked me off to Northern Station. Upon arrival, the officer that we called Jane Wayne taunted me from the precinct counter telling me that she would be 5150ing me into a psych ward as she jotted down something on a police form. Then she added, with her always stern expression, "You must be crazy since you won't stop feeding people even though you keep getting arrested."

A puddle of blood slowly pooled on the concrete below the bench I was cuffed to. Captain Richard Cairns swaggered into the booking room. He had a thing about Food Not Bombs, although really, he had a thing about activists. He was suspended after clubbing several Act-Up aids funding activists during the Castro Police Riot in October 1989. People called him Cocaine Cairns after that. His safari trips to Africa to kill elephants and lions were the subject of news reports.

Cairns slinked around the edge of the room like he was stalking big game, "I follow you everywhere. I can get you anytime," he bragged as he slowly crept, all hunched over, back to the far corner of the white-tiled room.

"Remember that day you and your wife parked at Ocean Beach? You think that it was an accident that that woman took your wife's glasses? It wasn't."

I thought back to that day. A woman peddling quickly along the Ocean Beach sidewalk slammed her front tire into Pluto as he jumped from our truck cab and dashed towards the beach, just as he had done dozens of times before. The Barbie-blond bicyclist wrapped in colorful spandex and matching helmet grabbed the prescription glasses off my wife Andrea's face and angrily demanded we pay to repair her bicycle. "I'm not returning your glasses until you pay to fix this," she said, jabbing her index finger towards her tire. Then she puffed up and pushed Andrea in what at the time seemed like an inexplicable overreaction. Not wanting to get in a fight we continued towards the beach letting her keep Andrea's $200 prescription glasses. A new pair would be less of a problem than a confrontation.

Cairns described this event in great detail. At the time the woman's hostility had seemed to be a random act of anger by an entitled yuppie in a deserted parking lot. Cairns slid along the row of cell doors still facing me now with one eye closed like he was taking aim. He described watching me have a conversation with Congresswoman Nancy Pelosi's San Francisco chief of staff Michael Yaki while tossing slobber-drenched tennis balls for our dogs at the Mountain Lake dog run.

His hunched-over sidestepping around the perimeter of the booking room amplified the dizziness increasing with each drop of blood that throbbed through my soaked paper bandage. His stories supported his contention that he was stalking me. After twenty minutes or so he stood up straight and darted out of the room.

Officer Jane Wayne swaggered over in her pseudo-Wild West manner and unchained me from the bench. "Step up to the counter. You are being charged with assault with a deadly weapon and possession of stolen property. Two more felony strikes. You're never getting out now," she gleefully reported.

The all-too-familiar North Station lockup was spinning. She cuffed me back to the bench. She made sure I understood that I would be facing twenty-five to life if convicted under the new Three Strikes law. Three violent or serious felonies and, just like the three empty swings of the bat in baseball, you're out!

The transporting officer stumbled into the room, lifted a heavy ring of keys from the booking counter, unlocked me from the bench and escorted me out to a police van waiting to deliver me to San Francisco General.

The lights at the hospital made the sterile and already blindingly white emergency room even whiter. Someone in a drab sports coat identifying themselves as a detective with the San Francisco Police Department hovered around the gurney like some dizzying carousel, further adding to my delirium.

The man flashed a badge too quickly to read. "I am here to get your confession," he announced with confidence, flipping open a notebook. I recall he stepped to the foot of the gurney and then scooted along my left to my head but it felt more like the hospital bed was spinning around the annoying investigator.

I ignored him, but the detective pressed on, "Ok Keith, we know you did it so just confess now and things will be a lot easier for you." I didn't respond. I couldn't respond.

The transporting officer intervened. "Leave Keith alone," he said. "Stop bothering him and get out of here."

The detective stammered something about it wasn't any of his business.

"Yes, it is. Now leave before I call your supervisor," the officer demanded. The detective muttered some meek protest and disappeared.

The officer asked me if I wanted to call my wife. I gave him my number and he dialed the phone nearest my gurney and handed me the receiver. She knew what to do. Call my lawyers.

An ER doctor stitched my wound closed and then I was off once again to the seventh-floor felony cells above police headquarters.

This is where the details get cloudy: the mercy, perhaps, of disassociation. I guess I must have been bailed out again because I remember taking a call from my attorney Dennis Cunningham while standing in my Clement Street flat.

"We have been ordered in for a bail revocation hearing at 9 a.m. in Judge Garcia's court. Prepare yourself for spending some time in jail. I suggest you dress in your best suit and tie. Bring rolls of dimes for the jail payphone. It could take some time to get you out."

Assistant District Attorney Chou made some unsubstantiated claims about my being a danger to society and requested my bail be increased to $250,000. Once again police lined the walls as if to provide visual evidence of Chou's argument that I was a threat to public safety.

"Granted," Garcia proclaimed.

Dennis blurted out, "No! Judge, that is too much. There is no way my client can raise that kind of money. You are giving him a life sentence."

I was shocked at both the bail amount and the passionate outburst from Dennis. Just as shocking was the Judge's reaction. He listened, and I have no idea why, but then reduced the bail to $57,000. Even so freedom was still out of reach.

"Return to this court on October 31, 1994, at 9:00 a.m.," Judge Garcia announced with a loud bang of his mallet.

I was escorted out of the courtroom in handcuffs past several helmeted bailiffs prepared for a riot. Drained of hope I struggled to breath. I glanced desperately at Andrea as I disappeared into the gloomy labyrinth of my incarceration. I was never getting out.

When you have to give up your street clothes in exchange for The Orange the feeling of doom is nearly always devastating, but that time it hit with uncommon force.

Gone forever would be the joys of beautiful blue horizons, breezes gently caressing the healing green of deciduous trees, sparrows flitting from delicate branch to flimsy twig, fresh salads and squash soups with friends. No more comfy beds to dream from, favorite music to select or the joy of returning home to Andrea and the guys. I mourned the pleasures that were being snatched from my future as I pushed one leg and then the other into the orange cotton pajamas of the caged.

I was the new man in the felony cell designed for twenty-four but crammed with thirty-two. Once again, I was relegated to a strip of urine-stained floor next to the toilet. Two days later I scored a top bunk.

A barely twenty-year-old tough guy quite full of himself returned from court. He was sentenced to twenty-five to life for various crimes, including stabbing pedestrians on Union Street. His cousin was locked in the neighboring cell. When the lights darkened, he stood at my bunk and, as loud as his voice would allow, started practicing what he said was his best original rap song past my head to his relative on the other side of the wall. "You slimy cunt bitch, fuck you, you skanky whore. You slimy cunt bitch, fuck you, you skanky whore," he shouted, hour after hour, interrupted only with a question to his cousin seeking a critique of his latest rendition. He wasn't interested in my pleas to quiet down. I imagined prison would change all that.

"McHenry, roll it up," startled me from a semi sleep at four in the morning. This time I knew this was not an indication of freedom. I was about to get treated to what the guards called "bus therapy." This was a program designed to reduce the fines to the county for the overcrowding that a judge had ruled was a violation of the Eighth Amendment barring cruel and unusual punishment.

I was removed from the cell before count and escorted to the basement with a dozen other inmates. It was a bit after four in the morning but under the blinding overhead lights it could have been noon, except for the fact that I was raggedly tired.

A huge guard who appeared to be impossibly stuffed into his brown uniform ordered me to strip. He snapped the fingertips of his blue surgical glove, ordered me to open my mouth and swiped his index finger around inside my cheeks. Then he told me to bend over. I did as he ordered, dazed by the conditions. He jiggled my testicles, wiped Vaseline on his index finger, and stuck it up my ass. Several other prisoners lined the hallway stripped naked. Guards were also probing the asses of those inmates. No contraband was to be found, so we dressed. Guards placed leg irons around my ankles and cuffed my wrists to a waist-chain. I struggle behind the other inmates, shuffled outside, and climbed onto the bus.

The bus crossed the Bay Bridge, turned around, and came back again. The guards carried out another body cavity search, then provided a baloney sandwich, another full cavity search and another ride on the bus. They did this over and over again, ten full cavity searches a day for a week. We slept on gym mats in one jail hallway or another with at least ten fingerings of the mouth and anus each day. I guess this wasn't considered cruel and unusual punishment.

The bus therapy finally ended with a march of leg-chained prisoners clanging along the narrow cement hallways into a sea of orange in the cramped subbasement of the North County Alameda Jail. Dozens of Black men chained together in the acid light of this windowless cavern suggested a twentieth-century version of a Middle Passage or plantation of enslaved workers. I remember the jolt of horror I felt at the image before me. The only other white prisoner had glommed onto me in a San Bruno Jail hallway. His terrified gaze must have been born from his racist hatred of Black people. As we stood waiting in a chilly underground parking garage at San Bruno, he leaned over towards me quietly asking if I thought he would be raped or killed by "the blacks."

An inmate on the far side of this squish of humanity remembered me. "Hey, aren't you the lunch crime guy?" he called across the suffocating dungeon. Yes, I am that guy, I said He then told the assembled detainees that I should run for mayor. "I'll vote for you!" he said and smiled. The room of thirty felons came to life promising me their vote, a vote that, if convicted, they may never get to cast.

The eternity of standing breath to breath and shoulder to shoulder came to an end. Six by six we were extracted from the subbasement holding unit and placed onto an elevator.

That desperate white prisoner and I were chained together, loaded onto the elevator and directed to a pod on the fifth floor. The white guy made sure he would bunk with me pushing into the cell the guards had assigned me. Fear seemed to inspire his unfiltered honesty. He was a truck driver from Missouri. He found his wife in bed with another man at a hotel in San Francisco and naturally had to beat the guy nearly to death. He admitted he was a racist and said he knew he would be killed if he had to be jailed with Black people. Tears came to his eyes as he shared his worries. I tried to assure him he would have nothing to worry about if he treated everyone with respect. He wasn't sure he could. Even though his nasty breath poisoned our hermetically sealed confinement that was not nearly as distasteful as his hatred of our Black neighbors. "You are on your own buddy, I'm not going to protect you," I said, making my position crystal clear.

The routine made itself evident. Your cell door buzzed open at regular intervals and if you wanted to be in the common room for food, TV, or conversation you had to move fast or you would miss your chance. The pie-shaped pod trapped twenty-four of us, two to a cell. A guard station in the center of the fifth floor provided a clear view of every cell door in every twenty-four-person unit.

I walked over to the window slit as soon as I entered the cell. There it was, that blue sky and puffy white clouds I could barely see through the thick wire mesh of my week on the bus. Interstate 880 curved to the Bay Bridge Interchange. Shipping container cranes and green, blue, and rust-colored boxes peeked above the highway overpass. Most interestingly, the slit overlooked a street that periodically attracted a line of people who appeared to be waiting for a free meal.

The door buzzed and unlocked and I headed for the common area. A strong blast of an ammonia urine stench greeted my arrival in the dining area. A TV struggled to emit sound through three inches of bullet proof plexiglass. The last thing I thought anyone would shoot would be the TV, but I'm not an expert in the science of corrections.

The repetition was relentless. The morning count, breakfast, and the variations of prison programing: a TV show uninterrupted by advertisements that featured twenty-four men in a space station that has lost contact with the earth and the question of who was going to be eaten first. Lunch and another program: twenty-four men trapped in a submarine that has lost contact with the surface. Who should they kill and devour? Dinner was always followed by a bloody kung fu movie. It was amazing how many variations of twenty-four men vying to determine whom to dine on first was possible. If you didn't wish to miss any of these captivating programs yet had to pee your only option was the showers. Otherwise, you had to use the steal toilet in your cell and if you didn't urinate quickly you would have to wait two hours until the door clicked open again.

The back pages of a paperback cowboy western written in Spanish that started at page 92 kept me occupied even though I know almost no Spanish. My commissary was empty. I didn't even have enough money on my books to buy the cheapest item, a plastic rosary. I snatched a pencil from the in-take nurse while her back was turned. I must admit that wasn't the first time I used that trick to secure a coveted pen or pencil. Since I couldn't buy anything from the commissary cart, I set up a jailhouse business trading my drawing skills for pieces of fruit. An orange or apple for a sketch of a woman's breast penciled to a slip of concrete wall just inside the cell and out of view of the guards. All your fruit for a week for a detailed image of a naked woman. Word spread and my vegan diet was rewarded.

The air was just as captive as the prisoners. My head pounded with the worst headaches I had ever suffered. My calls to the outside world were all that could escape those walls and those were limited to a couple of upsetting conversations with my father and an occasional encouraging word from my attorney about progress on securing bail.

I got my attorney Randy Baker on the phone. He told me that his partner Beth Sanders had spoken with People's Park activist and the owner of Berkeley's Ashkenaz Music and Dance Cafe, David Nadel. He offered to put up the title of ownership for his San Pablo Avenue property as collateral against my reasonable potential to flee the country if bailed. David trusted me with his life's work Ashkenaz while also knowing how corrupt the justice system I was lashed to could be. I was touched by his trust. Even so, the San Francisco District Attorney's office went before the judge and claimed that the five thousand square-foot building was valued at less than the bail amount. After several bail hearings my lawyers finally drew a judge that knew of the property and agreed it was clearly valued at much more than the amount needed for my release. A frustrated district attorney then argued that our bail insurance was fake. But after another day in court and testimony from an agent with the insurance company the judge ordered my release after nearly two months of fearing I would never breath fresh air again.

I had been released from jail over a hundred times but this time was different. A small group of friends greeted me with hugs on the cold damp steps of the Hall of Justice. Some had waited in the drizzle for hours. A Dutch woman visiting San Francisco who had learned of my plight cradled a bouquet of twenty-four white roses. "Welcome home," she softy said as she passed the flowers into my arms.

There was another pretrial hearing before the very unhappy Judge Garcia. He wanted to get this case over with and turned to the clerk to set a trial date, "How about setting this for the end of October? Are there any days free on the docket?"

"How about October 31?" he suggested and all parties agreed. I was blown away by the choice of Halloween. Maybe the clerk had been a secret supporter because what could be better than a spooky holiday protest?

Freedom from jail really increases one's ability to participate in one's own defense. The October 31 court appearance lent itself to a courthouse protest we called, "Unmask Corporate Greed," with the intention of shaming the mayor's corporate base into demanding an end to the cruel campaign of sweeping the homeless, the poor, and Food Not Bombs from the city.

It was typical sunny late-October Northern California morning in the South of Market district of San Francisco. A collection of ghosts, ghouls, and goblins gathered on the steps of the perpetually ominous haunted house known as the Hall of Justice. The costumed crowd had gathered to share breakfast and speeches with supporters and those who had come for their own court appearances or other law enforcement related business. Tom passed the bullhorn to me. "Corporate greed is scary so let's cast a spell against their cruelty and enjoy some ghoulish gruel," I said.

Columns of defendants, lawyers, witches, and pirates marched up the stairs towards the entrance and the first-floor metal detectors. A couple of young Black guys stepped out of line to take a bagel. A volunteer, Elizabeth, scooped blobs of oatmeal with raisins from a five-gallon bucket into cups. A few monsters and a werewolf enjoyed the hot cereal. A couple of other young men interrupted their trip before a judge to sample our fare.

Several costumed supporters had already made their way upstairs looking for Garcia's court. "Hey look what I found!" shouted red-nosed Tom, dressed as a clown. He held up a handful of trick-or-treat candy. "The courts are breaking the law. They're handing out free candy, I found this on the counter in a third-floor clerk's office." A second person was handing out candy he had collected at the traffic court chambers passing out Snickers, Three Musketeers, and peanut butter cups to the line waiting to enter the courthouse. He made sure the row of riot police witnessed the crime. More candy snatchers who had stuffed their pockets full of government sponsored criminal candy shared their contraband with the public. The police stood at attention ignoring the tricks and treats until they had a clear shot at the bagel and oatmeal servers. One, two, and then five were pushed to the steps by the police, handcuffed, and dragged into the lobby and then down the hall to the first-floor lock-up.

Goblins, ghosts, witches, and warlocks passed through the first-floor metal detector, chanting, "Food Not Bombs, Food Not Bombs," on their way up to the third-floor courtroom where they were met by a second metal detector placed at the courtroom entrance. Bailiffs staffing the courtroom entrance ordered people to remove their masks and demanded our supporters clean off their face paint. "Take that green paint off your nose," one of them grunted.

One of my lawyers, Mary Sterns, was stopped and ordered to remove her mascara. The walls of the courtroom were once again lined with sheriff's department officers making it clear that they intended to amplify the danger they claimed that I posed. An exasperated Garcia read over our proposed settlement of credit for time served, the dropping of all 47 felony conspiracy charges in exchange for a felony probation zone around City Hall. He needed time to review the proposal. We would formalize it on December 5, 1994 before Judge Saldamando.

But by early December it was clear the deal would be unworkable. It would be too easy for the police to claim I violated probation and I could be sent to San Quintin for six months at the word of a probation officer just for attending a protest or for my association with those feeding the hungry. After all, we were still getting arrested and charged with felony conspiracy when we shared our meals. "Police contact," is what the legal system calls it.

Judge Saldamando accepted our refusal and turned to the clerk to set a trial date. "How about February 14?" he asked the judge? The district attorney was agreeable so our next action was set for Valentine's Day.

A crowd of supporters and volunteers gathered on the Bryant Street sidewalk outside the Hall of Justice on that chilly February 14, 1995, morning. San Francisco's finest stood shoulder to shoulder across the top step of the courthouse. A line of lawyers, defendants, and civilians doing business in the building crawled up the west side of the expansive flight of stairs. A giant Food Not Bombs banner was unfurled across the top landing concealing all but the helmets and plastic visors of the police line.

Food Not Bombs activists rushed around filling their pockets with Valentine candy collected from bowls dotted around the counters and courthouse desks and defied the police by sharing the confiscated loot with the crowd.

I stood on the courthouse steps speaking through a bull horn about the purpose of our protest. A big brown and tan Berkeley Farms Dairy truck arrived with a police detective in the passenger seat and parked across Bryant Street. A commercially printed banner hanging from the refrigerator truck demanded we return their milk crates referring to the blue plastic crates we borrowed and returned from Ananda Fuara vegetarian restaurant that we used every day as a table for our meals and literature. These were the milk crates that we used to replace our folding tables that had been confiscated by the police. The milk crates that I was accused of stealing and thus resulting in my third strike and the potential of a twenty-five to life sentence.

I called out over the loud speaker to the dairy employee and invited him to speak to the community about the theft of his crates. He tried to wave me off but finally he reluctantly took me up on the offer and joined me on the stairs. I passed the bullhorn over to him. He meekly told the protesters that Berkeley Farms wasn't really all that worried about the milk crates but if you do have any please return them.

The San Francisco Mime Troupe gathered on the steps below the Food Not Bombs banner. The cast took their positions ready to perform Michael Sullivan's first Mime Troupe sketch, "Captain Bob's Hungry Heart, or A Bagel in the Hands Is Worth Two in the Bush." Several actors dressed in exaggerated San Francisco Police garb arrested Ed Holmes as Keith McHenry when he flung open his grey trench coat to reveal rows of contraband bagels and cheese dangling inside.

While the actors were dramatically arresting the Mime Troupe felons, real police start arresting real Food Not Bombs volunteers for sharing real bagels with those filing into the courthouse. San Francisco State Theater professor Joel Schechter later wrote in Theater Journal, "The same people who laughed at the Mime Troupe's police force shouted 'Shame, Shame!' at the second act's officers; and a few spectators became actors as they resisted the arrest of the bagel server and tried to pull him away from the police."

Many of those in the audience had already been arrested for sharing food so the police actions on the courthouse steps were not a surprise. We anticipated the arrests of those handing out bagels and oatmeal but were amused that the candy distributors were free, once again, to share their Valentine treats without interference, possibly because it would implicate the courts in the crime. The crowd filed past the metal detector and headed upstairs where we had to pass through another metal detector outside the courtroom. The judge tried to silence the party atmosphere thumping his mallet hard to the bench as he grumbled. I recall that he complained about the commotion but also indicated that he really didn't want his fingerprints on this case even though the district attorney said they would agree to the offer of credit for time served and dropping of my other felony charges in exchange for a guilty plea to assault, battery, and strong-armed robbery but he still wanted a at least a year on supervised probation. Like the judges before him he didn't seem to want his good name associated with this dubious high-profile prosecution. He ordered us to return to Judge Lucy McCabe's court the next morning. The crowd chanted, "Food Not Bombs! Food Not Bombs!" as it stormed out of the courtroom, stomped down the courthouse stairs and flooded out into the lobby where the rest of our confiscated Valentine candy was shared with an amused public.

The next morning, I stood before Judge McCabe. She was fearless and rumored to be a bit tipsy from a pre-court nip of the good stuff.

"I don't know why Jordan is bothering a good Irish boy like you. Let's end this case once and for all. Everyone knows this is political. It's a waste of time and money. Why don't we have you plead to a felony with time served? After all Mayor Jordan just wants to tell people you were convicted of a felony so he can look good to his friends at cocktail parties," she said.

She suggested that the district attorney drop the assault with a deadly weapon and stolen property charges as well as my felony conspiracy cases and agree to a conviction of felony assault, battery, and strong-armed robbery with credit for time served of five hundred days in jail and a year's probation that could only be violated if I was charged with murder or a bombing. "So, to be clear, if my client is arrested for feeding the hungry, he won't be in violation of his probation," my attorney Dennis confirmed. "Yes, that's right, he doesn't need to worry about that," Judge McCabe clarified.

I took the plea and headed out of town with my Dobermut Pluto, a five-watt FM radio station, my purple-fist-embroidered chef's hat and cook's jacket, a glass bowl, bolt cutters, and the story of Food Not Bombs on the Rent is Theft Tour. I sought to limit the possibility of additional legal problems with the San Francisco authorities by staying out of town on a speaking tour.

But the story of my having faced twenty-five to life in prison was not yet over.

My friend David Nadel, the man who trusted that I would not skip bail took a bullet to the face in the doorway of his beloved Ashkenaz. He succumbed to his injuries at Highland Hospital a couple of days later. The painful shock and lingering mystery of the tragedy rocked our community. There were questions about the two Berkeley Police officers who had been across the street at the time of the shooting and the possibility that the young man later identified as Juan Rivera Pérez had been egged on in an attempt to eliminate an important opponent of the city. A performer who had been barred from playing at Ashkenaz by David because of their dispute over the course of the University's Strategic Lawsuit Against Public Participation or SLAPP suit that designed to silence both of them pitted friends against friends.

David's family called me a year after his December 1996 murder. The city hadn't returned the title to David before his death. There would be one last appearance before the court, this time to ask that the city turn over ownership of Ashkenaz to David's family. It did so. The case was closed. But a dear friend was lost.

I think most of us wouldn't want to waste a second chance at freedom and I sure haven't.

Family watching their meal be confiscated at Golden Gate Park

PART FOUR: JOURNEYS

Keith's painting to promote the UnFree Trade Tour

Chapter 27

THE UNFREE TRADE TOUR

How is it possible that a person can vanish without a trace? How is it that someone can become forever lost in mystery? This drama started innocently enough in 1994 at a dingy Berlin club thousands of miles from my home in San Francisco.

Here's the story. A cold San Francisco wind chilled the small ACT-Up rally I was attending outside the Social Security office at United Nations Plaza. A friend named Michael saw me and hurried my way. "Keith, it's great to see you. Heinke and I did a small tour to highlight your case. We even made t-shirts," he told me.

He was excited. His partner Heinke booked a popular Kreuzberg pub during Michael's visit to Berlin and organized an event to build interest in my California Three Strikes case. The threat of a twenty-five to life sentence for crimes that included feeding hungry people and "stealing" milk crates must have been intriguing.

He described meeting an activist who had been sitting in the back of the bar listening to their presentation. The activist approached my friends and introduced himself as Manolo. He told them he was touched by my plight and suggested they join him in Spain. He offered to organize a couple of speaking events. Michael spoke warmly of his new friend Manolo. He was a serious radical and well connected in European circles. Michael would give me several news clippings about their presentations in the Basque country and an X Large t-shirt with "Free Keith MacHenry" silkscreened across the chest at our next meeting. I felt honored.

A few months later Michael excitedly presented me with a faxed letter in Spanish that he had just received from Manolo. I gave the letter to our volunteer Hugh Mejia to take to his father Jesse, who was fluent in Spanish, for a translation. Jesse let me know a small press called Talasa Ediciones in Madrid wanted permission to translate my first book into Spanish. The second page was a contract which I didn't hesitate to sign and return. I could only imagine what impact a Spanish edition of *Food Not Bombs: How to Feed the Hungry and Build Community* might have.

A year later Michael gave me another fax from Manolo. I took it to Jesse. The Spanish edition had been published. Manolo had heard I was coming to Europe and wanted to know if I could add a book tour in Spain to my travels.

Jesse added that Manolo's letter said that a friend of his, Ramón Fernández Durán's book against a single European currency and my title were "two of the most important books on the struggle against the globalization of the economy. We would be honored if you could add the Iberian Peninsula to your itinerary." Again, I didn't hesitate and responded with another fax agreeing to add Spain to my tour.

I met Manolo under the stunning vaulted lobby of Estación de Francia in Barcelona in October 1996. He was a wiry man perhaps in his forties, sporting a two-day stubble and wire-rimmed glasses that mimicked his frail frame. He located his well-traveled red sedan in the parking lot and we headed south gliding along the ridges above the turquoise waters of the Balearic Sea. He showed me his computer translator. We tried a few sentences. It made a clumsy but understandable translation. We both laughed.

Our tour took us to an Israeli Restaurant in the heart of Málaga. "Welcome to our establishment," said the owner, a smiling, down-to-earth woman with long brown hair and a sense of purpose. The large white-walled cafe was crowded. Manolo and I were seated on a top landing with a dozen others. Excited locals stopped by our table to greet us with a warm handshake and a kind word. The authentic middle eastern vegetarian meal promised by Manolo was served. There were rounds of welcoming toasts made with abundant Spanish wine. Laughter, chatter and the clanking of glasses mixed with the background music and then a midnight presentation about Food Not Bombs. "We only have one more event tonight," Manolo's friend Salva told me in all seriousness. "What? It's already two in the morning," I blurted out in surprise. Everyone in the room laughed. We would be settling in for the night.

The next morning, we headed out on the long flat drive across the treeless plains to Madrid. The open landscape was occasionally interrupted only by a towering black metal silhouette of a bull. Manolo and I would laugh and say, "El Toro, El Toro," each time the image rose on the horizon. Manolo and I were becoming friends.

The empty plains of golden grasses became the suburbs of Madrid. The dusk glow on the Prado added to the grandeur of the facade. Oh, how I wish I had the time to peek inside at the paintings I had only seen in my freshman year art history textbook: Francisco Goya, El Greco, and Titian. It wasn't long, however, before we found that evening's venue, an alternative bookstore in a stone building in one of the old sections of town.

The next day I found myself walking along the polished concrete sidewalks embossed with images of plump grape bunches to a huge auditorium of college students at the University of La Rioja. The headmaster gripped a microphone, stepped from behind the podium and spoke earnestly to several hundred of his young scholars. The translator whispered his accolades about my work and the organization I helped start. A sea of interested faces seemed to be soaking up each of my details, the protest in New Hampshire on May 24, the arrests in San Francisco, and the global spread of the movement. The loud clapping when I finished my presentation suggested that my impression of their attention was accurate.

The Basque sky was a gloomy and grey when Manolo and I climbed his stairs to his spacious third floor apartment in Vitoria-Gastei. We were greeted by a statuesque blonde with a serious air who was cradling a clay cup of tea when she answered the door. I had the impression she was an important figure in the Basque independence movement. I also thought she might have been Manolo's wife but this was never mentioned. I can't recall how I got that idea but it must have been gleaned from what little Spanish I know. Maybe it was mentioned by the translator at the last venue when sharing details of the day ahead. Manolo and his woman friend bundled me off to an interview in the sixth-floor office of a Basque newspaper.

I was excited. The reporter leaned back in his office chair, notebook and pen in hand. "So, what is the goal of your organization?" he asked. "We are working to build a movement that strives toward steering public funding away from the military and towards providing the real security of food, shelter, and other social services." The reporter continued, "So why have you come to the Basque country?" "To build international solidarity," I responded.

The reporter suggested we run over to a local radio station. Those arrangements had already been made by my host and after that it was over to another newspaper to finish the hectic day of interviews.

That was when our tour of the Iberian Peninsula came to an end. Manolo winded his borrowed car down the curvy mountain streets of Irún and pulled up outside a tavern. Row after row of photos of ETA prisoners looked down from a huge banner above the pub entrance. I would be catching a bus to Paris from there.

Manolo retrieved his computer translator from a bag, typed out a question, and handed me the message as he enthusiastically pointed at my chest then to himself. I believed he wanted to know if I could help organize a tour of North America for him. He typed that he wanted to introduce Americans to the dangers of the World Trade Organization. Of course, I said, jumping at the opportunity. I had been to the huge protests against the European Union and the Euro in Bonn. I had also organized opposition to the North American Free Trade Agreement. These were all institutions and policies likely to cause more poverty, increase the erosion of civil liberties, and speed up the destruction of the environment.

I typed out, "I will bring your proposal to my organization in San Francisco." We hugged and then he motored off into the darkness of coastal Spain and I continued on my European tour.

A few weeks after I had returned to San Francisco I marched to the top of Bernal Heights to visit with Heinke and Michael. Someone's legs were emerging from under a bus. It was Heinke and when I announced myself, she scooted into view, stood, and brushed the dust off her hands. "I am really struggling with this rusted fuel filter. I have been under there all day," she said. Michael heard us and appeared from behind their monster of a vehicle.

"I loved meeting Manolo. He asked if we would be interested in organizing a tour of North America," I proclaimed. They were eager to help. "Let's bring this proposal to our next meeting," Michael suggested.

An enthusiastic group of twenty or more activists sat around on a collection of old couches and rickety chairs at the back half of the dingy second floor punk space, The Epicenter Zone, on Valencia Street. That evening's sharing crew bounced in, all out of breath, and stashed an array of serving equipment in a corner. Everyone settled down and the meeting unfolded.

We followed our well-practiced agenda: introductions, agenda review, logistics and scheduling, and ending with the last item we called solidarity. This was my time to introduce the tour idea suggesting the title, "The UnFree Trade Tour." I explained a little about my visit to Spain, the film they wanted to show about the history that led to the formation of the World Trade Organization, and the potential for WTO policies to restrict civil liberties, increase poverty and ecocide, while leading to more hunger, more bombs, and more suffering.

Hugh indicated his support and offered to ask his father Jessie to continue translating our correspondence saying, "This is a great opportunity to build solidarity with the European movement." Ann added, "There might not be anything more important for us to get behind."

We all agreed. We would start by mailing a letter to each of the Food Not Bombs chapters we had a mailing address for and ask if their group would be interested in hosting such a tour. I drafted the letter introducing our allies as Spanish Anarchists and explained that they were active in protesting the globalization of the economy and had participated in the actions in the film we planned to show called, "Fifty Years is Enough."

Heinke and Michael offered the services of their bus if they would be able to get it road worthy by the start of the tour. Heinke also offered to translate since she also spoke Spanish. I would seek support from my friends at Global Exchange, Earth First, and the International Forum on Globalization hoping they would announce the project in their newsletters and send representatives of their organizations to our events. We started to make a plan. Hugh said he would continue to pass messages to be translated to his father and also offered technical support for the video showings.

It wasn't long before local groups started to respond to our letters and we were able to piece together an itinerary. I typed up our proposed schedule and mailed a copy to each participating group and faxed a copy to Manolo's group, Baladre, for approval.

Manolo's next fax confirmed the schedule. The only problem, however, was that he said the four of them would be landing in Los Angles instead of San Francisco. I assumed that they did not realize how large America is and had the impression that Los Angeles was near San Francisco and found that the tickets from Europe to LAX were less expensive than landing at SFO.

Our plans started to get complicated as the dates for the tour grew close. Heinke and Michael would not have their bus ready in time and Heinke reported that she had no choice but to rush home to Germany to help her East Berlin housemates defend their squat against an attempt by another group to seize their apartment. Michael would stay in town trying to nurse their bus back to life. Our transportation and translator were no longer available.

It seemed the best way to solve the translation deficiency was to write each host and ask them to provide a local person who spoke both English and Spanish to translate the presentation.

I had not planned to go on the tour myself but it was becoming evident that my participation would be essential. A young barefoot man stopped me one afternoon as I was walking along Harrison in the Mission. He recognized me from our meals. "I'm taking an oath of poverty," he said, telling me he was giving up money to live a life of service. He wanted to know if I would like to have his credit card. "Really, you don't mind if I use it to rent a van?" I asked surprised. That was lucky because I didn't have a credit card and I don't think anyone in our community had one either back then. It wasn't a time when you could use a debit card to secure rental cars.

That solved one big problem, our need to replace the bus.

I rented a forest green six-seat minivan at a South of Market lot and flew down I-5 to LAX to collect our "Spanish Anarchist" guests.

Manolo, Sara, and Salva, staggered out of customs in that post-intercontinental flight daze. The fourth guest, Andoni couldn't join them. I whisked them off to the comfortable bungalow of my friend Richard, a cohort from the Boston Food Not Bombs days. First order of business was a shower and a good night's sleep. Our touring musician, my friend Seth, was already sitting in Richard's yard sipping a beer when we arrived. We knew one another through his participation with the Long Beach collective and our involvement with Earth First!'s eco-defense actions.

The UnFree Trade Tour began with Manolo's requested press conference. Luggage Room Gallery co-founder Darryl Smith and I set out the podium and arched a row of folding chairs around the center of the airy second-floor hall. A cool blue light flooded the room through ceiling-to-floor windows. Manolo paced in thought while I showed Salva our low-watt FM station and unpacked the box holding a twelve-channel Radio Shack mixer, power supply, and a double-fist-sized FM radio transmitter.

The time for the media event arrived. A couple of my friends had climbed the narrow stairway up to the almost empty gallery, but not one journalist graced the space. The subject of "free trade" was apparently too esoteric for local media consumers even if it featured activists from Spain. While I was not surprised by the disinterest and had warned him, Manolo was clearly disappointed. He complained to his companion Salva that when he held press events in Spain dozens of journalists would attend. I had experienced that myself during our short tour of the Iberian Peninsula but this was the United States and media access has mostly been unattainable for those of us that question the logic of the corporate dystopian world.

Next it was time for our first presentation. We entered a packed venue called Long Haul in Berkeley. Legs dangled from the balcony. East Bay Food Not Bombs activists Judy, Elsa, and Joe darted around the small kitchen plopping spoonfuls of rice, beans, and salad onto thrift store dish-ware. Tattooed and pinned punks balanced plates of rice and beans and a bagel or slice of bread on their laps. Matt and Ian met us and directed our attention to the movie projector and the three chairs that constituted the "stage." Manolo quickly started to direct preparations. I recall thinking he had a more authoritarian energy than I was used to in my anarchist circles. When not responding to Manolo's requests I checked out Salva's progress with the task of hooking up the components of our five-watt pirate radio station and placed a couple of FM radio receivers around the hall. Sara stood before our assembled chairs nibbling on an apple as she spoke with our translator. Seth greeted old friends before setting up his guitar and music stand. He had some new material for the tour.

"Attention, attention, we are going to start now," Ian called out from the balcony.

That was the signal that the first stop on the UnFree Trade Tour was about to start. Seth stood before the crowd armed with his acoustic guitar, said a few words against corporate plunder and belted out one of his anticapitalist folk punk tunes.

It's against the law to feed the homeless.
It's against the law to sleep in the park.
It's against the law for you to see me.

I live outside.
I am a criminal.
I lived outside the law.

Fuck you, cop, I want to eat.
Fuck you, mayor, I live here.
Fuck you, law-abiding citizen, you put me here.
Fuck you, voter, I will never disappear.

All your systems will crash one day and you will crawl to me.

I thanked Seth and introduced Manolo, Sara, and Salva in my now scratchy voice. Sara sat next to Manolo facing the eager audience. Salva bounced around the room taking photos and adjusting radio tuners. I made a quick statement on the purpose for the tour and turned the program over to Manolo to share his analysis of the globalization of the economy. The translator repeated his presentation in English. At one point the translator had a confused expression about some of Manolo's statements and had to ask for clarification. A Spanish speaking audience member tried to seek clarity on an issue of bank coordination under globalization. I assumed Manolo's confused presentation had to do with translation difficulties, or possibly he had been hard to understand because he was so close to the subject.

Sara sat quietly with her hands folded in her lap listening until someone in the audience interrupted Manolo's somewhat incoherent ramblings and asked to hear from her. She smiled and noted that Spain was still a male-dominated society and continued by explaining that she volunteered with a prison abolition group and came to speak of the role of the police and prisons in maintaining liberal capitalism. I could feel a sense of relief flow across the crowded hall at Sara's compassionate presentation.

"Thanks, Sara and Manolo, so now it is time to view their documentary." I croaked.

People raced around turning off the lights as Joe switched on the projector. A grainy black and white picture of protesters behind the title, "50 Years is Enough," flickered against an old wrinkled movie screen. The film opened with a bit about the history of the Brenton Woods Conference, a gathering of seven hundred and thirty delegates from forty-four nations who met in the summer of 1944 in New Hampshire to form the World Bank, the International Monetary Fund (IMF), and the World Trade Organization (WTO). The film went on to profile the massive protest against these institutions on the fiftieth anniversary of the Brenton Woods Conference.

Our Spanish guests had been there in the streets protesting the economic bondage of the European Union and its single currency. They would be able to give first person accounts of the European actions projected across the screen. I had also participated in one of the huge demonstrations in Bonn, Germany in the early 90s.

The film credits rolled. The house lights were clicked on. A short discussion followed that mostly included ideas on how to organize resistance. "We should shut down the WTO if they dare hold a summit here in the US," suggested someone in the back of the audience. "That's right!" another responded. Seth agreed and played two closing tunes. We did it. "The UnFree Trade Tour" had begun and I had an idea of how to proceed over the next two months.

We woke to the drizzle of an incoming storm, ate breakfast, piled into the rental and scampered across the Golden Gate Bridge and north out of the Bay Area winding along an increasingly rainy US 101 to Arcadia. I had lost my voice by the time we reached Santa Rosa, so that ended my part in any conversation. It was during one of our first stops that Manolo began assigning van seating arrangements.

We stumbled, road weary, into the venue as the sun lost its glow behind the thick bank of clouds. I couldn't introduce Manolo. Seth would not only be our musician but would be my alternate voice. The small audience eagerly hung on every translated word. Sara got her chance to speak and Salva managed the radio station.

Our hosts took us to their collective's home, a two-story Victorian that overlooked a quiet residential street near the center of town. The after parties are often the most important part of any tour, offering excellent opportunities to build relationships.

Eight of us sat around a living room of trash-liberated sofas and chairs. Our South American translator was busy with a back and forth. Beers, cups of fruit juice, tea, crackers, olives, and chips were passed around. A long, bootleg Grateful Dead concert tape played softly in the background. The ecstatic energy was starting to fade when the room was startled back to life with the unpleasant screech of the doorbell. One of our hosts, Brian, popped to attention. The room went silent. We looked at one another inquisitively. Who could be to the door at 12:45 a.m. on this drizzly Humboldt County night?

All eyes turned towards the mystery arrival.

Brian stepped slowly to the door and turned the knob. A blast of damp air crept passed the three-inch-wide passage. A young man dressed in a crisp brown UPS uniform peeked through the threshold. A basketball-sized cardboard box rested like a trophy in the crook of his left arm.

Brian opened the door. "Delivery for Martin Murphy," announced the late-night visitor in a brown uniform who then handed the package to a puzzled housemate. "Please sign here," the UPS driver said, pointing to a dark x on a form snapped to a clipboard.

Brian signed.

"Are you Martin Murphy?" the driver asked as if that information wasn't really all that important. He didn't even look at the form to decipher the signature.

"No, but he used to live here. He drops by every now and then," Brian replied twisting the box back and forth trying to read the return address. "The sender isn't familiar," he said with a perplexed smile and setting the box behind the door at the end of a line of shoes. It wasn't long before we were shown our accommodations and went off to sleep.

Thankfully my voice had returned by the time we arrived in Eugene, Oregon. We were greeted with both excitement and a vegan feast with Spanish rice and lentils and a shepherd's pie prepared lovingly for our international guests before heading off to the event.

The hall was alive with activity when we arrived. A couple of people were adjusting the optics of an old projector. I set the tour's literature on a table near the stage. Salva assembled our low-watt radio station and placed our clunky old collection of FM radio tuners around the venue to provide a surround sound of the presentation and Seth's performance.

I realized after what I saw during our first two events that the program would be more effective if I gave an opening statement that expressed clearly the point of the tour to help make Manolo's lecture more understandable. I also decided to interrupt Manolo after about fifteen minutes since I could see that the audience would start to fidget and seem to lose interest by then. This would also give more time for Sara to speak about the work of feminist opposition to capitalism and her participation in the prison abolition movement in Spain. While Manolo was the main event if anyone was going to understand why we were on tour it would fall to me to explain the central points.

As planned our enthusiastic hosts welcomed us to their home after the presentation. Beer was served. Someone probably lit up a bowl of green bud. Chips and some dumpstered chocolate chip cookies graced a dented maple-red laminated coffee table. Our translator, a Chilean teaching at the university, sat with Manolo and Sara fielding questions on anarchism in Spain and global trade from the local activists. Cold beers continued to be opened and pipe loads of herb shared. It was well past midnight yet no one seemed to be getting sleepy.

Then we were jarred from our conversations by a loud knocking on the front door. One of the housemates answered and a uniformed postman handed him a small package. It seemed the mailman was running late, real late as it was, again, almost one in the morning.

Our tour took us north through the traffic and vibrant green pastures of the Willamette Valley to the City of Roses and a warm greeting and another tasty vegan meal. After we spoke in Portland our crew settled down for the evening at the home of several local Food Not Bombs organizers. We were treated to drinks and reheated leftovers from dinner. Housemates hung on every word that Manolo and Sara spoke. Salva was already starting to understand some English and was engaged in a conversation with a Latin American history student and her friend. The buzz of our late-night conversation was disturbed yet again, this time by the elegant ding-dong of the doorbell. A Portland utility employee in blue uniform needed to drop off some forms for the household to review. It was almost two a.m.

Our tour took us across Washington State, past the military bases and devastatingly logged forests to Seattle. Trays of tasty dishes lined a string of tables on one side of the hosting art gallery a block from Lake Seattle. My friend Carl Chatski filmed the event. The presentations were starting to jell. I helped Salva pack up our transmitter and receivers and our conversation with the local activists drifted out into the misty street before we headed off to the afterparty.

We retired to the living room of an old drafty Victorian up in University Heights. Housemates and friends fired questions at the Spanish interpreter eager to hear what their Castilian visitors had to say.

I was ready for bed. It was closing in on one-thirty in the morning, but the others still had at least another hour of life to contribute.

Thud, thud, thud. Someone was at the door.

I could see a stalky man in a crisp grey-blue US postal uniform standing under the acid-yellow glow of the porch light. He was holding a long white package bound up with red, white, and blue priority mail tape.

The conversation went silent and everyone had the look of disbelief. "That's odd, we have never received mail at one-thirty in the morning?" commented one of the young housemates. Seth turned to me and said, "These early morning deliveries are becoming a pattern."

The woman closest to the door got up and opened it. The mailman stood at the threshold for a minute or so and then handed her the box, quickly turned and bounced down the stairs into the night. She scrutinized the name on the address label. "Anyone know who Tim Rosenthal is?" she asked. "He might have lived here last semester" responded one of her housemates. She placed the box on the floor near the front door.

I had promised to make time for Manolo to email a report of the tour to his compatriots back in Spain. That was at a time in internet history before the ease we have now where we can email from our phones and laptops without having to think of the technology behind it. In 1997 the only way Manolo could reach his email account remotely was through a process called Telnet. We spent a couple of hours that morning in Seattle giving him time to type his report. Carl hooked him up to Telnet and the first cyber report of the trip was launched. Thankfully Carl was an internet pioneer. This process would never be so easy during the rest of our trip.

Manolo and I also had an agreement that we would pay for a weekly long-distance phone call to Spain using our 800 number Qwest Account. I would dial in the pass code on a payphone or someone's land line and hand him the receiver. Ten or so minutes later he would hang up seemingly satisfied. He made his first call that morning.

We scurried north to Peace Park and crossed the border into to Canada to join a rally to free Native American political prisoner Leonard Peltier. But we couldn't stay long as we had an event scheduled in Vancouver. We pulled up to Canadian customs and handed our passports to the officer standing at the window. He returns everyone's documents but mine. "Please come with me," the official ordered. He took me to a back room and questioned me about my arrests.

I told him I had been arrested for sharing meals with the hungry. He wasn't sure that was possible. He let me get a copy of my flyers and calendars that included photos of riot police guarding the food at the entrance to Golden Gate Park and making arrests at Civic Center Plaza in San Francisco. He warmed up to me. "That is insane," he decried, shaking his head as he told me I was free to go.

The late-night visits continued. There was a midnight visit from an employee with the electric company in Minneapolis and a car that followed us from our venue at Left Bank Books to our beds in Saint Paul. The sedan was still parked outside when we emerged the next morning. Two men in sports coats and sunglasses sat motionless in the front seats.

We had been on the road for nearly three weeks. The post-midnight deliveries and service calls continued. We headed south. Salva was driving and didn't realize how few gas stations there were in parts of Wyoming. The van puttered to a stop. We had run out of gas, but were saved by a Basque sheep herder who towed our van behind his flatbed truck. The bloody head of a freshly killed sheep bobbed off the back with its long tongue flapping in the wind and stared at us all the way to the first town. There we procured a full tank of fuel, a few rounds of brew, and a conversation with one of their own at a local bar.

Our tour had taken us to the center of the United States. We were the guests of the Leonard Peltier Defense Committee in Lawrence, Kansas. The staff person, Kathleen, who I would have to kick out a year later had already crept upstairs to bed. The three Spaniards, Seth, and I were sitting around the living room sipping tea and juice while discussing the next day's itinerary.

A loud ding-dong of the doorbell startled the room into silence. We glanced at one another in surprise at yet another past-midnight delivery.

I opened the door and asked, "Can we help you?"

A tall tower of a man in his late forties stood on the front stoop, his long black tie somehow emphasizing his stature. He had a clipboard under one arm and was mindlessly snapping the first inch or so of a thick yellow tape measure.

"I am here from the insurance company and I've come to measure the interior ceilings," he announced with an authority he punctuated with the snap, snap, snap of his tape measure.

"Really, at one-forty-five in the morning? Is that normal around here?" I asked, adding that the tenant had gone to bed and that he should return in the morning.

He ignored my comments and stepped past me, walking briskly to the stairway. He whipped out his tape and launches it towards the ceiling. I suggested he return in the morning when the tenant was awake. He continued ignoring me, made another measurement and marked it on his paper.

The late-night insurance measurements came to an abrupt end and he left as swiftly as he entered.

"This is getting pretty weird," Seth noted again with a look of concern.

The next morning, Sara was in the kitchen helping Kathleen clean up after a hardy breakfast. The men were sitting in the living room with their mugs of coffee and conversation. Manolo found a copy of the Kansas City Star left on an end table. He was particularly happy, leaning back in a leather recliner radiating a glowing smile of satisfaction. Even though he didn't speak any English he was absorbed in that morning's edition with particular interest in one story.

Seth asked Salva why Manolo was more upbeat than his usual anxious self. Salva was becoming pretty fluent in English. He believed Manolo was interested in a news story about an attack by the Basque group ETA that took place on the Guggenheim Museum in Bilbao, Spain.

It was my understanding during my tour of Spain that Manolo was an important Basque activist and supported the work of ETA. I assumed the news was good from his reaction. A victory for his people's independence or the release of an important member of the organization from prison.

He set the paper aside so I took it and opened it to the article. Members of ETA tried to bomb the museum intending to kill the King and other dignitaries who had come to celebrate the architectural monument's opening. The plot failed and the Basque fighters had either been killed or arrested. The intended targets were unscathed.

Salva, Seth, and I were all perplexed by his reaction to news that should have saddened him. Maybe he was happy that it had made the news and, in that way, he may have felt that the action was a success. Maybe he just didn't understand the story because it was in English?

Our hosts in Chicago welcomed us with dinner. "We made extra for you after hearing about your trouble getting meals," one of them said. Another utility company visited us after midnight and I woke to set up another early morning a Telnet connection for Manolo and his report. My roommate, Bobby, and I had organized a lecture at the Dr. Pedro Albizu Campos High School. We thought our Spanish guests would love to meet the Spanish-speaking revolutionaries and learn about the Puerto Rican Independence Movement. While Sara and Salva were captivated by the experience it was clear to me that Manolo found our visit tedious.

We cruised into to Detroit and found the Trumbullplex housing collective and show space. A banquet of delicious dishes graced the dining room table. "We are reading your travel log and are so sorry you have been going without food," someone said. I remembered wondering why they had thought we had been going hungry. Our van was packed with snacks and everyone made us delicious meals. Again, there was another late-night visit, this time by someone claiming to be lost.

We were greeted with concern in Cleveland. "We are so sorry you have been going without food. We will fix that," a host said, pointing to a huge pot on the stove and casseroles, chips, and fancy breads spread across the kitchen table. "Help yourself," she insisted and of course there was another midnight guest.

Manolo was distraught and with hand gestures let me know he tried to call Spain but the code for the Food Not Bombs long-distance service didn't work. I was stunned, how did he know the code since I had not shared it. I called Qwest from our guest's home phone and they told me that I had made $1,500 in calls to Spain and they blocked my service. They asked if I wanted to lift the block but I asked them to continue to deny access.

The auditorium at the University of Toronto was filled to capacity. This was the largest audience so far with four or five hundred people settling into their seats. I stood at the door speaking with the local organizers when the front desk staff called me over, nervously letting me know that I needed to wait for the Toronto Metro Police before starting. Sure enough, two officers appeared, walked up to me and asked, "So what do you have planned tonight?" One of the officers flipped open his notebook to a fresh page.

"Why do you ask?" I responded.

They insisted that they needed to know what I intended by coming to Toronto. I pressed them for an explanation for their question but they refused to say why. I told them we planned to speak about poverty and handed them both a flyer I found sitting on the reception counter.

"Are we done here? I need to start the presentation since the crowd is waiting," I said and stepped into the auditorium. The audience had witnessed the exchange through the open door and wanted to know what the problem was. "What was that about?" asked a college-aged woman sitting in the aisle. "Yes, what did they want?" an older man a few seats down chimed in concerned.

I started the event by assuring those assembled that all was well with the police and promised them that no one would be arrested.

Once again, we spent some time looking for a computer where Manolo could post a report to his organization in Europe. The digital world has changed a lot since those frustrating days of Telnetting and the gopher that blipped a puke greenish-yellow pixelated rodent across the monitor to fetch your email.

That next morning, I tried to accommodate Manolo's need to Telnet his travelogue. Fortunately for us several of the local Food Not Bombs volunteers were also students at the McLuhan Center for Culture and Technology and had been working on the frontiers of the internet. They had in fact created the process called a listserv and one of the first such interactive online lists was designed for Food Not Bombs called fnb@tao.ca.

I joined the students at their lab that morning preparing Manolo's account. I was at the center for all of ten minutes when Manolo and Salva arrived agitated. From what Salva was saying in his quickly improving English, Manolo believed someone had stolen all his money. Maybe he left it in his bag in the van and I needed to hurry back with the key.

The van seemed untouched and locked. I was confused. It didn't seem that anyone broke in but Manolo was desperate so I rushed and unlocked the vehicle. He removed Seth's expensive guitar from the top of a pile of luggage, lifted out two duffel bags and set them on the pavement revealing his suitcase. He dragged that bag to the edge of the hatchback, clicked it open, and franticly pulled out a smaller bag, and turned it inside out.

"No money, no money," he blurted out with a choppy Spanish accent shaking the empty cloth satchel for all of us to see.

Everyone expressed concern. Our Toronto hosts were devastated. I promised to make sure he could buy whatever he needed but this failed to console him. We agreed to meet that afternoon to address the crisis, all gathering in the basement of the Food Not Bombs house. We were settling into the couches and cushions and were about to start our discussion when there was an aggressive knock on the front door.

"Water department here. We need to check the pipes in the basement," a man announced, heading towards the stairway with unusual confidence. Our host suggested he return the next morning but the man insisted, pushed his way past the tenant and dashed down the stairs into the center of our meeting. He waved Sara aside and crouched on the cushion-covered bench and unscrewed a panel in the wall behind her. After a few minutes he needed to climb behind Seth to take a quick looked inside another panel then stepped through the middle of our meeting to look in a closet.

Manolo's missing money remained a mystery. How did the thief know that there was money hidden deep in our luggage? Or was the money taken before Manolo packed away his pouch. How did Manolo know the money was stolen when the bag was locked in the van? If taken from the van why did the thief carefully repack and lock the vehicle? Maybe this mystery was lost again in translation. So, believing there must be a logical explanation to these questions we decided to head off to the next lecture with a promise we would make sure the van was always securely locked.

The tour arrived in Buffalo, New York. Our host was concerned that we had been going without food. They had been reading the daily email reports. The last post said we hadn't eaten in days. The Food Not Bombs volunteers in Montreal had mentioned something about our needing food as had the people in Detroit but I thought nothing of it since we had been treated to huge community dinners at every stop and we had just arrived with two trash bags of bagels, apples, bananas, and granola.

We were welcomed in Waterloo and Montreal with both hosts sharing feasts with us. We were also met with attentive audiences and more middle of the night deliveries.

It was time to drive south through the frosty hay fields towards the Vermont city of Burlington on the eastern banks of Lake Champlain.

C.T. Butler, my long-time friend and Food Not Bombs co-founder, had helped organize the event and invited us to stay at his apartment. C.T. took me aside and said, "Keith something isn't right about the tour." He had become my long-distance phone connection after I allowed my account to continue being blocked. I had been calling his toll-free number from pay phones to ask him to call ahead to each venue. During these calls we would discuss the odd patterns, the late-night visits, and the email reports of inadequate food. "McHenry still isn't feeding us," seemed to be a repeated theme. C.T. had also unplugged his landline, hiding his phones in the basement. He didn't need an expensive phone bill. That turned out to be a wise decision. Manolo wandered around C.T.'s apartment mumbling "telephone, telephone," as he searched along the walls and furniture.

C.T. was as confused as I was about news of our having gone without food and he made a point of treating us to another feast. The venue was packed, the interpreter fluent, and the discussion lively. The volunteers stuffed our van with food blocking the rear-view window with boxes of organic produce and snacks to make sure that we wouldn't starve on our journey to Boston and beyond.

But when we got to Boston, we learned that there was another report that our party had been going hungry and our hosts were excited to provide us with fresh-baked vegan casseroles, a pumpkin stew, and a slew of pies.

Next it was south along Interstate 95, backed-up toll booths and thick traffic to the Big Apple. I had planned a real treat for our Spanish guests. A visit to the famous squat, Casa del Sol, in the heart of Spanish-speaking South Bronx. What could be more anti-capitalist and revolutionary? I was also excited that they would be able to carry out their presentations and follow-up conversations all without an interpreter.

I was familiar with the 136 and Cypress neighborhood and the squat where over a dozen families had been living rent-free for decades. I was first introduced to the area when collecting discarded food at the Hunts Point Produce Market. My contacts, Andrew and Paco, made the top floor of the squat their kingdom. Oriental carpets spread across the hard-wood floor. Two black oil barrel wood stoves made it t-shirt-comfortable even on the chilliest winter nights. Mammoth, high windows faced the Manhattan skyline and the snarl of highways and bridges that lead to the apartments and warehouses of Queens and Brooklyn. It was a cheery, light-bathed and vast common room of found furniture and posters from past community festivals.

I remember one bitter cold morning when two NYPD detectives climbed the six flights to the palace to investigate an assault that had happened outside the building and commented that their wives would be angry to know that people were living in such majesty for free.

Casa del Sol was a magical place, but it also had a harsh history. There were power struggles between the early squatters. It stood on Cypress Street surrounded by ruins from the days of the mafia insurance fires. What was left of the brick walls of past apartment buildings had become the fencing of vegetable gardens and orchards. I was impressed by the tall stand of birch trees that hugged one corner of the apple and cherry trees in the lot next the squat. The basement housed a theater and a bike repair shop.

Puerto Rican families occupied most of the units. Children ran laughing in the stairwells. Grandmothers sat out front on found chairs gabbing about their daily concerns. They always had a smile for me.

Andrew, a coordinator of the Cherry Tree Foundation, walked us over to the gardens that filled the block between 135th and 136th Streets. Our host had helped nurture the projects that fostered community in this rough section of America.

Andrew introduced our entourage to a group of older men who were happy to look up from their intense chess match to welcome us to their piece of paradise. Our arrival signaled that it was time to prepare for dinner and that evening's entertainment. Local children gathered scrap wood, mostly broken pallets, piling the splintered oak and pine near a circle of broken sidewalk slabs in anticipation of the cooking fire. A couple of young men ratcheted open a fireplug to provide our water as others gathered vegetables from the garden to make our soup. I balanced some discarded wooden planks in the concrete chunks near the fire pit to make our prep table. A young woman and her son filled plastic buckets with fire hydrant water. Children joined their grandmothers in the washing and cutting of the garden harvest filling giant plastic bowls with colorful slices of red and yellow peppers, rainbow chard, orange carrots, fire-truck-red tomatoes, and forest-green cucumbers.

I sparked the wad of paper bags beneath the pyramid of scrap wood and ignited the flames destined to cook our banquet. Andrew and his cohort Paco balanced two sixty-five-quart pots on the cement chunks that surrounded the conflagration.

Soon dinner was ready, and the sun would be disappearing behind a wall of still-inhabited apartment blocks. Dozens of neighbors meandered into the lot and set out folding chairs and milk crates to form a dining room. Two older women hauled in a pot of beans and rice. As the sun descended behind the tenements, we made ourselves comfortable sitting before a blank five-story brick wall enjoying our home-grown dinners. The children were restless, aware of the spectacle we would be treated to. I had the impression that everyone had anticipated this performance for days.

An Anglo couple bounced across the rubble-strewn dining area with several giant cardboard shadow puppets. The woman announced that the show was about to begin! They unfurled the intricately cut cardboard silhouettes. A street light illuminated the shadowy story of resistance to the gentrification of the South Bronx. Darkened flat images of gardeners swirled across the wall beating back the monster bulldozer with jabs of their spades, hoes, and pitch forks. The tool-armed community of lacy defenders danced across the brick side of a surviving apartment complex in victory. The neighborhood was saved.

We sped down FDR Drive towards the Brooklyn apartment where we would be spending the night. The woman we would be staying with sat in the front passenger seat turning to berate me over her shoulder. "How come you have been refusing to feed your Spanish guests? This is no way to run a tour," she squawked ignoring the fact that she had just enjoyed a feast with our crew.

She revealed that she had been translating Manolo's reports into English and was posting them to the Food Not Bombs list-serv. Did she intentionally change Manolo's posts or was she translating his reports accurately? She sure was angry with me.

News of our starvation worried our friends in Washington, D.C. where we were treated to another banquet and bags of groceries.

The following day we pulled into the Richmond Food Not Bombs house.

"We read about how you haven't eaten in days but it looks like you finally came across some food," one volunteer said, helping us unload five grocery bags full of pastries, bread, and fruit. I explained that we have arrived with food at all the other venues and that of course we are visiting Food Not Bombs chapters so we have been welcomed with a huge all-you-can eat vegan feast at every stop. "Maybe they feel they aren't eating because there is no meat?" I pondered out loud.

Our hosts headed off with Manolo to find meat. They returned with steaks, cheese, a gallon of milk, and sausage. Hopefully this would solve the problem.

C.T. and I spoke every day. He read a couple of the email reports to me. In one of the entries Manolo reported that we were almost killed by a group of Black youth in St Louis. The description suggested he confused a group of people waiting at a bus stop as dangerous thugs. C.T. was concerned that these emails were putting Food Not Bombs in a very bad light.

Our Spanish travelers took a look inside the accommodations in New Orleans and opted for a night in the van. Every inch of the walls in the shotgun house was pasted with images cut from magazines, packaging, posters, and scraps of found paper creating an intriguing collage interpretation of society. Salva greeted me in the morning shaking his head laughing. "We were surrounded by people teasing us. A heavy woman sprawled across the windshield. We thought they might kill us. It was frightening." It was a tough neighborhood that was clear. The convenience store across the street had a thick bullet-proof spinning window where you placed your cash and retrieved your purchase on one quarter of the two-foot by two-foot carousel.

They should have joined us inside. This would be a different story in Austin, the capital of Texas. We were guests of the Entropy House, the Earth First! central Texas hub. There was never a time when I stayed on their couch that I didn't find the walls, floor, and kitchen appliances crawling with enormous cockroaches. It was creepy. We had a few free days which I was blessed to spend with my high-school sweetheart Cullen. She was in Austin visiting her two elementary-school-aged daughters. Oh, dear Cullen, it was great to reconnect. She had a joyous spirit and had matured into a stunningly attractive Texas blond. I wish I could remember that sacrilegious joke that she shared as we toured around town in her top-of-the-line BMW. Her ten-year struggle against leukemia was starting to take a toll requiring a return to her hotel bed and a couple of more hours of news about the lives we didn't get to spend with one another.

I called C.T. from a wind-whipped payphone booth in Pecos, Texas. There was even more information that worried him. Manolo was becoming even more authoritarian, not satisfied just with telling us where to sit in the van but trying to control our stops and what we ate. He was angry now and his sulking in silence had become smothering. Salva, Seth, and I stood against gusty desert air discussing what we should do. We were all frustrated and angry with Manolo's controlling attitude. Seth seriously suggested we leave Manolo in the middle of the flat West Texas scrubland. "Let the Border Patrol arrest him," he said. We vetoed that. Salva told us that he thought there might be more to Manolo and his plan than he had originally understood when he agreed to join him on this tour. Maybe we should call off the rest of the tour.

We found the Greyhound Station in old downtown El Paso. It was decided that Salva, Sara, and Manolo would take the bus to LA to catch their flight to Spain. Seth and I would continue to Tucson and give a presentation there ending the tour.

Hugh Mejia was furious. He argued both in emails and, later, at our weekly meetings that I had embarrassed the Food Not Bombs movement by mistreating our Spanish guests. He pushed San Francisco Food Not Bombs to seek consensus on removing me from Food Not Bombs. Hugh said he had been following the tour through the English-language emails. "You didn't even have the courtesy to feed them," he railed week after week. Since I had never seen the posts and only heard snippets from our guests about our lack of food from our hosts, I was not clear why Hugh was getting so angry.

I got a phone call one freezing evening when I was staying at the Leonard Peltier Defense Committee house in Lawrence, Kansas. "I have been attending the weekly Food Not Bombs meeting here in San Francisco. There is always an agenda item about your behavior but I have no idea who you are," the caller said. The tour had been over for more than two years. "This guy Hugh threatened to burn the

Food Not Bombs video archives and often yells at us that we aren't doing enough to denounce you."

It wasn't long after that that I got news that Hugh had announced that, "he would not be long for this world." My friends reported that he had started to empty his tiny Tenderloin apartment room. They were distressed that Hugh might be having an emotional breakdown.

Journalist A.C. Thompson wrote about this tragic episode in the Bay Guardian, "A despondent San Franciscan named Hugh Erik Mejia mailed three identical letters to three friends, telling them he'd soon be dead. He wrote, 'If within 24 hours of receiving this document, you haven't been notified by the 'authorities' of my death, you may proceed to initiate the search for my remains. In all probability, my remains will be found in the S.F. financial district, the S.F. Bay, or on the coastal areas of Marin, San Francisco, or San Mateo counties.'"

"When I learned of his vanishing, I was stunned," writes Thompson, "How could a man who cared so profoundly for the wretched of the earth care so little for himself? Driven to pinpoint the forces that propelled him to his death or whatever, I started hunting for clues. Some pieces of the puzzle were easily uncovered; others would prove elusive."

Thompson continued, "Mejia blamed himself for the mess, but he also blamed another prominent FNB member. The dispute got ugly. Fittingly for an admirer of Vladimir Lenin, Mejia wanted the other guy purged from the group's ranks, which had dropped from a high of about 50 people to roughly a dozen. The grudge match dragged on for years." I was the "other prominent FNB member" but thankfully my only connection to the dispute during those days were my phone conversations with C.T. and his reports of Hugh's angst.

Just before Hugh disappeared, he emailed an announcement using the San Francisco Food Not Bombs email account claiming the group had come to consensus that I wasn't to have anything to do with Food Not Bombs. I was forbidden to claim I had co-founded Food Not Bombs, could not admit to designing the movement's logo or ever mention that I had anything to do with the movement. Another volunteer rushed out a reply to his post saying that the group had not in fact come to such an agreement.

"Hugh just saw Food Not Bombs losing credibility as a result of this tour not working out," Chris Crass told A.C. Thompson. "Everything got totally out of proportion. We're not talking about a huge event that changed the course of human history. We're talking about a tour that a few hundred people in the country went to."

I agree with Chris that everything got blown totally out of proportion but I disagree about the tour's impact. It seemed, based on what I experienced, that The UnFree Trade Tour played an important role in sparking an interest in resisting the policies the World Trade Organization. Many of those who first learned about the dangers of the WTO from the tour were the same people who would mobilize for the protest against the first WTO summit in November 1999 in Seattle.

While the tour drama was raging back in San Francisco I had become busy in Lawrence, Kansas with efforts to free Leonard Peltier. I volunteered to share meals each weekend with the local Food Not Bombs group while also responding to requests for information on our work or help locating or starting new local chapters.

My San Francisco roommate, Bobby, suggested I visit with Leonard Peltier's supporters in Geneva, Switzerland to talk with them about his case that was scheduled to be heard before the United Nations Human Rights Commission. He also encouraged me to represent the defense committee and Food Not Bombs at the founding conference of the Peoples Global Agenda, a two-week gathering of anti-capitalist activists from all over the world who would go to Geneva to formulate a plan to stop the policies of World Trade Organization.

I found accommodations in a squat on the top floor of a stately 1776 building on Rue de Ore. The makeshift kitchen featured the floor's only shower. Cooks rubbed elbows with nude bathers. My room had been an artist's studio facing north with a view of the Geneva River.

The chatter of global languages finally quieted down enough for the moderator to call the Peoples Global Agenda to order. After several hours of impassioned speeches in English, committees were formed and we joined in that morning's sessions struggling to create order out of the chaos. As it turned out the communist oriented groups decided to draft a manifesto and we anarchists met to organize a campaign of direct action.

I was soaking up the attention of an attractive photojournalist from a Madrid publication. She followed me everywhere jotting down my every comment and snapped pictures of me when she thought I wasn't looking.

When the organizing sessions paused for meals and breaks, I would find an empty table at a busy location to display my two hefty red scrapbooks, assorted flyers, Food Not Bombs buttons, and copies of my first book. One of the scrapbooks opened to several newspaper reports and photos of the press events organized in Spain by Manolo. Several reprints included grainy photocopied pictures of Michael, Heinke, and Manolo seated on a stage.

An activist from Spain with a serious air approached me as I was enjoying dinner and a conversation with two Food Not Bombs volunteers from Finland, "Excuse me sir, would you be able to meet with the Spanish delegation? We have something we want to speak with you about." I agreed to stop by their hotel that evening.

The man who had asked me to stop over stood stiffly at the top of a steep flight of stairs that climbed to the ornate hotel entrance. I followed him to a conference room off the lobby and was directed to a chair arranged to face twenty or so people who were already seated. My audience glared at me.

"We want to know how you know Manolo?" he said coldly in English with a heavy Spanish accent. I was caught off guard. Maybe Hugh was right all along and

I had damaged our relationship with our allies in Spain. I told them almost sheepishly that we had been on tour together noting that, "The tour didn't end well."

"Of course, it didn't end well," the man who invited me blurted out, "What were you thinking? You should do a better job of vetting the people you work with," he said, and then added, "Manolo is the most famous Interpol agent in Spain."

A woman stood up and said, "My best friend killed herself because of the strife he fomented in her organization." A second woman stood, held tight to a chair back and angrily described how her friend checked into a mental hospital after becoming a victim of Manolo's manipulation. A man standing towards the back of the room said Manolo worked with him in an antinuclear group and sowed so much ill will that the group fell apart.

The room burst into emotional tales, one person after another describing Manolo's impact. The man who invited me explained that Manolo was the only member of the ETA cell that tried to kill the king at the Guggenheim Museum in Bilbao that wasn't arrested. "He infiltrated a very secretive Basque cell. That's how useful he is to Interpol."

I was no longer under suspicion. It seems I may have taken an Interpol agent to meet North America's most revolutionary people. This might have had something to do with Hugh's sudden disappearance. I will never really know.

A.C. Thompson concluded his article "In the midst of this scene, sometime in 1999, Mejia and I got together for coffee. During our conversation he explained to me that nefarious forces within FNB were bent on destroying the organization. I've spent my life working for FNB, he said grimly, and now it's being wrecked."

Hawkman II self-portrait with a red hawk by Leonard Peltier

Chapter 28

SAVING THE PELTIER DEFENSE COMMITTEE

My 1998 speaking tour was over. I pulled into my usual shiny clean red and white QuikTrip Gas Station west of Saint Louis. After filling my tank, I ran in to use the restroom and grab a large hazelnut coffee from the assembly line of taps. A dozen foul smelling corndogs rotated on heat rollers taunting a plaid-shirted trucker whose giant fingers were struggling to operate the cheap plastic tongs provided by management. I knew from experience that this pitstop would have the lowest fuel prices and the last palatable coffee between there and Kansas City.

I pulled back onto Interstate 70 and joined the westward race. Eighteen wheelers, pickups, and passenger cars pressed hard over the rolling hills at eighty miles an hour flying past row after row of browning corn stubble and shiny green soybean bushes. I was planning to push on across the vast flats of Kansas and Eastern Colorado, across both the Rockies and the Sierras to my tiny dark Spruce Street room in the flat that I shared with my friend Bobby Castillo. My only stop would be at the Leonard Peltier Defense Committee in Lawrence, Kansas. I had promised my housemate Bobby that I would check-in at the office.

I pulled off the Kansas Turnpike at the first long sweeping Lawrence exit, paid the always pleasant toll taker, crossed the Kansas River and pulled up to the nondescript duplex that housed the Leonard Peltier Defense Committee.

Bobby and Leonard met when they were both locked down in the Marion Control Unit in Illinois. Conversations, often in passed notes between cells, with the Native American political prisoner had changed Bobby's life and inspired him to respect his own Apache heritage. Bobby won his freedom and left Leonard and the other political prisoners to the sterile cruelty of the control unit. Bobby was determined to help win his mentor's freedom.

Leonard was finally transferred to Leavenworth, Kansas. Journalist Scott Anderson interviewed Leonard in 1995. "If you have to be in prison, it's really not that bad," he said of Leavenworth. "I was at Marion until 1985, and that was hell, a twenty-three-hour lockdown. After Marion, Leavenworth is almost like getting parole."

Leonard was one of a number of young Native Americans that answered the call to participate in the defense of the traditional Lakota families at the Pine Ridge Reservation. The traditional Sioux of Pine Ridge were suffering from a violent campaign directed by tribal chairman Dick Wilson and his GOON squad, a paramilitary organization called The Guardians of the Oglala Nation. At least fifty opponents of Wilson were killed over a three-year period. The US government occupied the reservation for seventy-one days deploying armored personnel carriers, helicopters, and heavily armed swat police. On June 26, 1975, FBI Agents Jack Coler and Ronald Williams sped into the Jumping Bull Ranch where Leonard was among a group of young men guarding a camp of elders and children. A gun battle ensued and the two FBI agents were killed. Leonard was arrested, escaped to Canada, captured, extradited, tried, and ultimately convicted of the double murder. In 1998, he was serving two life sentences plus twenty-five years in Leavenworth Federal Prison.

I pulled up into a parking space outside the faded-brown, uninteresting duplex on an even less interesting street. I rang the bell and the defense committee staff person, Kathleen, answered.

"Come on in and make yourself at home," she said.

She led me down the plush carpeted stairs to the defense committee's basement office.

"I will be upstairs if you need anything," she said and quickly went back up to the ground floor.

The phone rang. After a bit it stopped and then rang again. I waited for Kathleen to get it but it kept ringing so I picked up the receiver. "Hello, Leonard Peltier Defense Committee. How can I help you?"

"Yes, I am with Qwest and I would like to speak with accounts payable."

I asked them to hold and went upstairs to let Kathleen know the phone company was on the line. I couldn't find Kathleen, so I returned to the phone.

"Let me take a message," I said.

The caller explained that it was necessary to pay $2,000 by five that day or the phone would be shut off. It was eleven-thirty in the morning.

The phone rang again. I answered, "Hello, Leonard Peltier Defense Committee. How can I help you?"

"It's Leonard. Who are you? I need to speak with Kathleen," a voice gruffly barked.

I told him that I was Keith McHenry, Bobby Castillo's friend.

"Oh yes, I have heard of you. Is Kathleen around?" he asked.

I told him I would get her. She wasn't on the first floor. I called up to the rooms on the second floor. No response, so I stepped outside. Kathleen was loading one of Leonard's paintings into an old, red sedan. I let her know that Leonard wanted to talk with her. She told me to tell him she would be down in a minute.

When I returned to the front door, I noticed that a letter had been taped there: a three days' notice of eviction.

"Leonard, I just spoke to Kathleen. She will be with you in a second. Are you shutting the defense committee down?" I asked.

"Why do you ask?" he responded.

"The phone company called saying the defense committee's phone will be turned off at five today if the past due bill of $2000 isn't paid and there is an eviction noticed taped to the door of the apartment," I told him.

"Where is Kathleen?" he asked bluntly.

"She is loading some of your paintings into a car," I said.

"No way, I am not shutting down the defense committee," he blurted in a shocked tone. "Go tell Kathleen to bring those paintings back into the house and tell her that I said she had to be out of the house by the morning," adding that he wanted me to do what I could to pay the phone bill and stop the eviction. "Don't let her out of your sight." He said he'd call again at five.

I rushed out to the parking lot and told Kathleen that I had just spoken to Leonard. "You have to bring the paintings back into the house and pack up all your belongings," I said, telling her that Leonard had just fired her and demanded that she leave immediately. She grumbled. I slid one of the paintings out of her car. She stomped back into the apartment. I grabbed the other two oil paintings and gently returned them to the basement.

I called Bobby to let him know about the conditions at Leonard's office. He asked me to pay the phone bill and promised me that the defense committee would reimburse me once things got settled.

I paid the phone bill and called the management company listed on the eviction notice and asked them what we needed to do to stay in the building. Not much it turned out. We had until the end of the month to pay the back rent.

Leonard called at five.

I reported that the phone bill was paid and that we could stay in the duplex if we were to catch up on the rent by the end of the week.

I walked upstairs to keep an eye on Kathleen. She was in her bedroom franticly stuffing makeup and clothing into bags. Two middle-aged men right out of a low-budget detective movie were cramming some of Kathleen's personal items into several old suitcases laid out on the second-floor hallway.

I stood guard at the bottom of the stairs to make sure the items they were packing belonged to Kathleen. It was midnight and the three of them were now collecting objects around the living room. A ceramic dildo in a nook next to the kitchen had replaced a porcelain statuette of Jesus I had noticed on my last visit to the office, thinking it was odd to have so many crosses in an office dedicated to an iconic Native American known for his defense of Indian culture. Kathleen swept her collection of stuffed bunnies from a windowsill into a crinkled paper grocery bag, grabbed two phallic totems from the living room cabinet, and dumped them into the paper sack. She left the Xerox copy of a nude Santa taped to the refrigerator for me to discard.

The two guys in sports coats seemed to live in the other half of the duplex. I saw them come and go from the apartment with small bags and assorted clothes hangers.

Soon it was five in the morning and I hadn't slept all night. I was demanding that Kathleen hurry up. "Get out of the house now already," I said as coldly as possible.

The last of her things that could fit were shoved into her car. The two men took the items she couldn't cram into her sedan to their apartment as she drove away.

Leonard called again in the morning before his breakfast. He would be allowed to make another call before he heading off to make government office furniture.

I let him know that Kathleen was gone and didn't get away with any of his paintings. I had made sure of that. He sighed with relief and said, "Thanks, I will call you after breakfast."

Bobby called. I gave him the news. "Keith, thanks," he said. "You saved the defense committee."

Now for the hard part, wining Leonard's freedom.

Missie B's Kansas City's home of good times, good friends and fabulous entertainment!

Chapter 29

CURRENT NEWS

My relationship with an amusement park insurance adjuster ended on her wide front porch on a sunny December in 1999 in the Brookside neighborhood of Kansas City.

"I bet you believe the United States has something to do with the Israeli Palestinian conflict," she said as we sipped coffee and read the Sunday Kansas City Star. A short article in Section A seemed to inspire her remark.

She added, "I can't be with you anymore. You make me feel uncomfortable. Either I quit my job and lose my home to join you in an altruistic effort to make our world a better place or we break it off and I save my job and home. It has to be the latter. Please leave now."

The drive towards Lawrence through bleak fields of snow-strangled corn stubble was crushing. I really liked Bonny and I had associated this back road journey with our enjoyable weekends together.

I stepped into my office and was greeted by more news from my coworker. Leonard Peltier had called the office depressed and was shutting down his defense committee. My assistance was no longer needed. Peltier's hope was tethered to a Clinton campaign promise of a pardon. He was crushed at news that the outgoing president wouldn't be good for his word.

My San Francisco housemate, Bobby, called me that same afternoon. "I just returned from Geneva," he said, "and found all our belongings out on the sidewalk. The landlord sold our building and we have been evicted."

I called friends and asked them to retrieve my history. My San Francisco Liberation Radio comrade Richard nabbed a few items from the damp pile of cardboard boxes, but he lived in a cramped studio and left the bulk to be collected by the Sunset Scavenger. My friend Robert Nores raced up from Santa Cruz and beat the garbage truck to the remains of my past and stored it for me to recover a decade later.

I was nearly penniless. I had spent my savings saving the defense committee. That phone bill was never repaid since the committee and Leonard's friends and relatives needed every penny we raised. I had no place to live when I returned to my well-paying poster distribution business in San Francisco and not much money for gas to get to California. But I had my ways with gas "donations" and planned to head west anyway.

My gas tank took me to Kansas City, Missouri to retrieve some items but my trusted Nissan pickup drove its last mile a block from the Country Club Plaza. My truck ended its life journey of over 400,000 miles at West 46th, just east of Madison Street and next to an unloved, weedy, vacant lot. I wouldn't be driving west to the financial security of my poster-taping enterprise even if I managed to make enough for fuel. The $1,100 engine computer had sent its last instruction to the motor of my truck.

I was homeless.

A red and white "for rent" sign was visible from my pickup's final resting spot. A local phone number was penned in black Magic Marker.

I dialed the number. "Sure, come on over," the pleasant voice responded to my inquiry.

That afternoon I walked leisurely around the outside of the one-bedroom apartment, investigating the surroundings while waiting to be shown inside. The building owner arrived in an old Ford 150, stepped out and gave me a welcoming handshake. He told me that his tenant would be moving out at the end of the month. He let me take a quick look at the interior then showed me the basement storage bin that came with the rental. I told him I liked it. Could I get him a deposit next week? That was fine. I left the meeting excited. This apartment was a huge improvement over my gloomy San Francisco room and conveniently located a block from the plaza. I now needed to get the $450 deposit.

I scooped up a copy of the local weekly, the Kansas City Pitch that same morning and found the help wanted ad, "Graphic Designer needed. Call 39th Street Copy."

I called and a distracted voice told me to stop in at the copy shop at 10 a.m. the next day. "We are at 811 west 39th," he said.

I said I'd be over then. The blaring TV in the background had me wondering if he even heard me, but that wasn't so important.

I crawled out of my almost-warm bundle of cheap Walmart quilts and assorted found blankets, squeezed past a bike tire, pushed open the camper shell's glass hatch and scaled down the back of my marooned pickup to the icy pavement. I walked briskly over the cracked slabs of sidewalk past a long collection of bottle-strewn lots of browned thistles several of which sported huge, "Will Build to Suit," signs. The cold silver sky hung over my focused journey to this potential design job and a promise to move to warmer accommodations.

"Do you know QuarkXPress?" Jerry O'Neal, the owner of Current News grunted in my direction as he shifted his gaze from an episode of The Golden Girls long enough to tell me his name.

Desperate for money I said yes and he told me the job paid $750 a week cash for six days of work. "Come back at one and we'll see how you do."

I had played around with a bootleg Kinko's version of the first edition of QuarkXPress for about an hour a year before but that wasn't enough to really say I knew the software. I walked as fast as I could to the Plaza Barnes & Noble bookstore, found a book on the program, sat down and started reading. I got an idea of how to open a page, find the text tool, and start a design before having to rush back to my one o'clock appointment.

Four young men sat around the smoky room waiting for directions from Jerry. Another rerun of The Golden Girls blasted from a TV high in one corner. Jerry was on the phone balancing the receiver on his shoulder and flicking embers into an overflowing ashtray as he moved a mouse back and forth on his desk. The stains in his grey t-shirt were visible in the wall of smoke-hazed mirrors that surrounded two sides of the cramped office.

Jerry hung up and slowly pushed himself from his cheap executive chair

.

"Ok," he said, "design a one-page ad using this text. I want to see what you can do."

I opened a blank file in QuarkXPress, quickly found the text icon and typed the headline, SAVE WITH BUTLER'S CLEANING SERVICE with Arial Bold in the largest type that would fit. I made a second text box and typed in the body text in twelve-point Times Roman and opened a final text box and keyed in the company name and contact details also in san serif Arial.

I searched for an image online that might be appropriate, saved it to the desk top and figured out how to import the photo of a Hoover vacuum into the advertisement.

A smart clean design.

"Here it is," I announced to Jerry.

He stepped over and took a look. "Great," he said, "you have the job. Now everyone, listen up. Save your files. Thanks for coming in. The interview is over."

The other applicants had obviously taken classes in the latest graphics programs and it seemed they were all confident new graduates from the design department at the Kansas City Art Institute. Two of the applicants continued at their computers, working on their fancy ads apparently not yet aware that they would not be offered the job.

"Come in at nine tomorrow and we'll get started," Jerry said with a grin.

I was relieved at how easy it was to find work. That next morning Jerry showed me where to find the previous week's file of his weekly full-color magazine called Current News, a disorganized publication highlighting the Kansas City drag queen community.

He explained that I needed to lift each week's News of the Weird from the Kansas City Pitch website. A local journalist would email an article and I would add some random stories copied from a newspaper's website out of Texas. He also insisted that I make room for Alison Bechdel's, "Dykes to Watch Out For," comic strip and, "Quote, Unquote," by gay syndicated columnist Rex Wockner. Other than those requirements the magazine was mostly a collection of ads for booze, bars, and dance clubs. Every issue featured a full-page ad for Missie B's announcing that week's well specials. I had to hand a hard copy of the sixty-four-page magazine to a currier every Saturday night at seven o'clock.

I would return six mornings a week at nine but that first day was the last time I would see Jerry at the office that early. He usually dragged in a little before noon with unshaved black stubble and weary bloodshot eyes. He'd toss a soft briefcase on an office chair next to his throne and plop a half-consumed Big Gulp next to the keyboard of his computer. He would be in an animated conversation with whomever was in tow, typically someone he had collected during an all-nighter at the casino boats. A cloud of cheap Giorgio Armani Cologne drifted across the room as he pranced towards his throne, only interrupting his chatter long enough to yell out something about needing coffee as he poured the previous night's pot of dishwater-weak Folgers into a cup along with several spoonfuls of sugar. While still yapping away to those who blew in with him, he would find the remote and click on The Golden Girls channel and light a Newport Menthol.

The 39th Street Copies and Printing office was ringed by a counter that held six PCs, several phones, and piles of papers made even more numerous by the mirrors that also wrapped around the room. Thick tobacco smoke would build to a yellowish haze by evening.

When I wasn't laying out the Current News, I designed church bulletins and resumes, photocopied documents for walk-ins and answered the phones. One phone line rang to the Kansas City Gay and Lesbian Helpline and it soon became obvious that I was the man on duty there as well. Most calls were from people worried that they might be gay who would ask me if one attribute or another was a sign. I hope I provided some comfort by sharing that it was fine if they happened to love people of the same sex or gender. Parents also called worried about the fate of their children. I was happy to help ease their concerns. One young man franticly called worried that he might be sinning. I didn't believe it was a prank judging from his tone of desperation.

"I have been sticking a screwdriver up my ass," he said distressed.

"Which end?" I asked alarmed. It turned out to be the handle and that seemed reassuring. His real concern was about sin. I suggested he speak with his pastor explaining that I had not read anything in the bible that would suggest it was a problem. He seemed a little more at ease when we hung up.

If Jerry overheard me talking with someone questioning their sexuality, he would ask how old the caller sounded. If old enough to be legal and young enough to be of interest he would take over the call and make arrangements to help the confused soul discover his true identity at a nearby park.

I put my first edition of the Current News in the currier's hands and Jerry counted out $750 in cash and handed me the bills.

I had arranged to meet my future landlord the next morning. He had shown me the empty basement storage unit and after paying him my deposit of $450 I asked if I could start to place my things in the wood-slated basement bin while waiting for the apartment to be free. That was no problem, he said.

So, I moved into the storage unit placing a yellow lawn chair mattress down in one corner behind a stack of what few belongings I had retrieved from the back of my pickup. That ended the discomfort of sleeping crunched up in the back of my truck struggling against the bitter Kansas City cold.

One of those belongings that I used as a screen for my mattress was my bicycle which I had started to use for transportation. I had signed up for a monthly membership at the YMCA in Shawnee Village as soon as I had moved into the back of my truck so I could continue my routine of taking water aerobics. As anyone who has been unhoused knows a gym membership is coveted for that all important shower.

I moved out of the storage bin and into the apartment after only two weeks in my makeshift basement den. It was a luxurious contrast to my queen-size mattress of a room in San Francisco. I had my own full kitchen, bathtub, and large windows that overlooked the Spanish architecture of the plaza and the tree-lined Brush Creek. I hadn't lived alone in years. I felt like a king laying on the wall-to-wall carpet below the south-facing windows, basking in the warm sunlight and my good fortune.

I was peddling along State Line to the Y one weekend morning when a woman about my age came rushing out of a house. "Help me! Help me!" she shouted running towards me franticly waving her arms above her head.

"Do you think my house is on fire?" she yelled, pointing to her ranch-style home nestled among several tall oaks, "Do you think that smoke is coming from my house?"

“Did you call 911?” I asked. She hadn’t.

I ran over to investigate. It seemed that a delivery truck was idling on the block behind her and blowing exhaust into her house through a back window. The smoke had a diesel truck smell and I couldn’t see any flames.

I gave her my report. She was relieved, enthusiastically wrapping her arms around me in an appreciative hug. She glided her hands down my forearms and asked if wanted to spend Sunday afternoon with her. Sure, I responded. She was a bubbly lady with thick, wavy black hair, a kind face and a toned figure and I was newly single. We agreed to meet in the parking lot at Jacob Loose Park at noon and exchanged phone numbers. She hugged me one more time, joked that I was her hero, and I peddled off on my way to my class.

I had spent nearly every waking minute of the prior couple of months surrounded by Kansas City’s gay community and was starting to believe that I might be the only heterosexual in the Midwest so I couldn’t have been more excited to spend the afternoon with a vivacious, single woman.

We met near the rose garden and headed out on our walk along the paved shoreline. Yellow dagger leaves from the park’s weeping willows drifted peacefully along the concrete banks of the pond. The electric gold of the blades that still clung to the branches were made even more vibrant before the bright blue fall sky. A brisk smell of decaying autumn leaf litter increased the exhilaration of our conversation.

She told me that she was a nursing professor at KU Medical and was originally from the Bay Area. The fact that we had that place in common was another promising development on an already pleasant afternoon.

I told her that I had co-founded Food Not Bombs, volunteered at the Peltier Defense Committee in Lawrence, and was now a graphic designer producing the city’s main Gay magazine, Current News. I wasn’t surprised that she had never heard of the publication. Worried she might think I was not available I made a joke about being one of the only straight people I knew in Kansas City. That was until I had met her, I smiled.

I also mentioned that I had been arrested for feeding the homeless in San Francisco. This for me was badge of honor that I was proud of sharing; it partly defined who I was. She told me about her path to becoming the head of the nursing department and a fragment or two about her Northern California childhood. She would be off to her family’s place in Marin for Thanksgiving and suggested we get together after the holiday. We gave one another a quick hug before she scooted into her silver Subaru waving with a flirtatious smile as she turned onto the park exit.

I was ecstatic when I picked up the phone and it was her. She wasted no time asking if I wanted to go out again. Wow, asked out on a date with a beautiful woman twice in a matter of a month. Bonnie’s ego-shattering front porch breakup was becoming a fading memory.

I suggested that we meet at Eden Alley in the basement of Unity Church at the plaza. She agreed.

My date seemed distant when we met outside the restaurant. There was no warm hug when we greeted, no smile, but rather blank eyes that avoided mine.

It wasn't a busy evening at the elegant vegetarian restaurant. Maybe two other tables had diners. I pulled out her chair and as she sat down, she said, "I had Thanksgiving with Nancy Pelosi and her family. We have known them for years. You lied to me. Nancy told me all about you."

The waiter came to take our order. She interrupted her comments, looked at the menu, and almost angrily ordered the Garnets and Greens salad and a cup of butternut squash soup before returning to her denunciation.

Pelosi told her that I was a violent criminal who had been arrested for assaulting city officials. The Congresswoman claimed I had refused to accept the permits offered to me by the city for free. "That's the real story about Keith McHenry," she said in conclusion and seeming to quote Pelosi verbatim.

I was stunned that a United States Congresswoman would have paid any attention to me. My first attempt to defend myself hoping to get a third date was quickly dashed. I said little after that and only asked enough questions to learn more about what else Nancy Pelosi had to say. Counter intelligence as to the personal opinions of America's most liberal politician seemed to be the best I could hope for then. Pelosi said that I had a dangerous agenda and seemed to have mentioned that I was an anarchist with an official terrorist designation. I got the impression the congresswoman was pretty animated in her denunciation.

The waiter kept our water glasses topped off and asked if we wanted dessert as he took our finished plates. My date's anger was about to boil over. The pressure of remaining polite and appropriate was starting to fray my nerves.

I asked for the check. The waiter returned seven or eight minutes later and said, "Mr. McHenry, the staff and I are so honored that you have chosen our restaurant for dinner that we have all agreed that your meal with your dinner date is on the house. Thank you so much Mr. McHenry for all you have done to make our world a better place."

The blood drained from my date's face, turning her complexion to a ghostly white. Her stunned eyes looked down at the table. I stood and pulled out her chair like the gentleman I am. She silently walked ahead of me. Once outside she made a slight motion of her hand to say goodbye and drifted out of sight.

I must have handed at least thirty issues of the Current News to the Sunday evening courier. He had ended his uneasy pacing a few issues back, once he realized that he would not be kept late as he had in the past. One morning after turning in the weekly, I answered my apartment phone to hear, "Hello, my name is Peter Waldman. I am a reporter with the Wall Street Journal. I am doing a story on Anarchism in the United States in the lead up to the World Trade Organization protest in Seattle and everyone I speak with tells me I should talk with you. I just got off the phone with John Zerzan and he strongly encouraged me to give you a call," he said, possibly flattering me to gain my confidence. The Wall Street Journal seemed to be an unlikely paper to have an interest in an anti-capitalist perspective.

He wanted a comment about anarchists using violence to destroy the political system. I agreed some anarchists support the use of violence but that I was dedicated to nonviolent direct action and mentioned mutual aid and the influence of anarchists like Emma Goldman and Peter Kropotkin.

The next morning was depressingly bleak and rainy. I was back at work. Drops of condensation left yellow tobacco streaks across the ceiling-to-floor lobby windows. Two tall, lanky men drifted into the lobby flipping rain from their grey London Fog coats and looking like movie versions of FBI agents. They made some homophobic statements under their breath to one another before asking me to make a copy of a two-inch-long cash register receipt for a 27-cent cup of coffee from Nichols Lunch, the dingy diner next door. I placed the scrap on the glass, tapped the green print button, and the machine spit out the nearly blank white page. I handed them the copy. One of them set a dollar on the copier and said, "Keep the change."

I was still considering a short trip to Seattle to participate in the November 1999 blockade of the WTO summit but my friends were adamant that I skip this one. It was too dangerous, they said. I would be a target since I had played an important role in making the protest a reality particularly because of my participation in the UnFree Trade Tour that encouraged audiences to join in protests against the WTO. The visit from these two FBI types solidified my plans. I was staying put.

But a week or so later I realized that the FBI may not have been there on my behalf.

Maybe they were actually interested in Jerry. I got the impression that he was driven to crime for crime's sake since it would have often been less work to employ a legal path than to struggle implementing his elaborate off-the-books schemes. But his crimes seemed too petty to warrant a visit by the Feds. I got the impression that Jerry had fun thinking up creative ways to skirt the law. Crime as art more than crime as profit.

A five-story-high mural proclaiming, "Metcalfe Lock and Key in business since 1912," towered over Main Street a few blocks from 39th Street Copy and Printing. The phone number, 816-931-5030 could be seen for blocks. Jerry snapped up that number as soon as it became available, had an additional phone line installed and changed the name of his key making company to Metcalfe Lock and Key.

Sure enough, the Metcalfe line started to ring almost as much as his other extensions. And so there I was, answering the office phones for the twelfth time that morning. There had been the anticipated calls for a locksmith. Then a representative from Universal Syndicate called demanding we stop publishing "News of the Weird." An earnest young man explained that they owned the rights and that the Kansas City Pitch was the only publication in the city licensed to run the weekly article.

"You are not the only content my boss tells me to use that may be stolen," I explained. I felt compassion for the caller who expected a rational response but I assured him there was nothing rational about the Current News or any of the other businesses that Jerry seemed to be running out of this suffocating office.

"You would be better off ignoring the issue as nothing really could be done to get my boss to stop," I suggested, adding, "He will just ignore your lawsuits, so why bother?"

Jerry had been paying me in cash for months but that suddenly changed. The first two paychecks cleared but the third was not from a real bank account. I threatened to quit unless he continued to pay me in cash. He did.

In a rare expression of compassion, Jerry responded to my complaints about the cigarette smoke and installed a fan and vent to reduce the nicotine cloud that filled the tiny room. The fog that accumulated from his chain smoking was causing me to suffer an increasingly painful sinus infection.

But the vent wasn't enough. The smoke was still oppressive and I let him know I was still finding the haze unbearable. Well, that was one complaint too many so he fired me. I was relieved.

I was unemployed for less than a week, taking a temporary job at Hallmark Cards as a digital finisher. On my first day my supervisor circled me around the massive, football-field-sized dark cavern. The dreary expanse was populated by less than a dozen people, each hunched over a light table. Rows of light tables waited for an infinity of digital serfs.

What my tour guide was most proud of sharing with me was her news that as Hallmark employees we had the coveted right to eat lunch in the apparently fabulous Hall Cafeteria. Such an honor was only dreamed of by most Kansas City residents she bubbled.

She had spent her life striping film for the great man Donald Joyce Hall but now she was teaching her replacement in the card culture of the Hall empire. I spent several months standing at a computer and companion light table in the dark waiting for Hallmark's top-secret server to reboot so I could assemble a cheap looking six color Bar Mitzvah card and a just-as-uninteresting confirmation greeting card with a rainbow-splashed cross dabbed with varnish and streaks of flex mixed with felt. I imagined that the poor child getting these monstrosities of sterility would be less than impressed.

After the rejection of the insurance adjuster and the nurse I had lost my usual confidence in romance. Even so I pushed through and placed a personals ad in the Kansas City Pitch, "Subterranean Balloonist," a headline I thought would discourage the typical Kansas City Chief's fangirl from responding. And I was right. I agreed to ring in the new century with an off-beat woman who made her living in collectables, action figures still in their original cellophane covered boxes. She didn't wear the Chief's gold and red but that wasn't, as it turned out, the crucial factor. There wasn't one magazine, newspaper, or book to peruse while she was busy getting dolled up. I remember finding her text-free apartment profoundly strange. We attended a gathering of her friends where I spent much of the time visiting with a woman who said she worked with an acquaintance of mine, the sex-positive performance artist Annie Sprinkle.

Meanwhile there was another respondent to my ad, a redhead named Marion, a web developer whom I had first asked to join me that New Year's Eve. She declined, saying that she would be busy sitting at a computer guarding the life of a day trader's website from the Y2K digital apocalypse. Instead, we agreed to meet on New Year's Day at a funky coffee house on 39th Street. From our phone conversations it seemed she had at least some leftwing credentials. More promising than miss collectable. Foremost was her mention of her master's degree thesis on the influence of Eastern European immigrants in the granite cutters union of Barre, Vermont.

Red is the color of this beauty who would become my second wife Marion. Midwestern fit and athletic. Red hair, red folk embroidered blouses, and red-hot enthusiasm. A mountain biking, cross country skiing hiker with a passion for Bulgarian asymmetrical rhythms. Slender fingers that caressed and expressed. Web creative for fun and pay. Her parents were too busy making a living to notice her brilliance and she was left in the care of her loving grandmother. Her circle of friends revolved around folk dancing and her Balkan band members.

Marion and I clicked and it wasn't long before we co-owned a large second story flat in a beautiful 1914 brick building on tree-lined Wyoming Street. Homeless to homeowner in twelve months.

Marion insisted that if we planned to grow old together, I should do my part and secure my own social security retirement check. I really felt trapped. The thought of formally attaching myself to a system I was dedicated to ending made me recoil. At the same time, I felt an obligation to be fair to my partner Marion. I broke down and drove over to the Social Security office to get the number and the promise of a monthly check in old age.

I was on the books.

I took a position as marketing director at the Piano Technicians Guild. The employment contract had five pages about sexual conduct in the work place. It wouldn't be long before I realized why. The office manager used flirting and more in a complex system that maintained her power among the important people in the Baldwin, Mason and Hamlin, and Yamaha empires. This strategy included pursuing the more significant office staff. When I rebuffed her advances, it put me on her bad side and resulted in my phone messages being withheld and my packages getting lost. A video cassette of the CNN piece the channel aired disappeared and messages to replace display ads in the journal or return calls to vender were never shared. Still, the job paid well and the director, Dan, and I worked well together. I produced a CD-ROM of the first twenty years of the Piano Technicians Journal and helped organize the national convention at Crystal City, Virginia. The pay was so good and my relationship with the director so solid that it was no trouble for me to take a month off to visit Bulgaria with Marion in search of authentic Balkan folk music. We met with Food Not Bombs activists in Sofia, spent magical days at the Rila Monastery and the sand cliffs near Melnik, hiked in the Pirin Mountains, and dipped in the warm Black Sea at Sozopol.

When Marion and I returned from our trip, the condo neighbor below our unit had hauled us to court claiming that Marion had injured her by tossing clumps of our cat Mourek's fur in to the hallway and thus causing her to have an allergic reaction. I was amazed that we lost the lawsuit but we were just the latest building occupant to suffer what our neighbors said would be a never-ending series of future suits. It seemed lawsuits for profit was this woman's game and court records showed she was quite successful.

The two of us started checking out properties in the southwest seeking to make our home in a better environment for the kinds of outdoor adventures like hiking and mountain biking that we liked to share. A camping trip to the bluffs above the Missouri River was disrupted by the loud music and laughter of a small Rainbow Gathering that blared across the forest throughout the night and the early morning volleys of musket fire from a local gun club. We then retreated to the wooded pond shores of a nudist camp outside Tulsa and made plans to move someplace where camping and hiking were close at hand. The southwest was in our sights. With the lawsuit over we rushed to put our place up for sale before another legal attack would make it impossible to put it on the market. But we didn't want to move right away so we set the price so high an offer would be unlikely before we were ready.

I got news that my father would be honored in Tucson with a lifetime achievement award by the organization he co-founded, The National Association for Interpretation. Marion and I flew to Tucson, took a room at the Congress Hotel, walked around downtown and Fourth Avenue and fell in love with the area.

The price of our Kansas City property wasn't set high enough to slow the sale and we had an offer of full price by the time we returned from Arizona. It was a windfall that we used to buy a sturdy little 1932 adobe house with nearly two acres of yard graced by a giant mesquite tree that shaded the back and a healthy Palo Verde in the front. My publisher Chaz Bufe lived a couple blocks away. It was perfect.

I was sitting at my computer one evening in our new Tucson home when an email from one of my Current News era associates dinged in my inbox. "Did you see this?" she asked. I opened the link. It was a November 22, 2001, Kansas City Pitch story called "No Flowers Please." The story went like this:

"People would call with $800 charges. Then we started getting calls from the FBI," says Weaver, who left when his last three paychecks failed to clear. "If someone told J.D. not to run an ad, he would continue to run it and then send them an invoice. I finally told him, 'I can't take any more. You've got the FBI calling. You've got too many issues.'"

Weaver must have been my replacement or he may have replaced the person after me. The article, by Deb Hipp, went on:

The Missouri Attorney General's office said O'Neal had put fliers for Metcalfe Lock and Key on the doors of several midtown businesses in September, then returned a couple of weeks later and squirted glue into their locks after hours in an attempt to drum up business from clients desperate to get inside their own stores. Video surveillance cameras captured (Jerry) O'Neal in the act, and his bizarre story made the evening television news October 16.

The next morning, a friend found O'Neal in the upstairs bedroom of his home east of the Plaza, dead from a self-inflicted gunshot wound, lying faceup crossways on his bed, his feet flat on the floor. A .38-caliber revolver lay nearby.

Keith's painting of Comida No Bombas in Monterrey Mexico

Chapter 30

THE HARDCORE PUNK ROCKERS OF MEXICO

Did we discover the dawn of existence in the colorful desert stones at kilometer 21 on the vast asphalt of Federal Highway 40 in Northern Mexico?

My seventeen uncomfortably unbathed punk-rocker tour mates and I knew it would be a long wait for fuel to get my twenty-eight-foot sky-blue Chevy school bus moving again. Such is the inconvenience of a broken gas gauge. The interruption would be long enough for the sacrament of peyote to reveal itself in the roadside rubble. The discovery of the green-grey cactus buttons pulled the memory of this origin story from my teenage past, a tale I would share as we finally started to rumble east towards our next concert in the city of Monterrey:

A sun scorched earth bites at the callused feet of a band of Tarahumara Indians desperate to find water in the vast, rocky Chihuahuan Desert. It is day six of their sprint north across the scalding pebbles through the maze of poison-tipped lechuguilla to the cooling green waters of the Rio Grande. A pregnant young woman struggles to keep up. A rising moon as round as her burden illuminates the cold nighttime march. But the blistering days are brutal. The dappled shade of the spindly creosote bushes provides no relief. Their mouths are white with the cotton of drought.

Finally, her ninth month of pregnancy is too heavy to bear and she falls to the searing desert floor under an unforgiving midday sun. But the band must survive so they continue to plod forward leaving her and her almost-child to wither and die.

But a violent labor gushes a tender life to the sweltering hard pack. In her delirium she claws at a grayish green sponge of a cactus nestled in the rocks and stuffs it in her mouth. The moisture satisfies. She claws at another cactus and gags down its bitter wetness. The cottony needles of strychnine jolt her to her knees. The first of all mothers stuffs another wretched peyote button between her chapped lips. She plucks yet another moist succulent and then a second, third, fourth, and fifth and wraps the treasures in her yucca sling. She rises to her feet, clutches the placenta-draped baby to her breast and starts to run north. She runs so fast she catches the others before the moon rises. She shares the acrid sacrament with the tribe and all of humanity is born.

At least that is how I remembered this genesis story.

Our journey to kilometer 21 started on Tucson's Congress Street on a pleasant winter night in 2002. I pulled open the glass door of our local DIY club, Las Sinfronteras, and stepped into a steamy break in the blaring hardcore concert. I must have been wearing a Food Not Bombs t-shirt because I was enthusiastically greeted by a young man who stumbled towards me panting and dripping in sweat.

"Food Not Bombs! Are you with Food Not Bombs?" I nodded yes and he blurted out, "You all are heroes in Mexico. Everywhere in Mexico, man." He introduced himself, "My name is Ivan Merma. What's yours?"

"Keith," I said and smiled.

"Oh, wow, you are the Keith. We have to go on tour with you. Do you have a bus?"

"No, but I was thinking of buying one as a matter of fact," I said, since I was struggling to stay housed.

It was a deal. That night I agreed to buy a school bus and tour Mexico with the bands La Merma and Suciedad Discriminada.

It wasn't even a week after my encounter with Ivan when I overhead a young man telling his friends at the Epic Cafe that he had to sell his puppet show bus and sell it quick. He explained that he needed to rush to Vermont to meet the love of his life. He wanted $2,000 for the twenty-eight-foot 1979 Chevy that he had bought a year before from the Tucson Unified School District. I told him I could pay $1,500 and that was enough. His girlfriend's birthday was bearing down and he couldn't miss that.

He had removed most of the vinyl green benches but if I wanted them, he would help me bolt them back. I didn't think that was necessary. I drove it around the block. It was a dream to drive. It had an automatic transmission with a powerful, purring engine and a high, wide view of the road. "The gas gauge isn't accurate so you will need to watch that so you don't run out of fuel," he warned. I counted out the hundred-dollar bills and he signed over the title.

I met Ivan in the parking lot outside the Nogales, Arizona McDonalds a few weeks after the transaction and settled into the passenger seat of his sun-bleached red Toyota pickup. His friends relaxed in the open back bed as we bounced through the border towards a meeting at Billares Barbarita. Ivan's band La Merma was among the acts playing that evening.

"Hey Ivan, what's this CIA guy doing outside our place all day?" the club owner laughed. "Are you planning an international incident or something?" My friends chuckled clinking their ice-cold bottles of Tecate together in response to her question. A group of pierced and tattooed punks played pool in the background as we discussed our plans. Ivan reported that he had spoken with the venue in Hermosillo. They just needed a date. Amílcar Peñúñuri had spoken with Emmanuel who had already started booking venues in Monterrey. We might be able to play in Chihuahua as well. By the time La Merma took the stage I was trying to sleep on a row of short, leather-strapped bar stools bracing against the high desert cold of Nogales with my arms tucked into my t-shirt. I had better make sure I didn't find myself in such discomfort on the tour.

I drove my blue bus down to the US side of the border on the appointed day cruising around a maze of produce warehouses collecting band members and scraps of discarded furniture to furnish our ride. The first concert was that evening in Nogales, Sonora. The billiard hall was packed. It stank of stale, yeasty beer and urinal ammonia. I gave a short speech about Food Not Bombs and Ivan translated. "My dream is that there could be a world where there is no war, where all live together, where all are healthy, happy and there is no poverty or hunger." The crowd cheered. The bands played. The first event was a hit.

We headed south towards Hermosillo. A caravan of ribbon-decorated sedans adorned with beauty queens sprawled out on the hoods crawled past us towards the center of Nogales as we chugged south. Minutes later we passed a traveling circus. Bears and a lonely tiger were chained to the back of flatbed trucks panting under the Sonoran sun. Brightly colored birds screamed in distress from cages. A twist of the bus as she groaned over a speed bump cracked a pane of mid-bus glass.

Ivan strummed his acoustic guitar, crooning popular Mexican folk songs. Two guys slumbered through their hangover on the foam mattress in the rear. We glided across the long flat plains reaching the Pemex Station at Benjamín Hill. Five hours later we pulled into the dusty Sonoran capital. We found the venue, a decaying old adobe saloon surrounded by dirt streets. A massive swamp cooler filled the center of the bar. The audience pressed against the loud contraption seeking relief from the Sonoran heat. The clang of the swamp cooler's fan was a metronome to the blaring punk of the bands. I said a few words that were again repeated in Spanish by Iván before La Merma and Suciedad Discriminada slayed the night.

The next morning, we snaked up the narrow switchbacks of the western slopes of the Sierra Madre Occidental gripping the thin ribbon of asphalt through the high pine forest. I pulled off in the tiny mining town of Cahuisori. Time to top off the gas tank. Our crew shuffled around a roadside taqueria devouring greasy tacos. There was a sense of victory in having made the climb.

My Bluebird bus was starting to smell like a traveling locker room. Another case of cheap beer was grabbed at an OXXO convenience store. Ivan strummed more ballads. Buchakas, Pingui, Richard, and Amílcar swayed back and forth with bottles of Pacífico raised to the arched ceiling as they sang along with Ivan.

The bus sputtered to a stop before we made it to the next petrol station. Pingui and Richard grabbed the five-gallon plastic gas jugs and headed east in search of fuel. I sprawled out on my foam mattress. Ivan serenaded a card game and Amílcar and José strolled along the highway checking out random stones and crumpled metal scraps flung aside from decades of traffic. Richard and Pingui returned, in the back of a pickup, victorious and smiling with their fifteen gallons of petrol. We were on our way again.

I was enjoying the bliss of coasting along on the open road five hours east of Torreón, Coahuila when Ivan got a call on his cell. We had left one of our drummers, José, at a remote Pemex Station. Ivan passed on the message that we would stop in the next town and wait for him. Even though he had wild purple hair and was barefoot he scored a ride and arrived several hours later to the grocery parking lot where we were busy scoffing down another round of cold, rice and bean tacos in the shade of the bus.

We again hit the open road, whizzing past mile after mile of creosote-dotted desert until my bus puttered to a stop on the last fumes of fuel at kilometer 21. Pingui and Ivan agreed to hitch east and off they went waving the empty five-gallon red and yellow plastic gas jugs heroically in the air. It would be another afternoon of waiting. It wasn't long before a couple of us wandered out into the desert to investigate the bright stones, pincushion cactus, and cholla.

Buchakas excitedly yelled for us to join him, "Over here, look, look!" The other desert investigators rushed to see what the excitement all was about. Peyote. Buttons as large as dinner plates. Soon arm-loads of the psychedelic plants were being stacked along the center of the bus. Buchakas and Héctor were eager to partake, gagging down bits of the wicked-tasting cactus. "Oh, fuck this is disgusting, water, water, I need water," Héctor pleaded with a smile.

The heavy jugs of fuel finally arrived. We funneled the gas into the tank and sailed off towards Monterrey. The excitement of the psychedelic alkaloid discovery temporarily distracted us from the discomfort of a third hot day without a shower. The line of open windows did little to relieve us of our own stench. It was at this moment that I told the musicians of my memory of a peyote creation story I had read as a teenager during my first days of ingesting the sacred succulent.

Twenty years later Ivan would remind me of the story in the Tucson living room of my friend Bill Mueller.

"We will never forget kilometer 21," he laughed.

Two of the cactus munchers dozed on the high bed at the back. No one puked. I felt like one with my bus gliding around slower vehicles as we dropped down into the valley and towards Monterrey, the capital of Nuevo León. The magic dreams of my comrades may have contributed to this bliss.

The first stop was a shower at a friend's house in a neighborhood of narrow streets. We were lucky to find a bus-length parking space across from our destination. My passengers fled the sweaty vehicle and hurried towards the toilets, the showers, and the possibility of cold beer stashed in their friend's fridge.

I backed the Bluebird against the curb. A helicopter hovered above and a convoy of five large white police pickup trucks pulled into the street. An officer with a general's hat, rows of gold stripes, and a badge sauntered up to the bus door. First, he asked me something in Spanish. When he realized I didn't speak Spanish he tried a little English. Something about what was I planning to do while visiting his city. A child witnessed the encounter and ran to the modest blue house that my passengers had just disappeared into. Ivan came out to see what was going on.

Ivan explained to me that the man with the imposing hat was the chief of the Monterrey Police Department and that he had asked about our intentions. Whatever Ivan told the officer must have been adequate because they drove off and the helicopter hurried out of view. News of the official police welcome put our tour on the map of Mexico's punk culture.

The first presentation was held in a huge dimly lit auditorium at the Autonomous University of Monterrey attracting some two hundred people. Emmanuel's friend Anna sat in the front row as he stood with me on the stage translating my presentation. I have a lot of experience having my presentations translated and find that those moments when I am silent help me prepare for my next statement, which will be intentionally brief for my translator.

Two musclebound men clad in polo shirts, khaki dockers, and dark sunglasses stood to my left on the stage with their arms crossed. As usual, I shared a short version of our movement's origin story, the arrests that inspired a global movement, and the three principles at our core: our meals are vegan or vegetarian and free to everyone; each chapter is independent and autonomous and makes decisions using consensus; and Food Not Bombs is not a charity and is dedicated to non-violent social change. Emmanuel not only relayed my message but added his own experience which I thought from the crowd's smiling, attentive expressions made the presentation all that more meaningful.

One of the first questions from the audience was about my two motionless companions standing at attention on the stage. "Do you know the two guys standing next to you?" Emmanuel asked, translating the young woman's question. "No," I said with a chuckle. The people in the hall roared with laughter.

A couple of people identifying themselves as Maoists asked me what Food Not Bombs would do to inspire an uprising and suggested that if we stopped feeding the poor, they would become so hungry and angry they would rise up and seize power. It was a good question. I agreed that hunger inspires desperation but said that I was not sure starving families would unite and have the clarity to improve their conditions. Food riots might be a good strategy to help a vanguard party rise to power but I don't have any interest in supporting such a "solution" to the economic crisis of poverty. I said that a well-considered transformation of society requires thinking beyond the next morsel of bread.

I have a special place in my heart for pirate radio and our next appointment had all the makings of another revolutionary broadcast. Anna, Emmanuel, and I hurried across town, through the narrow streets and to the studios of Radio Tierra y Libertad. Anna steered her pickup onto the sidewalk in front of the peeling magenta and ochre paint that announced the home of 98.5 FM. A student strike inspired the creation of Radio Tierra y Libertad in 2001. It operated independently of the state until nearly a hundred and fifty Federal Preventive Police (a militarized police force created and used to repress strikes and protests) raided the station in June 2008. One of the station's directors, Héctor Camero, would be prosecuted for operating without a permit and sentenced to two years in jail.

Our program host looked like Trotsky. He ushered the three of us through a room decorated with pictures of revolutionaries mounted snug against the ceiling. I found a seat on a squeaky office chair behind a battered and well-loved mic.

Anna and Emanuel squeezed in next to me. The low egg-carton ceiling, interrupted only by a row of harsh florescent lights, softened the background sound. Our host slid up the toggles, pulled his mic close, welcomed his audience, and then introduced the three of us. I don't know much Spanish but it was clear that it was a dramatic and glowing introduction. The questions flew. Emmanuel translated. How did Food Not Bombs start, what are my hopes for the movement in Mexico, how will we empower the peasants to rise up and, what can we do to push back against the poverty created by NAFTA? I shared short versions of the three founding stories: the delivery of my unsold produce to a public housing project across from a nuclear weapons lab in Cambridge; the raising of funds to repay money donated for bail by holding bake sales dressed as generals seeking to buy a bomber based on the poster, "It will be a great day when our schools get all the money they need and the Air Force has to hold a bake sale to buy a bomber;" and the theatrical soup-line outside the Bank of Boston's stockholders meeting. I expressed my belief that Food Not Bombs could be very popular in Mexico because of the country's rich history of activism and hoped that cross-border organizing could be an important part of resisting the impact of those cruel trade agreements.

The hour sped by. We wished the audience well and headed out towards our next adventure. Our host was ecstatic as he walked us to the street. And then we were off to the concert at the Telecommunication Workers Union in the historic district of Monterrey.

There was a buzz of excitement when we arrived outside the gigantic concrete union hall. Groups of friends all punked out in black were absorbed in animated conversations on the sidewalk. Clusters of tattooed youths milled up and down the long sweeping ramp that led to the basement parking lot. An elderly couple with weathered faces stationed themselves along the wall of the sloping garage entrance. The man's beat-up cowboy hat and the woman's colorful cloth wraps and glistening bright eyes said that they were proud to be part of the radical energy of that evening's event. Suciedad Discriminada and La Merma were already busy testing their sound and adjusting the amplifiers and mics.

I set up a literature table and placed stacks of my Spanish-language flyers, buttons, and patches across the surface of a heavy piece of office furniture. A blue Impala caught my attention as it coasted pass the garage and revealed two more buff men in sunglasses standing against the stone wall of the building across the street.

Then the fun began. The cement cavern of the garage vibrated from the deafening sounds of hardcore punk. The crowd pressed against the loading dock stage. An industrial blue glow back lit the musicians. A haze of cigarette and pot smoke curled in the light streams. The boundaries of band and audience blurred, the musical essence of our anarchist philosophy. The audience knew every word and belted out each song drowning out the amplified vocals of the band:

salarios mínimos niveles desorbitados de inflación
des-empleos enajenación, analfabetización, indiferencia
eso también asesina a nuestros hijos
eso también mata de hambre a nuestro pueblo

predicadores automatizados a su servicio una nueva cultura
ofreciendo beneficios que solo son derechos de unas cuantas personas
vendiendo una actitud un comportamiento y una conducta
un modelo a seguir ahora sé como debo ser

somos consumidos y a la vez consumidores
del desecho sobrante del llamado primer mundo
somos burdo reflejo de nuestros conquistadores
un modelo a seguir ahora sé como debo ser

An elastically thin, shirtless guy climbed onto the stage to share the mic. He was joined by a leather-clad woman with spiky flame-red hair. She reached into the trench below the loading dock stage and hoisted a stick of a girl to the slab. A flood of enthusiastic fans scaled the cement lip and before long much of the audience was crowding the stage. Ivan passed a guitar to an audience member midsong who continued without missing a beat while Ivan grabbed a beer off the nearest amp. The energy of possibilities engulfed the audience in that moment. This was the heartbeat of a determined resistance that grabbed at a person's soul and sustained them.

There was one last event and it took me to the intriguing two-level Macroplaza in the center of Monterrey. This is one of my favorite city parks and I have visited many. A long double-decker park lined with modern buildings that is impressive in its creativity. The park includes wide stretches of lawn, flowers, and colorful trees on a top expanse and more flowering trees are rooted on a lower deck that poke through large elliptical openings and reach towards the sun. I tell you this because my next venue was the newly renovated library, Biblioteca Central Del Estado Fray Servando Teresa De Mier, a modern tower alongside this city oasis.

A frazzled librarian greeted Anna, Emmanuel, Jesús, and the rest of my gang in the lobby and apologized repeatedly for the dust, explaining that the construction was scheduled to be finished before our event. We took the elevator to the ninth floor and stepped into a chalky construction site. Stacks of ceiling tiles lined one wall and clear plastic sheets had been casually draped across one end of the ninth-floor venue to protect the new bookshelves.

I stepped before the twenty or thirty people who were sitting attentively in folding chairs. The librarian introduced me. Two men again stood with their arms crossed to my left like emotionless statues looking out at nothing through their wraparound sunglasses. My message of peace and abundance may have been of concern to my two sentries whose presence provided a sense that we must be so effective that the authorities needed to keep close tabs on our work. The State's visible concern about our work provided the kind of credibility Comida No Bombas in Mexico needed.

Food Not Bombs Anti McDonald's protest in Belgrade

Chapter 31

BELGRADE TO BUDAPEST

I dragged my suitcase, filled mostly with copies of my book and flyers, along platform four at the Belgrade Central Rail Station. The click, click of my roller bag was a comforting counterpoint to the powerful rumbling of the shiny green and tan railcars preparing to depart. It was an exhilarating, crisp October Eastern European morning in 2003. I was on my way to meet Toxic and the other Food Not Bombs activists in Budapest for the first time. I had connected with Toxic by reaching out to the contacts at Budapest Indymedia. It wasn't a surprise that he volunteered for both the local Indymedia website and Food Not Bombs. I was excited!

I hauled my bag up the metal steps of a second-class car and stepped into the first cabin. A silver-haired older gentleman was sitting by the window on the forward-facing bench. His expensive dark suit suggesting a first-class car. We nodded to one another.

When the conductor arrived, I handed him my blue American passport and rail pass. "Keleti Station," the official stated while punching my ticket.

I could see my rail compartment companion recoil, pressing himself against the window at the sight of my passport. It looked like he wanted to hide behind the wall of forest green curtains as he handed his burgundy German passport to the controller.

"Where are you heading?" I asked him.

"I am returning home. I live in Germany," he responded carefully.

I offered that I was from San Francisco. He asked why I was traveling to Budapest.

"I am visiting my fellow activists. I helped start a movement called Food Not Bombs and we have a group in Budapest," I told him.

He started to relax and asked me more about Food Not Bombs. How did an American organization end up in Eastern Europe? I told him that we had been arrested for sharing meals on the edge of Golden Gate Park and people responded by starting groups in their own communities.

This seemed to interest him and I admitted, or perhaps even bragged, about having been arrested nearly one hundred times for sharing meals with the hungry in San Francisco. I told him that I had faced twenty-five to life in prison and added that the San Francisco police made nearly one thousand arrests in total for our providing food to the homeless and the poor.

"Amnesty International declared that anyone in Food Not Bombs who was convicted would be considered 'a prisoners of conscience' and had called for our unconditional release," I continued.

He then admitted that he was not comfortable when he first saw my American passport.

"The United Nations called me out of retirement to help draw up a new constitution for Kosovo. I practiced law in Germany for many years," he shared.

Then he surprised me. "You should be prepared to leave the United States," he said.

He told of how the US State Department officials he worked with reminded him of the type of people who were enthusiastic about National Socialism when he was a teenager.

"The US delegation displays the same arrogance as the Nazi bureaucrats of my youth. Even worse were the Blackwater Security Guards I had to engage with every time I entered the parliament building. You really don't have long before the borders to your country will be sealed," he said with authority, "you'd better prepare to leave before it's too late."

He told me of how even though Kosovo had a centuries-old legal tradition inherited from the Ottomans the US delegates didn't want to know anything about it and insisted that the new constitution include protections for things like intellectual property and a kind of corporate personhood based on their own interpretation of the US Constitution.

The train clicked across the border into Hungary. The German continued describing how his family had to grab what belongings they could and hike into the wilderness of the Swiss Alps when he was fourteen.

"We thought Hitler was a buffoon just like your President Bush," he continued. "We didn't take him seriously. After all, we were Germans. We lived in the Germany of great men like Beethoven and Martin Luther. And although our family was Catholic, even we weren't safe."

He might be right. There could be a time when escaping from the United State might be difficult yet necessary.

By the time the train chugged into Keleti Station we were allies.

Food Not Bombs in Budapest

Keith rebranded United Way of Tucson and Southern Arizona

Chapter 32

THE FIBROMYALGIA OF TUCSON

The sun glowed above the eastern slope of the Catalina Mountains warming the floor of another Sonoran Desert morning. My oatmeal breakfast was interrupted by the ringing of my landline. It was a friend calling from Washington, D.C. to say he was watching TV when the news program showed footage of a commercial jet piercing the World Trade Center. He wasn't sure if it was a simulation. I thought nothing of it. Surely it was another unimportant news story designed to capture more viewers or hype some government project. I hung up, hopped on my Motobecane and peddled off towards work.

Gamble's quail scurried across the asphalt path that meandered along the banks of the wash that had once been the Santa Cruz River. Stellar jays and mouthy crows screeched as I glided quietly through their neighborhood. I was known as the bicyclist by my coworkers because I was the only one who arrived in such luxury.

I spent my weekdays in a grey-carpeted cubicle on the second floor of an office complex. I was the in-house graphic designer for United Way of Tucson and Southern Arizona. Armed with the latest Mac, I was deployed to design heartstring-tugging packages of campaign materials to ease monthly contributions from Tuscan's gainfully employed.

The big Swedish American receptionist was not her usual happy self, tears streamed across her puffy red cheeks. A tiny American flag stood at attention from its black wooden base next to the ever-present vase of plastic flowers. "Didn't you hear? Muslim terrorists flew into the World Trade Center," she said sadly peering up from her desk. "Oh," I responded uninterested in the news and headed off to my workstation.

I flipped on my computer prepared to complete the previous day's design. My supervisor, who could have been confused for Farrah Fawcett, rushed up to my cubicle. "We have to kill those terrorists," she blurted out. No good morning or hello, just an expression of righteous anger.

"Didn't they die in the planes?" I asked adding that I was surprised something like that had not already happened considering the brutality America had inflicted on the rest of the world. If what little I had already heard from C.T. and the receptionist was true it seemed logical that the people who flew the commercial jets into the towers must have died along with the crew and passengers.

She stomped off confused.

By noon nearly every desk displayed the tiny, black-based American flag. The woman whose design I was finishing was franticly squeezing out God Bless America buttons. My design was no longer required.

An interoffice email a day later announced Red, White, and Blue Day, encouraging us to dress in patriotic colors and decorate our partitions in support of our nation. My supervisor stopped by first thing that same morning to let me know my poster with a peace dove and a peace button had to be removed. They were too controversial. A client might see them and could threaten to withhold their contribution. Tacking God Bless America signs and patriotic bunting to your cubical was encouraged. We were all New York strong, even in southern Arizona.

A week on and it was starting to look like the United States was planning to invade the far-off country of Afghanistan. The official story at that point was that the attack on the World Trade Center Towers was launched from a cave somewhere in that, "barbaric land of women-suppressing Islamists."

Time was of the essence. We needed to raise even more money than usual since we were required to help the New York City United Way campaign. The Vice President of community relations sat in the cubical next to me. She started to franticly call our financial recipients to make sure they understood that United Way would no longer be providing funding if we learned that any of their employees publicly expressed opposition to the proposed invasion. No names on petitions, no peace signs in apartment windows. No letters to the editor or participation in local protests. If our two largest contributors, Raytheon Missile Systems and Davis-Monthan Air Force Base found out that a United Way funded agency had employees that opposed the war it could jeopardize our contracts, she said.

I had designed the United Way Help folder and Raytheon Missile Systems was kind enough to print ninety-thousand copies for our agency. "Your brochures are ready to pick up," reported an employee at the print shop, "We will have them in the lobby."

I drove my Nissan truck south down Nogales Highway to the front gate. Solders greeted each vehicle. "ID please," one said and I passed my driver's license to the young man in desert camouflage while two others checked out my truck's under carriage with mirrors attached to aluminum poles. I was then free to pass and directed to the front office lobby.

It was a short walk from the passenger loading to the tinted glass doors. A businessman held the door for me on his way out. It wasn't difficult to find my order. A wall of cardboard boxes greeted me, all thirty marked in thick black with "Keith McHenry."

A day later I got a call from my friend Felice Cohen-Joppa to ask if Food Not Bombs could share food at their protest outside Raytheon's gates. Knowing how important a client Raytheon was for my employer, I went to United Way's human resources director to get her opinion before I agreed to the invitation. "Do you think it would be an issue if Food Not Bombs shared food at a protest outside Raytheon? I don't have to be at the scene if this would be a problem for United Way," I suggested. That conversation would lead to the end of my employment six days later.

Tim Vanderpool of the Tucson Weekly learned that I had been fired. My cubby neighbor, the vice president, had leaked the news. She would quit shortly after. Tim wrote, "McHenry says he dutifully removed the political stuff. Not long after, he was called by an activist buddy to help feed peace protesters out at the Raytheon plant on October 13. McHenry says he quizzed a human resources staffer at United Way about whether he'd get in trouble for going."

The article continues:

"I thought I should make the situation clear to them. I didn't want it to become a surprise, or for them to think I was doing something behind their back and get fired," he says.

The human resources person "told me it would probably be a conflict of interest," he says. "She said she couldn't order me not to go, but suggested that I should not go because if anyone identified me as being a United Way employee attending that demonstration, it could adversely affect funding from Raytheon."

I decided not to attend and told the organizers that while I would not be joining the protest, I would help cook the meal and that our other volunteers would go to share it. I couldn't afford to be fired. My wife Marion's employment was tenuous. Her employer's business plan was leading to bankruptcy and dissolution.

Then came a memo from the President of the local United Way.

Vanderpool continues:

Three days later, McHenry and his colleagues received a memo from Ed Parker, president of the UW of Tucson. "It has come to my attention," Parker writes, "that some of you may be participating in a demonstration at Raytheon... While I would like to discourage you from picketing one of our biggest donors, it is your right as private citizens to do so."

"Any conduct which reflects negatively upon United Way or which adversely affects our relationships with any of our donors is cause for disciplinary action up to and including termination," Parker continued.

"I and the United Way's managers support your right to free speech," the president concluded.

My sometimes-unjustified sense of optimism and fair play was reflected in the Tucson Weekly article. I told Vanderpool: "Decoding that missive is like reading tea leaves in a bucket of lint. I told my wife I got this memo, and we could go to the protest, and it wouldn't be a problem."

Marion had a more realistic interpretation. She looked at the memo and said, "No, I don't think that's what it's saying at all."

The article also noted that, "Six days later—about three weeks before the peace rally—Keith McHenry was given these options: resign or be fired."

The article ended with this:

Eleanor Eisenberg, executive director of the Arizona ACLU, has a few conclusions of her own. "I think it's deplorable," she said. "I would certainly hate to see this become a pattern. The idea of patriotism in my view, is not simply marching in step with the current administration, or the majority, for that matter."

"I think the argument could be made that the highest ideal of patriotism is to want to make your country better. And if you see your country doing something you don't think is the best way to do something, then you have an obligation to stand up and speak."

"Keith McHenry tried to fulfill that obligation. He was rewarded with a pink slip."

Thus, I was out seeking new work. The Western National Parks Association hired me to design, open, and manage their new headquarters bookstore in Oro Valley. I was given a budget to buy bookshelves, hundreds of titles, and high-end Native American rugs, kachinas, and jewelry through Hubble Trading Post. It was a $14-an-hour job. My father was pleased I had returned to the world of the National Park Service. He could stop telling his friends at his retirement home in Hingham, Massachusetts that I was a starving artist.

The eerie silence in the post 9/11 skies added to Marion's concerns. She bought a water purification system and stocked up on camping gear. She thought we might have to head south into Mexico. She was also worried that the next move by the government, now that I had been forced from my job, would be to seize our home. She thought we should get a temporary divorce and have the house be kept in her name only.

We had been restoring our simple 500-square-foot 1934 adobe with four square rooms. Like most Tucson homes, ours was cooled by a clanky swamp cooler. Our purchase came complete with a cluster of very nice men dedicated to smoking crack in the unfurnished living room and the original depression-era General Electric Refrigerator which I added to by installing a period Delta gas stove. I was impressed that my strung-out squatters respected the interior leaving the original wood window frames, plaster walls and lacquered floor in perfect condition.

I had also built a massive wooden roof over a cement patio slab out back replacing a Sears tin awning that had been torn from its moorings and was left in a crumpled mess at the far end of the nearly two-acre property. To attach the heavy roof, I had to drill holes through the two-foot-thick adobe. Black, red, and blond dirt piled below each hole revealing the rainbow of soil I found in excavated depression in our back yard. It was our authentic desert dream home, a house we could afford with the proceeds from the sale of our Kansas City condominium. The porn shop and desperate-looking hookers at the end of the block probably contributed to the lower price. We loved it.

Our squatters cheerfully moved onto the back of our land for a few weeks until they disappeared. They were replaced a few months later by some teenage neighborhood boys. Evidence of ever larger campfires and discarded vodka bottles was concerning so our solution was a six-foot-tall wooden fence.

Our neighbor to the east was an Olympic-class hoarder. A collection of barbed wire, 20-gauge rusted corrugated roofing, plastic toys, and automobile parts floated in mounds of white caliche dirt that cascaded into our yard. The only way I could set a straight fence was to toss the dirt-mixed debris back onto her property. It was a dusty but rewarding task. At one point my shovel clanged against a submerged piece of metal. I swept the discovery clean. It was two Spanish Colonial era iron kettles with gracefully thin handles. What would I find next?

The next day I woke to a searing sensation that felt like barbed wire being pulled vigorously between my skin and muscles. My loud screaming in pain was so disturbing that Marion moved me onto a mattress on the back porch where I continued to writhe in delirium yelling like a dying animal.

This was when my long journey for answers began. I struggled to breath. My legs and arms burned in unrelenting pain. Blood tests showed I had Valley Fever. I must have inhaled the spores of coccidioides fungi while shoveling my neighbor's trash back into her yard. I was prescribed Diflucan. Heavy doses of the fungicide promised to help me breathe, but the nature of the extreme pain in my limbs and the migraine headaches were not consistent with the diagnosis.

My breathing improved but the pain in my limbs increased. I toured doctors' offices. A folk dancer friend of ours was a doctor at the university and arranged a panel of blood tests not available to most. They said I had Rocky Mountain Spotted fever at one point in my life. Multiple sclerosis was ruled out. So was Lyme disease.

I was seeing double during breakfast one morning and this worried both Marion and I so we rushed to the Emergency Room. A doctor ordered a morphine drip. The suffering floated away and I was pain-free and relaxed for the first time in weeks.

Another specialist believed I might have Lupus. Marion and I returned home. We were sitting across from one another in our darkened living room. "Didn't your uncle Keith die from Lupus?" she asked adding in the same breath, "When is the life insurance policy at your new job going to take effect?"

I sat stunned before her.

I had succumbed to her pressure to get the temporary divorce but of course I had still included her in my life insurance policy.

A few days later I woke in my usual fog of screaming pain.

Marion announced that she had placed my computer and clothing into my truck. "You have to be out of here by noon or I will call the police," she said.

I stumbled out to my truck and drove over to my publisher's house. I asked Chaz Bufe if I could crash at his place until I found a new home. He made space in his laundry room and stretched out a foam mattress. I plopped down until it was time for me to drive out to the bookstore.

I found a listing on the board at the food coop on 4th Avenue. Hobbit House for rent in Oro Valley. Perfect, close to work; I rented it. It was a tiny foam igloo with a makeshift bathroom and kitchen. Flickers jarred me awake each morning pecking for bugs in the dried-out foam of the roof above my head. I patched the holes with pieces of mirrors that I fixed with mastic to the roof. It wasn't long before my shanty was a sparkling jewel.

Sales in my shop doubled in the second month. I packed the store's auditorium with live rattlesnake programs, Navajo weaving demonstrations, and a reading of Lazy B by Alan Day, Sandra Day O'Connor's brother, on their life in the Arizona desert. But it wasn't long before I was fired. My boss expressed frustration that my shop was doing better sales than the stores at the National Parks, he made it clear that he expected more enthusiasm from me when he showed his male staff pornography on his office computer, but used the excuse that he had found a blanket in the mechanical room where I would rest during my breaks.

I persevered and took a part-time position as the marketing director for Sun Sounds Radio for the Blind. The director, Mitzi Tharin, was a compassionate supporter of those with limited vision. I believe she lost her sight as a child. It was fitting that she directed a station dedicated to programing that aided people who could not read the printed word. Our volunteers read books and publications like the Arizona Daily Star at our little studio office at an east Tucson strip mall.

I was invited to speak in Lagos at an event in honor of Gandhi's birthday. I would be the guest of the Nigerian Vegetarian Society and the Consulate General of India. This would be my first journey to Africa.

Mitzi told me she was pleased that I would be taking a long week off. The budget was tight and she would need me to work overtime in the two weeks before our October Fest Fundraiser.

I returned from Nigeria inspired but I could sense something was bothering Mitzi when I entered. She called me into her office.

"I received a call from the Vice President of Raytheon." She had an uncomfortable expression as she continued. "He told me that you are on a blacklist and that I was not authorized to employ you. You have been doing a great job but I'm sorry I have to let you go."

Stunned, I slid my sketchbook out of my backpack and opened it to the inside front cover.

"Ok, Mitzi can you repeat that? What did the Vice President of Raytheon say?" I asked.

"He said you are on a blacklist and that I am not authorized to employ you," she added distressed, "I don't know what a blacklist is but that is what he said."

I wrote down every word and noted the time and date in my drawing book knowing it would be the most permanent place I could use to document this odd event.

"Mitzi, Raytheon is bombs not food and I am food not bombs. That might have something to do with this."

"Oh, I see, I guess," she replied still trying to understand.

Keith holding a Turkish language Food Not Bombs banner in Istanbul

Chapter 33

THE ORIENT EXPRESS

My solution to the employment ban and the suffering of fibromyalgia was to go on tour. I could cash college honorariums before the authorities could interfere and find enough relief from the pain by taking a tab of 512 Percocet before each lecture. That was when a young filmmaker from Australia emailed me about flying to the states for an interview.

Liz Tadic was all smiles, a bundle of enthusiasm, when I greeted her at the Tucson International Airport. She donned a crocheted Motown style cap and totted a tripod and a top-of-the-line Sony High-Definition video camera.

"Why not make the trip worth your while and join me on a spin around North America?" I offered. "You could interview our volunteers and those who eat with us." She agreed.

I got an email from the Italian punk band Kafka while we were parked at a truck stop outside Chicago. "The Italian edition of your book, Food Not Bombs: How to Feed the Hungry and Build Community has been published. Would you like to join us on a book tour of Italy?" A day later Liz was informed she had won an environmental award for her first feature-length film, Demon Fault, and was invited to receive her honor at a film festival in Spain. Liz was introduced to Food Not Bombs while filming the fight to stop a gold mine on sacred aboriginal land. The Melbourne group helped provide meals during the long blockade. "Let's continue our tour in Europe," I suggested. After we raised money for our airfare, we were off to our adventure in Europe.

The Zagreb main train station welcomes the traveler with a wide arching garden of an explosion of glorious red, pink, and yellow flowers. Liz Tadic and I stepped off the second-class carriage into the loving arms of our smiling host Darko. We rumbled our roller bags through the ornate station portal and into the sunny garden plaza. There was none of that sense of desperation we would experience at the other rail stations across eastern Europe. All was placid.

We ditched our luggage at Darko's apartment and headed off to collect discarded produce left scattered across the pavement at the central produce market.

Ivan, Marko, and Ana were already scavenging fallen carrots, turnips, cabbage, and peppers discarded to the asphalt by the venders who were packing up for the day. We lugged our baskets of produce to a thick-walled apartment in the city center. The kitchen was a buzz. Irene lifted a huge soup pot from the sink. A much-tattooed woman spun through the door with a jumble of wood and plastic cutting boards. The cigarette smoke was less oppressive than it could have been, possibly because of the high ceilings and poorly fitting window frames. I was introduced to each Food Not Bombs activist by city: Rijeka, Split, Slquonksi, Brod, as well as Zagreb. Our scavenged treasures were rinsed and delivered to the assembled volunteers, each balancing a cutting board on their knees.

I had the impression from the conversations and excitement that for them this was much more than the simple preparation of a vegan meal for the hungry. This was about defending a newly won peace against the war they had survived.

One young man wanted to know everything about anarchism in America. Did I know Bob Black? Did I read his essay, "The Abolition of Work," and, most importantly, did I throw rocks through that Starbucks shop in Seattle? Can I say more about anarchism that evening at Subversions? It was billed as "an evening of media guerrilla and poetry terrorism" at the community space ATTACK! Flyers described the modern multilevel venue as an "autonomous cultural factory." Of course, that was part of the plan. I shared the history of our movement. They shared their history of doing Food Not Bombs. Darko invited the audience to join us the next morning at their Anti-McDonald's Day action.

That was a time when our local chapters organized Anti-McDonald's Day actions all across the world. I had come across a flyer, "What's wrong with McDonald's: everything they don't want you to know," and information about a group of activists being sued in London for libel. The flyer accused the corporation of paying low wages, carrying out animal cruelty, and destroying the environment. Of course, I printed and distributed as many copies of the offending literature as I could.

London Greenpeace had handed out a few hundred copies of the flyers outside the McDonald's on the Strand and were sued for libel. Two of the young activists, Helen Steel and David Morris, decided to fight back. Their trial lasted ten years. They called for an annual protest and what could be more appropriate than our sharing fresh vegan meals outside McDonald's outlets across the country. Some literature I came across suggested that Helen and David picked October 16 because it was the day someone died in a fryolator, but I later learned that they picked it because it is World Food Day. I spent a couple days attending their trial at London's Royal Courts. It was inspiring to meet the defendants and humorous to watch the CEO of McDonald's UK periodically toss crumpled up cellophane candy wrappers at the back of the corporation's bald-headed barrister.

A chilly autumn sun struggled to warm the Zagreb streets. Our parka-clad crew pushed a cart-load of equipment towards the downtown McDonald's. We set up plywood tables. Darko and Irene tonged vegan burgers onto toasted buns and offered them to the curious pedestrians. Crispy sycamore leaves fluttered to the curb around us. Big-eyed children reached for the black balloons inked with the golden arches and the text "Eat Shit" in Croatian. A local animal rights group arrived with a freshly murdered cow head, its mammoth tongue dropping over the edge of a bloody silver platter. A small contingent of police stood nearby looking confused. A paper-capped employee locked the doors to the shop.

Leaving my Croatian friends was painful. In all honestly, I felt that way every time I had to say good bye to members of my family of activists. Yet it was time to move on and Liz and I climbed onto the overnight train east, flopped into our cabin, and struggled to fall asleep.

In those days when you stepped outside the central Belgrade train station the desperation blasted you in the face. A swirl of panicked men offered rides to hotels, pressured you to exchange your currency, and offered to show you around, anything to help you part with your money. A calm young man emerged from the chaos, "Hi, I am Rebel Red," he said, and off we went banging our bags through the clammer and rushing towards the city center arriving ten minutes later at a stately four-story brick mansion.

Rebel Red ran ahead. "We can get in this way," he declared gesturing to a rope hanging from an iron gate of the derelict manor. His enthusiasm was electric. We hoisted ourselves through the rusting metal doorway and past a scrap of weeds and trash. Broken stones from what once was an ornate wall were balanced just so providing a staircase to an alleyway of glass shards, discarded tin cans, and twisted ivy.

The three of us dashed over piles of broken roofing tiles and tangles of wire cable. White puffs of our breath punctuated our sprint. There was just enough daylight leaking through the soot-caked windows to find our way to a grand stairway.

We entered a maze of fallen concrete stabs and broken timbers. We squeezed through a jagged hole in a thick plaster wall and popped out into another stairwell leading to the third floor.

Rebel Red's flashlight struggled to pierce the drifting haze. Liz and I followed our host down a dark, cluttered hallway and burst through a filthy blanket into a dusty room lit with one yellow bulb that hung off a broken arm of an overused coat rack. An electric cord dangled from a bent nail in the ceiling and disappeared through a crack in the sheetrock to a power source in the neighboring building. Welcome to Rebel Squat.

Five or six people laid in a jumble of dirt-tan heavy jackets, thick scarves, and knit hats on a couple of stained mattresses. A kerosene flame balanced on a milk crate provided what little warmth there was.

Our arrival brought the snuggling squatters to life. The American had joined them at a time when people in Europe were quick to ask if we really owned arsenals of firearms as depicted in Michael Moore's movie Bowling for Columbine?

Oddly enough I had just finished reading a book of Moore's that I had picked up in Florence. I mentioned that Moore ends Hey Dude, Where's My Country with a chapter supporting General Wesley Clark for President of the United States.

The room erupted in angry denunciations of Clark and his war. They had survived his daily bombardments.

Emma sat straight up from her position in the pile, her red hair flickering in the pulsating light of the kerosene flame. She couldn't contain her emotions. She was a nursing student interning at a hospital for the most severely deformed children of NATO's storm of depleted uranium. My heart sank upon hearing someone that young having witnessed the sorrow of such permanent despair. "I work in a ward of seven hundred and fifty children," she said, her eyes becoming a moist blaze, "some were born with one eye, others with three ears, or thirteen fingers and webbed feet." Many will never learn to speak; some will spend their lives howling into the void.

"You just can't believe the suffering and these are just the first generation of damaged children. Thousands more could fill our hospitals. That's what Wesley Clark did for us," Emma said with fire and compassion.

Her mattress mate Rob piped in, "The war was madness, just madness. One day during the horror I woke up after a fitful night, walked to my family's kitchen and had to take a second look at the view that had been mine since birth. The mountain was gone." His mountaintop and his youthful optimism removed by Clark's cruise missiles.

He shared that he had stayed drunk during most of the bombing. "I remember sitting outside a bar on Admirala Geprata with my friends. We sat there with a sense of dread as we watched a cruise missile slowly lumber a few hundred feet above the street. We had seen enough to know it could swing our way. Thankfully, it abruptly turned into an office tower on the next block blowing a huge gash in its upper floors, mangling the metal frame, and raining fragments of architectural glass onto the sidewalk below."

Emma jumped in again. "I went to my mother's apartment during the opening hours of the air war. I found my mother staring at the TV rocking back and forth in horror, nervously biting the fingernails on both of her hands," she said, demonstrating the distressing image by placing her own fingers in her mouth.

It wasn't long before the televised explosions became real bombs and missiles landing outside her mother's twelfth-floor flat. Emma tells of pulling her mother from her favorite chair and leading her down the stairs towards the basement. The lights flickered out by the sixth floor. "Thankfully we didn't take the elevator," she told me; they had followed the suggested precautions drummed into every Serbian's head before of the tragedy.

"We made it into the basement shelter. There was a desperate banging on the door about ten minutes later," she continued, her expression becoming more somber. "It was my cousin. Shards of glass were still stuck in his forehead and face. Blood streamed from the gashes. It was awful, just awful."

Emma and her best friend Irene excitedly spoke over one another eager to explain a shared sense of dread: "We painted targets on our t-shirts and laid in a grassy park on the banks of the Danube daring the bombs, maybe even wishing that the bombs would take us out of our misery."

The stress was just too much. "I don't think you can understand what it is like to live under bombardment. Not until it happens to you. We sure had no idea until Wesley Clark launched his 'war of liberation' on us," Emma said sarcastically.

I soaked in every detail stunned by the horror my new friends had endured. No wonder they started a Food Not Bombs group. I was riveted by their stories but I couldn't ignore my need to relieve myself any longer and asked what they used as a restroom.

"You can use the crater on the other side of the building. That's what we do." Rebel Red lead me through the trash-strewn rooms to the twenty-five-foot-wide chasm. I stepped through broken timbers torn asunder from the impact of the undetonated cruise missile that had dropped through the roof and down to the ground below the basement. I positioned myself among the splintered rafters and flooring that fanned towards the starless sky trying not to slip onto the unexploded missile and added my urine to that million-dollar Raytheon product.

Rebel Squat had been the home of a wealthy Serb who fled to Paris before the war. Now it was home to a tiny band of anarchists, rats, and an undetonated satellite-guided missile.

Later that evening Liz and I were treated to a warm but smoky room at Irene's apartment at the end of a suffocatingly crowded bus ride. She told us that she was nervous about the police request to meet with her. She had been questioned by an officer during their October 16 Anti-McDonald's action and they had asked her to stop by to talk with their boss.

We returned to the city center and found the police precinct. What little English shared by the police captain along with his huge smile made it clear he was impressed by the protest outside McDonald's. It now occurs to me that his support may have stemmed from our taking action outside the very junk food establishment that is an iconic symbol of the America that rained terror on their community.

After the meeting we gathered outside in the sun. Irene explained that the captain had asked to be invited to help the next time they shared food. At the time, I wasn't sure if this was out of an interest in supporting our work or if he wanted to keep tabs on even the smallest protest.

Liz, Emma, Irene, and I found a warm corner in a café. Irene drew my portrait in my sketch book as we shared a coffee near the train station. Before long it was time for Liz and I to head off to Sofia, Bulgaria on the night train. Once again it was difficult to say our good byes. I can still feel that sorrow of parting. I sure hope we meet again.

The battered train clanked through the time-worn hills into the night. The poverty of war filled the coaches. Anything that could be unscrewed or pried off the once elegant train cars had vanished. Screw holes marked the memory of coat hooks and window curtains. The train lurched and swayed through the black mountain passes. Liz and I bundled against the cold, sharing the bleak railcar with a young couple who clung to one another for heat. A naked bulb flickered with the rocking of our Orient Express.

The train rumbled to a stop waking us at the Bulgarian border. Serbian officials checked our passports followed by two grumpy Bulgarian border guards. High rusting fences draped in razor wire connected abandoned lookout towers marking the border between the two former communist countries. What were they afraid of?

The beleaguered train limped into Sofia Central Station. We were greeted by five students smiling from the platform sporting a carefully drafted cardboard sign announcing, "Welcome Keith." Thankfully they had responded to our two-months-old email while we were in Belgrade but even so it was too late to change our plans so we were only able to spend the day with them before we had to again board our not-so-express Orient Express.

Liz and I moved from compartment to compartment seeking a warm cabin settling on the only occupied room where we were welcomed by a cheerful Sikh who quickly let us know he was from Modesto, California seeking a vacation from a fifty-seven-year marriage. "I arrived at the Turkish border with Euros and the guard sent me packing. He would only accept a $100 bill for the visa." He was hoping to enter this time. We lifted our bags onto the shelf above the seats and flopped to the bench across from the turbaned, grey-bearded, retired high school teacher.

Two Bulgarian National Police officers and their handcuffed companion boarded the midnight train at the first stop, Vakarel Station. They stomped up and down the train car entering each compartment. No light or heat in this one. No power or heat in the next until they finally joined Liz, the Sikh from Modesto, and me in the only warm, lit compartment on the second-class train car. The conductor must have checked our tickets but I don't remember.

The smell of smoke had been making itself known even before we arrived at Vakarel but the increasing intensity of the odor was concerning. I went to see if we were in danger. I checked the restroom. Clouds of smoke billowed from the toilet bowl. It seemed that the undercarriage of our train was on fire so I searched for a conductor. He wasn't at all concerned. The faster the train moved the thicker the smoke and before long the hallway was a grey cloud of bitter fumes.

Liz's family had immigrated to Australia from Bosnia and she had picked up a little Croatian and the larger, more relaxed police officer knew some English he had learned from the lyrics of popular rock tunes. From what I could understand the officers were transporting someone they called a "Kurdish terrorist" to Turkey. The animated official joked that Bulgaria was so poor that they had to pay the train fare out of their own pockets. They even had to buy a ticket for their terrorist.

The big Bulgarian, the Sikh, Liz, and I laughed and sang Beatle's songs while the alleged terrorist stared at the floor nervously wiggling his handcuffed fingers. For years I wore a Che button on my heavy coat which often invited a glowing smile from the Kurdish train passengers I would meet during my European journeys. That warmth was understandably absent from this poor guy on his way to a cold Turkish dungeon and the torture he probably knew was likely to endure.

The other officer remained serious and ignored the festivities of our cabin. I pulled my white chef's hat from my suitcase and popped it on my head. Our burly friend slid off his coat and removed his cap handing them both to me. I passed him my hat. I danced around the cabin sliding around in his giant blue National Police uniform pretending to admire the gold strips on his sleeves, tipping his police cap. The cop plopped my mushroom cap on his shaggy head and pretended to cut vegetables as we sang Give Peace a Chance. Liz filmed the party. I can't wait to see the footage.

When the festivities subsided the cabin companions were given a tour of the prisoner's fake passports and personal effects. The Sikh told us about how happy he was to take a break from his wife. "I love her but after nearly six decades together I really needed personal time," he laughed, "this is my first trip alone since we married." Liz soaked in the experience shooting clips and in her true journalist fashion quizzed our cabin mates. I eventually left to stretch out in one of the chilly empty compartments and catch some sleep.

Our Orient Express jerked to a stop in a nearly abandoned village. The 3 a.m. chill blasted across the car from the open train doors. The Kurd was escorted off the train and delivered to the Turks. I ducked behind the ruins of a building as directed by the conductor and found a man happy to take a crisp $100 bill sitting bundled in a tattered jacket on a wooden box behind the remains of the train station. He inspected the authenticity of my bill above the flame of a kerosene lamp, licked the back of a visa stamp and stuck it to a blank page in my passport. Istanbul here we come.

The train jerked across the border into a dark early morning Turkey. Two hours later the haunting call to prayer welcomed us to the Orient. Our rickety train snaked between the ancient walls of Constantinople and the milky Marmara Sea past rows of minarets rising through the golden mist into the timeless Golden Horn of mystery, tile facades, fragrant spices, and our first Food Not Bombs action in the crossroads of Anatolia.

Two days later we hauled pots of rice, lentils, and Kuru Fasulye and thermoses of sweet tea to the destination of the inaugural meal. Hundreds of red buses jostled around Taksim Square. Flocks of pigeons flapped out of the paths of the waves of pedestrians who were rushing towards the swanky shops on İstiklal Caddes or a bus to Ortakoy on the Bosphorus or to the poverty of the Tarlabaşı neighborhood.

Eight or nine friends excited to share our meal with the hungry gathered on the wide sidewalk outside the McDonald's on Tak-ı Zafer Cd. A flimsy portable aluminum table was unfolded into place, a tablecloth was draped into position, and our tasty vegan delights were placed lovingly with a stack of ceramic plates and napkin-wrapped flat wear.

A crowd of journalists armed with television cameras, microphones, and notebooks crushed in around us. A tall, middle-aged man in a brown dress suit that hung like a scarecrow from his bony shoulders stepped up and started our soup line.

He balanced his plate of casserole and salad and tasted a bit, then he took another bite and kept going until his plate was clean. Then he turned to the gathering, smiling ear to ear, and announced in Turkish that the food was excellent! A loud cheer spontaneously rose from his audience. He headed into the dark of the McDonald's and a few minutes later emerged with a line of young men and women dressed in the uniform of the fast-food establishment carrying plastic trays of ice-cream and sodas to share with our meal. The McDonald's employees beamed with joy as they glided around the crowd of a hundred inquisitive people handing out their refreshments for free. The manager's genuine show of solidarity and wise marketing was the cherry on top of a magical afternoon under the Turkish sun.

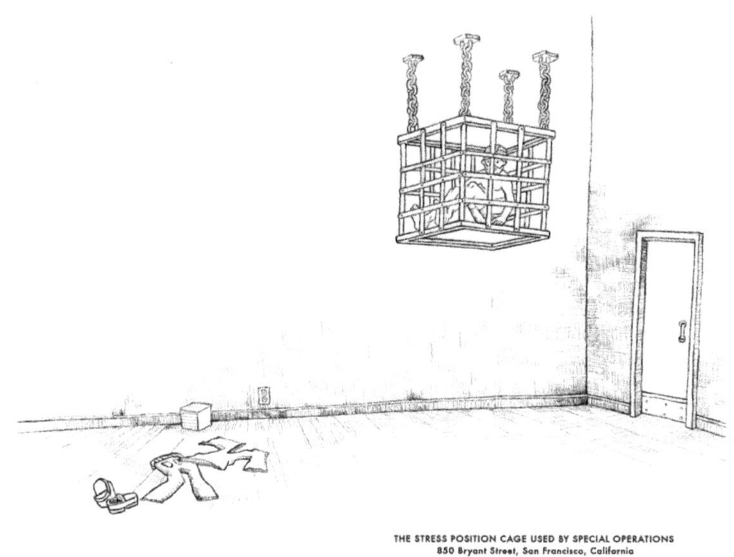

The stress position cage where Keith was placed in San Francisco

Chapter 34

ABU GHRAIB

The lights of Ortaköy sparkled on the dark waters of the Bosphorus. The outdoor cafes were animated with lively conversations that floated gently on the pleasant May breeze. Stars above the cafes shimmered in harmony with the waves lapping against the stone docks. A string of five-star restaurants offering seafood harvested that morning from the Marmara or the Black Sea stood next to one another along the southern edge of Europe. Asia was just a short ferry ride across the inky black.

My girlfriend, Canan, gave me the birthday gift of an elegant dinner with six of her best friends. One couple and four of Canan's girlfriends. The eight of us had participated in some of the No NATO protests that had become a weekly Istanbul ritual.

Canan's son Baris had emailed me in 2004 asking for help in starting a Food Not Bombs group so my documentary film companion Liz and I added Istanbul to our tour. By the end of the visit Canan and I had made plans for her to visit me in Arizona when I returned to the United States which evolved into my agreeing to live with her in her beautiful hill top apartment in the Levent district of Istanbul.

"How did the Food Not NATO action at Taksim Square go?" asked Aysun as she scooted closer to the white clothed table. "There were more media than protesters," I chuckled. We talked about the massive May Day rally in Üsküdar. Opposition to President George W. Bush's arrival at the NATO summit that June united the complex universe of the Turkish left. I didn't know much about the political differences between local activists but as the conversation continued it was clear that many things were not so different from our sectarian struggles in the American left.

It didn't take long before the subject of torture came up. News that the US tortured Iraqi prisoners at Abu Ghraib had just broken the month before. The now famous photo of black-hooded Ali Shallal al-Qaisi, standing with his arms outstretched on a box wired to a truck battery and images of US Specialist Lynndie England posing before naked detainees had been enlarged and mounted on foam core and greeted anyone passing through Taksim Square. Full color postcards of the grotesque images pre-addressed to the United Nations General Secretary and demanding a war crimes tribunal be formed were generously handed out to all who passed.

Canan's girlfriend Miray commented, "I am not surprised that the US tortures it's prisoners. The Turkish government is no better."

She shared that she had been jailed, beaten and smashed to the floor, her limbs ripped and her ligaments torn before she was placed in a cell so small, she couldn't extend her legs. She spent days in the cage, nearly naked, knees to her chest. The military arrested her for participating in a march against the war on the Kurds.

Ashti described a similar experience, captured for the crime of speaking her native tongue. Hawre told of having survived the tiny cell just for being Kurdish. The couple shared a similar account of their tendons and ligaments being torn before they were caged.

I asked everyone at the table if those administering the torture tried to get information from them.

"No, no they just tortured me," Miray said followed by the others concurring that they too had not been questioned.

Torturing to obtain intelligence might be a myth designed to justify torture to the public, at least that was my experience as I started to admit for the first time to anyone that I too was a survivor.

Plates of olives, dolmas, and hummus and metal platers of boney fresh fish were gracefully set before the us.

I started to share my experience.

"Police picked me up as I was driving to my apartment in San Francisco," I said, trembling to a memory that I had kept to myself. "I was shoved into a windowless van, driven to a basement garage and dragged down a maze of dimly lit hallways to a pitch-black room. I had the impression that five or six men had been waiting for my arrival. I was smashed to a cold concrete floor." I was already facing twenty-five to life in prison from the three cases I had caught in the first half of 1994.

A look of compassion radiated from Canan and her friends. The waiter glided around the table topping off our water glasses.

“They ripped off my shoes, pants, and shirt, grabbed me by my arms and legs, lifted me into the air, and then bludgeoned me against the cement floor.” I could hear my ligaments and tendons rip over the yelling of insults and profanity. What felt like a steel-toed boot crashed repeatedly into my ribs. Someone smashed his fist against the side of my scull screaming, “Fuck you, asshole!” so loud it almost drowned out the tearing sounds of the tendons in my legs and arms. My mind was spinning in surrender.

The vulgar insults continued as they lifted my pulverized body from the cold floor and shoved me in a tiny cell that felt like a cage hanging from the ceiling.

“Americans even torture their own,” Miray softly noted. We all shook our heads.

“Yes, I was never interrogated.” I added. Ashti nodded in agreement. “They could kill you but their goal is to send you out into the community to share your story to discourage people from supporting your work.”

I didn’t need to say more. The cake arrived with one huge burning candle. I made a wish that I no longer remember, cut pieces for everyone, and moved on to happier subjects.

But I couldn’t get that memory of the tiny stress-position cell out of my head. Just as the others attending my party must have done, I struggled to press my bare feet against the corner of the cage desperate to straighten out my legs. That seemed to be the only solution to the horrible pain. I tried turning onto my side but it was impossible and I became desperately obsessed with lengthening my legs. But I couldn’t.

Maybe an hour passed. Maybe it was five hours, I don’t really know but a moment came when I tried to come to terms with the impossibly of finding relief, discarding any hope of removing my knees from my chest. I drifted off into a fog of disassociation my eyes slowly adjusting to a dark barely illuminated by a slice of light that snuck under a door. I could see that my cell was in fact hanging by chains.

Hour after hour passed in silence interrupted by the occasional muffled thud of what might have been a door or the pinging of plumbing. The moments of unbearable pain and fear fused in a mental timelessness.

The terror cut to my bones when a sliver of light shot from under a metal door. A huge monster of a man stomped up to the cage. The clanging of keys clicked the iron bars free. The hulking silhouette whipped the cell door open and swiftly pulled me to the floor. The brute thrusted my blue jeans at my chest and pushed me out into the blinding light of a long hallway.

A uniformed police officer grabbed my other arm and joined the other guy forcing me to the front door and shoving me out into the cold drizzle on the top step of the police headquarters. I turned to see that the clock in the lobby said it was three o’clock in the morning. A taxi splashed down Bryant Street. I struggled to slide my aching legs into my jeans, in the first long seconds of what would become two decades of relentless pain in my legs and arms.

With no wallet or shoes, I started the long, miserable hike out to St Mary's Hospital believing that they would see me because I had been their guest in 1988. The emergency room receptionist was clearly unhappy to see a wet, shirtless, and shoeless man make an appearance. I recall that she asked if I was on drugs or had possibly stopped taking my meds. "No, I was beaten by the police," I insisted.

She was in a difficult position. A man with no identification stood before her marked with scrapes and bruises. She excused herself to find help. A nurse would see me she thought. "We are required to have the police interview victims of assault," the nurse said.

I asked to make a call to my attorney. After some back and forth she relented. I woke my friend and lawyer Randy Baker. "Don't say anything to the officer until I arrive," he reminded me.

The policeman and Randy found me waiting in a lobby chair draped in a blanket. The officer proceeded with his investigation. Who attacked me? I think it was the police but it was dark. I was released into the street outside police headquarters. The investigator's kind smile turned to a confused expression. When was the assault? I wasn't sure. Randy told the officer that I had failed to return home three days before. The officer noted this in his report. A nurse arrived and said, "we will see you now."

"Don't tell people about this Keith. No one will believe you and it could discredit your work," Randy told me on the way to my apartment. He would have to retrieve me from St Mary's two more times that year.

I was hobbling down Market Street during a protest one day. A friend, Holbrook Teeter, walked with me. "What happened Keith?" he asked since I was struggling to keep up with the march. I told him that I had recently endured yet another police beating. I knew Holbrook from his work as a mental health counselor in the Tenderloin. He asked me for details and I provided the basics. "You should stop in to see me. I see a number of Guatemalan and El Salvadorian torture survivors. What happened to you wasn't just police brutality, it was torture."

Keith speaking with Bas in Dasmarinas Cavite Philippines

Chapter 35

THE ARCHIPELAGO OF ANARCHY

That first blast of tropical Asian sun was unforgettable. Heat so powerful it seemed to evaporate the humidity. I was finally liberated from the suffocating twenty-hour transpacific journey from San Francisco.

The tall graceful man with a smile as warm as the hot sun standing at the Manila International arrival gate must be Cris. We both knew in that instant that we shared a common spirit of confidence and passion. His straight, black hair flowed to the center of his back. A thin mustache added drama to his glowing expression. He lifted my suitcase of literature and scant clothes onto a red city bus and we headed off to his place. I followed Cris off the bus and stooped into my first colorful jeepney, the ubiquitous independent public transportation that danced skillfully through the sea of chaotic traffic. This one was outfitted with sheet metal wings that flared across a red and yellow serpent design. I slid along the wooden bench crushing against my neighbor with my knees touching the passenger sitting across from me. Our heads caressed the low ceiling. Cris passed his coins to another occupant who handed them to yet another passenger who then dropped them into the conductor's hand in the cab. About twenty minutes later Cris let me know we needed to jump out at the next stop. We climbed out into the chaos of the working-class neighborhood of Pasig and bound through a mad tangle of pedestrians and motorized tricycles to a tiny lime green concrete storefront on a bustling side street: the home of the Etniko Bandido Infoshop, where Cris, Juey, Mel, and a revolving crew of radicals found refuge from capitalism's brutality.

A black and silver motorized tricycle sat under the tin porch roof. Cris let me know he would need to motor his fares around the clogged streets to collect a few pesos the first chance he got, but that right then our tour was his first priority. Mel was stirring a sizzling pan of vegetables and tofu on a little propane stove set near the door. A wooden windowsill painted light blue folded out of the storefront to become our dinner table. Cris' partner Juey was sitting in a tiny side room absorbed in reading one of the many political books that filled the floor-to-ceiling bookshelves. The main room was a perfect 10 x 10 x 10-foot-high cube.

I felt instantly at home surrounded by book spines that made the politics of this radical office obvious. Texts by and about my literary mentors, Emma Goldman, Mikhail Bakunin, Murray Bookchin, Errico Malatesta, John Zerzan, Voltairine de Cleyre, Ursula K. Le Guin, and a host of CrimethInc. titles and pamphlets invited guests into a world of anarchist ideas.

A parade of slow-dancing tricycle drivers—some beeping through the tide of pedestrians, some balancing packages on their heads, and others in conversation—passed the glassless window as we sat down to devour Mel's tasty vegan meal. A mobile hardware store peddled by, its driver smiling with a gold-tooth grin. Plungers, sponges, baskets of light bulbs, power cords, and more all dangled from the little plywood roof. A wide-eyed child clutched the remains of a mango, his face smeared in sticky yellow as he investigated the large white man in the window. The pleasant street chatter and laughter of children was the background music for our dinner conversation. Cris outlined our packed itinerary. They wanted me to see where Occupy Manila sat defiantly in the center of Rizal Park. I would finally meet the Christian Anarchist Asher whom I had been corresponding with for years. I would be speaking at the Eco Forum, the Third World Study Center at the University of the Philippines, and then fly to Davao City to speak at the Kinaiyahan Unahon Alternative Library. I would meet some of the Food Not Bombs activists called the Sagada 11 who had suffered a year in prison after being tortured into confessing to the killing of a member of the Philippine Army. My mind was spinning. I would be meeting some amazing community activists.

Birds called out into the dark. Mel slid our thin reed sleeping mats from above one of the book shelves and laid them out in neat rows across the cement floor of the main room. It was no problem falling asleep. It had been a long, long day.

A day later Cris and I crowded into another chrome-winged jeepney passing our pesos to the enthusiastic coin collector. We located our bus in a sea of seemingly impenetrable madness and headed north, soon arriving in the middle of a town at the edge of Metro Manila. A young man with a black baseball cap and black vest made from a well-used jean jacket greeted us. Cris left us and returned home.

"Welcome Mr. McHenry, my name is Jos," he said quietly reaching out his hand. I thanked him for his hospitality.

He didn't hesitate and I followed him into the maze of cramped blue-tarped and tin-roofed stalls. "The farmers need food too," explained Jos as we entered the market in central Baliwag, Bulacan, "so we ask each vender for a small donation to make sure no one family is impacted by our request."

We approached the first produce stall. A wrinkled man with a wispy grey beard sat on a wooden stool surrounded by piles of coconuts. Jos asked for a bag of shaven coconut meat. The farmer lifted one of the hard, hairy fruits and whacked it in half with one swift swing of a machete, flipped on his machine, and pushed one half into the whirling triangular blade. White slivers of coconut flesh fell into a bright red plastic bowl. A sweet woody smell flung from the spinning shaver. He repeated the maneuver with the second half. His bony fingers stuffed the curls into a plastic bag and handed it to Jos. His eyes beamed with joy from beneath his wide straw hat. He had donated before.

We visited another vegetable stall. A shy teenage girl sat dwarfed by sacks of onions, carrots, and garlic. We collected a bulb of garlic from her, then moved on to another seller for two carrots, then another for cabbage, and so on until Jos and I were struggling with several plastic bags of produce.

Another volunteer joined us at the entrance and grabbed the bags of donations. Once we passed through the entire market Jos hailed two motorized tricycles and we bounced off to a quiet street on the edge of town where we met Jos' family. His coy younger sister spied on us from the screen door to their simple concrete-block house. I caught her eye and she smiled. Sage-green palm fronds danced gently in the warm breeze.

Jos and I collected small branches scattered at the base of a long cement wall across the street. He piled the twigs, added some scrap boards and put a flame to a crumpled sheet of notepaper on a dirt patch in the family's front yard. Another volunteer placed cinder blocks next to the blaze and balanced a huge black kettle on the bricks.

Several friends arrived, excited to help. Like Jos they had the anarchist uniform of black jeans and shirts decorated with black patches featuring band logos and anti-authoritarian images screened in white. Three of us found cinderblocks and a plastic milk crate to sit on as we cradled cutting boards on our laps and chopped up our collected produce. Bubbling hot water was ladled into a bowl of coconut shavings. Jos stirred in grated ginger and lemon grass and whipped the concoction around with a fork until it was a smooth paste. He poured it into the kettle. I added my sliced cabbage and before long a tasty white coconut stew was ready.

Three tricycles sputtered to a stop on the street next to our kitchen. The drivers lashed the hot kettle to the vehicle's frame. I climbed into the low rear seat of the gas-powered rickshaw. A large blue plastic bowl of salad was placed on my lap. My seat-mate Tammy balanced a pot of sauce on her knees and off we bumped towards the city center.

Buses belched diesel as they struggled through a sea of motor bikes, tricycles, cars, and truck loads of construction materials. A cloud of black exhaust fogged the setting. Two of our cooks unfurled a huge black banner with a white

Food Not Bombs fist holding stalks of rice and tied it to the iron fence that surrounded a downtown elementary school. More black banners were stretched along the metal bars proclaiming that they "will not stop until every belly is full." The sound of honking, blaring car radios, and street chatter filled the hot humid air. People, mostly children, assembled to eat.

A middle-aged woman with glittery makeup told me her story of desperate poverty. Her eyes glistened with confidence. "Will you marry me?" she said, and smiled as she softy slid her slender fingers along my forearm. Two youngsters got my attention. "Look, look," they yelled as they jumped up and down holding rusty round bike rims above their heads, a treasure of the discarded. We finished the containers of stew and salads after a little more than an hour. The banners were removed and the equipment gathered for the bouncy ride back to the edge of town.

That evening I was treated to a queen-size mattress in a large block room at a sprawling house surrounded by lush green fields of rice. No wicker mat for me that tranquil evening. I asked about the huge portrait painted in grays and whites on the street-facing wall of my accommodations.

"Our friend Pong painted this mural when he stayed here after his accident," Jos explained. I enjoyed a peaceful sleep in that quiet house on an island of rice paddies. The big child eyes on Pong's picture watched over the still darkness as night birds sang me to sleep with their melodic lullaby.

In a succession of ever larger vehicles—a tricycle, two flashy jeepneys, then a crowded bus—Cris and I made our way to the town of San Jose del Monte. There we met with the smiling Asher, my first Filipino contact and a fellow activist with whom I had been corresponding since the early days of email. Asher was a teacher at his neighborhood primary school. He walked us around the lush bean stalks and bloated pumpkins cultivated by the students in his organic gardening class. A soccer field stretched beyond the garden below an impressive red and ochre school building.

We wandered slowly along a quiet street, absorbed in conversation. Asher asked: "Have you met the American Christian Anarchist, Shawn McCraney?" I hadn't met him but I knew of Shawn. "Is Christian anarchy popular in the Philippines," I asked. "No, it isn't," he said, "I only know of a few others." He wanted me to contact Shawn when I return to the States (which I would do). He led me to a small house and a simple white church nestled under swaying palms and towering bamboo.

Asher's mother was sitting at attention, dressed in a bright green smock and busy guiding cloth along the needle of her sowing machine. Her round face glowed, smiling in greeting as she looked at us from her elevated position on the family's front porch, without missing a stitch. Asher's father, the pastor of the little wooden church next door, welcomed us to his home. He pushed himself from his soft chair and extended his hand. He had a wise, dignified air fitting for a religious leader. He let us know we would be spending the night at his parish.

A stick of a silhouette stood at the church door the next morning. It was Asher's little sister investigating the sleeping bundles spread out on the shiny wooden sanctuary floor. The reflection of her frame drew a path across the hall. A rooster called from the bushes. The soft rustling of ficus leaves fluttered in the cool breeze. It was time to wake up.

I joined Asher and his friends on a steep steamy hike up a barren hill to the main city cemetery. Excited children ran along with us as we trudged along a dirt path that bordered a long row of cement and marble crypts. Asher pointed to a row of flowers outlined in fist-sized stones. "Our Food Not Bombs collective has been helping the families living on the edge of the graveyard with a number of projects," he said. They worked with the hillside community planting flowers along the path. "We taught them how to assemble bouquets to sell to the mourners who pass their shacks in funeral precessions," he noted, pointing to the thriving row of bright pink peonies.

A round-faced woman in a red apron tumbled from the first house. "Welcome, welcome," she called, waving. Two more older mothers emerged from behind her. "We are ready for you," the red-aproned lady announced. "We have enough wood and water," she said, gesturing towards a lashed stick wall that enclosed her kitchen.

A young Taho merchant, his tall silver tin of soft tofu and cane sugar hanging from his shoulder, floated up to us as we stood across from the kitchen outside one of the largest mausoleums. Asher hired him to provide a breakfast snack to the children. Several activists scooted the children together into the cool shade inside a marble crypt. A paper cup of the sweet silken treat was passed to each youngster.

"Ok everyone, I'm going to pass out drawing paper and colored pencils," the volunteer Sammy announced. The kids gobbled down their snacks, the youngest two pasting their face with globs of sweet brown cane.

"Welcome everyone. What is your favorite fruit?" Sammy asked.

"Mango! Banana! Pineapple!" they yelled, wiggling cheerfully into their neighbors and laughing.

"Ok, very good, can you draw your favorite fruit?" he asked as he spread colored pencils and sketch paper across the cool marble floor.

The cemetery mothers hustled around the cramped porch kitchen of their mud house across from the mausoleum art show. Armed with big spoons and heavy knives, they prepared our lunch over a stick-fueled fire. Asher and his friend Ana lashed a red and black anarchist flag across the outer wooden laths of the home.

Another volunteer stood before an attentive audience on the roof of the crypt holding a parenting workshop. I did my part by painting signs in white on black card board: "Food Not Bombs," "Mutual Aid Not Charity," "Another World is

Possible," and Asher's favorite slogan, "We are the Ordinary Radicals." The children would hold them for a photo or two after lunch.

The final touches of the fruit pictures were marked by the young artists. The kids giggled as they jostled for a space to tape their drawings on the mausoleum walls. "Who likes this picture?" Sammy asked. Everyone shot their hands up in glee. "Why do you like it?" he added and a rail-thin girl in the front row yelled, "It's a mango!" Another loved the red scribbles. Sammy asked about another image sparking more excitement. These kids were not shy about expressing their love for the colorful art.

Ana and Asher darkened the entrance: "Lunch is ready!" The boys and girls broke out in cheers. Sammy and another activist gently directed the bubbly kids into a line and passed a plate to each. One by one they stepped up and Asher and Ana spooned out the vegetable stew and potatoes. Then one by one they took their food and found a place to eat on the cool floor.

Every belly was full and it was time to relax in the shade of the tombs. The children commented on my beard so I invited them to run their fingers through my hairy face. I gave one child a high five. She smiled with satisfaction. Before long, a line of children had gathered to take their turn. "High five, high five," we said in unison as we dashed our palms together. We shed tears of laughter.

Cris and Juey were busy organizing another event when I joined them in Pasig. The street hummed with humanity. Coconut stew simmered on their propane stove and a noisy Yellow-vented Bulbul squawked from a wisp of a tree across the street.

Before traveling to Pasig, my friend Mary Beth gave me the phone number of Tita, the woman she stayed with when she was in the country as an election observer. "Have your driver take you to the Conspiracy Garden Café," Tita suggested. "Driver?" I asked, "I don't have a driver." "How are you getting around then?" "In jeepneys and tricycles," I responded. She was impressed. "A real man of the people," she said.

Tita met me outside her Quezon City condominium with a warm hug. The cafe was a short walk from her place. Sturdy tables and chairs rested under a canopy of banana boughs and lacy leafed balete trees. Tita was a member of a local communist party and the café's collective. The cook hadn't arrived so I was treated to pickled radishes. They were the best I had ever eaten, which was a good thing since the cook never showed and my dinner was several more bowls of that wonderful garnish. We agreed to hold an event at the café.

Our friend Bas popped in a day later and graced us with his wide, crescent smile. Cris handed him a cup of tea. "Do you know about the threat to Laguna de Bay?" he asked, "We will see the environmental destruction for ourselves."

A forest of spindly poles held a slum of cobbled together unpainted wooden dwellings thirty or forty feet above a plastic-filled slurry mudflat. The foul smell of fish rot and sewage really got your attention. Our crew followed Bas along an oil-drenched path to the shore. "Hey Bas," Jesus called with a sway of his arm.

Our guides led us through the trash-choked marsh where we were invited to climb into their long wooden canoes. Keeping your balance was a challenge for those of us new to the dugouts. The local fisher people poled us through the reeds and garbage out into the choppy freshwater waves. "Much of the waste water from Metro Manila pours into our lake through that concrete channel over there," said Jesus, pointing. Life was suffocated by the toxic soup. Dead fish bobbed up and down between blades of grass and discarded water bottles. It was a tragedy. Manila's fresh water was being poisoned.

Storm clouds built to the North. The smelly, white-capped waves clawed at the ax-carved hulls of our boats. It was time to return to land. "We once had an abundance of fish but we can't survive on our catch anymore," lamented Jesus as he tugged the last of the heavy canoes from the water.

Our entourage slogged back to the clamor of the nearest commercial district. A rusty, red, corrugated tin roof shaded a leathery grandpa from the midday sun. He smiled, his gold caps shimmering. Bas asked him for directions. The gentleman suggested we head south pointing his skeletally thin finger towards a maze of informal cinderblock structures of Dasmarinas Cavite, a town outside Manila. A swampy fish stench fought for prominence over the neighborhood trash fires.

We followed Bas through the concrete maze. A parade of motorized tricycles danced among the sea of pedestrians puffing their petroleum spice to the smothering air. Skinny-legged children laughed with the soccer kick of a one-liter, plastic Pepsi bottle as they scurried around the freshly puddled pot holes of their asphalt pitch. A pack of raggedy dogs tore at plastic sacks of refuse. A coin operated coffee vending machine marked the last turn before the dead-end dirt street of our destination. I knew I would need to remember its position when I woke. I fingered the pesos in my pocket to confirm I would be able to enjoy my morning cup.

Rain-spattered mud painted a skirt of red-brown on the solid cement walls of the legendary anarchist artist Pong's home. Pong had already made himself known to me through his portrait mural of grays on the wall of a home surrounded by swaying rice paddies on the outskirts of Baliwag, Bulacan. His name was invoked with reverence as I was shown my place on that soft mattress in the austere moonlit room. This man Pong must be amazing.

A flimsily wire-woven fence bordered the narrow walkway to a slightly ajar rust-red door. A wisp of a dog sniffed at our ankles as Bas and I popped up the steps and into the darkness of the little house.

Pong's glowing smile welcomed us to his hermitage. The spindly dynamo of a man returned to his seat on the rough planks of flooring and poured each of us a cup of water from a crinkly Aquafina bottle. I could tell that he had something to show me when he darted his hand through a pile of papers and magazine scraps. He found what he was looking for, grabbing a well-used plastic bag of stickers. A sliver of sun from the rear door illuminated the light pencil stroke ghosts behind each black-inked drawing of a fist gripping stocks of rice and the words Food Not Bombs penned in serif type. He fanned them out between us. All fifty or more stickers have been individually inked.

Pong lifted a reed basket from his left and placed it before me. He slid a detailed painting on cardboard of red, yellows, and blacks with chalky white highlights of Ronald McDonald eating a missile. He held up a second and then a third painting to the sunlight. "Check this out," he said, and grinned while sliding an image from his stash. This one proclaimed, "meat is murder," above bloody fangs and dollar-sign eyes. Next, he slid a painting before me that featured the McDonald arches turned into fighter jets and french-fry missiles. Drifts of smoke and dust floated in the mystical sunbeams that spotlit the gallery show. All the spike-studded punks in black attire clung to my every reaction. "What do you think of Pong's work?" asked the tattooed girl sitting closest to me. "It's brilliant," I responded.

Pong set each piece against the wall behind him but not before asking if I would like it. I chose a smaller portrait of Ronald and his striped socks sneering from a pirate chest of gold.

Pong could have continued showing me his pictures but he interrupted his art show to announce that it was time to organize the next community meal. He clarified a story I had heard before by explaining that his Food Not Bombs group started after the French punk band Container Crusties From Hell had toured the Filipino Archipelago. I had seen the heavy metal kettles left by the band as they traveled the country so I knew just what Pong and his friends were talking about when they asked that I help them get the proper equipment to initiate the Dasmarinas Cavite chapter of Food Not Bombs.

Pong uncoiled to his feet, sweeping his pictures to the side, and the two of us set off for the market. "We can find a pot in here," he said motioning to the Colic Trading shop. He rummaged through stacks of cheap household equipment until he located a metal caldron tucked behind a stack of brightly colored plastic tubs. I counted out the pesos, placing them one by one into the merchant's pudgy palm. Pong and I marched through the streets, lugging the thirty-pound prize back to his residence.

A crew of eight or nine young black-clad teenagers, most clutching bottles of San Miguel Beer were standing outside Pong's home engaged in an animated debate on which punk band they respected most when we arrived with our new pot. The conversation came to an abrupt end and everyone swung into action. Cutting boards and knives appeared and the chopping of the cabbage, carrots, and other vegetables they had collected all started in earnest.

Pong gathered four stones, each the size of a human head, from his back yard to form a foundation for the new brass-colored pot. A couple of us joined him in collecting scraps of wood and twigs that littered his muddy yard. He lit a fire between the stones and the two of us hoisted the new kettle onto the stones above the flames. "We get our water from my neighbor's tap," he remarked, handing me a pair of old two-liter plastic jugs. Before long we had prepared coconut stew followed by a vegetable stew.

A motorized tricycle bounced our heavy pots of vegan morsels down the pitted road outside Pong's dwelling and out into a wider neighborhood street. Our group quickly swelled to twenty, marching behind black cloth banners announcing, "Food Not Bombs," and, "Until every belly is full." A banner painted with the anarchist circle A was draped across the forest-green metal passenger roof of the tricycle. The parade trudged past small stores selling chips and sodas, electronics, and homemade meals. A few observers gave us a thumbs up. We snaked into a narrow ally traipsing down the damp soil path past wide-eyed children clinging to their mother's legs. A flock of scrawny white hens darted out of our way. Three frail white-haired men relaxing on plastic stools smiled their support for the excitement of our procession. We met up with our friends. They were guiding a class of eager child illustrators in the critiquing of their pictures that they had taped in colorful rows on a sheet of rusting corrugated tin.

The artists cheered in response to each child's description of their painting, bursting into applause at the culmination of the workshop.

Raj and Arar slid the lids off our collection of pots. Pong thrusted a ladle towards the crack of light cutting between the tin eaves yelling, "Dinner is served!" The young artists lined up below their gallery, each child grasping a plate in preparation for the meal. Arar scooped a dob of stew onto each platter and Raj ladled coconut soup over the vegetable mash. One by one they carefully carried their food to a seat on one of the concrete ledges buttressing the buildings and homes. A teenage girl helped a toddler take his meal to the safety of a bottom step. A hush descended over the street. The voices went silent as the kids devoured their supper.

The children collected their paintings from the tin wall and our team wandered back to Pong's place. His room was already packed with wall-to-wall friends. An orange glow from the low sun caught a sliver of smoke from a lit, hand-rolled cigarette. Slices of ripe mango and pineapple circulated through the snarl of black clothed humanity. Several people leaned against the back wall nursing bottles of cheap Filipino beer as they talked of the day's events. Others were absorbed in conversations about relationships, political theory, or past concerts. Pong found his place of honor and told me more about his vision for the anarchists of Dasmarinas Cavite.

Yellow smoke cured in the last rays of the fading sun. Pong glided around the room placing candles into cut-in-half plastic water bottles set into heavy copper wire wraps that he hung from the rafters or wooden ceiling support beams, lighting each wick as he went. Shadows and the gold of flickering flames danced across the walls from the two dozen chandeliers. A magical copper glow bathed the clusters of punks all busy in conversation. Pong had created a punk temple.

It had been another long day and I was ready to find a place to sleep. It came as no surprise that I was treated to the bed of honor: a dilapidated, horsehair love seat in the back yard with a threadbare, cloth cushion covering that provided no protection against the itchy prickles. The couch was only long enough to support my torso. My legs dangled off one end, but I was so tired I fell asleep quickly.

The rooster's call woke me as the first streams of sunlight filtered through the tree leaves. Someone had propped up my legs on a trash can while I was asleep. The dirt below me was obscured by rows of sleeping activists squeezed against one another and sprawled across the back yard. I carefully picked my way through, stepping on the few patches of damp ground not inhabited by Pong's friends and found my way to the nasty toilet with its leaky blue cistern before heading to the coin-operated coffee machine at the end of the block. Pong exuded the archipelago´s spirit of anarchy.

Keith helping share food with children in Lagos Nigeria

Chapter 36

ANYTHING CAN HAPPEN IN NIGERIA AND IT DOES

THE FIRST TRIP

"Anything can happen in Nigeria and it does!" is an understatement.

This Nigerian email was not the usual "I am related to Sani Abacha and need help with ten million dollars" type spam. The author introduced himself as Emmanuel, the president of the Nigerian Vegetarian Society. He explained that he was writing to invite me to speak at Gandhi's Birthday Celebration in Lagos. He attached a photo of himself standing stately before a neat stack of fifty-pound bags of rice that rose above his head and out of the picture frame. He wanted to feed Nigeria's hungry and he needed my assistance.

I agreed to help and requested funds for a plane ticket from my friend Dawn, the director of A Well-Fed World. I boarded the Virgin Air flight with twenty copies of my first book and $200 in cash. I was ready to make this happen.

The neatly dressed, moon-faced Emmanuel greeted me at the airport on a muggy September evening in 2005. We caught one of those justly famous yellow Volkswagen buses, then transferred to a beat-up blue auto rickshaw and bounced through the puddle-filled streets to our destination in the upscale Lagos Ajaoo Estate. Emmanuel grinned from ear to ear at the realization that it was my first rickshaw ride.

Two guards in pressed, grey uniforms stood below a flowering Royal Poinciana at the gates of the compound with their assault rifles relaxed and pointed towards the pavement. A brass sign identified the spacious property as the Gauranga

Foundation. Sweet-smelling tropical flowers that almost overpowered the smoky Nigerian diesel haze lined the driveway. Moonlight sparked on the estuary that caressed the banks of the manicured estate.

Emmanuel opened the door to the nearest building and a blast from the chilly, air-conditioned room engulfed us at the threshold. The humid warm outside air got the attention of the room's two occupants. They both struggled to lift themselves from the stuffed couches as Emmanuel, in a voice almost too soft to hear, introduced me to his friends, barrister Ayo Adebusoye and Guaranga Director Bolaji Rosiji.

Bolaji was a jovial West African with a proper British accent. The painted third eye on his forehead was my first indication he was a devote of Hare Krishna. His generosity was immediately apparent. He asked about my trip and offered me a place to sleep, laughingly asking a young man who appeared from a neighboring room to place a mattress in the guard house. That would be my accommodations.

Emmanuel had plans for me. Plans designed to impress. The next morning, he arrived eager to take me to meet his friends at the Bobnel Handicapped Child Support Project. He explained in his soft voice that I would be the guest of honor at the orphanage's Independence Day Celebration.

An enthusiastic, middle-aged woman named Cornelia Udoenoh greeted us at the gate with a bright smile. A small brass band stood at attention in the middle of the street banging out the Nigerian National Anthem. The marching band was soon replaced with a loud tinny sound system that blared Nigerian pop music. Twenty or so orphans jumped up and down to the music.

Cornelia's sound man turned off the music so the director could introduce me. I said a few words of encouragement to an audience of fifty little children mostly dressed in clean, white shirts. One of the older kids presented me with a green Nestlé mug that sang the Milo Chocolate Milk jingle. I handed out tiny wooden and string Dreamcatchers made by my girlfriend to the kids. "Let it catch your dreams when you fall asleep tonight," I explained sharing my interpretation of a Native American dreamcatcher story I had heard as a child. The squeaky sound system was reignited with more pop music. One girl about six years of age swished her frilly white dress with the music. I took her tiny hand guiding her around in twirls across the dusty dance floor. The kids roared with laughter and started to wiggle and gyrate to the music. The compound was vibrating with joy.

"Would you like to speak with the media?" asked a young man relaxing outside Bolaji's office when we returned and of course I took him up on his offer. First on his schedule was a live interview at the third-floor studios of Lagos TV. We found our way through a cavern of paint-pealed stairways and halls. A lighted sign shining "On Air" let us know we'd found our program. The host was visible from the hall sitting behind a familiar curved desk made TV special with a strip of glittered trim. Black scuffs and newspaper ink handprints honored the furnishings' well-used history. A cameraman slid his headphone off to greet us at the studio door directing me to an empty office chair next to our host. The energy and authority of the host made up for his lack of preparation. It was a lively thirty minutes on the basics of Food Not Bombs. Then it was off to a radio interview.

EKO's Akin Aiyedum was a superstar of Nigerian radio and he had a gift for making his guests the center of his popular program. Emmanuel's cell started ringing minutes after Akin Aiyedum finished wishing his listeners well. We crowded onto another yellow bus and scurried off to The Source, then a taxi struggled through the traffic to our interview at The Exclusive, and by day's end we were sitting at the desk of Tunde Oso at The Sunday Punch in their cramped office on Olu Aboderin Street. Not one journalist asked me for the traditional financial donation generally required for a media interview in Nigeria.

The big day arrived. The blistering hot October sun pressed down on the Guaranga compound. Krishna devotees hustled stacks of white plastic chairs to the lawn. I pitched in, helping them set the seats in rows before a stage rented for this illustrious celebration of Gandhi's Birthday. A local Reggae band practiced their new "Food Not Bombs" song in a gazebo near the still waters of the Lagos Lagoon. We didn't have to wait long before a parade of socialites and politicians arrived, all dressed in their churchgoing best.

The event was about to start. People found their places on one of the plastic chairs. An older woman in a purple, orange, and yellow gown franticly fanned herself under her flappy wide brimmed hat. Bolaji directed me to one of the seats on the stage next to the other dignitaries.

"Welcome, esteemed guests, to the Guaranga Foundation and the Food for Life kitchen. Now let me introduce you to India's High Commissioner to Nigeria, Shri H H S Viswanathan," said Bolaji. The audience clapped politely.

Shri H H S Viswanathan approached the podium, tapped on the mic to make sure it was still on and said, "Hello distinguished guests." He turned to Bolaji to thank him and then to his staff. He then looked towards me and said, "Let me introduce you to the honorable Mr. Keith McHenry. He is a descendant of Dr. James McHenry, a patriot who fought alongside George Washington in America's war for independence and who signed the nation's Constitution." This was when it first occurred to me that Nigeria, India, and the United States all shared a common history of liberation from the United Kingdom. "Please welcome an esteemed voice for nonviolence, Mr. Keith McHenry."

I stood before the attentive audience of dignitaries and shared the story and philosophy of Food Not Bombs. When I finished, I could see a young man raising his hand from the back. "Mr. McHenry, what you have said here today is of most importance to the youth of Nigeria. We need peace. Could I ask you Mr. McHenry if we can meet and start Food Not Bombs here in our country?"

"Yes, I would love to meet with you. What is your name?"

"Idowul, sir," he announced with pride.

After the questions and answers, the three of us stepped off the temporary riser onto the lawn. I shook the High Commissioner's hand, gave Bolaji a quick hug, and then walked quickly over to greet Idowul and his friends.

Thankfully there was still one copy of my book, Food Not Bombs, How to Feed the Hungry and Build Community, on the information table. The rest of the copies had been snagged by the other guests as they arrived. I gave Idowul my last copy and we agreed to meet at the Guaranga Vegetarian Restaurant later that week, the day before I was scheduled to return to the States.

Bolaji flitted around the garden wishing his guests well. He was clearly happy about the event and announced that he would treat me to a night at the three-star hotel next door where I could get a shower and a peaceful night's rest in air-conditioned luxury. My room featured a collection of stained brown chairs, a dented dresser, and a sagging mattress on a metal Hollywood frame. One sheet, no pillow-case, and no towels. The manager said they were out being laundered so I improvised using the corner of the thick golden drapery.

When I returned to Bolaji's office the next morning he was engaged in a heated discussion with a room of men worried about a crisis in Nigeria's fragile democracy and in particular the crisis in the Pro-Sovereign National Conference Coalition. Nobel laureate and playwright Wole Soyinka was threatening to pull out of the coalition. That morning's Punch quoted Bolaji saying, "We realized that we could not repair this country all alone. So, we supported an organization of like-minded Nigerians and formed the coalition." I had followed some of Nigeria's political history but to be an eye witness sure was an honor. Soon it was time to meet with Dr. Bekololari Ransome-Kuti to seek a solution.

Bolaji's driver was also a local police officer. He apologized but he wouldn't be able to drive us. "I am needed at the police station," he told us, distressed. A policeman had arrested a member of the Nigerian military for failing to pay a "toll" as the bus he was riding in crossed one of the bridges. Soldiers from a barracks came to free their friend and gunshots were exchanged.

Bolaji would not be deterred and took the wheel. As we approached the bridge onto the main island, we could see smoke billowing from a concrete building a few blocks from the highway. "That's the police station where they held the solider," he noted shrugging towards the fire.

We found the younger brother of Afrobeat Superstar Fela Kuti hunched over a dusty desk, chain smoking cheap cigarettes. Butts cascaded from a glass ashtray. He brushed away a chunk of ashes that had just fallen to the wooden desktop. He was clearly upset that Wole Soyinka was threatening to leave the coalition unless some conditions were met. Conditions I didn't really understand. It wouldn't be long before I would understand that conversations with vigor and excitement were a hallmark of Nigerian dialogue. After a contentious hour Bolaji finally expressed relief at their plan. Bekololari wasn't so sure, but there seemed to be nothing more to discuss so off we went.

Bolaji wove slowly through the Lagos traffic congestion telling me about his friend Charly Boy, one of Nigeria's most popular musicians. "You have to meet him, I will give him a call," he said, dialed the number and put his flip phone to his ear. "He says come right over." And thus, we were off and soon pulling up at the musician's modest house near the main highway leading out of Lagos. Bolaji asked if I had heard of the performer. I hadn't. "Oh, you are in for a treat. Charly Boy is big here in Nigeria. You see those guys on the motorbikes? They all work with Charly Boy. The last time he returned from abroad over a hundred thousand fans greeted him at the airport.

Traffic jockeyed past the bougainvillea-draped walls of his garden. A couple of dozen young men stood at their okadas, the motorcycle taxis that crowd the streets, waiting for fares. Bolaji buzzed the second-floor unit clanking open the iron door. A tail whipping pit bull lovingly licked my shoe tops as I stepped through and into the patio.

A beautiful, soft, northern light flooded Charly Boy's large front room. Healthy potted philodendrons positioned between doorways to the other rooms freshened the atmosphere. His wife, fashion designer Diane Oputa, emerged from the kitchen. Bolaji jumped from his seat to give her a hug. "Would you like a soda, coffee, maybe a beer?" she asked.

Bolaji introduced us mentioning that I had started Food Not Bombs in Boston. "I went to college in Boston myself, I know it well," Charly Boy said, smiling as he sat back down in what seemed to be his favorite chair. He told me that his girlfriend at the time was a white woman with long blond hair. They were walking hand in hand past Boston City Hall when two drunk white guys confronted his girl for being a race traitor. A few slugs to the face of the most obnoxious of the two and a lot of loud yelling attracted Boston's finest. They cuffed the Black man and hauled him off to a cell at Precinct A. "That is one racist city." he added.

"I've enjoyed an afternoon or two locked up at Precinct A myself," I said, hoping that a shared jail story was sure to create a bond between us. He shared his disdain for the leadership of Nigeria and spoke of the difficulty the opposition would have in coming to power.

He offered to arrange a stadium concert to promote Food Not Bombs. He laughed and said, "Anything can happen in Nigeria and it does!" He told me that this refrain was not only true, but part of the lyrics in one of his songs.

It was my last full day in the country. I sat at one of the long tables in the Guaranga Vegetarian Restaurant talking with several of the Krishna devotees. The two most enthusiastic students, Yinka and Idowul, arrived early, clutching the curled tube of the Food Not Bombs book I gave to them earlier that week. It was clear they had shared their copy with all of their friends. It was curled into a dirt fingered tube and sentence after sentence had been underlined in ink or pencil.

They asked me to clarify several ideas expressed in the book, turning to the page in question. They wanted to start a Food Not Bombs movement in Nigeria and suggested I return. I agreed to visit a year later for a month-long tour of the entire country.

They would send a plan and a budget. A few weeks later they emailed their proposal suggesting we buy two vans and hire a security force of five men armed with AKs. They estimated the cost would be $50,000. I responded that that amount of money was impossible to come by but that I could raise about $10,000 and that we would have to do without the armed security. I wired Emmanuel seed money. I would bring the rest with me.

THE SECOND TRIP

The Virgin Airways Airbus lumbered slowly through the black sky above Lagos on February, 15, 2006. A small collection of dim lights below gave the impression that this megacity of 16 million was really a village of a few hundred. Passengers wrapped in colorful West African prints placed their hands together, praying softly for a safe landing. Some held their hands towards God just as they had done before lifting off from Heathrow.

I almost skipped towards the customs desk I was so excited to see my friends. It was no surprise that I ran into the first scam of my visit before I even entered the country. Thankfully I had not one such encounter on my first trip. A uniformed man told me that I could pass through more quickly if I gave him a $100 for a visa. I knew better than to believe him. His movements through the lines of those waiting telegraphed his criminal intent and no one else was forking over the funds so I knew that this wasn't a new policy adopted since my first trip. Another official, probably a legitimate customs agent, told the guy to leave me alone.

Three other white passengers joined me in line. They were middle-aged guys dressed like civilian rough necks on their way to the oil rigs. One was still garbed in a heavy, plaid shirt, the other two in t-shirts. They were probably seen as tough characters back home in Great Britain but here they trembled with fear, all wearing that deer-in-the-headlights look pasted to their bleached white faces.

I tried to reassure them that not all Nigerians were dangerous but they weren't impressed. One guy was a Scott with a ruddy red color glowing from his chalky cheeks. He might have tried to drink enough to find the courage to step into West Africa.

"I hope security meets us outside," one Brit told the other, adding, "I heard it can be dangerous just getting from here to the helicopter." He told his coworker that if they could make it to their flight, he thought they would be safe once they arrived at the oil facility in Port Hartcourt.

A border inspector dressed like a general with a high swooping grey hat with burgundy trim reviewed my visa and quickly plunged the entry stamp on my passport several times for good measure. I was in!

Mountains of luggage cascaded across one end of the airport lobby. Agile men in traffic vests tumbled four-foot cubes of clothing and household items wrapped in mesh onto the pile. A mash of bedraggled passengers picked through the collection of standard and oversized yellow nylon bags and suitcases twisted in plastic wrap. I located my bag in the massive mound. Guards pulled a few would-be thieves aside, scolding them for their persistent attempts at unauthorized baggage retrieval.

The Australian filmmaker Liz Tadic was flying in from Dubai an hour after my arrival and a second cameraperson, Jill Gills from Tucson, was arriving soon after. They were coming to document the tour for the documentary Liz was making about Food Not Bombs.

I dragged my suitcase to the linoleum and set out into the muggy night. The smell of wood fires and diesel smoke stung my nostrils. Hundreds of people pressed against the Murtala Muhammed International Airport security fence. I saw my friends in the crowd. They were waving wildly and smiling with excitement. I pushed my way through the people jamming the exit.

We talked frenetically as we waited for the two other foreigners, Liz and Jill. Yinka and Idowul, told me they had lots of plans to suggest. They were excited to review their proposal with me in the morning. They had brought along eight other friends from the university. Emmanuel was there too, though he glared daggers at the enthusiastic students.

Liz arrived ready to get started on our journey even though she had flown from her home in Australia. My publisher's girlfriend and second camera person, Jill, staggered through the security gate frazzled and even more disheveled than usual.

My first host, Emmanuel, stood silently next to his cousin Winston who gave off a strong scam artist vibe. Emmanuel's movements were slow and deliberate. His voice was always soft. Winston, on the other hand, was pushy and combative. He tried to bully some perceived financial advantage based on an illogical pretense. A sideway glance sneering at being too generous with the food we were preparing like it would somehow benefit him if we cooked less.

I hugged my young Nigerian friends goodbye and they headed off to town on one of the myriad yellow Volkswagen vans that flood the streets of Lagos. Emmanuel haggled the price down on a private taxi and took his three foreign guests through the dark streets to the Airport Marriott Hotel.

The hotel was a Marriott in name only. A neatly painted plywood sign faithfully copied the hotel chain's logo in red, but otherwise it was just a rundown old hotel whose best features were running water and a lovely front patio graced with potted palms and hanging arbors bursting with flowers.

Jill spent the first night rummaging through several grocery bags of personal items. Someone swung open the door to our room, dashed past Liz's suitcase, clipping the bag with one foot. He stumbled, caught himself on a corner of my bed, lunged through a second door and out into the hotel's hallway.

We survived that first uneasy night. A songbird flitted from flowered limb to limb of a tangled vine as Liz and I talked over cups of Nescafe. We agreed our first task was to change our money.

Emmanuel arrived with Winston in tow. He agreed to help us exchange our currency and took us to an old crumbling building made of thick stone blocks. Emmanuel assured me that the men inside could be trusted. "They are Muslims," he whispered. "The Muslims are the only trusted money changers in Nigeria." This was a refrain I would hear often during our movements across the West African country. Even the Christians told me that the Christians couldn't be trusted in financial matters.

We entered an ancient-looking hovel and seemed to be stepping back in time. Smoke and dust swirled in the beams of light streaming through the entrance. A dozen or so leather-faced men with long, stringy, white beards and dirty looking turbines sat along the rock walls on dusty reddish carpets. I imagined that their ancestors had spent their days on woolen rugs waiting for dhows to dock in the Lagos harbor or camel trains to arrive with heavy loads of silk and treasures. An elder that exuded a grace of confidence sat cross-legged in the center on a yellowish Oriental rug surrounded by neat stacks of crinkly tan Naira. His wealth of gold capped teeth glistened when I approached. A medieval-looking balance holding a kilo weight sat to his right.

I crouched on the dirt floor and counted out ten crisp $100 bills. The otherwise placid old men sighed in unison with the drama of seeing the last bill placed on the money changer's brass platter.

Row after row of well-fingered Naira were stacked before me, each pile equaling $100. I slowly counted each heap and placed it into a plastic bag I had brought for the occasion. I stood and bowed to each of the men and gave them all a hardy hand shake. I promised I would return and I did.

Emmanuel and I returned to the hotel. He let me know he planned to hold a press conference at his office and promised to help me locate a van. He informed me that he had big plans for me.

But a few days passed and we had no word on either the media event or the van. Emmanuel insisted it wasn't safe to work with the students. They would rob me, he said, adding that he was the only person I could trust. Meanwhile, my limited time in Nigeria of one month was slipping away at the Airport Marriott and the students hadn't arrived as planned.

Liz and I were sitting on the patio sipping our lukewarm instant coffees when I heard Idowul call my name from beyond the hotel gate. His glowing smile was a welcome sight after four days of dour Emmanuel and bitter Winston. The students, Idowul told me, had been kept away by Emmanuel's claim that I didn't wish to see them.

They, however, were eager to share their plans with me. Emmanuel tried to derail their proposal that we get moving, saying we had to wait for the press conference. I disagreed and insisted that we get on with the tour. The students suggested we meet Senator Adeseye Ogunlewe at his home in Lagos while we worked out the logistics for purchasing a van. The senator had also recently been appointed as the Minister of Public Works for Nigeria. He promised to pave the intercity highways within a year.

Golden rays of sun struggled to burn through the early morning haze. We joined forty or fifty people, mostly men, standing in the side yard of the senator's huge, nearly treeless compound on Victoria Island. Knots of men dressed in a variety of Western business suits and traditional West Africa prints stood in clumps speaking softly to one another. A polite young man in a business suit assured us it wouldn't be long before our meeting with the senator. He continued to drift past us every ten or fifteen minutes to reassure us that we had not been forgotten. Soon the house no longer shaded the courtyard from the cruel midmorning sun and the diminishing crowd grew restless.

After waiting for a couple of hours, we were ushered into a huge room off the patio. Several rows of white plastic chairs sat in the center of the hall facing a wall decorated with banners, a table and several more chairs. The senator warmly greeted our entourage and I suspect, since I was the only white man in the room, the senator walked up and gave me a hardy handshake saying, "Welcome to Nigeria."

Idowul passed my business card to the senator who asked if we would agree to being on TV. "What you are doing is very important. We must tell all of Nigeria about your program," he stated with authority.

We agreed that would be helpful. "Come this way," the senator gestured and led me to an area before to a long table. A green and yellow flag hung centered on the wall behind. The cameramen from NTA and LTV adjusted their tripods and focused their lenses. Several photographers crouched before us. Senator Adeseye Ogunlewe put his arm around my shoulders, faced the cameras and announced "it is an honor to meet a white man from America like you who has come here to Nigeria to feed the hungry."

He encouraged all of Nigeria to support the work of Food Not Bombs and turned with a smile to shake my hand. I thanked the senator for his support and said a few words about how happy I was to participate in the founding of Food Not Bombs Nigeria.

The cameramen packed up their equipment and slid quickly out of the room. The senator and I drifted over to Idowul and Yinka, whom the senator lovingly grabbed around the back of the neck, saying, "You must visit me in Abuja. I will be in the capital at the end of the week. Please stop by." He ended our meeting with a firm handshake and then said, "Wait right here. I have something for your journey."

A young man walked up a few minutes later and discreetly handed Idowul an envelope stuffed with $500 in Nigerian currency. My friends were excited. Our visit was a success. It was time to buy a van.

Liz and I met Emmanuel and his preacher friend on the narrow street outside my host's second-floor office. Five men were mixing a mound of concrete with old shovels on the dirt. A tangle of power and phone lines laced from poles and building corners formed a web above the drama. A family was grilling fish over a small fire of discarded wood scraps. Waves of people flowed past. Stately women balanced baskets and bundles on their heads as they glided through the chaos. The preacher joined us. He seemed distracted and his greeting had an insincere air. Soon he rushed off to get our van. I returned to my playful interaction with the wide-eyed children who made this block their playground.

An hour later the cagey preacher returned with a dented white van. Emmanuel wandered around the vehicle trailing his soft fingers along the metal while repeating that he didn't think it would work for our purposes. The preacher showed us the features of the van while also complaining that the van was no good. This re-enforced the image I had of him as someone not to be trusted. Why waste our time looking at a van that none of us are interested in, I thought to myself? He insisted he had a better van lined up for us. It seemed that the preacher had been recruited to give me the impression that I could trust the transaction. This was odd, however, since Emmanuel himself had said that I could only trust Muslims. I thought it was possible that the fellow was not only a man of the cloth but also a used car salesman.

The preacher drove us in his car, bouncing along a crumbling highway near the Port of Lagos. Vehicles were strewn along the side of the road, lodged between chunks of concrete and smoldering tires. Monster-sized cranes dangled above a collection of rusting cargo ships across the five-mile-wide milky channel. The emptied cable spools used by so many Nigerian vendors were nestled between the vehicles and debris, offering small collections of fruit, batteries, colas, and socks.

"There he is!" said the pastor. A man was flailing his arms above his head. He was standing on a slab of cement next to a grey Mitsubishi van. The preacher pulled in front of the vehicle. He introduced us to the owner of the van. The vehicle was emblazoned with Danish bumper stickers that gave me the impression it might have been stolen from a European family.

The hood was open. I pulled on wires and checked to see if there was oil on the head or dripping on the engine. All clean. We investigated the tires and the interior. It was $7,000 just like the first van. This vehicle had newish fabric seats with high backs. It was unstained and could seat our whole crew. I was handed a key and some papers indicating ownership. I counted out $7,000 US on the passenger's seat. We were square. Emmanuel drove us back to our hotel and I reluctantly let him drive the van to his family's home hoping I would see it again.

Emmanuel met us at the hotel the next morning assuring me that the van had been safely parked in a compound and adding that the press conference would be postponed again.

I couldn't waste another day at the Airport Marriott so I pressured Emmanuel to schedule the press event for the next day. Emanuel suggested the customary payment be 3,000 Naira than changed that to 5,000 Naira. I agreed to 3,000 knowing from speaking with the students that amount was the going rate for an interview. Five or six reporters followed one another up to Emmanuel's tiny second-floor office. He sat like an emperor behind his solid wooden desk. I sat to his side. Emmanuel made sure the students were not invited.

The reporters scooted the collection of chairs into position sliding out notebooks and tape recorders from their bags as Emmanuel distributed his press release introducing himself as the director of Food Not Bombs Nigeria.

"Thanks for taking an interest in Food Not Bombs," I said before sharing our three principles and stressing that we didn't have any leaders or directors. The journalists were polite but I got the feeling they weren't really interested in more than our cash and franticly packed their papers jamming their envelopes of money into their pockets before speeding off to another story.

Now that the frustration of the delayed press event had passed it was time to get this tour on the road. The chaos of the street flowed past as the students joined us outside Emmanuel's office. While we were discussing our plans a man silently joined our gathering. Emmanuel introduced me to this person saying that he would be our driver, James. It was clear that I would need to figure out the relationship between James and my host. We agreed to start by sharing a meal with the most desperate people of Lagos who lived in an abandoned market near the old port.

Emmanuel offered his family's small, neat neighborhood restaurant. A rough unfinished board with red lettering that said, "The Moonshine Café," hung across the thin unpainted porch facade. Two red, plastic tables with matching plastic chairs sat on a plywood deck that bridged over a foul-smelling and garbage-filled cement channel. A cloth-draped door opened into small room with two more plastic tables and chairs. Emmanuel's oldest sister Eleanor, the proud owner of the café, emerged from a back room wiping her hands on a towel before reaching out to welcome us. The establishment was neat and inviting with black and white checkered table cloths over the standard plastic tables and decorations centered between doors or windows.

A sparse room that doubled as a living room and sleeping space provided us with a place to chop the vegetables and fruit. Emmanuel's sisters directed the preparation. The men watched in amazement as I sliced tomatoes and peppers. They didn't realize men were capable, or maybe more to the point, willing to cook a meal. For them, that was women's work. Liz drifted quietly around the room filming the colorful preparations. The sisters took turns stirring a pot of vegetable stew bubbling over a small propane burner set in the alley to minimize the heat of the already suffocatingly hot, windowless room.

Soon the dishes were ready. Winston and I lugged the pots of stew and rice to our van. Eleanor tucked our serving equipment next to the meal.

James drove us to a location near the wharfs known to be safe for the city's outcasts. A puddle-strewn courtyard walled in by shallow loading docks and tin porch roofs was occupied by dozens of wiggly children.

We found the elder sitting like a king draped in bright yellow, red, and green prints, his head crowned with a matching Kufi, and surrounded by courtiers of men. He joyfully greeted us. "We have cripples, the blind, and lepers. Cripples, the blind, and lepers. You can feed them all," he said, and elegantly gestured towards the crumbling compound.

Several teenagers responded to the conversation by dashing around the yard gathering the children. The kids jumped up and down waving their plastic bowls. A five- or six-year-old girl hopped up and down waving a red, plastic bowl yelling that she wanted tomatoes.

The youngsters were enthusiastic but also careful not to push one another as each child stepped forward to have their bowl filled with rice and vegetable stew. The food ran out in fifteen minutes leaving dozens of other children to go without.

My Nigerian friends got an introduction to the magic of Food Not Bombs. It was time to seed the movement across West Africa.

The next morning Emmanuel came by the Airport Marriott in our new van. It was clear from Emmanuel's face that he was disappointed to find me sitting in the patio speaking with Yinka and Idowu and their friends. He brought his shady cousin Winston and James, our driver. Emmanuel was the only Nigerian with luggage. The rest travelled with just the clothes on their backs. I would learn they lived in a concrete office building sleeping on the hard floor. They were undergraduates at the University of Lagos. They owned almost nothing other than a second change of clothing.

James pushed through the city traffic to the southern border of Lagos. We passed an exit to Prayer City and whizzed past a few hundred rows of benches interrupted by old TVs perched atop a stack of boxes and then continued to drive alongside fifteen or twenty minutes of such rows of rickety pews waiting to be occupied by the faithful.

We lost our way a few times. There were heated discussions about the best route. We came upon a recent traffic accident outside Benin City. There were mangled cars half submerged in the jungle foliage. Survivors staggered about in the street, wailing and flailing their arms. Bodies were strewn motionless across the roadside weeds. The tragedy was painful for Jill and she wanted to turn back. We took Jill back to Lagos and the hostel run by Catholic nuns St. Agnes Catholic Church in the heart of the Maryland district. She would make this her home for the rest of the month.

Our first stop engagement was the annual meeting of the National Association of Nigerian Students.

Police stopped us at a checkpoint. The young officers insisted that our vehicle was not properly registered. There was a lot of yelling between our party and several police officers. Are we under arrest I asked or do they just want money? I demanded to see the chief. After we refused to pay a fine the commander ordered us to follow him to police headquarters, a compound that resembled a sixteenth century stone fort. They marched us over to the Police Chief's office.

A middle-aged man dressed in a pressed grey uniform was sitting behind an unimpressive wooden desk. His air of authority dominated the brightly lit room. Light white drapery swayed gently in the cool breeze behind him.

I stepped confidently to his desk and introduced myself. "I am an author and co-founder of a global program that feeds the hungry," I said. I held out a copy of my book and explained that I had just bought the van that week in Lagos. We were assured that we had obtained the proper paperwork. I directed his attention to my associate, Liz Tadic and her high-end digital video camera. I let him know that Liz is an important Australian journalist. I told the chief that we would like to film him receiving a copy of my book. I could see he was impressed. An American with a book and his own camera person.

Liz readied her camera on her tripod. I stood next to the chief and Liz indicated that the camera was filming. I thanked him for his warm welcome to his state. He said he was honored we came to visit him. We shook hands. The chief handed me his business card saying if I ever need anything to please call him. He crossed out the phone number printed on the front and turned the card over. "Call me on my cell," he said, writing out one long number. "If that doesn't work try this number," he said again and so on until he had written out five phone numbers where I would be able to reach him.

After two sweltering sweaty days our tired crew bumped out of the dense jungle into the little village of Katsinina - Ala. A huge brown barn-like building sat at the center of the town. It was the heart of Government College Katsina-Ala, said to be Nigeria's oldest and most prestigious school of higher education.

Several young men from the National Association of Nigerian Students or NANS, greeted our entourage at a little house across the street from the barn where the national annual meeting was busy discussing the powerful group's future. The student leaders invited us to clean up and relax from our journey. But I didn't want to miss the opportunity to address one of Nigeria's most respected institutions and our hosts whisked me across the street into a hall where hundreds of students were sitting on neat rows of wooden benches.

Idowu whispered to one of the student leaders sitting behind a long wooden table stretched across the stage. Food Not Bombs Nigeria was soon next on the agenda.

Idowu introduced me as, "a white man that has been incarcerated more than you or I." I then gave a short presentation and thanked the students for the honor of sharing a little about the history and purpose of Food Not Bombs. The assembly discussed a proposal to support the formation of a Food Not Bombs movement in Nigeria. The entire room voted in favor. Word of the vote would make the national news. Students asked me how to get involved. My friends believed our visit to have been a huge success.

But Emmanuel was visibly distressed at the support we received in Katsina-Ala. I could see that he feared that he was losing control and wanted us to leave town as quickly as possible and head for Calabar and his scheduled meeting with Olumba Olumba Obu, the Sole Spiritual Head of the Universe.

A small group of security guards huddled under a patch of shade outside the freshly painted white walls of the headquarters of the Brotherhood of the Cross and Star. James guided the van under a huge white arch decorated with three interlinking red zeros. Bright enameled pictures of Olumba Olumba Obu the father graced the top of one column and that of Olumba Olumba Obu the son peered down from the left column.

A woman dressed in a white gown stood in the parking lot waiting to greet us. She introduced herself at the producer of Starcross TV and in less than five minutes was pushing me to pay the Brotherhood $500 to be interviewed on their station. I refused.

She finally seemed to realize I wasn't going to give her any money and agreed to let us meet the Sole Spiritual Head or the Son of the Son of God.

We climbed to the top floor of a five-story building, one of the tallest structures I had seen in Nigeria. The marble stairs ended at a cramped room filled with a plexiglass box that covered an architect's model of a cathedral. The first white men I had seen since arriving stood with their backs pressed to the wall dressed in long white robes. The TV producer introduced them as the personal aids of the Sole Spiritual Head but I also learned that they were the sons of a British Scientist who found Olumba Olumba Obu while studying primates in the jungles of Cross River. The round-faced man relaxing majestically in a stuffed chair also cramped against the back wall was the very man we came to see, the leader of the Brotherhood, Olumba Olumba Obu

Emmanuel fell to his knees and crawled towards Olumba Olumba Obu with his hands in prayer. Not the image I had hoped to see from someone representing a movement whose principles rejected both masters and charity. The gentle leader stood from his cheap throne smiling warmly as he reached out to shake my hand.

According to Emmanuel, Olumba Olumba Obu was an important Nigerian vegetarian who, like Food Not Bombs, fed the hungry. This was someone that I had to meet, but his dedication to the vegetarian diet and ending hunger seemed to change during our conversation. His forty-hector yam farm helped him feed the poor every month or maybe once a year or was it every day? The Brotherhood's popular vegetarian stew included a sufficient amount of ham to sustain his flock. Even so, I could see how people might want to believe he was God's grandson. He had an ephemeral spirit and gentle smile as well as food and a place to sleep. all good qualities in the eyes of the desperately poor of Calabar. "You can give the sermon tomorrow morning. I think this would be good," he said softly.

Well, as odd as this was, I thought this was an opportunity to introduce more people to Food Not Bombs and could prove to be interesting so I agreed to speak to his congregation.

Our Starcross TV woman woke us at 4 a.m. as promised. Emmanuel, Liz, and I sleepily staggered behind her across the compound to the sanctuary.

People draped in clean, white robes were sleeping in the high-walled pews, giving the impression that we had entered a New England Meeting House occupied by sleeping ghosts.

The parishioners stirred to life as the Sole Spiritual Head of the Universe stepped to the altar and begin the service. An LED light scrolled above his head telling his followers that they had to deposit their ten percent into Zenith Bank account 288-64-24-8571377. A cheap circular fan hidden behind a short wall softly blew his shear, white robe providing an ephemeral almost god-like impression.

After several animated hours on the theology of the Brotherhood, the TV producer whispered that it was time for my sermon. I followed her into a glass box furnished with a microphone and lectern. I shared a short story about Food Not Bombs, described our three principles emphasizing our dedication to inclusion of those who eat with us in the decision making of each local group, and ended by saying I hoped to start a chapter in Calabar.

My sleepy audience was visibly moved. I returned to my pew as the congregation started to march around the temple hunched over with their arms swaying in front of them mimicking an elephant's trunk. The parade passed a bathtub-size brass bowl. Each of the faithful would swing their trunk arms over the bowl dropping their tithe to the bottom with a clink.

Once everyone had a chance to make their contribution the congregation marched out into the sun. Everyone knew to sway back and forth in unison and clap their hands as they sang a hymn. The precession danced around the church grounds and swayed out on to Ambo Street.

That was enough for me. I could see the horror on the faces of people selling fruit and other items along the muddy street. I stopped, turned to those following, loudly thanked Olumba Olumba Obu and his community for the opportunity to meet, and announced I had to rushed off to the University of Calabar.

A pleasant receptionist welcomed our entourage and directed us to Deputy Vice Chancellor Zana Akpagu and Dean Joseph Asor. After a short meeting with the university administrators, we headed over to the classrooms.

The dim lights flickered off. We found our way through the mammoth fortress of school buildings illuminated by shards of sunlight that slid past the glassless window slits. "The national electric grid failed again," said Yinka with a laugh.

I stood before a sea of students sitting in a dimly lit cavern. I almost had to yell to reach those who seemed to be sitting nearly fifty yards away at the back of the lecture hall. I shared my story of Food Not Bombs and then opened it up to questions.

A young woman sitting near the front waved her hand, wildly excited to share her story. She stood before the audience to tell her classmates that she had met Food Not Bombs during a visit to America. Yinka and Idowu later described the lecture this way:

"Keith addressed over one thousand students at the University of Calabar and was almost mobbed for his brilliant emotion-laden speech. Then, something incredible happened in the lecture room. One of the students listening to Keith admitted she had known Food Not Bombs since she last visited US with her husband. This made Keith's assignment easier and credible."

Liz was not only filming the tour but working on a story about the counterfeit drug market in Nigeria. The students arranged for us to visit the staff at the University of Calabar Teaching Hospital.

The hospital stood above a lush valley of fields and forests. The head physician welcomed us in the lobby and led us through a maze of hallways to the malaria ward. Children with sunken eyes and bone-thin limbs laid on plastic covered mattresses; IVs were suspended from Sears green, metal bed frames. A mother dabbed her daughter's forehead with a damp cloth.

"These children are infected with malaria. Their mothers thought they were giving them Chloroquine but it was nothing more than chalk," the physician explained. "More than 4,500 children and mothers die from malaria every year here in Nigeria. We could reduce this number if it were not for the counterfeit drugs."

Our visit to Calabar had come to an end and we headed out to visit a subsistence farm. The journey was long. We were running low on gas and noticed a roadside fuel vender sitting on a log. We agreed on a price and he siphoned petrol from a plastic gallon jug into our van. He indicated with a nod of his head that he wasn't pleased when Liz filmed his skilled transfer. Still his laughter let us know he wasn't really all that concerned about the legal ramifications.

James located the turn to his friend's community and bounced down a rutted dirt road to a village of yam farmers in rural Enenchele Delta State. Cassava plants struggled to survive in the red dust. Children emerged from mud-walled huts to greet the unusual guests. After introductions we toured the fields. We were told the soil was dead and needed modern fertilizers if they hoped to grow enough food to sustain the village. A young girl held my hand as we returned to the shade of a giant Iroko tree. The village leader honored me with a kola nut and a 2,000 Naira note. We gave them plastic bottles of fresh water.

I wished we could stay longer with these welcoming people of the land but we had appointments in Port Hartcourt. We got back on the road and two hours later we came to what Nigerians call a go slow. Two lanes of traffic became five, then eight, then more. The road became a jumble of trucks and vans navigating deep tire ruts and assorted debris, often passing or waiting only inches from one another. Members of our group got out of the van to help James back and file around the neighboring cars. Old women hung from van widows franticly fanning themselves with magazines. Four or five hours of inching through town and we hit a more open road. The high midday sun had by then disappeared into the forest.

Then it was dark, that jungle darkness that absorbs any hint of moonlight. We desperately needed to refuel. James said he thought we were coming up to a station. The lights of our van soon illuminated the desperation of dozens of young men sitting in the pitch black perched on the cement islands and stoops of a savaged Shell Station that long ago had lost its pumps, pipes, wires, and glass. Each man guarded a collection of plastic water and soda bottles filled with golden gasoline that shimmered in our headlights. The whites of the vender's eyes glowed like frightened stars. Fumes blanketed the tense darkness. It seemed like some quiet glimpse of a hellish post civilization future. But of course, it was their present.

James negotiated a price with the first boy he approached. We bought his liter. We bought three liters from a sullen old man and more from a third. No one smiled. The gas vapors were so biting I thought we would torch the crowd just by restarting the van. We were then in the heart of Nigeria's Bonny Crude oil industry.

Emmanuel had arranged a night at the local Krishna Temple in a settlement outside Port Hartcourt. The next morning, I pressured a reluctant Emmanuel into buying food and water for the people of Alesa Eleme. I got the impression he believed that money should belong to him. My crew loaded the rear of our van with cases of fresh water and canned food. The only provisions available in the tiny tin grocery.

We bumped through puddles of greasy crude passing lines of tanker trucks, tangles of trash, and flaring steel chimneys that scorched the sky. Hundreds of families survived in the community of Alesa Eleme beneath the towering refinery stacks in small tin shacks surrounded by ditches of bubbling toxic soup, lime green chemicals, and slicks of rainbow black oil. The village elder, Igwe Ejireyl greeted us at what could be considered a city hall, a collection of discarded billboards cobbled together to make a three-sided kiosk. Igwe Ejireyl was a soft-spoken man of maybe thirty. We followed him along planks of wood that hovered above the poisons. A sweet little girl grasped tightly to my hand as we zigzagged between the huts and darted past smoky trash fires.

Our guide softly shared that a helicopter gunship had flown up and down the neighboring river firing on villagers that morning. He believed it was an effort by the CIA to force the release of several oil industry hostages. He said there were no firm details on the number killed. News later that week would report the hostages were released and that they were telling the media they were well treated by members of Movement for the Emancipation of the Niger Delta. "We ate much better than the people that captured us," they said and suggested that their hosts had legitimate demands.

He was clearly proud to introduce us to his community. I was heartbroken, wishing we had more to share. I gave him a copy of my book, bottled water, and canned foods but that seemed so inadequate. Igwe Ejireyl ended our visit with the Bob Marley lyrics I heard so often on this journey, "A hungry man is an angry man."

The van survived another rough ride through fossil fueled hell. It seemed like we had traveled to another country even though we had only traveled a few hours from Alesa Eleme returning to our Krishna accommodations.

James and I spent a pleasant evening under the stars eating fufu and peanut stew at a simple cafe. He shared bits of his journey to Europe. He feared he would drown on an overcrowded ship to the Canary Islands and spent months in a Munich jail for the false accusation of bus fare evasion. A kind judge apologized and released him onto the cold streets of Germany. He had written a book about his desperate attempt to improve his lot. I hope it will be published.

After an unusually good sleep we headed off to the nation's capital, Abuja. It was a pleasant drive. Liz fell asleep, resting her head against a van window. We were soon arriving at the Niger River City of Onitsha. Yellow Volkswagen vans snaked in and out of traffic, copilots standing in the side doors calling out for passengers. It wasn't long before the colorful bustle turned to an ominous grey. We passed lines of ashen grey oil trucks smoldering along the road. The street was covered in thick grey ash. Everything had been torched. The air was stiff with the smell of burned wood and smoldering bodies. We had arrived at what had been the main market of Onitsha.

I thought I saw several charred bodies, but that might have been more out of fear than reality. Someone had warned us that there had been retaliation for the Danish Cartoon riots in the east, this time killing nearly one hundred Muslims in Onitsha. We had no other option than to pass through Onitsha to cross the Niger River.

The New York Times journalist Lydia Polgreen reported that, "Dozens of charred, smoldering bodies littered the streets of this bustling commercial center on Thursday after three days of rioting in which Christian mobs wielding machetes, clubs, and knives set upon their Muslim neighbors."

Twenty or so lanky young men milled around the main intersection of this massacre. Smoking tin market stalls as grey as the trucks and pavement stretched out before us. Burned carpets coated in ash clung to the remains of a flimsy Hausas shop.

The "Area Boys," as gangs are called in Nigeria, stood in our path. Two guys banged on the hood with their fists screaming at us to stop. Several other men smacked the roof with long wooden poles. James stopped and argued with two of men who had approached his open window. He stepped out in anger and left the key in the ignition. The rest of my Nigerian friends poured out of the van to confront the intimidating group. The gang demanded we buy a medallion from them. It would allow us to pass through the city to the bridge over the river. Our party wasn't convinced. They believed we would be forced to buy another pass at the next intersection. I stepped out to speak with the two traffic police monitoring the intersection. A plump woman with a kind expression on her face and her male companion both dressed in grey police uniforms let me know that they couldn't help. They lived in the area. They had families. There was nothing they could do.

Idowu told me to get back in the van: "It isn't safe, please return."

Minutes after I returned to the front passenger seat, one of the Area Boys reached through the open passenger side window across my lap and grabbed the key out of the steering column. He was quick and I was caught by surprise. I clutched tight to his arm and tried to pin it to the door frame. He had the advantage of standing outside and broke free of my grip and quickly tossed the key over the van to one of his friends who jumped into the driver's seat, turned on the engine and pressed the gas pedal to the floor. The van raced past the two traffic officers onto a side street of garbage. The rest of my party stood among the gangsters in shock.

The van careened over potholes, knocked over a motorbike, and scraped the sides of several parked cars before fishtailing up a steep narrow street. As you might imagine I was in a state of shock. Liz was awake now, clutching her camera under a cloth she had been using as a cover. The van swung up a steep hill plowing through piles of trash until we bounced to an abrupt stop at a dead end.

Dozens of excited people rushed into the street. The driver took the key and stepped out into the noisy crowd. I got out and kept my eyes on the key. An older man demanded I give him $25 million. I assured him he wasn't going to get that. No matter, I guess I am white and must have access to millions. He kept yelling that he wanted $25 million. The crowd agreed with him, screaming that I give up the money. People were swirling around waving their arms and bumping into one another in a frenzy. "Give him the money, give him the money!" they yelled.

I noticed Idowu and Yinka rushing up the hill towards the altercation. The rest of our group was running behind them with three men in clean white dress shirts each armed with an AK-47.

Idowu yelled to me that he had found three men he believed might be State Police officers. My party joined in the yelling. Idowu interrupted his harsh words to the kidnappers to let me know if I promised to pay the armed men 2,000 Naira, they agreed to ride with us to the Niger River. I started to negotiate with the armed men interrupting our discussion to negotiate with the man holding the key.

"I'll pay you 1,000 Naira for the key," I yelled, adding, "Look at how small the key is; 1,000 Naira is a good deal for a tiny key."

I turned to the three automatic weapons totting men and said, "I can pay you 2,000 Naira if you ride with us to the bridge."

The presence of guns seemed to have reduced the Area Boy's enthusiasm. The key man's friends hovered around him meekly suggesting he hold out for the $25 million but I could see that even they were starting to realize they weren't going to succeed. I continued to loudly claim he was getting a great deal selling a small key for so much money. He wouldn't be embarrassed by such a profitable exchange.

One of the armed men told the guy with the key that he should except the deal. That seemed to do it. I took out 1,000 Naira in crumpled cash and held it out towards him with one hand and placed the open palm of my other hand towards him. He set the key in my hand and took the money. The street went silent.

My entourage scrambled back into the van. I climbed into the driver's seat and turned over the engine. The three guys packing heat squished into the side door. One clutched to the door frame swinging his gun towards the ground.

I skidded the van down the hill, through the trash, and out into the smoldering market towards the Niger River crossing. We came to another cluster of Area Boys. They got the message and we passed without incident. We came upon one more gang and arrived at the foot of the bridge. I handed 2,000 Naira over to one of the gun men and they stepped out.

I then sped across the river and pulled up next to the entrance to a gas station next to the unusual existence of a real green lawn. Everyone in our party evacuated the van and fell to the grass in relief. We survived.

Idowu and Yinka later wrote a report on that day's events:

THE ONITSHA KIDNAP - Keith and Liz proved fearless when they were waylaid by the AREA BOYS (street urchins) at the dreaded Onitsha Market in Anambra State. Nigerian members on the trip were forcefully displaced from the van and it took the timely intervention of the officers of the State Police Command to secure their release, though demands were made for the release. Keith and Liz would later reason that it is cheap to secure your release when hijacked in Nigeria, just 3000 Naira (including police).

Once we recovered our composure and splurged on snacks from a gas station vender we headed north into the jungle. We had to cross the forest before sun fall or risk a wreck or another kidnapping attempt.

We glided through a forest of tropical trees wrapped in leafy vines that fluttered as we sped past. The van was bathed in the ever-present smell of burning jungle.

It wasn't long before we approach a blockade of fallen logs and large rocks. Five young men were standing guard, each clutching a five-foot-long two-by-four with huge menacing spikes sticking out like a medieval mace.

“Oh no, I can’t face another kidnapping today,” I announced. There was nervous laughter. James stopped the van about twenty-five feet before the checkpoint. I jumped out and walked quickly towards the toll collectors with a fist full of Food Not Bombs flyers.

“Hi guys, you probably saw us on TV, we are on our way to Abuja to see the Minister of Public Works,” I said, handing each guard a leaflet in as friendly a manor as possible. The young men suggested authority in their bright green traffic vests with “Treasury Department” silkscreened on the back.

I repeated that we had been on national TV and that we had an important meeting in the capital. The men took my flyers nodding as though they had really seen us on TV which is unlikely as there was little access to electricity let alone TV reception that deep in the bush. I shook everyone’s hand and they said they would be honored to let us pass for free. We were celebrities after all. They rolled the logs and stones to the road side and waved us through saluting as we passed.

The orange sun was low in the hazy western sky when we found Senator Adeseye Ogunlewe’s Abuja compound: a contemporary three-story mansion tucked into a neighborhood of impressive homes.

“Oh, did the Area Boys scare you?” laughed the senator as he handed me a glass of orange juice. He suggested I speak with Mrs. Toyin Adetunji, the Special Adviser to the President on Food Security. “I will give her a call,” he said.

It isn’t long before she arrived. The senator invited her to join us in his stylish living room. We sat together on the senator's large, beige leather couch that wrapped around his carpeted family room. The adviser draped her arm casually across the couch back, her tan gym sweats almost matched the furniture. She suggested I go to her office the next day. The special adviser bid us good evening and vanished and just as quickly the senator called a local motel to reserve a room and handed me ten freshly photocopied $100 bills. They almost looked real if it wasn’t for the glossy sheen of the copier paper.

We settled into the hotel. The new cash worked and the change was in real Naira. We visited an internet cafe on the ground floor of an imposing three-story office building. Two young men had rented the computer next to ours. Their screen was close enough to see: a spread sheet of credit card numbers and other details from people in Pennsylvania and a second window displaying Visa and Master Card logos. The computer operators bought items as fast as they could, moving from line to line on the spread sheet. They stopped after exactly one hour. A power cut ended our session twenty minutes after they left.

The next morning it was off to save the world. We found Mrs. Toyin Adetunji’s office in a collection of dilapidated cement government buildings. She was a farmer and knowledgeable about hunger.

Presiding before three of my Nigerian comrades she warmly discussed Nigeria's regional role in food policy. "Most people in the West don't realize this but Nigeria provides most of the food relief to Sudan, Chad, and Niger. People think the food aid comes from the United States and Europe but that is not the case," she said, before going on to explain how many tons of grain was transported by truck to each of those countries. She then offered to help our work in Nigeria.

She stood to wish us good travels closing with, "Keith you must attend the Shehu Musa Yar 'Adua's Memorial Lecture." "It's very important," Yinka enthusiastically agreed. She planned to leave for the democracy library dedication as soon as our meeting wrapped up.

James delivered us to the Shehu Musa Yar 'Adua Foundation building, a huge modern white structure with a glass dome and stately white columns. Security guards in sharp black suits and sunglasses stood with their arms crossed in the shade of a towering portal. Liz and I passed through a line of black limousines, up the marble stairs, and joined a group of dignitaries busy chatting. The two of us followed the crowd into the building and drifted into a large auditorium filled with people dressed in their best. People stood to shake my hand as I passed down the center aisle. Liz filmed the crowd and my movements through the room. A camera person from NTA asked if I had any birthday wishes for President Olusegun Obasanjo. I wished him the happiest of days and good health.

The ceremony started and everyone took a seat. Foundation director Atiku Abubakar opened the event by thanking Mr. Gary Samore, Vice President for Global Security and Sustainability of the John D. and Catherine T. MacArthur Foundation, for making the Olusegun Obasanjo Research Library collection on Democracy a reality. He then introduced the head of the foundation, Hajia Binta Yar'Adua.

"Good afternoon, ladies and gentlemen. On behalf of the Board of Trustees and the Yar'Adua family, I wish to welcome Her Excellency, Mrs. Ellen Johson-Sirleaf of Liberia and her entourage. We especially thank you for finding the time to be with us today to honor the memory of my late husband."

She then continued, "It is an opportunity to offer our heartiest congratulations for successfully winning your country's election to become the first elected woman president in Africa. We are proud of you as this will motivate our women to seek high political office. I am sure being a woman and an economist will give you motherly sensitivity to the difficult task of re-building your war-ravaged country."

She closed her introduction with, "We wish you God's guidance in the task ahead of you and a very safe journey back home."

The crowd stood as Mrs. Ellen Johson-Sirleaf walked to the podium. "I am most pleased to be a part of this very important occasion of honoring a true hero of Nigeria – and a noble Pan-Africanist," she said. "And I thank you, my brother, His Excellency, President Chief Olusegun Obasanjo, for your kind invitation to me to participate in this solemn but festive celebration of a life well spent and dedicated to nation and people."

She spoke highly of General Yar'Adua: "I am informed that in a conversation with a prison mate at Kirikiri where he was incarcerated, the general, ever the gallant soldier, described his commitment to Nigeria as 'unquestionable.' Men like this never really die – and like all old soldiers, they just fade away."

The audience of hundreds laughed politely.

She ended by saying, "My dear brother, President Chief Obasanjo, the world looked then to your country for leadership. And the Federal Republic of Nigeria answered the summons, and Liberia today has been given the opportunity for a rebirth. My countrymen and I thank you and your people."

The crowd jumped to their feet applauding in appreciation of the moving speech by this world leader.

President Olusegun Obasanjo, the former dictator of Nigeria took the podium. "The first thing I want to do is to thank my sister, Madam Ellen Johnson-Sirleaf, first of all for what you have done for Liberia, for Africa, and indeed for the world," he said. "She has tried to give us a glimpse into her life. Looking into Ellen's life is an inspiration to women folk of our continent and to all of us who believe in the fact that what other races can do, an African should be able to do."

He went on to say, "Now, Africa is passing through a very interesting and exciting period. And I believe that God has designed that this period will in fact be Africa's. So, I like to say God is a Nigerian. And when you see what has happened and what is happening in Liberia, you will probably agree that if God is a Nigerian, He frequently visits Liberia. But sister, I think He is partly a Nigerian and partly a Liberian… My sister, thank you very much for coming. You have boosted all of us up and if you had actually worked and lived with Shehu Yar'Adua as some of us have done, you would not have been able to describe him, his ideals, better than you have. We appreciate you and we wish you a very happy journey back home.

The audience stood in another ovation. The dignitaries mingled among themselves on the stage. The pile of books donated by the MacArthur Foundation stood as a monument to Nigeria's struggle for democracy. I sneaked several copies of C.T. Butler's book On Conflict and Consensus into the stack. My small contribution to the country's promise.

Our work in the capital was done. We had an uneventful drive back to Lagos. I booked a room at the St. Agnes Catholic Church. An unusually pleasant Nigerian place to sleep with high walls and vast lawns that provided tranquility from the noisy street life of the Maryland District.

I would leave in a few days so this was my opportunity to secure the cooking supplies for Lagos Food Not Bombs.

James came to the cathedral to collect me and the crew. We headed out into the empty streets. It turned out that there was a state law that made it illegal to drive on the last Saturday of the month. All of Lagos was supposed to be cleaning the streets. You could face a fine if you were caught outside without holding a broom, rag, or other type of cleaning supplies. I was shocked to see the vibrant metropolis become so peaceful.

Sunday was another matter. The city was back to its usual chaos. Two amputees stood on the medium strips of Ikorodu Road shacking cans and seeking coins. Every manner of newspaper, wall map, candy, or battery was being hocked in the streets.

James found an empty space outside the Oshodi Market. Emmanuel, Winston, Idowu, and Yinka led Liz and I through a labyrinth of stalls. I had to duck under the tarp ceilings. The allies were hardly wide enough for a person to navigate and I had to walk sideways when anyone passed. There wasn't one surface of any side of any stall that was not covered with merchandize. I got the feeling that many of the items were destined to join the mountains of smoldering garbage at municipal dumps or part of the debris found floating in the open sewers and streets. Vendor after vendor balanced on rickety stools or crates smothered in a deluge of plastic this-and-thats. The chaos of post-trash morphed into a mile or more of astonishingly vibrant textile market of West African cotton prints.

We finally found the restaurant supply district and secured a huge iron kettle, knives, cutting boards, and coolers. Our crew marched triumphantly to the van lugging our new equipment. Lagos Food Not Bombs was ready to start.

I soon discovered that this would be Emmanuel's last chance to profit from my visit. I didn't possess some necessary forms required to transfer ownership to the local group. I discovered that Emmanuel had the documents all along and when I asked for them, he refused to turn them over. I found the local police captain and explained my problem. He walked over to Emmanuel's office where he compelled Emmanuel to join us at the police department.

Emmanuel and I sat before the captain. After some reluctance the captain was able to convince Emmanuel to give me the documents suggesting it would be the best for all involved. A very sad Emmanuel handed over the papers. The three of us shook hands. I thanked them both and headed off to an office behind a tailor's shop where I was able to transfer the title of the van to Idowu and Yinka.

My enthusiastic friends saw me off at the airport the next morning. Liz stayed behind to film their first meal. Idowu and Yinka managed to collect enough produce and rice, recruited a group of cooks and prepared a huge dinner that they shared with a mob of hungry Nigerians.

So yes Charly Boy, anything can happen in Nigeria and it did.

THIS INFORMATION MUST BE PROTECTED AND NOT DISSEMINATED OUTSIDE THE FBI.

Details: On Tuesday, 05/02/2006, FBI Chicago at ORD was contacted by USCBP at ORD regarding the arrival of Jonathan Keith McHenry, male, white, date of birth: 05/06/1957, 4060 N. Fremont Avenue, Tucson, Arizona, on American Airlines Flight #47 from London Heathrow International Airport, London, England.

McHenry was referred to USCBP, Secondary Investigation Area, for a review of his luggage which was negative for any restrictive items. McHenry was traveling under U.S. Passport #057621796 which was issued under his name. McHenry was traveling with [redacted] female, white, date of birth: [redacted] U.S. Passport [redacted] A copy of the documents that McHenry and [redacted] were traveling under were made and enclosed.

b6 per OGA
b7C

McHenry advised USCBP that he traveled for nine days to Istanbul, Turkey accompany [redacted] who was interviewing for a

An FBI memo filed after being questioned

Chapter 37

CHICAGO O"HARE

Our week-long transnational "date" inspired by her invitation for a job interview as an English Literature Professor at Turkish University landed awkwardly at Istanbul International Airport in late April 2006. I became friends with Laurie several years before when she invited me to meet her fellow Food Not Bombs volunteers at her beautiful Santa Fe-style home in Las Cruces, New Mexico.

Laurie's luggage was lost. Her perfect hire-me-as-a-professor-of-English-Literature-professor suit, evening sweater, and personal effects were apparently circulating in a labyrinth of conveyor belts and luggage wagons in some European airport.

Her initial shock turned to adventure in the clothes racks of water-front boutiques nestled between seafood restaurants along the Bosporus. All angst vanished on the completion of the interview. Laurie and I finally free to soak in the Byzantine mosaics of the Chora, the geometry of The Blue Mosque, and the subterranean mysteries of the cisterns of Constantinople.

Our shared love of pigment and plaster flashed to an end at the beginning of a long winding ticket line at the international terminal.

There was a problem. Laurie was nervous. I assumed it was a problem with the Turkish Airline computer. Finally, things were resolved and we boarded our flight to Heathrow, waiting the many hours one does when passing through that awful British shopping mall. We had no trouble getting on the flight to Chicago. We were heading home.

A pleasant male voice came over the loudspeakers, "Welcome to Chicago. Please remain seated with your seatbelt securely fasten until the seatbelt light is turned off and we have come to a complete stop. Thanks for flying American Airlines. Please enjoy the rest of your day."

The jumbo jet plane coasted to a stop at the gate and the announcer returned and in a much less cheery voice to say, "Please have your passports ready to show as you exit the plane onto the jetway. Thanks for your cooperation."

Dazed from the flight we staggered to the door, passports in hand. Two large U.S. Border and Customs Protection officers in dark blue uniforms greeted us. "Follow us to luggage. When you get your bags, we will tell you what to do next."

The carousel of baggage rotated past the weary crush of travelers. "If I don't answer please call the ACLU and tell them you got this card at Chicago O'Hare and that the person on the card may be in trouble with the authorities," I quietly told each person as I handed them my business card. The steely looks of our two uniformed chaperones confused our fellow passengers.

Our bags slid into sight. I lifted our suitcases from the conveyer. "Follow us," the female officer said coldly.

The four of us entered a huge windowless cavern with two-story-high, grey walls. The woman officer took me to the first line of stainless-steel tables. The male officer walked Laurie to a row of tables at the far end of the bleak chasm.

My officer opened my suitcase and shuffled through my dirty pants, shirts, and underwear before turning towards me. "Give me your wallet," she said. Stunned, I retrieved it from my back pocket and handed it over.

"How do you make a living," she asked.

I absentmindedly responded, "I am a graphic designer."

"How do you know C.T. Lawrence Butler?"

"I wrote a book with him," I again said in my fog.

"What is your role in the violent group Food Not Bombs?" she barked.

"Ma'am, it's Not Bombs. We aren't violent. We are called Food Not Bombs," I reminded her.

She walked over to a computer. An older man in a sports coat sat on a high stool behind the monitor.

"What about that Aspen Fire?" he blurted out with a smile, suggesting he may be an out of context forest fire hotshot, "Burned 132 square miles."

"That sounds terrible," I said just loud enough for him to hear.

"That Horseshoe 2 Fire was really something wasn't it?" he continued.

The Border and Customs woman fanned my bank and business cards ac ross the table in front of her keyboard.

"What's this?" she asked leaving the keyboard to hold the card in my face.

"Why do you have the director of the ACLU's business card?"

"I know her," I responded unthinkingly.

I must have said more than I remembered. I sat in Ryan Shapiro's sunny West Side Santa Cruz apartment overlooking the Pacific on a chilly spring morning in 2016. Ryan is one of America's top experts on the Freedom of Information Act.

"Keith we can tell by this number here that this report was sent to FBI Headquarters. I like those the best but look here," he said pointing to his computer screen. "This number here shows you were the subject of an FBI investigation for your connection to Earth First." Two Joint Terrorism Task Force documents reported that my blue school bus had arrived at an Earth First gathering in Southeastern Arizona. Then there was this May 9, 2006 memo, "THIS INFORMATION MUST BE PROTECTED AND NOT DISSEMINATED OUTSIDE THE FBI."

Subject EARTH FIRST, dba, ET AL; (Redacted)

"McHenry stated that he is the founder of Food Not Bombs which is now based in Tucson, Arizona. Food Not Bombs is a peaceful protest group which was founded 26 years ago by McHenry. McHenry advised that Food Not Bombs has 20,000 members worldwide."

The memo has the exact name and address of the school Laurie had interviewed at but claims that I had planned to teach there in a year and a half from the interrogation. The FBI agent followed by writing, "McHenry has been all over the world and arrested numerous times. McHenry stated that he has been arrested for 'feeding the homeless.'"

The FBI report said they found a blank check in my wallet and noted the check's details including the routing and account numbers in the report.

The memo goes on, "McHenry was carrying the e-mail address of (redacted) and phone number of (redacted) McHenry also had the e-mail address of (reacted) at (redacted) @email.com (and two more lines of redacted text.)"

The memo ends with, "McHenry was carrying multiple copies of two flyers: What's Wrong With McDonald's and Food not Bombs. McHenry provided USCBP with a copy of each flyer which are enclosed."

The ten-year mystery of my Chicago Wildfire enthusiast was finally revealed. I was part of the FBI's investigation Operation Backfire that eventually caught up with my friend Bill Rogers who was charged with torching of the multi-million-dollar Two Elks Lodge at the Vail Ski Resort in the Colorado Rockies.

PART FIVE: THE STREETS

A man seeking money on a Santa Cruz, California street corner in the rain

Chapter 38

STREETS

There is a hierarchy of our homeless.

There are those who travel with just a blanket under one arm. A donated blanket that they have successfully protected from theft. Not yet confiscated by the police. Not yet taken by another desperate person to shield themselves from the chill. Those who have a backpack to tie their blanket to are doing even better. The lucky ones drag a roller suitcase along the sidewalks. No weight lashed to their tired backs.

Then there are the people who balance their survival property on a bicycle. They can own more. Maybe their paintings, extra shirts and socks, a blue tarp or maybe some items they were able to secure on their way out of their last residence with a key. Bikes, bicycles with trailers, baby strollers, and four-wheeled walkers are starting to replace the more upscale shopping carts. Yet even though subject to aggressive recovery as a stollen item, the shopping cart can hold more personal belongings and doesn't have to be constantly steadied. The iconic shopping cart can rest without aid of its guardian, a cherished step up from the bicycle. Bikes need substantial ornamentation of rope, plastic flowers, stuffed toys and what nots to discourage the thief. Such a bicycle is too much work even for the restless Methhead.

But the once operating car is obviously a huge improvement over the shopping cart. For people able to save ownership of their vehicle and find a place less likely to fall victim to the tow truck's hook, the idle car not only provides shelter for the owners worldly possessions but may offer a safe harbor for the single woman who might otherwise endure a late night groping or god forbid, a savage doorway rape.

Those who own a running vehicle are the wealthiest on the streets, though even so there is a hierarchy. Small working cars are no challenge to a surviving SUV or even better, the camper van or RV. Then there are those that have a long-term agreement to nest on a family or friend's couch or back porch. Some even have a section eight housing voucher to cling their hopes on.

The morning after the election of George HW Bush, I was speaking with a resident of Civic Center Plaza. He lived under an American flag stretched between two shopping carts in the shadow of San Francisco City Hall's golden dome.

He was pleased with the election results: "I would rather be homeless in America than have an apartment in another country."

The American Exceptionalism of those who live on the hard streets.

People know their place in this hierarchy, living and dying by the curb. Human refugees wandering in search of a place to exist in the lands of the not so free. It's always time to move. To become someone else's problem requiring yet another 911 call and another slithering of the soul to the sanctuary of another alcove or hedge bush strategically chosen for its obvious neglect.

We are all on a kind of global migration, some of us comfort ourselves in the belief that a safe place to rest is our destination. But what's under our blankets? Are we really a person who has arrived home?

Being housed or not housed is a hierarchy that everyone knows. A broken home or broken body away from losing the safety under the shingled rafters. Most have trusted that they will always have a roof. Yet really, we are all people of the streets.

Instead of all streets leading to Rome as the saying goes, the street I most often frequent now leads to the Monterey Bay. It starts at the confluence of Water, Front and Mission Streets. An hourly bell rings this is the time at the Town Clock of the headwaters.

It could be any paved path. The cobblestones of Europe where Africans and Syrians huddle under cardboard scraps and blue tarps. Always those blue tarps. Thousands struggling for protection from the cold European rains.

Millions are wandering on streets unpaved by war, seeking shelter under the universal blue tarps that line the roads of the Yemens, Syrias, Iraqs, Libyas, Afghanistans, and Somalias of our world. Well-worn trails. Footprints often erased to the winds on the human river against the seemingly ever rising tides of violence and hunger.

This migration is not limited to those fleeing foreign wars and faraway starvation. This migration is here on the highways of my homeland. A nation founded by my immigrant forefathers. The nation whose national anthem was written about the flag that was still flying over Fort McHenry. A star-spangled banner now used as a tent by one of our county's homeless veterans.

Like the lands of Africa, Latin America, and Asia, America has a growing army of urban campers pitching tents and tarps under the bridges of the 101 in Hollywood and the hundreds of other over passes from the San Fernando Valley to the mouth of Interstate 5 as it empties into Mexico at the San Isidro Border Crossing. Those who cluster in hiding against I-5 struggle on its banks from Mexico to the 49th parallel. Our own internally displaced.

Feral humans shuffling along our streets in search of a place to be. Maybe a place to curl up in a drainage tunnel under Phoenix or Las Vegas. Possibly a patch under an architectural lip could be shelter from the elements in the great cities of New York, Chicago, or Denver. Sometimes a corner of a leaky sewer is better than freezing to death under the steely winter sun.

A manhole cover rises from a downtown Seattle street. Men from public works set it back into place. They are called later that day to remedy the situation again. The iron cover just won't stay in place. It's time to find out why. The public workers descend below the asphalt. It isn't a gas leak, it's a colony of children, young Americans dwelling under a King County street surviving in the underbelly of the great society.

My street is Pacific Avenue and its tributaries: a street life rich in the dreams, despair, and dignity of those who make this artery of Santa Cruz their universe. A transient home to the schools of tourists, shoppers, students, and the housed who drift along Pacific with the rhythm of a tide. The avenue is flooded with pedestrians who lap against the retail walls and sidewalk curbs at noon. High tide is always on Friday and Saturday nights. They are more transient than the transients.

Pacific Avenue is more permanent a home to those who strum their guitars, sell their gems, beat their drums, announce their god, or bare their hearts to the public river of humanity that flows just a block from the banks of the San Lorenzo River.

A thoroughfare that is always threatened with sterility by those at the Economic Development Office and the warm the chairs at City Hall. My agora that continues that human tradition "of going downtown."

The waters of migration slow outside O'Neal's propelled only by the spinning white bowling pins of Juggling John. The rapids of the boulevard can be found swirling around the hubcaps of Curtis's vehicle, where Curtis himself can be found dancing to Motown atop his red and white Peace trailer, dressed to the nines in a pressed white tux and matching white bowler hat.

My late evening strolls along the cement banks of Pacific draw me to the acoustic eves outside the Palomar Hotel. Ricardo, Jack, Rick, Jay, and Cooper don't busk for dollars, they busk out of a sacred love of the Grateful Dead, the Eagles, and the Beatles, the songs that pulled them to the street decades before. This is a soundtrack to a vision of freedom that drowns out the anger of car horns, idling 18 wheelers, and the angry hell and damnation of the self-identified Christians selling salvation.

The soundless of the avenue too sprawl out, like Jeff who has chosen vodka over oxycodone to soften the misery of a work-related mishap. He might even say, when he can speak, that his vodka induced comma is his way of showing respect to his ancestors that may have laid drunk on the cobblestones of Cork or Derry. He has no remorse. This is his life.

Rose and Dianthus flower peddles swirl in the breezes above the Pacific Avenue rapids. Nature's colorful pallet flung joyously from the frail fingers of Linda Lue, the gentle woman who made floral arraignments from blossoms quietly snatched from the yards of the better off. A daily box of cheap wine secreted out of CVS in her walker takes her liver one afternoon at the Lauden Nelson Senior lunch. A reminder that Jeff's next pint could also be his last.

Chris holds down his bench outside Zoccoli's Delicatessen marking the ebb and flow of his Pacific Avenue. He is the king of the headwaters bundled in layers of dark grey coats often resting his guitar like a baby in his ample lap.

Tears of a beauty concealed flood over Melissa's muddy cheeks. She can't take it anymore. Distressed that she found bugs captured in her long beautiful hair after a shower at the Homeless Service Center. They are eating her alive. Maybe creatures from her bed of weeds on the banks of the San Lorenzo or maybe it's just too much meth. That happens.

But I listen to her. She reminds me that she is a very attractive young lady that has learned to disguise her figure under oversized jackets and coveralls.

"I would take two showers a day if I could."

Her tears are dry now. The desire to die has faded.

Cezar coasts up on his bike, "Mellisa your things are still over at the empty bank."

Another traveler along Pacific was Michael Mears. A motorist found him nearly dead of hypothermia a block from the St Francis soup kitchen. Medical personnel told his sister Jerry that his body temperature was only 70 degrees when he was discovered soaking wet and unconscious on Potrero Street. The rain was harsh that week. Michael was born in Tulsa, Oklahoma and left home after high school, travelled America by thumb and landed in California. A spinal injury resulting from being run over by a car at age 5 caused his feet to curl under. Suppling him with new socks was a weekly pleasure. He was smart even though his quiet slurred voice and struggle to hobble around fooled many. He lived in libraries, memorized the bible, both New and Old Testaments, and was a wealth of information on a world of subjects. I overheard him countering a text on Ancient Greek Art that he found at our weekly Really, Really Free Market at the headwaters of Pacific Avenue.

We held a memorial service outside City Hall before a meeting of the City Council. David from Peace United Church opened with words and a short prayer. I set up his alter with recovered Trader Joe's flowers and photos donated by his friends at Goodwill.

A friend of 99 Bottles of Beer shared a story of rebuffing Micky until a bar tender tipped him off to the fact that he only bought a beer so he could participate in the games of trivia; he was an honored trivia contestant. That waitress followed with her tales of Micky and his sophisticated sense of humor. The staff of Goodwill shared the fun they had when Michael spent his afternoons "dressing up." The funny pictures on our alter attest to that. Ranger John lumbered up to the front of the 50 or more attendees and told of his many years of conversations with Micky and his knowledge that those who knew him loved him. Wes live streamed the hour-long celebration of Michael Mears' life to his family in Oklahoma. His sister thanked me.

There are big fish on Pacific Avenue. Artists that have become globally loved performers and visual artists. Artis the Spoonman was discovered on the sidewalks by Frank Zappa. The Flying Karamazov, Tom Noddy's Magic Bubbles, and The Great Morgani all started as regulars on the cement of their Surf City.

The Great Morgani announced he would no longer perform in downtown Santa Cruz "due to the recent strict enforcement of current ordinances," passed by the Santa Cruz City Council. Six months later the "blue boxes" of free speech began to disappear.

Artists discovered that their favorite locations had been erased. In August, artists began to resist the elimination of their "free expression" zones by creating their own. According to journalist Bradley Allen, "The action of painting blue boxes comes on the heels of two well-known artists, Joff Jones and Alex Skeleton, being arrested by Santa Cruz Police on August 20 for displaying art in front of the Forever 21 clothing store which, as of recently, is not allowed since the boxes there were removed. A few days later on Sunday, the artists defiantly returned to the sidewalk in front of Forever 21 dressed in colonial attire with displays of their artwork and a painting of the First Amendment. They were not arrested a second time."

Joff Jones explains, "My art expresses my social, religious, and existential views. My first amendment guarantees me the right to express that in a public space. My friend Alex and I were arrested yesterday for exercising these rights. . . Stand up for your rights!"

I joined the torrent of those jailed in the battle to defend the First Amendment snatched from Chris's memorial and charged with felony vandalism and conspiracy to commit a crime. Officers said we had spray-painted new blue boxes in 33 locations throughout the downtown area.

I made my mark on this street. Santa Cruz police spokeswoman Joyce Blaschke told the media that, "The blue corner marks that Abbi Samuels and Jonathan Keith McHenry made were similar to official city markings for street vendor areas. Authorities noticed the 33 markings and caught the pair by reviewing surveillance footage. In addition to vandalizing the city sidewalks, the act undermines the city's program to establish safe, orderly and fair use of the downtown sidewalk space."

The morning after the new blue boxes appeared, city officials were outside Forever 21 in a state of confusion, as they tried to figure out why the performance spaces they had removed a week or two before had suddenly reappeared.

And what harm came from this? Low-income people have places to earn a few dollars. A guitarist sang in glory outside New Leaf, excited that a new blue box had been placed at exactly the right location for him to reach his appreciative audience.

The City Economic Development employees and police spent the day trying to determine which blue box was real and which had to be removed. Once determined an orange dot was sprayed on each false corner.

I bought a can of orange spray paint and made sure every blue box was marked for removal. Public works followed directions. All the Free Speech boxes vanished.

The life of Pacific Avenue blossomed that Labor Day weekend. Performers and street artists had unrestricted access to their own public space and the weekend tourists.

There is one rock that the city sterilizers have not been able to dislodge and that is Marghe McMahon's 1978 sculpture of anarchist street performer Tom Scribner that stands in defiance outside Bookshop Santa Cruz. A monument to the very street culture the city seeks to eliminate. City officials replacing the life of the street with his bronze memory.

"As a matter of fact, we're almost certain that ghouls and werewolves occupy high positions at City Hall" reflects Corey Feldman as Edger in The Lost Boys. Edger may be on to something.

Not everyone in my community of the Pacific can aways be found sleeping under the stars. My housed friends Gail, Dennis, and Jean review the latest political crisis at the sidewalk tables outside the Coffee Roaster. They have the long view of capitalism's crushing punishment. I can relate. A comforting reminder of my early sectarian mentors who took to the streets of Cambridge.

The official in charge of this street is Chip. Just Chip, no last name. The visible face of the Downtown Association. Always friendly even though his organization is often cruel. His handlers see the street as a money-making venture. Property that they alone own. Don't do anything to upset the money from Silicon Valley. I secretly believe Chip wants to ease the flow around the boulders of affluence but he has a job to do.

This slow-motion Great Depression is flooding the streets with our humanity. The thirty years of falling through the cracks of Trickle-Down Economics is taking its toll. One war, one extreme weather event, one lost job, a divorce, a medical emergency, a sinking into depression or other mental health crisis throwing our neighbors out onto the hard pavement, becoming America's Internally Displaced.

We are refugees in a sea of wonderers.

Santa Cruz Food Not Bombs at the Town Clock

Chapter 39

A TEMPORARY AUTONOMOUS ZONE

A seagull wobbles on the still air laughing towards the Pacific Ocean. A panel-truck chugs up Mission Street. The faint scent of fishiness drifts in on the last feathers of morning mist. The otherwise quiet empty space at Front and Water Streets is interrupted by a postal customer climbing the steps to pick up their mail.

Henrietta Shore's Depression-era murals silently ignore the stamped correspondence and their destinations. A resident of the concrete benches at the Clock Tower drifts past on their way to the rest rooms at Bookshop Santa Cruz. A discarded LuLu's Cafe cup is the only occupant of the intersection.

Robin's bright white locks and beard are the first sign the corner is about to be transformed. He clutches his blue, cloth bag at the ready. He steadies a handlebar of his transportation against the chain-linked fence that protects the sandstone US Post Office from those who once slept beneath the portal arcade. Robin has come mostly to collect some battered apples for the family of deer who expect him to arrive home before dark. He will wave off each motorist who seeks to park in the corner space.

By now Rick has locked his bike to a meter on Water Street. Rick is our bread man. He ate with us for several years before he started to volunteer. He is also our astrologer. He can often be found dancing at Ocean and Water streets with a cardboard sign proclaiming "stop violence against women." And will be found later this evening joining the sidewalk buskers at the Palomar Hotel. Our white flowing hair artist friend Robin announces, "There she blows," when the white Food Not Bombs van turns on Mission Street.

Rick stations himself near the curb. He waves the van-load of that day's meal into the corner parking spot, directing the driver as though he were conducting a symphony, sweeping his hands dramatically and ending with outstretched palms signaling the end of the parking song.

Shawn coasts into the emerging drama, leaning his bike against one of the red granite columns that once held a brass Santa Cruz Sister City relief, a monument that might have been stolen for its recycling value or as a fraternity prank. This has become Shawn's own personal pillar always at the ready to support the heavy load perched over a milk crate wired to the rear bike rack. He will lash a bundle of baguettes above his crate of treasures. He will also tear chunks off a loaf to share with the rats that dwell under the post office wall worried that his rodent friends might go hungry.

I slide from the driver's seat, stuffing a red counter in my pocket gripping a serving spoon in one hand. I will pass the clicker to Travis and slip the spoon into a metal band on the corner light pole. Travis will swing the braided wire cord of our Food Not Bombs sign behind the scoop. The stage is being set.

New Blue pulls up in an old white van that doubles as both home and storage for an odd array of items he has tied to the roof. Pots, gardening tools, hoses, bike parts, and a huge blue ball he retrieved on his descent from a rental to the streets. Old Blue is sure to slide up on a bike or tricycle and ask, "Papa do you have any duct tape?" or another such request for material support. New Blue is older than Old Blue but Old Blue has been a fixture since he was emancipated from foster care. New Blue would be our only bright spot one day at Open Streets while being chased around by city officials for not having registered for a community event we assumed would be welcoming.

A crowd is forming around the van. Shawn slides open the side door. Blue joins Paul, Breadman Rick, and the others clambering to extract a knot of plastic folding tables, pop up tents, totes of bread, and produce.

I set out stacks of literature, books, buttons, and a donation can on top of a tablecloth displaying the Food Not Bombs logo. The other tables are forming a buffet line.

Rick calls out, "I need two more people over here."

He and New Blue are struggling to set up one of our canopies. Travis and Paul step in to help. They maneuver the tent over the serving tables.

Our often quite grumpy Travis is still complaining that someone had stolen his false teeth during the night. He insists that he had placed them in his shoe and repeats that there are no rats at the parking garage where he sleeps. A seagull might have taken them but he doubts it. "Don't ask me to smile for a photo," he reminds me again.

Joy arrives with a car-load of yellow Trader Joe lugs filled with organic greens and fruit that she gathered from the Live Oak Farmers market. She has been busy at the Monterey Community TV station finalizing her documentary about the 35 years of our movement.

If it wasn't for her, we would have never been able to secure our relationship with the Second Harvest Food Bank in Watsonville. I met her again earlier this week at the warehouse to help her gather up the food bank's heavy cases of broccoli, cabbage, and sweet potatoes. The two of us hoisted fifty-pound bags of onions, carrots, and russets on to our cart and wheeled the load to the scales. Once accounted for, we stuffed the van with our loot ready to head back to Santa Cruz.

Paul is our volunteer of reason. We can depend on him to provide a sober opinion on any question that may arise, as they often do. He has volunteered with Santa Cruz Food Not Bombs on and off since 1992. His position has evolved into a Saturday and Sunday van coordinator artfully adjusting the Rubik's Cube of paper products, dry goods, and other items we would likely forget if it wasn't for his attention to detail. He investigates the ingredients of any suspicious items for violations in our dedication to sharing vegan food. He also offers wise council on issues of political impact and is a solid advocate of nonviolent direct action. Every Food Not Bombs group needs a Paul.

Two University of California college students, Kaoline and Melissa, set out the compostable paper trays, sporks, and napkins and join in the march to lift the steaming hotel trays of vegan dishes to the serving tables. Five-gallon, green buckets of tossed and fruit salads are set next to the paper products followed by a hotel tray filled nearly to over flowing with a curry and cauliflower-based stir fry and a silver tray of fried potatoes, very popular whenever served. The devotees of the Zen Center appear with their pot of vegetable stew and famous end-of-the-month corn bread.

"The corn bread is here!" Anna Rose announces as Rick quickly makes space next to the loaves of bread. That gets everyone's attention.

The Town Clock shows that it is five minutes to four. A wall of people eager to eat winds along the sidewalk towards River Street. They are not the extras of this theater. They are the stars of our twice weekly show. I walk along the line of nearly fifty people, most are my friends, some are new to the streets. Many balance backpacks on a shoulder and others drag all kinds of carts or carriages stacked with worn trash bags, tarps, and suitcases. Many have nothing more than a need to eat.

I welcome those in line to another meal with Food Not Bombs, walking along the row of diners to give high fives or hardy handshakes to my friends. I return to the tables and ask the line of volunteers armed with serving spoons and ladles if they are ready to serve. To a person they beam with pride at their position behind a steaming silver restaurant tray.

"Ok, get ready, get set." The bell on the clock tower rings four times. "Go! It's time to eat!" I yell with a more than a pinch of levity.

One by one my community of the streets steps up, takes a bowl, spork, and napkin. Many are relieved to wash their hands under warm water draining from our home-made hand washing station.

"Would you like salad?"
"Yes, please."
"Fruit Salad?"
"Sure."
"Rice?"
"Can I have an extra spoonful?"
"Why, yes of course."

A four-year-old stands on a milk crate dishing out spoonfuls of the fruit salad she made with her mother. Rick makes sure you get the piece of bread or slice of pie you desire. He might have something special that he is holding back for you. His is a kind of Sandwich Syndicate.

One person after another passes down the table balancing a compostable bowl of Sunday feast. Many find their place on the sidewalk using the new "Anti-homeless" fence as a back rest. A circle of friends makes a dining room of the cement next to the payphone balancing their bowl of food on their laps as they chat about that day's business. Maybe they are reminiscing about the time they saw the Grateful Dead at the Oakland Coliseum or perhaps one of them is sharing the tale of the time the waves dashed them to the rocks breaking their arm under a long board. Ariel surf pioneer Kevin Callahan laughs. He has more than one story of dramas at the Steamer Lane lineup.

Back at the literature table Stanton walks up with his decorated bike. His wavy, sandy hair cascades towards his hunched shoulders, "My sister is doing it again with her voodoo. I can feel it," he reports repeating that his sister had collected his social security checks for twenty-seven years.

"Do I look like no such person?" he asks again showing me a copy of the envelope with the message scrawled above his name. "No such person."

Uncle Jeff staggers up pulling a small suitcase, "Where's Buddy Boy? Where's Buddy Boy?"

Jeff has a long scraggly beard that will soon be decorated with bits of today's dinner. He takes the folding chair and leaves his bag under our literature table. I let him know Buddy Boy will be here soon. That brings a smile to his dirt-smudged face. Jeff studied at Otis College of Art and Design in Los Angeles. Somewhere along the line he became a hard liquor man but he is still a sharp tack, smart as the day he took his first sip. He's always up-to-date with the news and spends his days reading in the back corner of Bookshop Santa Cruz. He used to spend his nights in one of their never-used doorways but then the management fenced it closed. These days he can be found sleeping in the high brush outside the County Jail. He will share that evening's dreams. The little men that came to talk with him, people from Heaven 2.0. He asks me if I know what they call their libraries. "Truthbaries, that's what they call them in Heaven 2.0."

Uncle Jeff will walk Buddy Boy around downtown. He might ask me for four dollars to buy a pint. Just enough to help him sleep he will tell me. He comments that the people living outside with bike loads of belongings are crazy. "What are they doing with all that stuff anyway?" He travels with one found bag or another, always stolen or lost by the month's end when he will then find a replacement. The bridge of his nose and his forehead are blistered by his years in the sun, covered in red scabs.

Bob is one of those who pushes his belongings around town on a bike. A post shopping-cart-era strategy that is common now that the grocery stores have implemented an aggressive shopping cart recovery program. A beacon of pride glows from his proud eyes that are surrounded by a long mane of flowing bright white hair and a beard to match. He is strong. I often see him standing shirtless facing the afternoon sun. I have never known Bob to drink or use drugs.

"Did you hear about the rebel advances on Tripoli. What is up with there being three governments claiming to rule Libya?" he reports from last night's BBC radio news program. If the Forty-Niners are playing, I know I can find him on the sidewalk outside Woodstock's Pizza glued to the sports channel. Bob told me he was a master carpenter but had to leave his union job to help a family member. "I took a nonunion job in Montana. A terrible cut in pay." He looks away hinting that something terrible had happened and he now found himself unable to escape the sidewalks of Santa Cruz. This seems to be story he would rather not share. I will spend months during the pandemic trying to find him a room in a hotel where he could plug in his C-pap machine. He will be found passed out, clutching his bicycle outside the Health Department office on Emiline. Heart failure will be the diagnosis with still no place for my 69-year-old friend to rest. I will be busy passing out tents when I get the news that Bob has died on the pedestrian foot bridge outside Trader Joes. He didn't make it to the hotel.

Ron fumbles with his music stand and finally sets up the remains of a tattered book of sheet music. "All donations go to Food Not Bombs," announces the carefully lettered strips of cardboard wired to his cart. He strums his guitar with the vigor of someone determined to make a difference while wailing, "All you need is love."

If Ron fails to arrive, Musical Mike is happy to take the stage. Mike can be found crouching before his moving Christmas Tree of a bike. The gems of the discarded street scores dangle like prizes from his tower of hats. Some days lime green socks disappear under his rainbow of shorts. Purple and reds are the main theme of today's outfit. His lyrics detail the theater swirling around us interspersed with tooting on his latest discovery, a plastic horn.

A loud commotion threatens to drown out Mike's concert. Eric is scolding his wife in torrents of loud accusations. A marital spat exposed to the elements but there is Mike crouching next to his worldly possessions exuding a contagious bliss.

"This too will pass," he sings, "like the night turns to day, like the night turns to day in Keith's theater of love. In Keith's theater of love."

Robin spreads out the blue tarp. I call it the Really, Really Free Market. The library of the discarded is placed in neat rows. Books, shoes, dresses, pants, shirts, household appliances, a rubber radiator hose, and the pieces of unloved furniture grace the tarp. Old Blue takes the grungy electric can opener. He returns it ten minutes later. Maybe the radiator hose will be more useful. These are the modern Gleaners of a Millet panting, people bent at the waist picking for the grain of usefulness.

Mikey is sprawled across an empty area of the free tarp reading a Gardner's edition of The Art of the Ancient Greeks. I catch a mumble "that isn't an ionic column." The unfamiliar might discount the knowledge of this road scholar with his curved under feet hobbling around Santa Cruz in stocks that require a parade of stocking donations.

A few months later we'll learn that Mikey was found dead in the weeds of Potrero Street a block from the Saint Francis Soup Kitchen wrapped in a rain-drenched blanket.

Our pews of chairs will sit in neat rows on City Hall's brick plaza. We won't borrow enough seats to accommodate the memorial. Pastor David will open with a prayer. The young bubbly bartender Amy from 99 Bottles will step before the altar, a plastic table draped in black cloth and a framed photo of Mikey at his best surrounded with bouquets of flowers from Trader Joes. "Mikey would wander in on trivia night and buy just one beer. It was his ticket to compete. You might call him the encyclopedia of Santa Cruz."

The manager of 99 Bottles will steps before the mourners and say, "I almost ejected Mikey the first time I saw him in my bar but Amy and the other patrons stopped me and I'm glad they did because we became good friends."

The Goodwill staff loved to indulge Mikey's experiments in dress up. "His playful spirit won't be forgotten." Then Park Ranger John, dressed in his uniform, will step before the altar and speak, "I knew if I came across him on the levee it wouldn't be long before he was teaching me about the path of a migrating duck or a unique species of river reeds." We'll livestream the service to his family in Tulsa, Oklahoma. I will miss Mikey.

But here at the meal an explosion of anger slices the calm. Julie says something as she often does and most have learned not to take it personally but this time someone objected to her snarling accusations, "Stop looking up my vagina, you racist."

She won't tell me her sweet pit bull's name. Julie has blond dreads and nice clothes. She makes some money from the local merchants washing windows and sweeping the curbsides on Cedar Street. This income is essential. She requires organic smoothies made to specification to help her maintain a degree of mental stability. She tells me about her parents and their research in electronic surveillance at Honeywell. She shares that the boys on Pacific Avenue are looking up her crotch.

Julie's energy is contagious today and Chief scares the uninitiated when he blasts someone for touching that day's bike. The superficial excuse to wake everyone up with fiery eyes, a booming yelp and the swinging of a broom handle. I give him one look and he relaxes. And then, with a huge smile, he runs over to give me a hug. I know him as the wild dark hair, short beard, and healthy frame who dances not so gracefully through life. On occasion can be seen floating down Pacific Avenue like a cloud, hugging each friend he comes upon.

Our messiah, Baba Ito, slides his scraped and dented white station wagon into his regular parking space. His eyes and an almost imperceptible hand gesture pull me to his vehicle. He hands me a pink crystal and explains, "If I could just fix this car, I would go over to my friends in Silicon Valley and talk with them. They would give us $30 billion just like that," he grins rubbing his hands softly together. "I need a new water pump and they told me it will be $275. Where am I going to get that type of money?" he asks rhetorically.

I stand by the literature table, center stage at the bow of our festivities. Sarah sits next to me radiating pleasure at the heaps of orange sweet potatoes on her plate. "Keith what do you think of the political theories of Noam Chomsky?" she asks and then quotes a sentence that impressed her enough to memorize it, "In sum, neoliberalism is the immediate and foremost enemy of genuine participatory democracy, not just in the United States but across the planet, and will be for the foreseeable future." Her husband, John, is juggling bowling pins next to their caravan of bike carts and their large family of patient pug dogs.

A bicyclist in spandex thankfully interrupts Sarah's breathless analysis of imperialism. He flips through a copy of my book, "Hungry for Peace," takes some flyers and drops a dollar in the donation can. "Do you know about Food Not Bombs?" I ask. He doesn't and just then a couple steps up to investigate the literature. Travis interrogates them, noticing an accent and asks them where they were from. "San Francisco," they smile but that won't satisfy Travis and they admit they're Polish. I can't help myself, "Do you know of Food Not Bombs in Poland?" They do and I let them know I that I have visited chapters in Poznan and Gliwice. "I have a friend from Gdansk named Vegan Lucas. He joined me in Ethiopia. He rode his bike from the Baltic Sea to South Africa."

They step back. "No way, my best friend knows Vegan Lucas," the girl says surprised.

Dirty brown fabric stitched together with thread and safety pins is the unmistakable uniform of the crusty punk travelers. Only two of the five have woven bird bones and clay beads into their tangled dreads. All have a ring dangling from their nose. An excited black lab waggles with the tribe onto the stage. "Awesome! Food Not Bombs! We helped out in Kansas City and Denver. You guys are every place we go," one says as they lean their heavy backpacks against the post office fence before stepping to the back of the still pretty long line.

The action never stops. A long white van bumps gently to a stop at the curb and one, two, and finally six people emerge dressed in crisp white t-shirts with the name of their mission, Iglesla de Jesucristo Palabra Miel Salinas and a cross silkscreened in red across the front. They start pulling out boxes of blankets and clothing.

I notice their arrival and interrupt the man I am speaking with, "You can place the clothing on our blue tarp or hang them off the fence as you wish. Thanks so much for helping." They tell me they hope to start a shelter in Salinas. We all stand together for a picture. The crusty punks ignore the treasures, not crusty enough for their aesthetic.

Tall Robert finds a long silk slip and lifts it to his chest to see if it would fit, gently caressing the frilly helm. "Beautiful," he says over his shoulder glancing towards me with a smile and seductive glint. Robert is wearing his latest Goodwill purchase from the women's section and it is obvious he is really pleased to find exactly what he wanted for free at our Really, Really Free Market.

Santa Cruz's colorful defender of the people of the streets, Robert Nores, backs his Volvo station wagon covered in bumper stickers into a space on Water Street. Once settled, he enters the performance with his recorder at the ready striding up to Dream Catcher. Robert knows he will have news on that week's police actions against the crime of sleeping and an inventory of the confiscated belongings.

"They did it again; they took all my paintings, my blanket, and my clothing," he says, waving his outstretched arm across the sky to illustrate he means everything. He also reports that the First Alarm patrol woke him up three times last night and had to move from the doorway at the Women's Health Center to the alley near the Tea Room.

Robert will get around to interviewing me but only after getting the scoop from those struggling against police contact, the scorn of the "haters" and most urgently, the elements. He will also quietly slip a twenty into the donation can, often the only contribution of the day.

A volunteer has arrived with Buddy Boy, and Uncle Jeff is giddy like a school boy on Christmas morning. He places what's left of his meal on the sidewalk next to the bag he stashes under the literature table and off he goes stumbling behind the little white Coton de Tuléar. Buddy Boy is the other Jeff's dog but he gets too drunk to safely care for him. Uncle Jeff tries to educate me, "I'm a sipper but he's a chugger, that's the problem." Shuffling off towards Pacific, he says, "I'll be back in an hour," with a toot-a-loo flick of his hand.

Kim slides softly into the drama stage left, attracting my attention with a smile. "I found some photos from the early days of Santa Cruz Food Not Bombs," she says, opening a tattered black folder. "There is the truck Tony bought and Robert Flores is smiling behind the serving table," she adds and turns to another page of colorful pictures. There is Paul holding a serving spoon to the heavens. Those were the days of food arrests and sit-lie sit-ins.

Kim worked at San Lorenzo Garden Store for almost two decades. She is squatting an abandoned house downtown. "I won't put up with all that crap" she says with the pride of a true rebel. Kim is the thread that binds today's theater to the first Food Not Bombs meals in Santa Cruz.

Vikki screams, "Fuck you," at a new guy. She smashes a ceramic travel mug against the sidewalk. Shards spatter. No one is hurt. A devious smile lights up her face. All is fine.

Vikki hurls a second plaster coffee cup to the pavement. Who let her have those anyway? The new guy loses interest in taunting Vikki and disappears up Pacific. She is tough, tough as a grandmother bear. And she is family, even if a little bit wild today.

The sun hovers above the sycamores that tower above the Bank of the West. The Clock Tower bell rings five times. There are just ten people in line, no, wait, now fifteen. One hotel tray of stir-fried vegetables is empty. "What is this?" Jimmy asks holding a sautéed brown cube to the sunset. That is Eric's tasty fried tofu, and it sure seems to be a hit today.

The hotel tray of potatoes has been empty for ten minutes now. Our comfort food is never long for the serving table. Our star performance was a twenty-four-quart pot of coconut milk soup now reduced to a white coating. Time to send that over to Roberta's soapy gloves at the three-basin washing station.

Robin introduces me to a middle-aged woman named Karen. "Can you help her. Last night was her first night on the streets. She needs a safe place to sleep tonight."

Karen steps close and whispers that she was sexually molested. Her tired lips sketch the basics of the crime, her beleaguered face shows that she has survived a cold night awake. "I slept in a doorway on Cedar but a couple of young guys waved their cocks in my face demanding I give them head. I can't spend another night on the streets."

"Did you try the Homeless Service Center on Coral?" She had, but she didn't qualify. "How about the Walnut Street Women's Center?" They couldn't help.

"I can get you a bus ticket home."

"I am home. I've lived in Santa Cruz my whole life."

"I can ask Larry if you can join him. He shares the door at University Copy with Linda Lue. He's a gentleman. You would be safe with him," a Santa Cruz solution to a woman's safety.

Portuguese Tony hasn't been seen in weeks. He's probably spending another term locked up at the Santa Cruz County Jail. The last time he disappeared he had been arrested for telling off a Park's Department employee, Michael, who objected to Tony's use of the Clock Tower fountain to wash his clothes.

“I fought for this country you motherfucker. You aren’t going to tell me what to do,” he’d said in a bark that was louder than his bite.

Tony spent most of a week hidden in plain sight under an unfortunately placed tarp that spanned what would be the center of our operation but oddly enough he had vanished before we set up, leaving a mound of random cascading debris across the dining area. He returns as I am pushing a cellophane cover to a pack of cigarettes towards the tarp. “I am going to stab you, you son of a bitch. I mean it, you touch my stuff and I will kill you!” he yells with such passion all those assembled fear for my life.

“Sorry Tony, but your stuff is spread all over. A smaller footprint at the corner would be fine,” which was enough to inspire a loud torrent of realistic sounding death threats. His audience thought he was serious but he failed to intimidate me. A week later he would tell me a little about his journey to the corner of Front and Water Streets. The IRS ruined his contractor’s business in the late 1990s. Once he recovered it, it only took a couple of more years before he was out of business again and since then he hasn’t been unable to climb from the streets. Alcohol and salty language are not helping him any, but I find his spunk a breath of fresh air in its own unique way.

For the last year Chris has been Tony’s nearest neighbor, making the bare dirt next to the three drive-by mailboxes his home. I was walking by Woodstock’s Pizza one day when Chris quietly told me he had retrieved his amplifier and wanted to know if I would like to hear him play one of his songs. I did. And, wow, is he a great guitarist.

“I played with the Jetboys. You can find a YouTube video of me on guitar.” Sure enough, there he is slamming it on “Feel The Shake.”

He told me his trip to the three mailboxes started when the producers of “Feel The Shake” pocketed most of the proceeds. Bitter about the unfair financial arrangement, he says he joined a private security company which assigned him to the deserts of Kuwait and the task of blowing up vehicles traveling to Iraq. He mumbled at one point, “I killed nineteen people in one attack.” He claims to have returned to Santa Cruz and joined the police department. But says that he was soon fired after discovering that the drug ring he was investigating had its roots in the police force. “I’ve been on the streets ever since.”

Leigh is always stationed at the western edge of the Sister City Circle, nursing a hand-rolled cigarette in one hand. “Check this out,” he says, showing me a photo of teenage Leigh running from New York’s finest who are chasing him on horseback through Central Park. I enjoy his Lower East Side knowledge of the New Left and the stew of Trotskyists, Maoists, and Yippies, with a pinch of Lyndon LaRouche that was the New York of my early activist years. He really doesn’t like the meth heads at all and can have some harsh suggestions on how to deal with them. He doesn’t love the cops any more than the drug addicts. “Toss a gas bomb their way,” he jokes.

"Leigh let me say this loud and clear: we don't joke about violent revolution around here," I say. I've seen that get a lot of people in deep trouble.

Several people are sitting on the Post Office steps smoking pot. "The Post Office wants us to smoke pot on the Water Street side of the building," I announce with all the seriousness of a comedian. "Please smoke pot on Water Street."

Jessie is still giving Billy a massage on the table he carted down to the meal on a bike trailer. Billy was a golden glove boxer, Jessie, a vet with a southern drawl and a kind heart. "Are you cold?" he asks Diane as she scuffs by his public massage parlor. She is freezing, she admits. Jessie stops pressing on Billy long enough to pull his shirt over his head and hand it to Diane.

Daniel is starting to assemble clean buckets and yellow Trader Joe's totes. He lives on Pacific Avenue and works for Wikipedia. I enjoy his German accent as he asks for direction about what to load into the van. "You can put the empty buckets behind the cooler."

Another hotel tray is emptied of its last spoonful of bread pudding. The last tray of corn bread is finished. Zen Center Patrick wishes everyone well and says goodbye as he heads off to his car with his empty baking pans.

We are down to less than half a tray of stir fry, fast coming to the bottom of the second pot of soup and have a little tossed salad left. The Clock Tower bell rings six times. Anna Rose and Rick scoop the remaining food into our to-go containers. We know more people will be arriving late and hungry.

Golden sycamore leaves quake in the last rays of sun. Mark and Oscar join Roberta at the wash bins to help scrub the empty hotel trays. Rick hands Oscar the bread pudding tray, wipes the tables clean and as though choreographed, Rick swings each table to its side, snaps it closed and in one swift motion leans each one against a light pole. He knows any empty table is a magnet for loose items.

The stack of compostable bowls is tilting west into the five-gallon bucket of uneaten food. Brent and Tom are on patrol for discarded evidence of another stellar performance at Food Not Bombs.

Travis is sweeping the area around the compost buckets. The bowls, sporks and cups are stuffed into a five-gallon bucket to be added to the special bin next to our compost pile out at the Homeless Garden Project.

Now all we have left is to pack the empty Trader Joe's trays.

A couple, one of whom carries an infant, rushes up. "Do you have any food left."

They are new to town and just learned of the meal when seeking food at the Homeless Services Center. Daniel hands them two takeout containers of food. "Do you want some bread? We have lots of bread." They take a loaf.

Two of our regulars, Russel and Cooper, arrive. They are relieved that we still have food. Ricardo also speeds towards us. They were busy busking on Pacific and didn't notice that it was getting late.

Click, click and click, on our counter, a total of 218 people joined us for dinner. I take a photo of the sidewalk and tree trunks in front of the Post Office to protect from the regular accusations of litter. Not a scrap of paper in sight.

Now for the last two photos, one of that day's survivors, the volunteers that made it to the very end followed by a picture of the counter.

The siren of a passing ambulance splits the chilly air. Jessie loads his massage table in his wagon, wishes me well and peddles off towards the Water Street Bridge. A lonely crow joins the sycamore roost at the Bank of the West. The diners have returned to rest in their doorways and river banks. Seven rings of the Clock Tower mark the return of the empty corner. The drama of our Temporary Autonomous Zone vanishes as quickly as it appeared. That is until next week when it all happens again.

Sharing coffee and snacks at the city's COVID triage cage for the homeless

Chapter 40

THE GREAT TURNING

We are the millions struggling for the basics for life: food, shelter, companionship, and dignity. Some might us that "basket of deplorables," as Clinton described but we know better. We are the foundation of society and the casualties of exploitation. The collapse has opened a portal to a transformation. An end to participating in our own repression. They misjudged those they detested.

When they need us the vultures of capital call us heroic essential workers but really the celluloid avatars of power sitting at their Zoom meetings believe we are nothing more than digital ones and zeros. Out of work, out of money, out of comfort, but not out of dignity and disdain for the thieves of Wall Street. Nothing to lose, burdens cascading into memories.

The winds of March 2020 blew away the past, flinging open the tattered curtains of the Great OZ illusion. The exploitations of the past now blow like ash towards the heavens. Power of the privileged evaporated. Our dawn has risen and burned clean the pinstriped suits of opulence and greed. They have left their crumbling souls on the cold rocks of our dreams.

The uprising is global.

The plunder will end. Governments and their moneyed thieves maybe scattered to the winds of ash. Their rule is evaporating in our minds, a trillion-dollar-a-day illusion has vanished. It had been a lie all along. We are pushing off power the power button on their Great Reset.

Millions have sheltered in place in the silence of doorways and highways of the failed state. Finding warmth in the back seat of a derelict car or under a collection of cardboard and tarps. And now we are becoming cities of the penniless.

The pandemic served up the gift of unanticipated freedom to mold our own future. A return to humanity prepared to fill the spiritual void of the dystopian corporate plans of the monsters of finance and war. The billionaires will bunker behind their blank walls of concrete, praying that their minions resist the urge to eliminate them.

The Google warlords and their hedge fund friends are power and they demand cruelty. Santa Cruz City officials believe that they can respond to the crisis of lockdown by corralling our homeless friends into the chain-link triage cages they erected in parking lots across the silent downtown. That is the first of what will become years of pandemic failures.

Amidst their panic to protect the housed of our community, we forced the screaming health experts to plead a case for all unhoused to retreat to vacant motel rooms.

And while local officials don't believe that the vermin transients really deserve the comfort of a warm bed, they do feel the need to pretend to put their tax-paying base at ease with their rule by headlines. The media blare the news of $500 million to quarantine the street creatures away from the good people.

Please don't spread your unclean breath of viral death onto the unbleached surfaces we may have to touch on our rare trip for an undeliverable necessity. A windfall for the few with billions of our dollars skating into the offshore accounts of the conspirators. But they will never have what those of us on the streets will enjoy, the freedom of heart.

So I set out to entice the city to comply with Getty-boy Governor Newsom's promise of Project Roomkey, hotel beds for the unhoused, vulnerable, and elderly. All my friends are people worthy of a bed and shower. I will do my part to make a change in civic conscience.

I speak with motel managers reluctant to rent to the homeless. Hotels clinging to the illusion of vacationing pandemic guests resist renting to the unwashed but I pry loose 81 beds on Ocean Street and Riverside at $100 per room.

The word of a shower spreads faster than a virus. At least 100 storm the Santa Cruz Clock Tower. The seas of desperation smash against the promise of a night in a hotel. Fuck social distancing just get me off the streets. Officers of the Santa Cruz Homeless Union march off with their platoon of the grateful to the Islander, the River Side, the Mission Inns and the first mattress and hot bath of the pandemic. Police Chief Mill's declares our hotel voucher distribution a violation of social distancing. He also hints that I am passing counterfeit vouchers. But they are real, I made them myself and the criminal investigation fogs into mist just like all the empty promises mouthed by the state. Second Harvest Food Bank responds by cutting off our food until they learn it was just a ban from the Town Clock.

We prove ourselves on the first night and word spreads among the guardians of the empty hotels. The policy the authorities called "social distancing" was tolerated on the second night with the knowledge that so many would be able to shelter in place even if it was only for a night. Several hundred of the calm and hopeful gather out of the rain at garage 10 on River Street. Homeless Union officers now have 180 people of the streets to welcome at the rooms of temporary bliss. Emergency 911 dispatch wants to know if we have more vouchers. Dominican Hospital wants to discharge a patient into one of our beds. We are the reality the old system never was.

City officials grunt their lies. It's too late for them, they had their chance before the world flipped upside down. The city fathers and mothers stare empty at what they imagine is their San Lorenzo River of cholera and future pandemics. They yell why did the feral people defecate on our soil as they cowered under their Costco towers of toilet paper and grumbled angrily at the thought of providing toilets for the homeless. They don't yet realize their silver and gold will a thing of the past. There will be a time near when food and safe water is the only valuable asset. Their world of privilege will be over. Maybe we are all in this together.

Day three and the fortunate 180 won't have to return to the streets until the 11 o'clock check.

It's day four of the great hotel voucher crusade. Thirty-six of our communities proud unhoused stand at six-foot intervals in the wet mud of the Santa Cruz Benchlands. We are operating by the street lights behind the County Court House. Cold drizzle, COVID-19, and the uncertain future drape us in sorrow.

Jake is a refugee of Police Chief Andy Mills' morning of the lockdown sweep of the Post Office. But even though he lost his shoes in the day-long police action and stands barefoot for our rice and beans he is one of the lucky twelve who the city has placed in a hotel room for a week's stay.

Sandra clutches our pink plastic clipboard and signs up for a room at the Riverside adding a cursive "God Bless You, Keith" below her signature. We share a smile of relief.

Lauren shivers in a beautiful lacy brown dress. It is her turn for the sacred hotel voucher for that one night at the inn. Tears cascade across her cheeks. She hasn't bathed in days she whispers and sobs gripping her voucher for dear life with moist eyes of thanks as she joins her hotel mates.

I run out of rooms. My heart breaks as I report the desperate news and hand out blue tarps to the unfortunate. Melissa suggests I ask for their names. Put them first in line for Friday's warm showers and soft bed and I hope their wish comes true.

A young bedraggled Venessa finds a seat on the sliver of pavement next to her boyfriend Seth looks up towards me and tells me not to worry. You did your best, they cheerfully add.

Mark grumbles the truth what everyone on the streets knows. The governor passed out $500 million to place those without housing in California's hotels. That bought Chief Mills a week for twelve at the Motel Santa Cruz and his half dozen abandoned chain-link cages of the city's parking lot gulags of triage. Maybe it was a psychological preparation for that final solution to the problem of our town's useless eaters?

I leave ten of us to the frost.

But the sun shines again this time on a new world. The sparkling diamonds of icy crystals evaporate from the blades of grass like city officials fleeing under their million-dollar roofs. How many years before their once wealthy neighbors murder them in their sleep as they bury their starving dead? Why weren't you prepared for the great calamity they might ask?

It's six feet under not six feet apart for those too arrogant to let go of the old world and join the army of the free. Maybe they will survive the energetic stabbings, 45 caliber bullets, and the torching of their palaces and find themselves standing quietly in lines of the gaunt waiting their turn with the other unwashed for their taste of a sacred plate of rice and beans.

All has changed during the great turning and yes, the poor will finally inherit the earth.

Human Rights activist Kathleen Lynch shows Martin Sheen El Salvador during the war

Chapter 41

THE LAST HANDSHAKE

Flight CM0382 touches down at SFO at 12:08 AM on March 11, 2020. I have returned from three weeks of writing in Flores, Guatemala and was excited to hold my girlfriend Kathleen in my arms and return to the keyboard to complete the text of this book.

News of a deadly virus infecting the vacationing passengers has forced the Grand Princess to sit quarantined off the coast of San Francisco. Video of police blocking the roads to Lombardy, Italy, of first responders garbed in Hazmat suits and caskets being lowered into graves all scream across the internet and news programs. The Grim Reaper is knocking. It's time to lockdown. Terror sweeps our streets empty of all but the unhoused. Triage cages are erected in silent parking lots to corral the homeless of Santa Cruz. The indoor soup kitchens and public restrooms are shuttered. Fear rules. I sit down this first week to type these words:

It might have been a tasty bat. Did its outstretched wings sizzle in cheap peanut oil or was the nocturnal meal grilled? Was it that family's weekend treat? We will never know for sure but the questions will linger heavy like the fog of sorrow that fallows the invisible soldiers of COVID-19 in the war to save humanity from itself.

As in any war, the first casualty is truth. These liberators don't lie. Even though we can't see or hear these battalions they can sweep across continents like a bubonic blitzkrieg. First China, how about Italy and Spain but no now there is a North American front marching. Their bugle sings "nature bats last!"

But we might discover that bats weren't on the menu or even available for sale in the stalls of the Hunan Seafood Market. Was it a biowarfare research program that leaked into the DNA of a globe already in crisis? Would Huang Yanling, a young scientist that had worked the Wuhan Institute of Virology be confirmed as patient zero or would we embrace the comfort of international capital's mantra of trust us as they forced a frightened people to cower in loneliness? Would we discover that the fear on the winds was designed to enslave humanity to the electric chains of those who know what is best for us?

Yes again, as in any war, the first casualty is truth.

The first truth exposed was that all our Emperors stand naked fearing that their yellow brick roads will lead to the ripping aside of their curtain concealing the mirage of their power. We know that the hard grey pavement and flapping blue tarps never lie.

The second truth is that I am blessed to share the smashing of illusions in the arms of my brave Kathleen Lynch. Sharing the horrors of system control and propaganda warfare.

Wisps of fog caress the cedar above Peace United Church on Tuesday, May 15, 2018 as I hand out news of the 38th anniversary celebration of the movement I helped start

"Did you know Carol Lynch?" asks an attractive women waiting to attend the first night of the Right Livelihood Conference. "My sister worked with Food Not Bombs at Golden Gate Park in the eighties." I did remember her name but I didn't recall meeting her.

The Saint Francis soup kitchen, the Monday night Coffee House at the Little Red Church is ordered to close and the Louden Nelson senior meal is no more. The great lockdown of social engineering has arrived. Our weekend meal is the only hope of food for hundreds unable to shelter in place. Our crew meets at LuLu Carpenters to discuss our response to COVID -19. A floor opens at Good Samaritan Hospital. Patients draped under plastic tenting are wheeled past Kathleen's station. I give her a call during our meeting and she outlines the pandemic safety protocol she had learned that week at work over speaker phone.

The days of turmoil and panic turn to weeks, then months and years. Cars return to the streets but fear rules. The pandemic drama will be replaced with Yellow and Blue flags and the promise of a glorious global war. We are a cyber attack, a flood, economic failure or the crashing of Pacific waves away from the next distraction. The just evicted stare blankly into an uncertain future. Essential worker volunteers fill the void of government failures.

The house of cards floats in the tornadoes of delusion. This is the 25th floor jumping type of storm for those who had consumed the poison of easy money. This is when facts are unfurled. Digital dollars in the trillions flood the accounts of the money changers at the temples of doom while the prisoners of the boardroom elite cower under house arrest waiting for their stimulus crumbs. The "we don't care act" is celebrated on the top floors of State Street, Vanguard, and Black Rock while we squeeze our last pennies into a tank of desperation praying the eviction sheriff won't be visiting today. The ones and zeros of unreality are evaporating into our post-apocalyptic haze.

There was no one better to weather the whipsaw of crisis with than Kathleen. She knows danger, having experienced six years of bombs and bullets in San Salvador and in the liberated zones of Morazán during the US war in El Salvador.

I am blessed with Kathleen's nightly greeting of "change into some relaxing clothing," a glass of water and favorite drink placed at my seat of honor and her heart felt "I love you," when I dragged in drained from the chaos of hunger and desperation at the Santa Cruz Homeless Union COVID-19 Relief Center and Food Not Bombs meal.

Our rituals sustain. I make sure she wakes to her phone, glasses, and a hot cup of coffee lovingly placed for her morning constitutional. A silent tune serenades our daily dance of defiance as we glide across our rust red kitchen tiles on the tidal waves of the great awakening.

Our truth can be found in the rain and sun. In the shared past of empathy for the suffering. In our embrace. In our liberation. In that handshakes the tyrants claimed would never be. We are free.

SPECIAL THANKS

Andy Couturier, Nick Flynn, Kathleen Lynch, Gail Page, Paul Lee, Dennis Bernstein, John Gibler, Elizabeth Tadic and Chaz Bufe

SOUP STREET

A memoir by Food Not Bombs co-founder Keith McHenry

Written and designed by Keith McHenry

OTHER PUBLICATIONS BY KEITH McHENRY

Hungry for Peace: How You Can Help End Poverty and War with Food Not Bombs
by Keith McHenry - April 1, 2012

The Anarchist Cookbook - October 1, 2015
by Keith McHenry (Author), Chaz Bufe (Author),
Hedges Chris (Introduction) and preface by William Powell

Anarchist Cook Substack
keithmchenry.substack.com

Anarchist Cook Word Press
anarchistcook.blog

Food Not Bombs
PO Box 422, Santa Cruz, CA 95061 USA
menu@foodnotbombs.net
www.foodnotbombs.net
1-800-884-1136

www.ingramcontent.com/pod-product-compliance
Ingram Content Group UK Ltd.
Pitfield, Milton Keynes, MK11 3LW, UK
UKHW062312290726
14090UKWH00018B/1022